Bulusu Lakshma

Oracle and Java Development

A Division of Pearson Technology Group
201 West 103rd Street, Indianapolis, Indiana 46290

Oracle and Java Development

Copyright © 2002 by Sams Publishing

All rights reserved. No part of this book shall be reproduced, stored in a retrieval system, or transmitted by any means, electronic, mechanical, photocopying, recording, or otherwise, without written permission from the publisher. No patent liability is assumed with respect to the use of the information contained herein. Although every precaution has been taken in the preparation of this book, the publisher and author assume no responsibility for errors or omissions. Nor is any liability assumed for damages resulting from the use of the information contained herein.

International Standard Book Number: 0-672-32117-3

Library of Congress Catalog Card Number: 00-111030

Printed in the United States of America

First Printing: August 2001

04 03 02 01 4 3 2 1

Trademarks

All terms mentioned in this book that are known to be trademarks or service marks have been appropriately capitalized. Sams Publishing cannot attest to the accuracy of this information. Use of a term in this book should not be regarded as affecting the validity of any trademark or service mark.

Warning and Disclaimer

Every effort has been made to make this book as complete and as accurate as possible, but no warranty or fitness is implied. The information provided is on an "as is" basis. The author and the publisher shall have neither liability nor responsibility to any person or entity with respect to any loss or damages arising from the information contained in this book.

Executive Editor
Rosemarie Graham

Acquisitions Editor
Angela Kozlowski

Development Editor
Kevin Howard

Managing Editor
Charlotte Clapp

Project Editor
Carol Bowers

Copy Editor
Michael Dietsch

Indexer
Rebecca Salerno

Proofreader
Jody Larsen

Technical Editor
Joe Greene

Team Coordinator
Lynne Williams

Interior Designer
Gary Adair

Cover Designer
Alan Clements

Page Layout
Ayanna Lacey
Stacey Richwine-DeRome

Contents at a Glance

Table of Contents

Part III Building Reusable Java Components

About the Author

Bulusu Lakshman is the author of the book *Oracle Developer Forms Techniques* from Sams Publishing. He holds an Oracle Masters credential from Oracle Corporation and is OCP-Certified. He also holds Master level BrainBench certifications. He has more than nine years of experience in using Oracle and its associated tools in the development of mission-critical applications. Most recently, he has used Oracle 8i and its related technologies for developing applications for a Fortune 400 client. He has lectured at different national and international conferences and authored technical articles for lead publications in the United States and United Kingdom. Currently he works for Compunnel Software Group Inc., a leading technical consulting firm in New Jersey and can be reached at `balakshman@hotmail.com` or `blakshman@compunnel.com`. He lives in Edison, New Jersey, with his wife Anuradha and writes poetry during his free time.

Dedication

This book is dedicated to the memory of my brother Bulusu Harihar Mallikarjuna, whose loving words still ring in my ears.

Acknowledgments

I thank my lovely and sweet wife Anuradha and my brother B.K. Visweswar for providing help in preparing part of the manuscript.

I thank my parents, Prof. B. S. K. R. Somayajulu and Smt. B.Sita for their constant encouragement throughout.

I thank Mr. Paul Wu, Director, MIS, Associated Press, the client company for which I am consulting, for providing me with necessary resources to write this book.

I thank the publisher and various editors at Sams Publishing, for the opportunity to publish my book.

My sincere gratitude goes to all concerned for their help and advice.

Tell Us What You Think!

As the reader of this book, *you* are our most important critic and commentator. We value your opinion and want to know what we're doing right, what we could do better, what areas you'd like to see us publish in, and any other words of wisdom you're willing to pass our way.

As an Executive Editor for Sams Publishing, I welcome your comments. You can fax, e-mail, or write me directly to let me know what you did or didn't like about this book—as well as what we can do to make our books stronger.

Please note that I cannot help you with technical problems related to the topic of this book, and that due to the high volume of mail I receive, I might not be able to reply to every message.

When you write, please be sure to include this book's title and author as well as your name and phone or fax number. I will carefully review your comments and share them with the author and editors who worked on the book.

Fax: 317-581-4770

E-mail: feedback@samspublishing.com

Mail: Rosemarie Graham
Executive Editor
Sams Publishing
201 West 103rd Street
Indianapolis, IN 46290 USA

Introduction

Oracle has emerged as the world's first Internet database with the introduction of Java in the database. The latest release Oracle 9i and its previous release, Oracle 8i, have made significant advancements in the areas of Java, e-commerce, and business-to-business (B2B) and business-to-consumer (B2C). The combination of Oracle 8i and Java provides a robust and effective environment for development and deployment of applications. Oracle 8i incorporates a Java Web server in the RDBMS (Relational Database Management System) that enables a wide variety of database functions using Java. Basically, these fall under three main categories:

- Database access from Java
- Building reusable components
- Deploying Java in a Web environment

This book covers the Oracle Java technologies involved in these three areas. If you're developing applications incorporating these Java technologies or you're migrating from older technologies, you can benefit from this book. This book is divided into four parts with thirteen chapters as follows:

Introduction

This includes Chapter 1, "Introduction to Oracle Java Technologies," describing the particular Java technologies that are relevant from an Oracle perspective, categorized in three ways described earlier. A brief description of each technology is presented.

Database Access in Java

This part comprises five chapters highlighting three different technologies for accessing an Oracle 8i database using Java.

Chapter 2 covers Java Stored Procedures. Chapters 3, "Basic JDBC Programming," and 4, "Advanced JDBC Programming," cover the basics and advanced aspects of Java Database Connectivity (JDBC). Chapters 5, "Basic SQLJ Programming," and 6, "Advanced SQLJ Programming," cover the ins and outs of yet another technology for database access from Java, namely, SQLJ.

Building Reusable Components

This part comprises five chapters that discuss the technologies for component-based development such as JavaBeans, Enterprise JavaBeans, and Business Components for Java.

Chapter 7, "Using JavaBeans," covers JavaBeans and how to use them with Oracle. Chapters 8, "Using Enterprise JavaBeans," and 9, "Developing and Deploying Enterprise JavaBeans," cover the advanced technology of Enterprise Java Beans (EJBs) and provide a detailed account of development and deployment of EJBs using Oracle 8i. Chapters 10, "Using Business Components for Java (BC4J)—Introduction and Development," and 11, "Using Business Components for Java (BC4J)—Deployment and Customization," highlight the Oracle-specific technology called Business Components for Java (BC4J) and present the details of the specifics involved therein.

Deploying Java in a Web Environment

This part comprises two chapters that describe the technologies of employing Java in a Web environment to produce dynamic Web content with Java. Specifically, Java servlets and Java Server Pages (JSPs) are discussed. Chapter 12, "Java Servlet Programming," discusses Java servlets and their relation to Oracle. Chapter 13, "Using Java Server Pages," outlines the development and deployment of JSPs in Oracle 8i.

INTRODUCTION TO ORACLE JAVA TECHNOLOGIES

ESSENTIALS

- Java technologies can be incorporated into the Oracle8i database in three ways, namely, database access in Java, building reusable Java components, and employing Java in a Web environment.
- Database access in Java is by using Java Stored Procedures, Java Database Connectivity, and SQLJ.
- Building reusable Java components is by using JavaBeans, Enterprise JavaBeans, and Business Components for Java (BC4J).
- Employing Java in a web environment is by using Java Servlets and Java Server Pages.
- Oracle8i provides a seamless environment where Java and PL/SQL can interoperate as two major database languages. Java Stored Procedures can reside in Oracle8i and JDBC and SQLJ applications can access the database. In addition, Enterprise JavaBeans, CORBA objects, BC4J objects, Java Servlets, and Java Server pages can be deployed in the Oracle8i database.

Java technologies, based on the multi-tier component-based model, currently dominate the scene of Internet application development. Java, JavaBeans, Java Servlets, and Enterprise JavaBeans (EJB) Technologies constitute the most fundamental architectural change in software development in the coming years. Oracle8i has positioned itself as a tool for developing Web-commerce megasites using the popular paradigm of component-based multi-tier applications. It makes use of Java technologies to achieve this.

This chapter explains the Oracle Java technologies available and gives a brief description of each. It offers an outline of how Java technologies can be incorporated into the Oracle8i database in three ways: database access in Java, building reusable Java components, and employing Java in a Web environment. Database access in Java is done by using Java Stored Procedures, Java Database Connectivity, and SQLJ. Building reusable Java components is achieved by using JavaBeans, Enterprise JavaBeans, and Business Components for Java. Employing Java in a Web environment is done by using Java Servlets and Java Server Pages.

Oracle8i database server has an Oracle JServer that includes a Java Virtual Machine (JVM) called Aurora, a Java runtime environment, and supporting Java class libraries. The Oracle JServer is a server-side Java engine for the Oracle8i database. A JVM is a Java Virtual Machine that takes care of compiling and executing Java code. The Oracle JServer along with the contained JVM is embedded in the Oracle8i RDBMS and is integrated with SQL and PL/SQL. It enables interoperability of Java and PL/SQL inside the database. Oracle8i also has the capability of handling CORBA components and EJB support. In addition, Java Server Pages (JSP) and Java Servlets can be deployed in the Oracle8i database. Both Java and PL/SQL (Procedural Language/Structured Query Language) can interoperate as two database languages. Java applets and applications can access Oracle8i using Java Database Connectivity (JDBC) or SQLJ. These Oracle Java technologies are discussed in-depth in the remaining chapters of this book.

Database Access in Java

Java Stored Procedures—PL/SQL Calling Java

Java Stored Procedures are the Java counterpart for PL/SQL stored procedures in the traditional Oracle8i database. Oracle8i provides a seamless environment where Java and PL/SQL can interoperate as two major database languages. Java Stored Procedures are an example of PL/SQL calling Java. Procedures written in Java are loaded into the database. Once loaded, the Java Stored Procedures are published in the Oracle Data Dictionary. These published stored procedures can be invoked from PL/SQL code, database triggers, and top-level code. Oracle8i allows access control on the Java stored procedures.

Chapter 2, "Java Stored Procedures," describes the steps for developing, loading, and invoking Java Stored Procedures. The chapter demonstrates the `loadjava` utility for loading a Java Stored Procedure into the database.

The mapping between Java and PL/SQL data types is also described. Examples illustrate how a Java Stored Procedure can be invoked from PL/SQL blocks, database triggers, and top-level code and object type methods.

JDBC—Java Calling SQL and PL/SQL

Java Database Connectivity (JDBC) is the Java Application Programming Interface (API) for communicating with databases. It is a Java API for providing vendor-transparent access to databases through a standard interface. From an Oracle8i perspective it provides a way for Java applications to call SQL and PL/SQL. Oracle8i supports the standard JDBC 1.0 and 2.0 features. In addition, Oracle8i has Oracle-specific extensions to support advanced Oracle8i data types and other performance related functionality. The JDBC API consists of a high-level API and low-level drivers for connecting to different databases. Java applications can access an Oracle8i database by establishing a connection to a particular schema using one of the Oracle JDBC drivers. The driver is registered first and then a connection is obtained. Once a connection is obtained, SQL statements or blocks of PL/SQL code can be executed against the target database using standard JDBC API and the results of the SQL operations can be processed in the Java application. Data can be passed to and from an Oracle8i database and Java application.

Chapter 3, "Basic JDBC Programming," describes in detail the Oracle-related aspects of JDBC programming. It starts by highlighting the basic steps involved in accessing an Oracle8i database and then goes on to discuss issues such as performing Data Manipulation Language (DML) using JDBC and Exception handling. The Oracle JDBC extensions are discussed in detail. The method of calling stored procedures from JDBC programs and result set functionality is explained.

Chapter 4, "Advanced JDBC Programming," discusses the support for Oracle objects in JDBC. Finally, it also describes the performance extensions in JDBC.

SQLJ—Java Calling SQL and PL/SQL

SQLJ is an emerging standard that lets the use of embedded Structured Query Language (SQL) database requests and statements into Java. It provides a set of programming extensions to Java that enable database access from Java applications. Using JDBC is the other way of doing this. The difference lies in that SQLJ is static embedded SQL for Java whereas JDBC provides a dynamic runtime SQL interface for Java. A source program is written in Java with static embedded SQL statements. A SQLJ translator is run on this source program that converts the SQLJ program to a standard Java program, replacing the embedded SQL statements with calls to SQLJ runtime. The generated Java program is compiled using any Java compiler to obtain Java executable/Java bytecode and then run against a database.

The second component of SQLJ is the SQLJ runtime environment. It consists of a SQLJ runtime library that is implemented in pure Java. This library uses JDBC and hence retains the features of vendor independence and portability. However, the Oracle-SQLJ runtime library is a thin layer of pure Java code that runs above the JDBC driver.

Advantages of Using SQLJ

- SQL statements are checked at compilation time rather than at run time. Also, optimization of the SQL statements is done at compilation time. This provides a significant speed improvement.
- SQLJ provides strong type-checking of queries and other return parameters. Strong type-checking ensures that data types of all variables and parameters involved are strictly compatible.
- SQLJ provides more efficient runtime execution using SQL precompilation techniques.
- SQLJ is higher level than JDBC. In SQLJ programs, SQL statements are not hidden in method calls.
- SQLJ programs offer flexible deployment configurations. Once developed, they can be deployed in any configuration such as on a thick client, on a thin client, in an application server, in a Java application, in an applet, or in an Oracle8i database server as an SQLJ Stored Procedure.
- SQLJ conforms with ANSI standards, is vendor neutral, and is portable.

Chapter 5, "Basic SQLJ Programming," explains the use of SQLJ for database access in Java. It starts by discussing the fundamentals of SQLJ and then proceeds to outline SQLJ query processing, DML processing, and exception handling. Chapter 6, "Advanced SQLJ Programming," presents advanced topics such as handling object types, large objects, and collections in SQLJ and SQLJ performance extensions. The chapter closes with a brief discussion of SQLJ in the server.

Building Reusable Java Components

JavaBeans

JavaBeans are Java classes designed to serve as reusable components. Beans are the basic component model in Java applications. Individual component Beans can be easily integrated to form complex applications. A Bean Development Kit (BDK) can be used to make the development and deployment of a Bean easier.

A Java class can be converted to a Bean by changing it to adhere to the JavaBeans specification. A good example of a JavaBean is one that performs a validation based on certain input.

In an application, it is a good idea to design most of the GUI-related components as Beans even though some Beans need not be related to the GUI. This is because the GUI-related components, once developed as a Bean, can be reused in multiple Java applications and are easily "pluggable" in existing pieces of code and become part of the application.

An example of a GUI-related JavaBean is a Bean that displays a progress bar. The progress bar can be used anywhere a process completion status needs to be displayed.

A Bean has a set of properties, some (or all) of which define the state of the Bean. The properties can simply be class variables of the Bean. The Bean provides accessor methods to set and retrieve the values of these properties. When these properties change, the Bean can trigger events and notify listeners about the change. This allows the listeners to react to the events. A Bean can also respond to external events (possibly generated by other Beans). For example, the progress bar can have a property named Percentage that provides how much percentage of the process has been completed. This property once set defines the state of the bean as working or completed. Here, "working" and "completed" define two states of the progress bar. Also, the value of the percentage property can be stored in a bean class variable. When the value of the percentage property is set to a specific value, the change event is triggered and the progress bar moves in the forward direction as a result of the change. Here the process in question is said to trigger the change event and the progress bar is said to listen to this change and act accordingly.

There are a series of steps that the Bean developer must follow in order to write a robust, functionally complete and easily interoperable Bean. These steps include:

- Defining the set of events that the Bean will trigger and respond to.
- Defining the listener interface. All listeners must implement this interface.
- Writing the Bean class to contain its properties, property accessors, and listener registration methods.

Bean properties can be constrained or bound. For constrained properties, the Bean sends out messages to listeners before the property is changed. Any of the listeners can veto the proposed change and thus prevent the change. For bound properties, the Bean sends out messages after the property is changed so the listeners will take action to accommodate the change in property. In the progress bar example, the percentage is a bound property. After its value has been incremented, the progress bar responds to this change.

In order for the Bean to be persistent, both the Bean and the properties that define its state must be serializable. Persistence is the property by which the state of the bean can be stored and retrieved from persistent storage (for example, a database). The mechanism that makes persistence possible is called *serialization*. A bean is serializable if all its properties can be converted to a data stream and written to storage. The bean's properties can be restored to back to the persistent data stream by deserialization. Since a Bean can be used by multiple threads at the same time, care must be taken to make the Bean thread safe. The simultaneous executions of various threads share the same data of the bean. Therefore the coding of the bean should be done in such a manner that the threads do not interfere with each other's execution. This is what is meant by the term *thread safe*.

A BDK uses the Introspection API to find out meta-information about the Bean. Meta-information gives details about the metadata such as the name of the Bean, the name of the Bean properties, the name of the events and listeners, and so on. The Introspection API has the BeanInfo class for the purpose of holding all the meta-information about the Bean. It then displays this information visually and allows it to be modified dynamically. The Introspection API depends on certain naming conventions of the accessor methods and also the textual descriptions of the methods that the Bean developer is expected to provide. A Bean must have one constructor that does not take any arguments so that the BDK can instantiate it. A constructor is a class that allows you to define an instance of the Bean class and initialize it as an object.

Beans can be used anywhere in the application but their primary use is in the GUI components like applets and JSP code.

Chapter 7, "Using JavaBeans," discusses JavaBeans in detail. The method of creating a JavaBean and the various ways of adding properties and events to a JavaBean are discussed. Finally, using Beans in an applet is described.

SET UP ENVIRONMENT FIRST!

The first thing to do while using the Java technologies such as Java Stored Procedures, JDBC, SQLJ, JavaBeans, Enterprise JavaBeans, Java Servlets, and JSPs is to correctly set up the environment and make sure that all the required components are installed.

This might seem to be as trivial as including basic files in the PATH and CLASSPATH variables but it is not trivial in practical cases. The difficulty lies in determining which files should be included for a particular technology to work. Note that some variables might be set while installing the software. In such cases, these variables might need modification or their values need to be appended with additional input.

So the moral is "to locate all the environment variables and set their values perfectly and then start to use the technology."

Enterprise JavaBeans

The Enterprise JavaBean (EJB) architecture is a specification from Sun Microsystems for a comprehensive server-side component model. It is a Java standard for building three-tier applications. It combines the best of Internet technology, distributed component model, and platform-independent coding. In terms of distributed computing, it has an advantage over Common Object Request Broker Architecture (CORBA) since it shields the application developer from the low-level distributed application development details. For example, a Person EJB can be designed to provide information about a person's name and age. The details of how to store, retrieve, and modify this information is transparent to the developer. By invoking methods on the EJB, a client program can be written to obtain and change the person's name and age.

An Enterprise Bean resembles any other JavaBean in the sense that it has properties that can be introspected and it also follows the JavaBeans conventions for defining accessor methods for its properties. However, an enterprise Bean also inherently has the capabilities required for most business components—transaction processing, security, persistence, and resource-pooling. The Bean gets these capabilities from the EJB Framework environment in which the Bean runs.

The EJB model involves three components: The EJB Client, the EJB Container, and the Enterprise Beans themselves. The EJB client is a program that accesses the EJB. It interacts with the EJB to get data from an EJB or provide data values pertaining to the EJB to be stored in the database. The EJB Container is purely a server-side entity. It provides functionality for transaction processing, security, persistence, and resource-pooling. The Bean developer can use these readily available features. However, the Bean developer is insulated from the details of these services provided by the EJB environment.

When an EJB is deployed, the Bean developer specifies exactly how he wants to use the various services provided by the EJB environment. This specification is called the deployment descriptor for the Bean. Since the deployment descriptor is not embedded in the Bean Implementation, the same Bean can be deployed differently in different environments. For example, the EJB can be deployed in a database server such as Oracle8i or in the middle-tier on an application server.

Chapter 8, "Using Enterprise JavaBeans," discusses the EJB architecture model in detail. It demonstrates an example of how to create an EJB and use it in an application. It discusses the various types of EJBs with appropriate examples. Chapter 9, "Developing and Deploying Enterprise JavaBeans," discusses the development and deployment of EJB in an Oracle8i environment. Various types of transaction management features are discussed. Finally, Oracle8i EJB tools such as `deployejb` and `ejbdescriptor` are described in this chapter.

Business Components for Java

Oracle Business Components for Java (BC4J) is Oracle JDeveloper's programming framework for building scalable, multi-tier database applications. The EJB model provides services like transaction, security, persistence, and resource management. But it does not make development of business logic any easier nor does it provide services for reusing business logic across multiple applications. The BC4J framework facilitates the development of the business logic tier of the application. The principle behind this is that the business logic of any application is closely tied to the underlying database design. The BC4J framework adds another layer on top of the database for coding the business logic of an application. It does this by allowing you to define specific business components that interact with the database as well other components. Once defined, these components can be reused in any application that needs to access the relevant data and thus provide a "write once, use anywhere" interface.

Business logic developed using BC4J can be deployed as an EJB server object in the Oracle8i JServer. Thus BC4J rides on the popularity of the EJB model rather than competing with it.

BC4J offers the following advantages:

- BC4J facilitates development of business logic.
- It allows reuse of business logic across applications.
- It provides an easy interface between the front end (HTML (Hypertext Markup Language)/Java code) and the data views.
- It allows layered customization of business logic after deployment.

Chapter 10, "Using Business Components for Java (BC4J)—Introduction and Development," discusses the details of BC4J architecture and its components. The chapter gives an example illustrating how to design and develop the various BC4J components for a real-world application. Chapter 11, "Using Business Components for Java (BC4J)—Deployment and Customization", gives an account of how to deploy a BC4J application.

Employing Java in a Web Environment

Java Servlets

Servlets can be viewed as logical extensions of the Web server. In this respect, they serve as a Java-based replacement for CGI scripts. The Web server is the back-end software that receives the requests from the Web browser (for example, Netscape or Internet Explorer), services the request, and sends the HTML response back to the browser. Initially, Web servers only had the capability of serving static HTML pages. With the advent of CGI, the Web servers developed the capability of building dynamic HTML pages. The Web server would invoke a CGI application which would generate the HTML code on the fly. So CGI can be viewed as an extension of the Web server. Servlets are a Java-based replacement for CGI applications. The Web server invokes the servlets which in turn generates the HTML dynamically.

Servlets can be invoked from HTML code exactly in the same way CGI programs are invoked. However, unlike CGI programs, servlets are persistent across invocations and hence are much faster than CGI programs. Being written in Java, servlets have access to all the APIs of the Java platform and are portable across operating systems.

The servlet model works in the following way:

1. The user makes a request of the Web server.
2. The Web server invokes a servlet designed to handle the request.
3. The servlet fulfills the request. They servlet may invoke other Java APIs to achieve this.
4. The servlet returns the results to the user (in HTML format).

Since the servlet is persistent across invocations, it is initialized only once. This initialization process can set up I/O intensive resources like database connections which can then be used across multiple invocations thus saving the overhead of doing the initialization for each request to the servlet.

Java provides a servlet API which makes life easy for the servlet developer. Among other things, it takes care of tasks like decoding HTML form parameters and dealing with sessions and cookies. It also provides classes which can be used for communication between the Web server and the servlet. A cookie is an object that contains client-side information as well as information describing the state of the user session. The cookie is passed back and forth between the client and the server which enables the server to keep track of the client information as well as the session information.

Chapter 12, "Java Servlet Programming," discusses the Java servlets framework in detail. Apart from the details of servlet design and development, it also discusses error handling, security, thread safety, and session tracking using cookies and session objects.

Java Server Pages

Java Server Pages (JSP) are Sun's solution for developing dynamic Web sites. JSP allows developers to mix regular static HTML with dynamically generated HTML. The dynamic part of the code is enclosed in special tags. The JSP page looks more like a HTML page and is normally stored using the .jsp extension. But behind the scenes, the JSP page gets converted into a servlet with the static HTML simply printed to the servlet's `HttpResponse` object. There is nothing that JSP allows which cannot be implemented using a servlet.

The following is a very simple example of JSP code. It displays a Web page with the current date and time.

```
Hello! The time is now <%= new java.util.Date() %>
```

When the above JSP is invoked, the static HTML is returned as such to the output. But the dynamic code (between the <% and %>) is executed and the result is sent back. Typically, the JSP uses JavaBeans to retrieve all the data it requires. This allows an HTML programmer to design a Web page without worrying about the details of data retrieval. A Java programmer can independently code the backend JavaBeans.

The JSP page gets translated to a servlet the first time it is accessed. Subsequent requests to the JSP page use the servlet. Since translation is not done for every request, JSPs are significantly faster than CGI programs.

JSP offers the advantage of separating the front-end components from the business components. A JSP/HTML programmer can write the JSP code. The code can make use of JavaBeans which can be designed and developed independently by a Java programmer.

Chapter 13, "Using Java Server Pages," discusses JSP programming in detail including JSP Syntax, scope of variables and Beans, predefined variables, and session management.

Summary

This chapter outlined the various technologies of incorporating Java in Oracle8i. Specifically, it dealt with database access in Java using Java stored procedures, JDBC, and SQLJ. It also detailed the technologies for building components using Oracle8i namely, JavaBeans, EJD, and BC4J. Finally, it discussed Java servlets and JSP and their use in an Oracle8i environment.

JAVA STORED PROCEDURES

ESSENTIALS

- Java Stored Procedures are one method of incorporating Java in the database, a method of SQL and PL/SQL calling Java. A Java Stored Procedure is a Java method written and compiled as a Java class, published to SQL, and stored in the Oracle8i database.
- Developing a Java Stored Procedure involves writing the Java method by creating a custom Java class to achieve the desired functionality, loading the Java method into the RDBMS and resolving external references, publishing the Java method into the RDBMS by writing a PL/SQL call spec, granting the appropriate privileges to invoke the Java Stored Procedure, and calling the Java Stored Procedure from SQL or PLSQL.
- To load the Java method into the Oracle8i database uses the *loadjava* utility from the command line. This utility can be used to load .java source files, .class files, .jar files, .sqlj files, and Java resource files.
- Publishing the Java method is done by writing a PL/SQL procedure, function, or member method using the AS LANGUAGE JAVA NAME clause and specifying the fully qualified Java method name including parameter data types.
- The runtime contexts that can invoke Java Stored Procedures are stored packages, functions and procedures, database triggers, object-relational methods, anonymous PL/SQL blocks, and SQL DML statements.
- Java Stored Procedures can also be called from a Java client via JDBC or SQLJ, Pro*, OCI or ODBC client, or an Oracle Developer Forms client.

This chapter explains the use of Java Stored Procedures for database access in Java. It highlights the method to incorporate Java in the Oracle 8i database using Java Stored Procedures. The various methods of creating Java Stored Procedures starting from writing the Java class to executing the Java Stored Procedure from the Oracle 8i database are described in detail.

Overview of Java Stored Procedures—PL/SQL Calling Java

Oracle 8i provides a seamless environment where Java and PL/SQL can interoperate as two major database languages. This section delves deep into this aspect of Oracle Java technologies and details the tricks-of-the-trade involving the creation and use of Java Stored Procedures.

A Java Stored Procedure is a Java method published to SQL and stored in an Oracle 8i database. Once a Java method is written and compiled as a Java class, it can be published by writing call specifications, abbreviated as *call specs*. The call specs map Java method names, parameter types, and return types to their SQL counterparts. A call spec simply publishes the existence of a Java method. The Java method is called through its call spec and the runtime system dispatches the call with minimum overhead.

Once published, the Java Stored Procedure is callable by client applications. The stored procedure when called can accept arguments, reference Java classes, and return Java return values. The type of the application that can invoke a Java stored procedure is determined by the runtime context. Any Java method that does not include the GUI methods can be stored and run in the RDBMS as a stored procedure. The runtime contexts that can invoke Java Stored Procedures are

- Functions and procedures
- Database triggers
- Object-relational methods

Procedures can be used for *void* Java methods and functions can be used for methods returning values. Also packaged procedures and functions can be used as call specs.

Java methods published as procedures and functions must be invoked explicitly. They can accept arguments and are callable from

- SQL CALL statements
- Anonymous PL/SQL blocks, stored procedures, functions, and packages

Java methods published as functions are also callable from SQL Data Manipulation Language (DML) statements (i.e., `INSERT`, `UPDATE`, `DELETE`, and `SELECT` statements).

Database triggers can use the `CALL` statement to invoke a Java method to perform a particular action based on the triggering event.

Object types can be defined with attributes and methods that operate on these attributes. The methods can be written in Java.

Java stored procedures can also be called from

- A Java client via JDBC or SQLJ
- A Pro*, OCI or ODBC client
- An Oracle Developer Forms client

Advantages of Java Stored Procedures

Using Java Stored Procedures offers a number of advantages, the primary ones being:

- Incorporation of complex business logic that cannot be handled by PL/SQL, into the database. A good example of this is the use of logic involving multidimensional arrays which otherwise are very difficult to handle in PL/SQL. Java stored procedures combine the powerful 3GL and object-oriented language features of Java otherwise unavailable by PL/SQL with SQL to provide better flexibility of coding.
- Java allows for a safer type system and automatic memory management that provides tighter integration into the RDBMS.
- Java Stored Procedures offer the same advantages as PL/SQL stored procedures in terms of better performance, scalability, and easy maintainability.
- Java Stored Procedures provide broader access to share business logic across applications in that they can be developed using any Java Integrated Development Environment (IDE) (i.e., a software tool for coding, compiling and testing the Java Stored Procedure) and then deployed on any tier of the network architecture. Moreover they can be invoked by any standard interfaces such as JDBC, EJB, SQLJ, and so on.
- Oracle 8i provides a seamless environment for Java and PL/SQL to provide a high degree of interoperability. Java provides full access to Oracle data. PL/SQL applications can call Java Stored Procedures directly. Conversely, Java can call PL/SQL using embedded JDBC driver.

Comparison of PL/SQL Stored Procedures and Java Stored Procedures

Though Java and PL/SQL are integrated into the Oracle 8i database as two major database languages, there are a few subtle differences between Java Stored Procedures and PL/SQL stored procedures. The following highlights some of the differences:

- Any procedure written in PL/SQL can be written in Java but not vice-versa.

- Unlike PL/SQL stored procedures, Java stored procedures are executed by default with invoker rights.
- The Java code though residing in the database, is still executed by a Java 2 bytecode Interpreter and associated Java runtime system embedded in the Oracle JServer.

Developing Java Stored Procedures—An Overview and Case Study

Developing a Java stored procedure involves the following steps:

1. Writing the Java method by creating a custom Java class to achieve the desired functionality.
2. Loading the Java method into the RDBMS and resolving external references.
3. Publishing the Java method into the RDBMS by writing a PL/SQL call spec.
4. If needed, granting the appropriate privileges to invoke the Java stored procedure.
5. Calling the Java stored procedure from SQL and/or PLSQL.

Each of these steps is explained in detail in the sections that follow with a simple case study.

Case Study

The case study consists of two parts. The first part explains how to write a simple Java class to demonstrate the aforementioned steps:

- A Java class named `Slength` that includes a function `compute_length` that returns the length of an input string
- A Java class named `Slengthtest` that tests the above Java method as a standalone Java program
- A PL/SQL function that publishes the above Java method into the Oracle 8i database

The second part of the case study uses the following schema definitions and Java methods to illustrate the ins and outs of Java stored procedures:

- Database objects (tables and object types):

The `Dept` and `Emp` tables store information about departments and the corresponding employees in each department. The `dept_audit` table stores the count of employees in each department. This count is incremented or decremented each time an employee record is inserted or deleted.

The address object describes an object type representing an address in terms of an address ID, line1, line2, city, state, and ZIP code. The addresses table stores all addresses of address type. The definition of these database objects is given below.

```
CREATE TABLE dept (deptno number(4) primary key,
                   dname  varchar2(20) not null,
                   loc    varchar2(15) not null);

CREATE TABLE emp (empno number(10) primary key,
                  ename varchar2(40) not null,
                  job   varchar2(15) not null,
                  mgr   number(10) references emp(empno),
                  hiredate date not null,
                  sal   number(12,2) not null,
                  comm  number(4),
                  deptno number(4) references dept(deptno));
CREATE TABLE dept_audit (deptno number(4) primary key references dept(deptno),
                         cnt_emp number(10) not null);
CREATE OR REPLACE TYPE address AS OBJECT
                               (add_id number(10),
                                line1 varchar2(20),
                                line2 varchar2(20),
                                city  varchar2(15),
                                state varchar2(2),
                                zip   varchar2(11));
/
```

(This type is later changed to include member methods.)

```
CREATE TABLE addresses OF address;
```

- A Java class empMaster with methods hireEmp, fireEmp, transferEmp, and hikeEmpSal
- A PL/SQL package pkg_empmaster with procedures hire_emp, fire_emp, transfer_emp, and hike_emp_sal to publish the above Java methods into an Oracle 8i database
- A Java class DeptAudit with method DeptAuditRow
- A PL/SQL procedure p_dept_audit to publish the above Java method into Oracle 8i database
- A database trigger dept_audit_trg
- A Java class addressMaster with methods createAddress and changeAddress
- A SQL Object Type address with member methods create_address and change_address to publish the above Java methods into the Oracle 8i database

The environment used of compiling and executing SQL and PL/SQL code is SQL*Plus. Also, all PL/SQL commands should be terminated by a ';' and '/'.

Writing the Java Method

This consists of writing the Java method to achieve the desired functionality. Consider a method called `compute_length` declared as part of a class named `Slength`, that computes the length of a string passed to it as an argument. The code looks like the following:

```
// File name Slength.java

// declare a classpublic class Slength { // declare a method with a String
argument
  public static int compute_length(String string) { // create an instance of a
String and initilaize it with the parameter value
      String astring = string; int retval = astring.length(); // compute the
length of the string
      return retval; // return the computed length
   } // method compute_length
 } // class Slength
```

Note that the `length()` method of the `String` class cannot be directly called from PL/SQL and a custom Java class is necessary. There are two reasons for this:

- A Java method is executed on a specific object instantiated from the class. Exceptions are class methods declared as *static*.
- There is no direct mapping between data types in Java and data types in PL/SQL.

The custom Java class

- Instantiates an object of the String class
- Invokes the length() method on that object
- Returns an int value that PL/SQL can interpret

Once the custom class is written, it is saved as a .java source file. The next step is to compile and test it before loading it into the RDBMS. To compile this class use the javac command from the command line with the source filename as the argument. Note that the current directory should be the directory where the source file resides. Also, the PATH and CLASSPATH environment variables should be set so as to include the current directory. Alternatively, an IDE such as IBM's Visual Age for Java can be used with proper setup done, compile the Java class.

```
C:\javasrc> javac Slength.java
```

This results in a Slength.class file.

To test this class, you should include a `main` method with proper arguments and recompile the class so that it can be executed as a standalone program. The `main()` method is one of the primary methods to execute a Java application from the command line. The code looks similar to the following:

```
//File name Slengthtest.java
// declare a class
class Slengthtest { // declare a main method that takes a string as argument
  public static void main (String args[]) {     Slength test = new Slength(); //
Instantiate the Slength class
// Invoke compute_length() method on the above instance
   System.out.println(test.compute_length(args[0])); } // Main method
} // Class Slengthtest
```

Recompile this class and run it as follows:

```
C:\javasrc\javac Slengthtest.java
```

Run the compiled class using the `java` executable, as follows:

```
C:\javasrc\java Slengthtest "This is a test class"
20
```

The length of the string "This is a test class" which is 20, is displayed as the output of the program.

Loading the Java Method into the RDBMS and Resolving External References

Now that the above Java method is tested, it has to be loaded into the RDBMS using loadjava. `loadjava` is a command-line utility provided by Oracle to load Java code files (.java source files, .class files, .jar files) into the database. The command when invoked looks like the following:

```
C:\javasrc> loadjava -user SCOTT/TIGER -oci8 -resolve Slength.class
```

There are a lot of options to the loadjava utility; -user, -oci and -resolve are some of these. These and other options are explained later.

To verify that the class has been loaded, we query the data dictionary view USER_OBJECTS to obtain user-defined database objects of type 'JAVA CLASS', as shown here:

```
column object_name format a30;
select object_name, object_type, status, timestamp
    from   user_objects
```

```
where  (object_name not like 'SYS_%'
  and   object_name not like 'CREATE$%'
  and   object_name not like 'JAVA%'
  and   object_name not like 'LOADLOB%')
  and   object_type like 'JAVA %'
order by object_type, object_name
/
```

What follows is the output from the above query:

```
OBJECT_NAME                   OBJECT_TYPE       STATUS  TIMESTAMP
----------------------------- ----------------- ------- -------------------
Slength                       JAVA CLASS        VALID   2000-03-19:22:24:01
```

Publishing the Java Method into the RDBMS

After loading into the RDBMS, the Java method is to be published in the Oracle Data Dictionary by writing a PL/SQL call specification. The call spec maps the Java method names, parameter types, and return types to their SQL counterparts. The call spec is written using the CREATE PROCEDURE, CREATE FUNCTION, CREATE PACKAGE, or CREATE TYPE statements.

Methods with return values are published as functions and void Java methods are published as procedures. Inside the function or procedure body, the LANGUAGE JAVA clause is specified. This clause maintains information about the name, parameter types, and return type of the Java method. The following code illustrates the publishing of the Slength Java method described earlier:

```
CREATE OR REPLACE FUNCTION f_Slength(string IN VARCHAR2) -- create a function
called f_Slength
RETURN NUMBER -- Specify the Return type
AS LANGUAGE JAVA -- Specify the AS LANGUAGE clause
NAME 'Slength.compute_length(java.lang.String) return int'; -- Specify the full
definition of the Java method
```

Notice how the Java method is specified using the classname.methodname syntax. The Java full name of the method has to be specified here. Also the parameter list for the Java method has the fully qualified data type name specified instead of the parameter name. Thus *java.lang.String* is the *String* class with the full name of the package containing this class. The fully qualified Java type names and the call spec parameters are mapped by position and must correspond one-to-one. (The *main()* method is an exception to this rule). Also the RETURN clause for the Java method simply specifies *int* for integer, a primitive Java data type. The function f_Slength once compiled publishes the Slength Java method in the data dictionary.

Calling the Java Stored Procedure from SQL or PLSQL

Once published, the Java method is called from SQL and/or PLSQL using the standard procedure for calling PL/SQL procedures or functions. The code for calling the `f_Slength` Java Stored Procedure is given below. The SQL*Plus environment variable SERVEROUTPUT should be set to ON to display the output on the screen. The DBMS_OUTPUT.PUT_LINE procedure can be called to display informative messages as well as debug messages while working with stored sub-programs.

```
DECLARE
/* Declare a variable of NUMBER type to store
   the return value of f_Slength function */  ret_val NUMBER; BEGIN
-- Invoke f_Slength function that in turn calls the Java method  ret_val :=
f_Slength('This is a test class'); -- Display the return value from the function
dbms_output.put_line(to_char(ret_val)); END;
/
```

Running the above script in SQL*Plus yields the value 20, which, in fact, is the length of the string "This is a test class".

By default, Java stored procedures run with invoker rights. Thus, references to schema objects are resolved in the schema of the invoker. However, this default behavior can be overridden by specifying the loadjava option *definer.*

This section illustrated a simple example of creating and using a Java Stored Procedure. The sections that follow present a detailed description about the ins and outs of each step.

Loading the Java Method into the Oracle 8i Database

Using `loadjava`

Loadjava enables you to load the following type of files created on the client-side:

- Java source files (.java files).
- Java binary files compiled outside the database (.class files or .jar and .zip files). Archive files should be uncompressed and non-nested. .jar and .zip files cannot be stored as schema objects, and loadjava loads these files individually. Only the latest modified files are uploaded.
- Java resource files.
- SQLJ input files (.sqlj files).

The command for loadjava assumes the following form:

```
loadjava {-user | -u} username/password[@database]
[ -option_name -option_name … ] filename filename …
```

where `option_name` stands for the following:

```
{  {andresolve } |
   debug              |
   {definer }      |
   {encoding } encoding_scheme_name |
   {force }        |
   {grant } {username | role_name} [, {username | role_name}] … |
   {oci8 }         |
   oracleresolver     |
   {resolve }      |
   {resolver } "resolver_spec" |
   {schema } schema_name |
   {synonym }      |
   {thin }         |
   {verbose }   }
```

Multiple options or files must be separated by spaces and multiple usernames or role names must be separated by commas.

Table 2.1 describes the loadjava command-line options.

Table 2.1 The* `loadjava` *Command-Line Options

Option	Description
andresolve	Compiles uploaded source files and resolves external references in each class file as it is loaded. This option can also be specified as -a.
debug	Generates and displays debugging information.
definer	Overrides default execution with invoker rights and executes the uploaded class methods with definer rights. This option can also be specified as -d.
encoding	Sets (or resets) the option encoding in the database table JAVA$OPTIONS to the specified value. Here, encoding refers to the character-encoding scheme and JAVA$OPTIONS is a table that stores the compiler options. It is owned by SYS and can be seen in DBA_OBJECTS or ALL_OBJECTS when logged in as SYS or SYSTEM schemas. This option can also be specified as -e.
force	Loads Java class files irrespective of whether they have been loaded before. By default, previously loaded files are discarded. This option can also be specified as -f.
grant	Grants the EXECUTE privilege on uploaded classes to the listed users. This option can also be specified as -g.

Table 2.1 Continued

Option	Description
help	Displays the loadjava help screen.
oci8	Uses JDBC OCI driver to communicate with the database. This option can also be specified as -o.
noverify	Disables bytecode verifier so that uploaded classes are not verified.
oracleresolver	Binds newly created class schema objects to the following predefined resolver spec: `"((* definer's_schema) (* public))"`
resolve	Resolves all external references in those classes. This option can also be specified as -r.
Resolver	Binds newly created class schema objects to a user-defined resolver spec. This option can also be specified as -R.
schema	Uploads newly created Java schema objects into the specified schema. If this option is not specified, then the logon schema is used. This option can also be specified as -S.
thin	Uses the JDBC thin driver to communicate with the database. A thin driver is a 100% Java driver for client-side use without any Oracle installation. This option can also be specified as -t.
verbose	Directs loadjava to display progress messages. This option can also be specified as -v.

The loadjava utility first creates a system-generated database table named create$java$lob$table, into which Java can be loaded. Next it loads the Java binaries into a BLOB column of this table. Finally, it implicitly executes the CREATE JAVA... command to load Java from the BLOB column (Binary Large Object column) into database library units. There are three issues to be discussed here, namely, how external references are resolved, the manner in which files are loaded, and how compilation is done.

DEFAULT CONNECTION IS BETTER THAN NO CONNECTION!

It seems easy to write a Java Stored Procedure after going through the outlined steps. Write the Java Method, publish it using a call spec, and invoke it. That's it, isn't it? No. When accessing an Oracle database from the Java method, an important step is how to connect to the database to access the data. Obviously, like any other JDBC program, register the driver and obtain a connection using a particular schema. This doesn't work. Hey, what have I just done? Why didn't it work?

It didn't work because a Java Stored Procedure requires using a default server-side connection using the defaultConnection() method rather than an explicit connection.

Resolving External References

External references are resolved only after all Java classes are loaded. This is because the Java Development Kit (JDK) requires separate source files for each public class. Also, Java classes can refer to each other, hence name resolution is not possible until all the files have been loaded. Also all references must be resolved before the classes can be used.

Loadjava performs resolution when the resolve option is specified. Java uses the ALTER JAVA CLASS ... RESOLVE statement to resolve uploaded Java classes. If the resolve option is not specified, resolution is done at runtime and the ALTER JAVA statement is executed implicitly at run time. If, for a particular class, all its references to other classes cannot be resolved, that class is marked as invalid.

The loadjava utility can also take a RESOLVER specification as an argument, which is used to resolve Java classes. This is similar to the CLASSPATH environment variable which JDK uses to locate a class by searching in the list of directories specified in the CLASSPATH. However, a resolver spec lists schema names instead of directories. To specify resolver specs, the option resolver has to be used. Resolver specs are specified as follows:

```
-resolver "((name_spec schema_spec) [(name_spec schema_spec) ] . . . )"
```

Here name_spec stands for the full name of a Java class, a package name that with its final element specified as * or just * itself. The elements of a name_spec must be separated by / and not the dot notation. For example,

```
-resolver "((java/lang/* SCOTT) (* PUBLIC))"
```

specifies all classes in the java.lang package and residing in SCOTT schema as well all classes in the PUBLIC schema.

A schema_spec can be a schema name or the wildcard "-". The wildcard tells the resolver not to invalidate a class even if a reference cannot be resolved. This is at load time. However, all references are resolved at runtime if not resolved at load time.

For example, the following statement loads the `Slength` class and resolves the external references by searching for all classes in the java.lang package in the SCOTT schema and then in the PUBLIC schema.

```
loadjava -user SCOTT/TIGER -oci8 -resolve -resolver "((java/lang/* SCOTT) (*
PUBLIC))"
Slength.class
```

The Manner in Which Files Are Loaded

By default, previously loaded class files are not loaded. However, the force option enables to load previously loaded class files. But, if a source file has been loaded, -force cannot be used to load the corresponding class file. The source schema object has to be dropped first. To determine whether a class file has been loaded or not in a given schema, loadjava queries a hash table named JAVA$CLASS$MD5$TABLE. This table is called the "digest" table. Every time a Java schema object is loaded, the digest table is updated and only the most recent files are loaded. So all files not changed since the last load are skipped. Also, before reloading, `dropjava` command must be used to remove the corresponding entry from the digest table.

(The `dropjava` command is explained later). However, with the force option specified, the digest table lookup is bypassed.

How Compilation Is Done?

It is a better practice to compile all Java source files outside of the database. However, all Java source files when loaded are compiled when the resolve option is specified. The compilation errors are inserted into the USER_ERRORS table.

Options such as the JDK encoding scheme and whether online or not can be specified during compilation. Encoding refers to the character-encoding scheme. Online or not is an option when specified enables online semantics checking for SQLJ source files only. The encoding of the uploaded source file must match the specified encoding. The default value for this option is *latin1*. Specifying the resolve option in the loadjava command forces compilation of all Java source files while they are loaded. In this case the options can be specified in the command line such as the encoding option. A second method of specifying compiler options is using a database table named JAVA$OPTIONS, called the "options" table. This table is owned by SYS and can be seen in DBA_OBJECTS or ALL_OBJECTS when logged in as SYS or SYSTEM schemas. Options set in the options table are overridden by options specified in the command-line.

The value for the various compiler options can be set, retrieved, and reset in the options table by invoking the packaged procedures and functions in a package called DBMS_JAVA. These procedures and functions are

```
PROCEDURE set_compiler_option
          (name VARCHAR2, option VARCHAR2, value VARCHAR2);
FUNCTION get_compiler_option
          (name VARCHAR2, option VARCHAR2);
PROCEDURE reset_compiler_option
          (name VARCHAR2, option VARCHAR2);
```

These are the procedure and function specifications giving the signatures of the respective procedures and functions in the DBMS_JAVA package.

Here name stands for the name of a Java package, the full name of a class or an empty string. While compiling, the compiler selects the row that most closely matches the full name of the schema object. In the case of an empty string, it should match the name of any schema object. The options table is created when the procedure DBMS_JAVA.SET_COMPILER_OPTION is called.

TIP

A class once loaded with the loadjava command, should be dropped with the `dropjava` command. Otherwise, the digest table is not updated properly.

Dropping the Java Method

Once a Java object is loaded into the database, it can be dropped using a command-line utility called `dropjava`. `Dropjava` converts filenames into schema object names, drops the schema objects, and then deletes their rows from the digest table. As when you're using loadjava, the names of Java source, class, and resource files; and SQLJ files; and JAR and ZIP files can be specified with `dropjava`. Filenames not ending with .java, .class, .ser, .properties, .sqlj, .jar, and .zip are assumed to be schema objects.

TIP

Java schema objects should be dropped the same way they are uploaded. For example, if a .class file is uploaded, use the same filename to drop it.

The command for `dropjava` assumes the following form:

```
dropjava {-user | -u} username/password[@database]
[ -option_name -option_name … ] filename object_name filename …
```

where option_name stands for

```
{  {h | help}
 | {o | oci8}
 | {S | schema} schema_name
| { s | synonym }
| { t | thin}
| { v | verbose} }
```

For example, to drop the `Slength` class from the SCOTT schema, use the following from the command line:

```
dropjava -user SCOTT/TIGER Slength.class
```

`dropjava` does the inverse of loadjava. If a source file is specified, it finds the name of the first class in the file and then drops the corresponding schema object. In case of .class files, it finds the name of the class in the file and then drops the corresponding schema object. With .sqlj files, it does the same thing as a .java file. Lastly, with .jar and .zip files, `dropjava` treats the individual archived files as if they were entered in the command line.

Creating the Java Stored Procedure and Publishing It

Defining Call Specifications—Basics

As mentioned earlier, Java methods must be published in the Oracle data dictionary. Loading a Java class into the database does not publish its methods automatically. This is because, at load time, Oracle does not know which methods are safe entry points for calls from SQL. Java methods are published using call specifications. A call specification is defined as one of the following:

- A standalone PL/SQL procedure or function. This is at the top-level. Procedures can be used for *void* Java methods and functions can be used for Java methods that return values.
- A packaged PL/SQL procedure or function.
- A member method of a SQL object type.

TIP

A call spec is not a wrapper program as it does not add a second layer of code to be executed. It just publishes the existence of the Java method.

TIP

Only *public static* methods can be published with one exception. As an exception, public instance methods can be published as member methods of a SQL object type.

TIP

Only top-level and packaged procedures and functions can be used as call specs.

TIP

Call specs included in a package can be overloaded. This means the same procedure or function can be defined more than once with the same name but with a different signature.

While publishing Java methods using call specs, three issues need to be taken care of:

- Mapping SQL types to Java types
- Mapping SQL parameter modes to Java parameter modes
- Determining privileges under which the Java methods will execute

Mapping SQL Types to Java Types

While calling Java methods from PL/SQL via call specs, data is passed to and from SQL to Java. Java and SQL support different data types and hence these data types should be mapped from SQL to Java or from Java to SQL. This ensures that the parameters and function results in a call spec have compatible data types. Java native types include BYTE, SHORT, INT, FLOAT, and DOUBLE while SQL native types include NUMBER, CHAR, VARCHAR2, and DATE. Table 2.2 shows the allowed data type mappings between SQL and Java.

Table 2.2 The Mappings Between SQL and Java

SQL Type	Java Class
CHAR, NCHAR, LONG,	oracle.sql.CHAR
VARCHAR2, NVARCHAR2	java.lang.String
	java.sql.Date
	java.sql.Time
	java.sql.Timestamp
	java.lang.Byte
	java.lang.Short
	java.lang.Integer
CHAR, NCHAR, LONG,	java.lang.Long
VARCHAR2, NVARCHAR2	java.lang.Float
	java.lang.Double
	java.math.BigDecimal
	byte, short, int, long, float,
double	oracle.sql.DATE
DATE	java.sql.Date
	java.sql.Time
	java.sql.Timestamp
	java.lang.String
NUMBER	oracle.sql.NUMBER
	java.lang.Byte
	java.lang.Short
	java.lang.Integer
	java.lang.Long
	java.lang.Float
	java.lang.Double
	java.math.BigDecimal
	byte, short, int, long,
	float, double
RAW, LONG RAW	oracle.sql.RAW
	byte[]

Table 2.2 Continued

SQL Type	Java Class
ROWID	oracle.sql.CHAR
	oracle.sql.ROWID
	java.lang.String
BFILE	oracle.sql.BFILE
BLOB	oracle.sql.BLOB
	oracle.jdbc2.Blob
CLOB, NCLOB	oracle.sql.CLOB
	oracle.jdbc2.Clob
OBJECT	oracle.sql.STRUCT
	oracle.SqljData
	oracle.jdbc2.Struct
REF	oracle.sql.REF
	oracle.jdbc2.Ref
TABLE, VARRAY	oracle.sql.ARRAY
	oracle.jdbc2.Array
any of the above	oracle.sql.CustomDatum
SQL types	oracle.sql.Datum

SQL native types can be mapped directly to Java native types. However, there are two problems with this:

- There may be loss of information when SQL native types are mapped to Java native types. For example, mapping a SQL NUMBER type to a Java short or int type could result in loss of information when dealing with large numbers.
- The ability to handle NULLs also poses a problem. In SQL, data can have NULL values. Native types in Java which are also scalar types cannot accommodate NULL values. In cases where Java scalar type parameters receive NULL arguments, a NULL CONSTRAINT exception is raised before invoking the Java method call.

TIP

NULLs values are supported by using Java classes corresponding to the Java scalar types. Thus the Java method parameters can be defined of type java.lang.Integer, java.lang.short, and so on. This allows NULL values to pass in the call spec. However, there may still be loss of information.

TIP

The type UROWID and the NUMBER subtypes (INTEGER, REAL, FLOAT) cannot be mapped.

To address both these issues, Oracle 8i boasts the oracle.sql Java package that provides Java wrapper classes for native SQL types (oracle.sql.NUMBER, oracle.sql.DATE, and so on). The mappings to oracle.sql classes preserve data formats without having to do conversion to Java native format and without having to do character-set conversions. Also null values can be stored.

Mapping SQL Parameter Modes to Java Parameter Modes

Java supports call-by-reference when objects are passed as parameter. Call-by-reference enables the value of an argument to be available in the calling environment. However, in Java, a method cannot assign values to objects passed as arguments. So, to achieve call-by-reference, parameters in the call spec should be declared as an OUT or IN OUT parameter. The corresponding Java parameter should be declared as a one-element array. For example, an IN OUT parameter of type NUMBER can be mapped to a Java parameter of type

```
int[]  I
```

Then a new value can be assigned to i*[0]*.

TIP

All Java parameters and call spec parameters must correspond one-to-one. An exception to this rule is the *main()* method. The String[] parameter of main() can be mapped to multiple VARCHAR2 or CHAR parameters of the corresponding call spec.

TIP

If the Java method has no parameters, an empty parameter list has to be specified for it but not for the PL/SQL procedure or function.

TIP

Boolean parameters cannot be specified for the PL/SQL procedure or function. A workaround can be to pass a corresponding of type NUMBER. A non-zero value is interpreted as TRUE whereas a zero value is taken to be FALSE.

The following sections elaborate on the three ways for defining call specs in order to publish Java methods.

Defining Top-level Call Specs

A standalone procedure or function can be used to define top-level call specs. As mentioned earlier, procedures can be used to publish *void* methods and functions can be used for methods with return values. The general syntax is as follows:

```
CREATE [OR REPLACE]
{  PROCEDURE procedure_name [(param [, param] ..)]
 | FUNCTION function_name [ (param [, param] ..)] RETURN sql_type}
[AUTHID {DEFINER | CURRENT_USER}]
[PARALLEL_ENABLE]
[DETERMINISTIC]
{IS | AS} LANGUAGE JAVA
NAME 'method_fullname (java_type_fullname[, java_type_fullname] ..)
      [ return java_type_fullname]';
```

Here param stands for

```
parameter_name [IN | OUT | IN OUT] sql_type
```

The *AUTHID* clause determines the privileges under which the stored procedure or function will execute and whether any unqualified references to schema objects are resolved in the schema of the definer or invoker.

The NAME clause string should specify the full name of the Java method. Also, the fully Java type names and the call spec parameters are mapped by position and must correspond one-to-one. An exception to this rule is the main method. An example of defining a top-level call spec has been outlined above using the Java method Slength.compute_length and the PL/SQL function f_Slength.

Defining Call Specs as Part of a Package

A packaged procedure or function can also be used to publish a Java method. The individual procedures inside the package body use the NAME clause (described above) to publish the Java method. The following example illustrates this concept:

Consider the following Java class *empMaster* with four methods: hireEmp, fireEmp, transferEmp, and hikeEmpSal. The hireEmp method creates a new record in the EMP table. The fireEmp method deletes the corresponding row in the EMP table based on an input EMPNO. The transferEmp method transfers the input employee from the current department to the input ip_todept. The hikeEmpSal method updates the SAL column for the input EMPNO.

```
// Import the relevant packages
import java.sql.*;
import java.io.*;
import oracle.jdbc.driver.*;

public class empMaster {
// Define Java Method to insert a record
  public static void hireEmp(int    i_empno,
```

```
                                  String i_ename,
                                  String i_job,
                                  int    i_mgr,
                                  String i_hiredate,
                                  float  i_sal,
                                  float  i_comm,
                                  int    i_deptno,
                                  String[] msg)
  throws SQLException {
    // Get default Oracle connection
    Connection conn = new OracleDriver().defaultConnection();    // Define
SELECT to query input empno
String sql1 = "SELECT empno FROM emp WHERE empno = ?" ;     //Define INSERT to
input the emp record
String sql2 = "INSERT INTO emp VALUES (?,?,?,?,?,?,?,?)";int ret_code;
    try {        // Initially check to see wether record with input empno exists
ot not.
       PreparedStatement pstmt = conn.prepareStatement(sql1);
       pstmt.setInt(1, i_empno);
       ResultSet rset = pstmt.executeQuery();
       if (rset.next()) { // If exists, display a message and end the program
         msg[0] = "This employee already exists.";
         rset.close();
         pstmt.close();
         }
        else // if record with input empno does not exist,INSERT the new record
         {
         pstmt = conn.prepareStatement(sql2);
         pstmt.setInt(1, i_empno);
         pstmt.setString(2, i_ename);
         pstmt.setString(3, i_job);
         pstmt.setInt(4, i_mgr);
         pstmt.setString(5, i_hiredate);
         pstmt.setFloat(6, i_sal);
         pstmt.setFloat(7, i_comm);
         pstmt.setInt(8, i_deptno);
         pstmt.executeUpdate();
         rset.close();
         pstmt.close(); }
       } catch (SQLException e) {ret_code = e.getErrorCode();
                                 System.err.println(ret_code + e.getMessage());}
   }
```

```
// Define Java method to delete a record
  public static void fireEmp(int i_empno)
  throws SQLException {
    // Get default Oracle connection    Connection conn = new
OracleDriver().defaultConnection();String sql = "DELETE emp WHERE empno = ?"; //
Define DELETE statement
    int ret_code;
    try {
         PreparedStatement pstmt = conn.prepareStatement(sql);
         pstmt.setInt(1, i_empno);
         pstmt.executeUpdate();
         pstmt.close();
       } catch (SQLException e) {ret_code = e.getErrorCode();
                                 System.err.println(ret_code + e.getMessage());}
   }

//Define Java method to update a record - update deptno
public static void transferEmp(int i_empno, int i_todept)
  throws SQLException {
    // Get default Oracle connection
    Connection conn = new OracleDriver().defaultConnection();    // Define
UPDATE statement
String sql = "UPDATE emp SET deptno = ? WHERE empno = ?"; int ret_code;
    try {
         PreparedStatement pstmt = conn.prepareStatement(sql);
         pstmt.setInt(1, i_todept);
         pstmt.setInt(2, i_empno);
         pstmt.executeUpdate();
         pstmt.close();
       } catch (SQLException e) {ret_code = e.getErrorCode();
                                 System.err.println(ret_code + e.getMessage());}
   }

// Define Java method to update a record - update sal
public static void hikeEmpSal(int i_empno, int i_comm)
  throws SQLException {
    // Get default Oracle connection    Connection conn = new
OracleDriver().defaultConnection();    // Define UPDATE statement
String sql = "UPDATE emp SET sal = sal + (1.25*?) WHERE empno = ?";
    int ret_code;
    try {
         PreparedStatement pstmt = conn.prepareStatement(sql);
```

```
            pstmt.setInt(1, i_comm);
            pstmt.setInt(2, i_empno);
            pstmt.executeUpdate();
            pstmt.close();
          } catch (SQLException e) {ret_code = e.getErrorCode();
                                      System.err.println(ret_code + e.getMessage());}
   }
}
```

A package is the ideal program to publish these four related methods. The following package PKG_EMPMASTER includes four procedures HIRE_EMP, FIRE_EMP, TRANSFER_EMP, and HIKE_EMP_SAL for defining the call specs to the respective methods hireEmp, fireEmp, transferEmp, and hikeEmpSal.

```
CREATE OR REPLACE PACKAGE pkg_empmaster
IS
/* Define PL/SQL prccedures corresponding to
   hireEmp(), fireEmp(), transferEmp() and hikeEmpSal() Java Methods.
   The specifications are defined here. The implementation details are
   defined in the package body. */
  PROCEDURE hire_emp(ip_empno NUMBER,
                     ip_ename VARCHAR2,
                     ip_job   VARCHAR2,
                     ip_mgr   NUMBER,
                     ip_hiredate DATE,
                     ip_sal   NUMBER,
                     ip_comm  NUMBER,
                     ip_deptno NUMBER,
                     msg OUT VARCHAR2);
  PROCEDURE fire_emp(ip_empno NUMBER);
  PROCEDURE transfer_emp(ip_empno NUMBER, ip_todept NUMBER);
  PROCEDURE hike_emp_sal (ip_empno NUMBER, ip_comm NUMBER);
END pkg_empmaster;
/

CREATE OR REPLACE PACKAGE pkg_empmaster
IS

/* Define the implementation details of the procedures
   defined in the package specification */
  PROCEDURE hire_emp(ip_empno NUMBER,
                     ip_ename VARCHAR2,
                     ip_job   VARCHAR2,
```

```
                     ip_mgr    NUMBER,
                     ip_hiredate DATE,
                     ip_sal    NUMBER,
                     ip_comm   NUMBER,
                     ip_deptno NUMBER,
                     msg OUT VARCHAR2)
  IS LANGUAGE JAVA
NAME 'empMaster.hireEmp(int, java.lang.String, java.lang.String, int,
                        java.lang.String, int, int, int, java.lang.String[])';

  PROCEDURE fire_emp(ip_empno NUMBER)
  IS LANGUAGE JAVA
  NAME 'empMaster.fireEmp(int)';

  PROCEDURE transfer_emp(ip_empno NUMBER, ip_todept NUMBER)
  IS LANGUAGE JAVA
  NAME 'empMaster.transferEmp(int, int)';

  PROCEDURE hike_emp_sal (ip_empno NUMBER, ip_new_sal NUMBER)
  IS LANGUAGE JAVA
  NAME 'empMaster.hikeEmpSal(int, int)';

END pkg_empmaster;
/
```

Defining Call Specs as a Member Method of a SQL Object Type

A member method of an object type can also be used to define a call spec and publish a Java method. This is to accommodate object features and publish Java methods that require you to process objects. For every object type involving methods, an object type body should be specified giving the method implementation details. However, for publishing Java methods as member methods of an object type, there is no need to define an object type body. The body of the methods is defined as methods in a Java class.

Consider the following Java class *addressMaster* with two methods: create_address, which populates an instance of the above-mentioned Java class, and change_address, which alters the values of the attributes an instance of the same class. The corresponding call specs are implemented as MEMBER procedures of the object type *address* and are used to insert and update rows in the object table *addresses* based on the object type *address.*

```
// Import revelant oracle and Java packages
import java.sql.*;
import java.io.*;
```

```
import oracle.jdbc.driver.*;
import oracle.jdbc.oracore.*;
import oracle.jdbc2.*;

public class addressMaster implements SQLData {
  private int add_id;
  private String line1;
  private String line2;
  private String city;
  private String state;
  private String zip;

  public void createAddress
                              (int    i_add_id,
                               String i_line1,
                               String i_line2,
                               String i_city,
                               String i_state,
                               String i_zip)
  {
    add_id = i_add_id;
    line1  = i_line1;
    line2  = i_line2;
    city   = i_city;
    state  = i_state;
    zip    = i_zip;
  }
  public void changeAddress
                              (int    i_add_id,
                               String i_line1,
                               String i_line2,
                               String i_city,
                               String i_state,
                               String i_zip)
  {
    line1  = i_line1;
    line2  = i_line2;
    city   = i_city;
    state  = i_state;
    zip    = i_zip;
  }
```

```
// Implement SQLData interface
  String sql_type;

  public String getSQLTypeName() throws SQLException {
   return sql_type;
  }
  public void readSQL(SQLInput stream, String typeName)
  throws SQLException {
    sql_type = typeName;
    add_id = stream.readInt();
    line1  = stream.readString();
    line2  = stream.readString();
    city   = stream.readString();
    state  = stream.readString();
    zip    = stream.readString();
  }

  public void writeSQL(SQLOutput stream)
  throws SQLException {
    stream.writeInt(add_id);
    stream.writeString(line1);
    stream.writeString(line2);
    stream.writeString(city);
    stream.writeString(state);
    stream.writeString(zip);
  }

}
```

The corresponding call spec can be defined using a CREATE TYPE statement in the database. This is demonstrated below:

```
/* Define the object type with attributes and member methods */
CREATE OR REPLACE TYPE address AS OBJECT (add_id number(10),
                                line1 varchar2(20),
                                line2 varchar2(20),
                                city  varchar2(15),
                                state varchar2(2),
                                zip   varchar2(11),
  MEMBER PROCEDURE create_address
                   (i_add_id number,
                    i_line1 varchar2,
```

```
                    i_line2 varchar2,
                    i_city  varchar2,
                    i_state varchar2,
                    i_zip   varchar2)
   IS LANGUAGE JAVA
   NAME 'addressMaster.createAddress(int, java.lang.String, java.lang.String,
                                   java.lang.String, java.lang.String,
                                   java.lang.String)'
   MEMBER PROCEDURE change_address
                   (i_add_id number,
                    i_line1 varchar2,
                    i_line2 varchar2,
                    i_city  varchar2,
                    i_state varchar2,
                    i_zip   varchar2)
   IS LANGUAGE JAVA
   NAME 'addressMaster.changeAddress(int, java.lang.String, java.lang.String,
                                   java.lang.String, java.lang.String,
                                   java.lang.String)'
   );
/
```

The calling of these object type methods is outlined next in the sub-section "Calling from PL/SQL" of the section "Calling the Java Stored Procedure". Here an object table *addresses* based on the object type *address* is used.

TIP

Static Java methods are specified as STATIC member methods and non-static Java methods are specified as MEMBER procedures or functions in the call spec.

TIP

To access the attributes of an object type, the Java class that implements the SQLData interface is created. The SQLData interface is a Java interface for accessing the object attributes of an object type. To do this, the methods readSQL() and writeSQL() (as defined in the SQLData interface) are used. These are executed by the JDBC driver to read and write values to and from the database and the instance of the Java class.

TIP

The `SELF` parameter associated with the object type method corresponds to the `this` parameter of the Java method. Here, the SELF parameter denotes the object whose member method was invoked in SQL and PL/SQL. The corresponding parameter in Java is `this` and denotes the object whose Java method was invoked.

Granting Access Privileges

Regarding the privileges under which the Java methods will execute, all Java stored procedures execute with invoker rights. This allows for late binding to tables, i.e., binding at runtime rather than at compile time; also, the procedures are executed within the scope and authorization of the caller of the procedure.

Calling the Java Stored Procedure

This section outlines the details of calling the Java stored procedure from SQL or PLSQL. Once loaded and published, a Java stored procedure can be called from one of the following contexts:

- The top level, that is, from an anonymous PL/SQL block and not as a procedure for function called from another procedure or function
- Database triggers
- SQL DML
- PL/SQL

Calling from the Top Level

The SQL CALL statement enables to call Java stored procedures from the top level.

```
CALL [schema_name.] [{package_name. | object_type_name.}] [@dblink_name]
{procedure_name( {param[, param] …) |
 function_name ( {param[, param] …) INTO :host_variable};
```

Host variables should be prefixed with a colon and each host variable must appear only once in the same CALL statement.

For example, in SQL*Plus, the Slength.compute_length() method can be invoked by calling the corresponding published function f_Slength using the following CALL statement:

The statement below declares a numeric variable named len to store the return value of the function:

```
SQL> variable len NUMBER;
```

The CALL statement executes the function and assigns its return value to the variable len.

```
SQL> CALL f_Slength('This is a test class') INTO :len;

Call completed.
```

The above is what SQL*Plus displays after the execution of CALL statement. To check the output from the above execution, we display the value of the len variable as follows:

```
SQL> print len

      LEN
---------
       20
```

The value of len is displayed as above.

Calling from Database Triggers

Calling a Java stored procedure from a database trigger involves making a call to the corresponding call spec in the trigger action block with the CALL statement. In the CALL statement, column names must be prefixed with :NEW or :OLD. The following example illustrates this:

Consider a DEPT_AUDIT table that stores the DEPTNO and the count of employees in each department. This table was created earlier (in the case study) and its definition looks like the following:

```
CREATE TABLE dept_audit
(deptno NUMBER NOT NULL,
 cnt_emp NUMBER NOT NULL);
```

The Java class *DeptAudit* is given below:

```
// Import relevant oracle and Java packages
import java.sql.*;
import java.io.*;
import oracle.jdbc.driver.*;

public class DeptAudit {
  public static void DeptAuditRow(int i_deptno)
  throws SQLException {
// Get default Oracle connection    Connection conn = new
OracleDriver().defaultConnection();// Define SELECT to query input deptno
```

```
String sql1 = "SELECT deptno FROM dept_audit WHERE deptno = ?" ; // Define
INSERT to insert a new row if row with input deptno doesn't exist
String sql2 = "INSERT INTO dept_audit VALUES (?,?)";// Define UPDATE for
existing row
String sql3 =
     "UPDATE dept_audit SET cnt_emp = nvl(cnt_emp,0) + 1 WHERE deptno = ?";
    int ret_code;
    int x = 1;
    try {
       PreparedStatement pstmt = conn.prepareStatement(sql1);
       pstmt.setInt(1, i_deptno);
       ResultSet rset = pstmt.executeQuery();
       if (rset.next()) { // If row exists, then update
         pstmt = conn.prepareStatement(sql3);
         pstmt.setInt(1, i_deptno);
         pstmt.executeUpdate();
         rset.close();
         pstmt.close();
         }
        else // else INSERT
         {
         pstmt = conn.prepareStatement(sql2);
         pstmt.setInt(1, i_deptno);
         pstmt.setInt(2, x);
         pstmt.executeUpdate();
         rset.close();
         pstmt.close(); }
      } catch (SQLException e) {ret_code = e.getErrorCode();
                                 System.err.println(ret_code + e.getMessage());}
    }
}
```

The class spec for the above Java method is defined as follows:

```
CREATE OR REPLACE PROCEDURE p_dept_audit(ip_deptno NUMBER)
AS LANGUAGE JAVA
NAME 'DeptAudit.DeptAuditRow(int)';
/
```

This class is used in an AFTER INSERT database trigger on the EMP table, whenever a new employee is hired. The trigger text is given below:

```
CREATE OR REPLACE TRIGGER dept_audit_trg
AFTER INSERT ON EMP
FOR EACH ROW
CALL p_dept_audit(:NEW.deptno)
/
```

The above creates a database trigger named dept_audit_trg that calls the p_dept_audit procedure whenever a new row is inserted into the EMP table.

Now we insert rows into the employee table to see the result of our Java method. First, we check for the existence of records in the dept_audit table with the following query:

```
SQL> select * from dept_audit;
```

The output from the above query is displayed as follows indicating that there are no rows in the dept_audit table:

```
no rows selected
```

Next, we insert a row into the EMP table as follows:

```
SQL> insert into emp values
     (1111, 'JOE', 'ANALYST', null, sysdate, 7000, null, 10);

1 row created.
```

We have added a row to the EMP table for deptno 10 and the system has verified that one row was created.

Next we select from the empty dept_audit table and see that one row was created for deptno 1- with cnt_emp = 1. The query and the corresponding output are shown below.

```
SQL> select * from dept_audit;

   DEPTNO   CNT_EMP
--------- ---------
       10         1
```

We then add a second row to the EMP table for the same deptno. The INSERT statement for this is shown below.

```
SQL> insert into emp values
     (1112, 'STEVEN', 'ANALYST', null, sysdate, 8000, null, 10);

1 row created.
```

Checking the dept_audit table once again yields the fact that the cnt_emp column has been updated to two for deptno 10. The SELECT for this and the corresponding output are shown below.

```
SQL> select * from dept_audit;

   DEPTNO    CNT_EMP
--------- ---------
       10          2
```

Finally, we add one more row to the EMP table for deptno 20. The INSERT statement for this is shown below.

```
SQL> insert into emp values (1113, 'MIKE', 'ANALYST', null, sysdate, 9000, null,
20);

1 row created.
```

Checking the dept_audit table now shows us that another row has been inserted. The new row is for deptno 20 and the cnt_emp = 1. The query and the corresponding output for this are shown below.

```
SQL> select * from dept_audit;

   DEPTNO    CNT_EMP
--------- ---------
       10          2
       20          1
```

Calling from SQL DML

Java methods published as functions are callable from SQL SELECT, INSERT, UPDATE, and DELETE methods. For example, consider the Slength.compute_length() method and the corresponding published function f_Slength described above. The function f_Slength can be called from SQL SELECT statement as follows:

```
SQL> select ename, f_Slength(ename) len from emp;
The output of the above SELECT statement is as follows:
NAME            LEN
---------- ---------
SMITH             5
ALLEN             5
WARD              4
JONES             5
MARTIN            6
BLAKE             5
CLARK             5
SCOTT             5
KING              4
TURNER            6
ADAMS             5
JAMES             5
FORD              4
MILLER            6

14 rows selected.
```

The following restrictions apply for calling Java stored functions from SQL DML:

- The method cannot have OUT or IN OUT parameters.
- The method cannot modify any database tables.
- When called from an INSERT, UPDATE, or DELETE statement, the method cannot query or modify any database tables modified by that statement.
- The method cannot execute any DDL, that is, Data Definition Language, statements, transaction control statements such as COMMIT, session control statements such as SET ROLE, or system control statements such as ALTER SYSTEM.

Calling from PL/SQL

Calling Java methods from PL/SQL amounts to calling the corresponding published procedure or function from PL/SQL. The call spec is called similar to the manner in which any stored or package procedure or function is called from PL/SQL. Consider again the Java method and its call spec f_Slength. f_Slength can be called as follows:

```
DECLARE
  ret_val NUMBER;
BEGIN
  ret_val := f_Slength('This is a test class');
  dbms_output.put_line(to_char(ret_val));
END;
/
```

The above code defines an anonymous PL/SQL block that makes a call to the f_Slength function. This invokes the `Slength.compute_length` Java method that executes to yield the length of the input string.

Calling f_Slength in the above manner executes the Java method Slength.compute_length inside the Oracle 8i database.

Coming to the object type *address* and the object table *addresses* created earlier, its member method create_address can be called from PL/SQL as follows:

```
declare
  address1 address := address(null,null,null,null,null,null);
begin
  address1.create_address(1,'19 Reading Rd','# J','Edison','NJ','08817');
  insert into addresses values (address1);
end;
/
```

The above code defines an anonymous PL/SQL block that declares an instance variable of the object type address and instantiates it by using the default constructor. It then makes a call to the create_address function. This invokes the `addressMaster.createAddress()` Java method that executes to insert a row into the `addresses` table.

The output of the above PL/SQL block can be tested using a SQL*Plus query as follows:

```
SQL> select * from addresses;
```

The output of the above query is as follows:

```
   ADD_ID LINE1              LINE2              CITY          ST ZIP
--------- ------------------ ------------------ ------------- -- -----------
        1 19 Reading Rd      # J                Edison        NJ 08817
```

Similarly, the member method change_address can be called from PL/SQL as follows:

```
declare
  v_address address; -- declare a instance of address object type
begin
/* Select the value of the object row into the defined instance variable */
  select value(a)
  into   v_address
  from   addresses a
  where add_id = 1;

/* Invoke the change_address procedure on the defined instance */
  v_address.change_address(1, '30 Carlton Avenue','# 32D','Sunnyvale',
                           'CA','97848');

/* Update corresponding row in the addresses tabke with the changed address */
  update addresses a
  set    a = v_address
  where  a.add_id = v_address.add_id;
end;
/
```

Querying the object table addresses yields the following:

```
SQL> select * from addresses;
```

The output of the above query is as follows:

```
   ADD_ID LINE1              LINE2              CITY          ST ZIP
--------- ------------------ ------------------ ------------- -- -----------
```

Summary

This chapter outlined the use of Java Stored procedures for database access in Java, as a method to incorporate Java in the Oracle 8i database. Essentially, the various methods of creating Java Stored Procedures starting from writing the Java class to executing the Java Stored Procedure from the Oracle 8i database were described in detail.

BASIC JDBC PROGRAMMING

ESSENTIALS

- Java Database Connectivity (JDBC) is a method of Java calling SQL and PL/SQL. The DML operations of SELECT, INSERT, UPDATE, and DELETE as well as calling PL/SQL procedures and returning of resultsets can be done using JDBC.
- Oracle8i provides JDBC drivers for Java programs to interface with the database.
- Java programs can call SQL and PL/SQL using the classes in a standard package java.sql.* and two other Oracle supplied packages oracle.sql.* and oracle.jdbc.driver.*.
- The basic steps in creating a JDBC application involve importing JDBC packages, loading and registering the JDBC driver, opening a connection to the database, creating a statement object to perform a query, executing the statement object, returning a query resultset, processing the resultset, closing the resultset and statement objects, and finally closing the connection.
- To process INSERTS, UPDATES, and DELETES, create a PreparedStatement object.
- To invoke PL/SQL subprograms create a CallableStatement object.
- Transaction processing involving COMMIT and ROLLBACK is done by setting the auto-commit mode to OFF and then using the commit() and rollback() methods on the Connection object.
- To manipulate ROWIDS and REF CURSORS use the Oracle Extensions supplied by the classes in the oracle.sql.* package.

This chapter explains the use of Java Database Connectivity for database access in Java. It highlights the method to incorporate Java in the Oracle 8i database using JDBC. The various methods of using JDBC starting from the querying and returning of resultsets to executing DML from the Oracle 8i database are described in detail. The Oracle JDBC extensions are discussed. A case study is presented to illustrate the concepts.

Overview of JDBC—Java Calling SQL and PL/SQL

This section gives a brief outline of JDBC and the various JDBC drivers. It also highlights the JDBC 2.0 features. The details of the case study used to illustrate the various JDBC concepts throughout are presented.

About JDBC

JDBC provides a standard interface for accessing a relational database from a Java application regardless of where the application is running and where the database is. From an Oracle 8i perspective it provides a way for Java applications to call SQL and PL/SQL. In other words it is a way to execute SQL statements and also call stored database procedures. One important feature of JDBC is location independence. Java programs with database access can be written and deployed as an application or as a Web-based applet. The ease of development, robustness, and security of Java programs makes it a good choice for writing database applications in Java. Moreover, the early compile-time checking and dynamic runtime checking goes in sync with the dynamic SQL interface of JDBC for Java. JDBC consists of a high-level "thin" API and multiple low-level drivers for connecting to different databases. There are four types of drivers defined by JDBC as follows:

- **Type 1: JDBC/ODBC**—These require an ODBC (Open Database Connectivity) driver for the database to be installed. This type of driver works by translating the submitted queries into equivalent ODBC queries and forwards them via native API calls directly to the ODBC driver. It provides no host redirection capability.
- **Type2: Native API**—This type of driver uses a vendor-specific driver or database API to interact with the database. An example of such an API is Oracle OCI (Oracle Call Interface). It also provides no host redirection.
- **Type 3: Open Protocol-Net**—This is not vendor specific and works by forwarding database requests to a remote database source using a net server component. How the net server component accesses the database is transparent to the client. The client driver communicates with the net server using a database-independent protocol and the net server translates this protocol into database calls. This type of driver can access any database.

- **Type 4: Proprietary Protocol-Net**—This has a same configuration as a type 3 driver but uses a wire protocol specific to a particular vendor and hence can access only that vendor's database. Again this is all transparent to the client.

Figure 3.1 shows a typical implementation of a JDBC application.

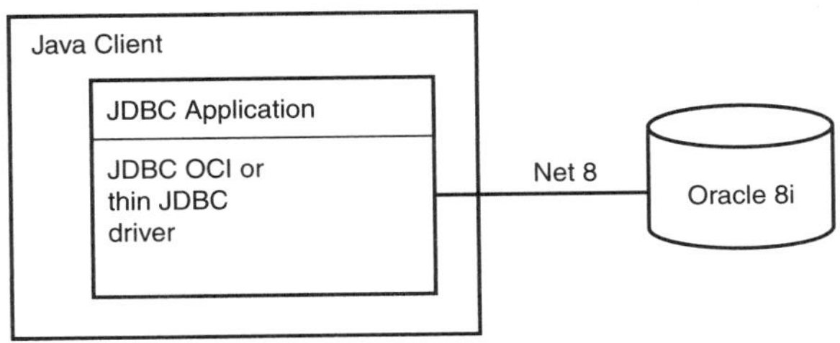

FIGURE 3.1
A typical JDBC application.

Basically a Java program implementing JDBC performs the following functions:

- Load a JDBC driver.
- Establish a database connection.
- Optionally interrogate the database for capability subset.
- Optionally retrieve schema metadata information.
- Construct a SQL or callable statement object and send queries or database tasks.
- Execute the database tasks or process resultsets.
- Close the statement object and resultset.
- Close the connection.

Oracle JDBC Drivers

Oracle 8i provides four types of JDBC drivers, namely, thin drivers, OCI drivers, server-side thin drivers, and server-side internal drivers. These client-side and server-side drivers provide the same functionality and have the same syntax and APIs and they share the same Oracle extensions. The difference lies in how they connect to the database and how they transfer data. The server-side internal driver supports JDK 1.2.x/JDBC 2.0 whereas the other drivers support JDK 1.1.x/JDBC 1.22 with Oracle extensions for JDBC 2.0. The following gives a detailed description of each of these drivers:

Client-side Oracle JDBC Thin Driver

This driver is a Type 4 (Proprietary Protocol-Net) driver and is written in 100% pure Java making it platform independent. It allows a direct connection to the database. It implements the TCP/IP protocol that emulates Oracle's Net8 and TTC (the wire protocol of OCI) on top of Java sockets. Java applets are good candidates that make use of this driver. This driver gives the maximum portability. Figure 3.2 shows a client-side JDBC thin driver.

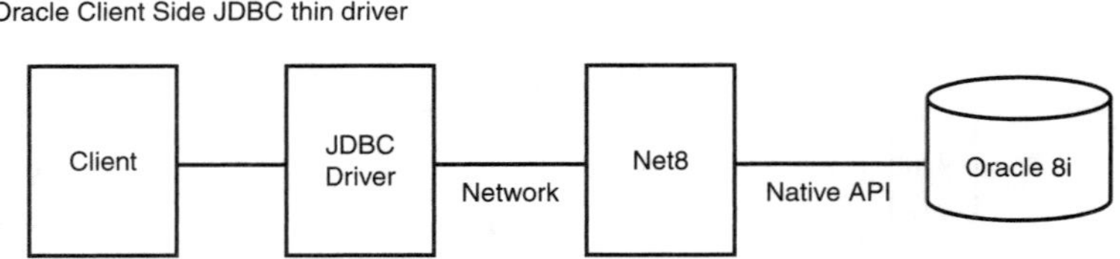

FIGURE 3.2
A configuration of an Oracle client-side JDBC thin driver.

Client-side Oracle JDBC OCI Driver

This is a native-API Type 2 driver that is suited for client-server Java applications. It is Oracle platform-specific and requires an Oracle client installation. This driver converts JDBC calls into calls to the Oracle Call Interface using native methods. These calls are then sent to the Oracle database server using Net8. These drivers support protocols such as IPC, named pipes, TCP/IP, and IPX/SPX. This driver gives the maximum performance for an Oracle client application.

Server-side Oracle JDBC Thin Driver

This driver has the same functionality as the client-side thin driver except that it runs inside Oracle 8i and accesses a remote database. This driver can also be used to access data in the same database as the database connection. An example of using this driver is when accessing an Oracle server from inside of a Java stored procedure.

Server-side Oracle JDBC Internal Driver

This driver supports any Java code that runs inside a target Oracle database such as a Java stored procedure and must access the same database.

JDBC 2.0 Support

Oracle 8i Release 2 provides JDBC drivers that are fully compliant with Java 2 and JDBC 2.0. Applications can use these features in exactly the same way as with earlier versions of JDBC. All four Oracle JDBC drivers support these changes. We will discuss JDBC2.0 support under the following headings:

- JDK Support
- JDBC 2.0 Features

JDK Support

Oracle 8i Release 2 supports JDK 1.2 and JDK 1.1. As regards the former, the JDK 1.2 versions of the JDBC drivers are fully compliant with JDBC 2.0. The implementation is by means of the interfaces in the standard java.sql package included in the file classes12.zip. On the Oracle side, these interfaces are implemented as appropriate by classes in the oracle.sql and oracle.jdbc.driver packages. The files java.sql.* and oracle.sql.* need to be imported for JDK 1.2.

As regards JDK 1.1.x, the file classes111.zip is needed. The implementation of JDBC2.0 functionality is by means of the package oracle.jdbc2 still included in classes111.zip. Features such as objects, object references, arrays, and LOBS can be used by importing this package. The files java.sql.*, oracle.jdbc2.*, and oracle.sql.* need to be imported for JDK 1.1.x.

The package java.sql.* comes with JDK; the packages oracle.sql.*, oracle.jdbc.driver, and oracle.jdbc2 come with Oracle's drivers.

JDBC 2.0 Features

The following are the JDBC 2.0 features supported by Oracle 8i Release 2:

- Resultset enhancements

  JDBC 2.0 supports scrollable resultset capability under three major headings, namely, forward-only, scroll-insensitive, and scroll-sensitive. Each of these resultsets can in turn be Read_only or Updatable. Forward_only/Read_only is feature of JDBC 1.0. The remaining five kinds are additions in JDBC 2.0. All these kinds are supported in JDK 1.2 and JDK 1.1 through an Oracle extension.

- Batch Updates

  Oracle 8i Release 2 supports two types of batch updates, namely, automatic batch update of Oracle style and explicit batch update of JDBC 2.0 style.

- Advanced Data Types

  The advanced data types such as objects, object references, arrays, LOBS, SQL Data, and Struct are now supported by JDBC 2.0. With JDK1.2 compatible drivers, these are available as part of the java.sql package. While porting code from JDK1.1 to JDK 1.2 drivers, oracle.jdbc2 should be replaced with java.sql in the source and then recompiled.

- JNDI

The Java Naming and Directory Interface (JNDI) is an interface to obtain network resources in a vendor independent fashion. This is available as part of the JDBC2.0 Optional Package (JDBC 2.0 Standard Extension API) and implemented by means of javax.sql package. As of Oracle 8i Release 2, this is available for both JDK1.2 and JDK1.1.x.

- Connection Pooling

  Connection pooling is a method where multiple consumers share a limited set of connections instead of each having to create new connections. This also includes connection caching. This is implemented by means of javax.sql package. This is available for both JDK1.1.x and JDK1.2 drivers but only in the OCI and thin drivers. The server-side Oracle JDBC driver does not have connection pooling as the server driver can have only one connection which is to the logged-in session.

- Distributed Transactions

  A distributed transaction is a combination of two or more related transactions that execute in a coordinated manner. All the individual transactions might take place in the same database, but typically, the individual transactions are in different databases and often in different locations. For example, a distributed transaction might involve a change in a transaction record in one table and an automatic creation of an audit record in another table in a different database located in a second location. Distributed transactions are defined as a JDBC2.0 standard extensions API and are also implemented by means of javax.sql package. On the Oracle side, support for distributed transactions is provided by means of two packages: oracle.jdbc.xa.client for client-side OCI and thin drivers and the server-side thin driver; and oracle.jdbc.xa.server package for server-side internal driver.

- Other Features

  Other features include fetch size/row prefetching. Fetch size is part of JDBC2.0 and includes methods to define the number of rows retrieved by each database fetch. Oracle row-prefetching can also be used as an equivalent of JDBC2.0 fetch size. These features can be used in Oracle 8i Release 2 and JDK 1.2 and JDK 1.1.x as an Oracle extension.

Case Study

We will use the schema `oratest/oratest@oracle` (where oracle is the tnsnames alias in tnsnames.ora). This is for tools such as SQL*Plus. As part of the case study we will use the same schema objects as defined in case study of Chapter 2. These are reproduced here for convenience:

Database objects (tables and object types):

```
CREATE TABLE dept (deptno number(4) primary key,
                   dname  varchar2(20) not null,
                   loc    varchar2(15) not null);

CREATE TABLE emp (empno number(10) primary key,
                  ename varchar2(40) not null,
                  job   varchar2(15) not null,
                  mgr   number(10) references emp(empno),
                  hiredate date not null,
                  sal   number(12,2) not null,
                  comm  number(4),
                  deptno number(4) references dept(deptno));

CREATE TABLE dept_audit (deptno number(4) primary key references
dept(deptno),
                         cnt_emp number(10) not null);

CREATE OR REPLACE TYPE address AS OBJECT
                               (add_id number(10),
                                line1 varchar2(20),
                                line2 varchar2(20),
                                city  varchar2(15),
                                state varchar2(2),
                                zip   varchar2(11));
/
```

(This type is later changed in Chapter 4, "Advanced JDBC Programming," to include member methods.)

```
CREATE TABLE addresses OF address;
```

In addition, the following schema objects are also used and should be defined in the above schema:

- Database tables and objects

```
CREATE TABLE emp_with_type
                (empno number(10) primary key,
                 ename varchar2(40) not null,
                 etype varchar2(10) not null,
                 job   varchar2(15) not null,
                 mgr   number(10) references emp(empno),
```

```
                  hiredate date not null,
                  sal   number(12,2) not null,
                  comm  number(4),
                  deptno number(4) references dept(deptno));

CREATE TABLE emp_with_addr (empno number(10) primary key,
                  ename varchar2(40) not null,
                  job   varchar2(15) not null,
                  mgr   number(10) references emp(empno),
                  hiredate date not null,
                  sal   number(12,2) not null,
                  comm  number(4),
                  deptno number(4) references dept(deptno),
                  emp_addr REF address);
```

This is used for describing Object REFS in Chapter 4.

```
CREATE TYPE address_id_varray IS VARRAY(20) OF NUMBER;

CREATE TABLE address_id_list(address_id_list address_id_varray);
```

The above created type and table are used in describing collections in Chapter 4.

```
CREATE TABLE lob_tab
(id NUMBER PRIMARY KEY,
 blob_data BLOB,
 clob_data CLOB,
 bfile_data BFILE);
```

This table is used in describing large objects in Chapter 4.

```
CREATE TABLE tab1 (col1 NUMBER);
```

- PLSQL packages and procedures:

```
CREATE OR REPLACE PACKAGE pkg_refcur IS

  TYPE bonus_refcur IS REF CURSOR;

  FUNCTION f_refcur(ip_etype VARCHAR2) RETURN pkg_refcur.bonus_refcur;

END pkg_refcur;
/
```

This package is used in describing Oracle REF CURSOR in the section "Features of Oracle Extensions."

A procedure `p_highest_paid_emp` is used in the section "Calling PL/SQL Stored Procedures," later in this chapter.

The above schema objects are used to describe the ins and outs of JDBC programs.

Fundamental Steps in JDBC

The fundamental steps involved in the process of connecting to a database and executing a query consist of the following:

- Import JDBC packages.
- Load and register the JDBC driver.
- Open a connection to the database.
- Create a statement object to perform a query.
- Execute the statement object and return a query resultset.
- Process the resultset.
- Close the resultset and statement objects.
- Close the connection.

These steps are described in detail in the sections that follow.

Import JDBC Packages

This is for making the JDBC API classes immediately available to the application program. The following import statement should be included in the program irrespective of the JDBC driver being used:

```
import java.sql.*;
```

Additionally, depending on the features being used, Oracle-supplied JDBC packages might need to be imported. For example, the following packages might need to be imported while using the Oracle extensions to JDBC such as using advanced data types such as BLOB, and so on.

```
import oracle.jdbc.driver.*;
import oracle.sql.*;
```

Load and Register the JDBC Driver

This is for establishing a communication between the JDBC program and the Oracle database. This is done by using the static `registerDriver()` method of the `DriverManager` class of the JDBC API. The following line of code does this job:

```
DriverManager.registerDriver(new oracle.jdbc.driver.OracleDriver());
```

JDBC DRIVER REGISTRATION

For the entire Java application, the JDBC driver is registered only once per each database that needs to be accessed. This is true even when there are multiple database connections to the same data server.

Alternatively, the `forName()` method of the `java.lang.Class` class can be used to load and register the JDBC driver:

```
Class.forName("oracle.jdbc.driver.OracleDriver");
```

However, the `forName()` method is valid for only JDK-compliant Java Virtual Machines and implicitly creates an instance of the Oracle driver, whereas the `registerDriver()` method does this explicitly.

Connecting to a Database

Once the required packages have been imported and the Oracle JDBC driver has been loaded and registered, a database connection must be established. This is done by using the `getConnection()` method of the `DriverManager` class. A call to this method creates an object instance of the `java.sql.Connection` class. The `getConnection()` requires three input parameters, namely, a connect string, a username, and a password. The connect string should specify the JDBC driver to be yes and the database instance to connect to.

The `getConnection()` method is an overloaded method that takes

- Three parameters, one each for the URL, username, and password.
- Only one parameter for the database URL. In this case, the URL contains the username and password.

The following lines of code illustrate using the `getConnection()` method:

```
Connection conn = DriverManager.getConnection(URL, username,  passwd);
Connection conn = DriverManager.getConnection(URL);
```

where URL, username, and passwd are of `String` data types.

We will discuss the methods of opening a connection using the Oracle JDBC OCI and thin drivers.

When using the OCI driver, the database can be specified using the TNSNAMES entry in the tnsnames.ora file. For example, to connect to a database on a particular host as user oratest and password oratest that has a TNSNAMES entry of oracle.world, use the following code:

```
Connection conn = DriverManager.getConnection("jdbc:oracle:oci8:

@oracle.world", "oratest", "oratest");
```

Both the ":" and "@" are mandatory.

When using the JDBC thin driver, the TNSNAMES entry cannot be used to identify the database. There are two ways of specifying the connect string in this case, namely,

- Explicitly specifying the hostname, the TCP/IP port number, and the Oracle SID of the database to connect to. This is for thin driver only.
- Specify a Net8 keyword-value pair list.

For example, for the explicit method, use the following code to connect to a database on host `training` where the TCP/IP listener is on port 1521, the SID for the database instance is Oracle, the username and password are both oratest:

```
Connection conn =
DriverManager.getConnection("jdbc:oracle:thin:@training:1521:Oracle",

 "oratest", "oratest");
```

For the Net8 keyword-value pair list, use the following:

```
Connection conn =
DriverManager.getConnection("jdbc:oracle:thin@(description=(address=

(host=training)(protocol=tcp)(port=1521))(connect_data=(sid=Oracle))) ",
"oratest", "oratest");
```

This method can also be used for the JDBC OCI driver. Just specify `oci8` instead of `thin` in the above keyword-value pair list.

Querying the Database

Querying the database involves two steps: first, creating a statement object to perform a query, and second, executing the query and returning a resultset.

Creating a Statement Object

This is to instantiate objects that run the query against the database connected to. This is done by the `createStatement()` method of the `conn` `Connection` object created above. A call to this method creates an object instance of the `Statement` class. The following line of code illustrates this:

```
Statement sql_stmt = conn.createStatement();
```

Executing the Query and Returning a ResultSet

Once a `Statement` object has been constructed, the next step is to execute the query. This is done by using the `executeQuery()` method of the `Statement` object. A call to this method takes as parameter a SQL SELECT statement and returns a JDBC `ResultSet` object. The following line of code illustrates this using the `sql_stmt` object created above:

```
ResultSet rset = sql_stmt.executeQuery("SELECT empno, ename, sal, deptno FROM
emp ORDER BY ename");
```

Alternatively, the SQL statement can be placed in a string and then this string passed to the executeQuery() function. This is shown below.

```
String sql = "SELECT empno, ename, sal, deptno FROM emp ORDER BY ename";
ResultSet rset = sql_stmt.executeQuery(sql);
```

STATEMENT AND RESULTSET OBJECTS

Statement and ResultSet objects open a corresponding cursor in the database for SELECT and other DML statements.

The above statement executes the SELECT statement specified in between the double quotes and stores the resulting rows in an instance of the `ResultSet` object named `rset`.

Processing the Results of a Database Query That Returns Multiple Rows

Once the query has been executed, there are two steps to be carried out:

- Processing the output resultset to fetch the rows
- Retrieving the column values of the current row

The first step is done using the `next()` method of the `ResultSet` object. A call to `next()` is executed in a loop to fetch the rows one row at a time, with each call to `next()` advancing the control to the next available row. The `next()` method returns the Boolean value true while rows are still available for fetching and returns false when all the rows have been fetched.

The second step is done by using the `getXXX()` methods of the JDBC rset object. Here `getXXX()` corresponds to the `getInt()`, `getString()` etc with XXX being replaced by a Java datatype.

The following code demonstrates the above steps:

```
String str;
while (rset.next())
  {
    str = rset.getInt(1)+ " "+ rset.getString(2)+ " "+rset.getFloat(3)+ "
"rset.getInt(4)+ "\n";
  }
byte buf[] = str.getBytes();
OutputStream fp = new FileOutputStream("query1.lst");
fp.write(buf);
fp.close();
```

Here the 1, 2, 3, and 4 in `rset.getInt()`, `rset.getString()`, `getFloat()`, and `getInt()` respectively denote the position of the columns in the SELECT statement, that is, the first column `empno`, second column `ename`, third column `sal`, and fourth column `deptno` of the SELECT statement respectively.

SPECIFYING `get()` PARAMETERS

The parameters for the `getXXX()` methods can be specified by position of the corresponding columns as numbers 1, 2, and so on, or by directly specifying the column names enclosed in double quotes, as `getString("ename")` and so on, or a combination of both.

Closing the ResultSet and Statement

Once the `ResultSet` and `Statement` objects have been used, they must be closed explicitly. This is done by calls to the `close()` method of the `ResultSet` and `Statement` classes. The following code illustrates this:

```
rset.close();

sql_stmt.close();
```

If not closed explicitly, there are two disadvantages:

- Memory leaks can occur
- Maximum Open cursors can be exceeded

Closing the `ResultSet` and `Statement` objects frees the corresponding cursor in the database.

Closing the Connection

The last step is to close the database connection opened in the beginning after importing the packages and loading the JDBC drivers. This is done by a call to the `close()` method of the Connection class.

The following line of code does this:

```
conn.close();
```

EXPLICITLY CLOSE YOUR CONNECTION

Closing the `ResultSet` and `Statement` objects does not close the connection. The connection should be closed by explicitly invoking the `close()` method of the `Connection` class.

A complete example of the above procedures using a JDBC thin driver is given below. This program queries the emp table and writes the output rows to an operating system file.

```
//Import JDBC package
import java.sql.*;
// Import Java package for File I/O
import java.io.*;
public class QueryExample {
  public static void main (String[] args) throws SQLException, IOException
{
       //Load and register Oracle driver
       DriverManager.registerDriver(new oracle.jdbc.driver.OracleDriver());
  //Establish a connection
  Connection conn =     DriverManager.getConnection("jdbc:oracle:thin:
  @training:1521:Oracle", "oratest", "oratest");
  //Create a Statement object
  Statement sql_stmt = conn.createStatement();
  //Create a ResultSet object, execute the query and return a
  // resultset
  ResultSet rset = sql_stmt.executeQuery("SELECT empno, ename, sal,
  deptno FROM emp ORDER BY ename");
  //Process the resultset, retrieve data in each row, column by column
  //and write to an operating system file
String str = "";
while (rset.next())
  {
    str += rset.getInt(1)+" "+ rset.getString(2)+" "+
    rset.getFloat(3)+" "+rset.getInt(4)+"\n";
  }
  byte buf[] = str.getBytes();
```

```
OutputStream fp = new FileOutputStream("query1.lst");
fp.write(buf);
fp.close();
//Close the ResultSet and Statement
  rset.close();
  sql_stmt.close();
  //Close the database connection
  conn.close();
  }
}
```

Processing the Results of a Database Query That Returns a Single Row

The above sections and the complete example explained the processing of a query that returned multiple rows. This section highlights the processing of a single-row query and explains how to write code that is the analogue of the PL/SQL exception NO_DATA_FOUND.

NO DATA FOUND EXCEPTION

NO_DATA_FOUND exception in PL/SQL is simulated in JDBC by using the return value of the `next()` method of the `ResultSet` object. A value of `false` returned by the `next()` method identifies a NO_DATA_FOUND exception.

Consider the following code (this uses the `ResultSet` object `rset` defined in the above sections):

```
if (rset.next())
  // Process the row returned
else
   System.out.println("The Employee with Empno "+ args[1] + "does not exist");
```

Instead of the while loop used earlier, an if statement is used to determine whether the SELECT statement returned a row or not.

Datatype Mappings

Corresponding to each SQL data type, there exist mappings to the corresponding JDBC Types, standard Java types, and the Java types provided by Oracle extensions. These are required to be used in JDBC programs that manipulate data and data structures based on these types.

There are four categories of Data types any of which can be mapped to the others. These are:

- **SQL Data types**—These are Oracle SQL data types that exist in the database.
- **JDBC Typecodes**—These are the data typecodes supported by JDBC as defined in the `java.sql.Types` class or defined by Oracle in `oracle.jdbc.driver.OracleTypes` class.
- **Java Types**—These are the standard types defined in the Java language.
- **Oracle Extension Java Types**—These are the Oracle extensions to the SQL data types and are defined in the `oracle.sql.*` class. Mapping SQL data types to the `oracle.sql.*` Java types enables storage and retrieval of SQL data without first converting into Java format thus preventing any loss of information.

Table 3.1 lists the default mappings existing between these four different types.

Table 3.1 Standard and Oracle-specific SQL-Java Data Type Mappings

SQL Data types	JDBC Type codes	Standard Java Types	Oracle Extension Java Types
Standard JDBC 1.0 Types			
CHAR	java.sql.Types.CHAR	java.lang.String	oracle.sql.CHAR
VARCHAR2	java.sql.Types.VARCHAR	java.lang.String	oracle.sql.CHAR
LONG	java.sql.Types. LONGVARCHAR	java.lang.String	oracle.sql.CHAR
NUMBER	java.sql.Types.NUMERIC	java.math.BigDecimal	oracle.sql.NUMBER
NUMBER	java.sql.Types.DECIMAL	java.math.BigDecimal	oracle.sql.NUMBER
NUMBER	java.sql.Types.BIT	Boolean	oracle.sql.NUMBER
NUMBER	java.sql.Types.TINYINT	byte	oracle.sql.NUMBER
NUMBER	java.sql.Types.SMALLINT	short	oracle.sql.NUMBER
NUMBER	java.sql.Types.INTEGER	int	oracle.sql.NUMBER
NUMBER	java.sql.Types.BIGINT	long	oracle.sql.NUMBER
NUMBER	java.sql.Types.REAL	float	oracle.sql.NUMBER
NUMBER	java.sql.Types.FLOAT	double	oracle.sql.NUMBER
NUMBER	java.sql.Types.DOUBLE	double	oracle.sql.NUMBER
RAW	java.sql.Types.BINARY	byte[]	oracle.sql.RAW
RAW	java.sql.Types.VARBINARY	byte[]	oracle.sql.RAW
LONGRAW	java.sql.Types.LONGVARBINARY	byte[]	oracle.sql.RAW
DATE	java.sql.Types.DATE	java.sql.Date	oracle.sql.DATE
DATE	java.sql.Types.TIME	java.sql.Time	oracle.sql.DATE
DATE	java.sql.Types.TIMESTAMP	javal.sql.Timestamp	oracle.sql.DATE
Standard JDBC 2.0 Types			
BLOB	java.sql.Types.BLOB	java.sql.Blob	Oracle.sql.BLOB
CLOB	Java.sql.Types.CLOB	java.sql.Clob	oracle.sql.CLOB

Table 3.1 Continued

SQL Data types	JDBC Type codes	Standard Java Types	Oracle Extension Java Types
user-defined object	java.sql.Types.STRUCT	java.sql.Struct	oracle.sql.STRUCT
user-defined reference	java.sql.Types.REF	java.sql.Ref	oracle.sql.REF
user-defined collection	java.sql.Types.ARRAY	java.sql.Array	oracle.sql.ARRAY
Oracle Extensions			
BFILE	oracle.jdbc.driver. OracleTypes.BFILE	n/a	oracle.sql.BFILE
ROWID	oracle.jdbc.driver. OracleTypes.ROWID	n/a	oracle.sql.ROWID
REFCURSOR type	oracle.jdbc.driver. OracleTypes.CURSOR	java.sql.ResultSet	oracle.jdbc.driver. OracleResultSet

Exception Handling in JDBC

Like in PL/SQL programs, exceptions do occur in JDBC programs. Notice how the `NO_DATA_FOUND` exception was simulated in the earlier section "Processing the Results of a Database Query That Returns a Single Row."

Exceptions in JDBC are usually of two types:

- Exceptions occurring in the JDBC driver
- Exceptions occurring in the Oracle 8i database itself

Just as PL/SQL provides for an implicit or explicit `RAISE` statement for an exception, Oracle JDBC programs have a `throw` statement that is used to inform that JDBC calls throw the SQL exceptions. This is shown below.

```
throws SQLException
```

This creates instances of the class `java.sql.SQLException` or a subclass of it.

And, like in PL/SQL, SQL exceptions in JDBC have to be handled explicitly. Similar to PL/SQL exception handling sections, Java provides a `try..catch` section that can handle all exceptions including SQL exceptions. Handling an exception can basically include retrieving the error code, error text, the SQL state, and/or printing the error stack trace. The `SQLException` class provides methods for obtaining all of this information in case of error conditions.

Retrieving Error Code, Error Text, and SQL State

There are the methods `getErrorCode()` and `getMessage()` similar to the functions `SQLCODE` and `SQLERRM` in PL/SQL. To retrieve the SQL state, there is the method `getSQLState()`. A brief description of these methods is given below:

- getErrorCode()

  This function returns the five-digit ORA number of the error in case of exceptions occurring in the JDBC driver as well as in the database.

- getMessage()

  This function returns the error message text in case of exceptions occurring in the JDBC driver. For exceptions occurring in the database, this function returns the error message text prefixed with the ORA number.

- getSQLState()

  This function returns the five digit code indicating the SQL state only for exceptions occurring in the database.

The following code illustrates the use of exception handlers in JDBC:

```
try { <JDBC code> }
catch (SQLException e) { System.out.println("ERR: "+ e.getMessage())}
```

We now show the `QueryExample` class of the earlier section with complete exception handlers built in it. The code is as follows:

```
//Import JDBC package
import java.sql.*;
// Import Java package for File I/O
import java.io.*;
public class QueryExample {
  public static void main (String[] args) {
   int ret_code;
  try {
       //Load and register Oracle driver
       DriverManager.registerDriver(new oracle.jdbc.driver.OracleDriver());
  //Establish a connection
  Connection conn =     DriverManager.getConnection("jdbc:oracle:thin:
  @training:1521:Oracle", "oratest", "oratest");
  //Create a Statement object
  Statement sql_stmt = conn.createStatement();
  //Create a ResultSet object, execute the query and return a
```

```
  // resultset
  ResultSet rset = sql_stmt.executeQuery("SELECT empno, ename, sal,
  deptno FROM emp ORDER BY ename");
  //Process the resultset, retrieve data in each row, column by column
  // and write to an operating system file
String str = "";
while (rset.next())
  {
    str += rset.getInt(1)+" "+ rset.getString(2)+" "+rset.getFloat(3)+
    " "+rset.getInt(4)+"\n";
  }
  byte buf[] = str.getBytes();
OutputStream fp = new FileOutputStream("query1.lst");
fp.write(buf);
fp.close();
//Close the ResultSet and Statement
  rset.close();
  sql_stmt.close();
  //Close the database connection
  conn.close();
} catch (SQLException e) {ret_code = e.getErrorCode();
  System.err.println("Oracle Error: "+ ret_code + e.getMessage());}
  catch (IOException e) {System.out.println("Java Error: "+
  e.getMessage()); }
  }
}
```

Printing Error Stack Trace

The SQLException has the method `printStackTrace()` for printing an error stack trace. This method prints the stack trace of the throwable object to the standard error stream.

The following code illustrates this:

```
catch (SQLException e) { e.printStackTrace(); }
```

INSERT, UPDATE, and DELETE Operations Using JDBC

Prepared Statements

The DML operations of INSERT and UPDATE—that is, the write operations—are done by means of the `prepareStatement()` method of the Connection object created above. A call to this method takes variable bind parameters as input parameters and creates an object instance of the `PreparedStatement` class.

The following line of code illustrates this:

```
String sql = "INSERT INTO emp VALUES (?,?,?,?,?,?,?,?)";PreparedStatement
dml_stmt = conn.prepareStatement(sql);
```

The input parameters are bound to this object instance using the `setXXX()` methods on the `PreparedStatement` object. For each input bind parameter, a `setXXX()` method is called. Here `XXX` stands for `Int`, `String`, and so on. The following line of code illustrates this:

```
dml_stmt.setInt(1, val);
```

Here 1 denotes that the first bind parameter is being set and `val` denotes an integer variable holding a value.

Once a `PreparedStatement` object has been constructed, the next step is to execute the associated INSERT or UPDATE statement. This is done by using the `executeUpdate()` method of the `PreparedStatement` object. The following line of code illustrates this using the `dml_stmt` object created above:

```
dml_stmt.executeUpdate();
```

The differences between `Statement` object and `PreparedStatement` object are the following:

- A `Statement` object cannot accept bind parameters, whereas a `PreparedStatement` object can.
- A `PreparedStatement` precompiles the SQL and hence the precompiled SQL statement can be reused. In this way, it optimizes the database calls.

PREPAREDSTATEMENT OBJECTS

It is recommended not to use the methods `executeQuery(String)` or `executeUpdate(String)` on `PreparedStatement` objects as there might be a chance of the Oracle driver throwing an exception at runtime.

A complete example is shown below. This example first checks whether a given `empno` exists in the `EMP` and if not inserts rows into the `EMP` table.

```
import java.sql.*;

public class InsertExample {
  public static void main(String[] args)
  throws SQLException {
```

```
int ret_code;
Connection conn = null;
  try {
       int i_empno[] = {1001, 1002, 7788};
       String i_ename[] = {"JOHN","DAVID","ORATEST"};
       String i_job[] = {"MANAGER","ANALYST","CLERK"};
       int i_mgr[] = {7839, 1001, 1002};
       String i_hiredate = "01-JAN-01";
       float i_sal[] = {10000,6000, 4000};
       float i_comm[] = {2000,1000,500};
       int i_deptno = 10;
       //Load and register Oracle driver
       DriverManager.registerDriver(new oracle.jdbc.driver.OracleDriver());
  //Establish a connection

    conn = DriverManager.getConnection("jdbc:oracle:thin:@training:1521:
    Oracle", "oratest", "oratest");

    String sql1 = "SELECT empno FROM emp WHERE empno = ?" ;
    String sql2 = "INSERT INTO emp VALUES (?,?,?,?,?,?,?,?)";

    PreparedStatement pstmt1 = conn.prepareStatement(sql1);
    PreparedStatement pstmt2 = conn.prepareStatement(sql2);
   for (int idx=0;idx<3;idx++)
   {
       pstmt1.setInt(1, i_empno[idx]);
       ResultSet rset = pstmt1.executeQuery();
       if (rset.next()) {
         System.out.println("The employee "+i_empno[idx]+" already exists.");
         rset.close();
         }
        else
         {
         pstmt2.setInt(1, i_empno[idx]);
         pstmt2.setString(2, i_ename[idx]);
         pstmt2.setString(3, i_job[idx]);
         pstmt2.setInt(4, i_mgr[idx]);
         pstmt2.setString(5, i_hiredate);
         pstmt2.setFloat(6, i_sal[idx]);
         pstmt2.setFloat(7, i_comm[idx]);
         pstmt2.setInt(8, i_deptno);
         pstmt2.executeUpdate(); }
```

```
        } // End of for loop
          pstmt1.close();
          pstmt2.close();
        conn.close();
         } catch (SQLException e) {ret_code = e.getErrorCode();
           System.err.println(ret_code + e.getMessage()); conn.close();}
    }
}
```

UPDATE and DELETE operations are similar to the INSERT operation described above. However, if there are no bind parameters involved, a `Statement` object can be used instead of a `PreparedStatement` object with the values hard-coded directly in the DML statement.

Callable Statements

Callable statements are used for calling Oracle stored procedures from Java and are discussed in a separate section "Calling Stored Procedures in JDBC Programs," later in the chapter.

Using Transactions

A transaction is a collection of DML statements that are executed as if they are a single operation. A JDBC application that needs to execute multiple SQL statements targeted towards a specific function, can make use of JDBC's transaction services. Transactions might need to be grouped in situations where multiple updates are needed and the entire set of transactions is to be committed or the entire set undone in case of a single failure.

Transaction services basically include beginning the transaction, executing the SQL statements that make up the transaction, and either perform a commit on overall success of each SQL statement or rollback the transaction as a whole if one of the SQL statements fails.

A second issue with transactions occurs when changes to the database become visible to the rest of the application system. This is termed isolation level. For example, in a multi-user system, when do changes performed by one user become visible to the remaining users? Transactions can operate at various isolation levels. At the highest isolation level, the changes to the database become visible only when the transaction is committed.

Transaction management in JDBC is handled to some extent by the Connection object. Whenever a new Connection is opened, the transaction auto-commit mode is turned on. In auto-commit mode, every SQL statement is executed as a single transaction that is immediately committed to the database. To execute multiple SQL statements as part of a single transaction, the auto-commit is to be disabled. The next section explains more on this.

Committing

Committing of DML INSERT, UPDATE, or DELETE statements in JDBC programs is done automatically. The auto-commit is set to ON by default in JDBC and a COMMIT is issued after every SQL operation. However, if you choose to set the auto-commit mode off, you can do so by calling the `setAutoCommit()` of the `Connection` object as follows:

```
conn.setAutoCommit(false);
```

The above line of code should appear immediately after the connection has been established. This is shown below.

```
//Load and register Oracle driver
       DriverManager.registerDriver(new oracle.jdbc.driver.OracleDriver());
  //Establish a connection

    conn = DriverManager.getConnection("jdbc:oracle:thin:@training:1521:Oracle",
"oratest", "oratest");

//Disable auto-commit mode
conn.setAutoCommit(false);
```

Once the auto-commit mode is turned off, an explicit COMMIT or ROLLBACK should be done to commit any unsaved database changes. COMMIT or ROLLBACK can be done by calling the `commit()` or `rollback()` methods of the `Connection` object as shown below.

```
conn.commit();
```

or

```
conn.rollback();
```

TIPS:

Explicit COMMIT or ROLLBACK is done for a transaction and not for individual DML statements.

Closing a connection before an explicit commit automatically COMMITs the transaction, even if auto-commit mode is turned off.

Executing a DDL statement automatically COMMITs the transaction even if auto-commit mode is turned off.

Disabling auto-commit improves performance in terms of time and processing effort as a COMMIT need not be issued for every SQL statement affecting the database.

The following gives an example program to illustrate transaction management:

```
import java.sql.*;

public class TransactionExample {
  public static void main(String[] args)
  throws SQLException {
int ret_code;
Connection conn = null;
  try {
      //Load and register Oracle driver
       DriverManager.registerDriver(new oracle.jdbc.driver.OracleDriver());
  //Establish a connection

    conn = DriverManager.getConnection("jdbc:oracle:thin:@training:1521:
    Oracle", "oratest", "oratest");

//Disable auto-commit mode
conn.setAutoCommit(false);

    String sql1 = "SELECT empno FROM emp WHERE empno = ?" ;
    String sql2 = "INSERT INTO emp VALUES (?,?,?,?,?,?,?,?)";
    String sql3 = "UPDATE dept_audit SET cnt_emp = nvl(cnt_emp,0)
    + 1 WHERE deptno = 10";

    PreparedStatement pstmt1 = conn.prepareStatement(sql1);
    PreparedStatement pstmt2 = conn.prepareStatement(sql2);
    PreparedStatement pstmt3 = conn.prepareStatement(sql3);

       pstmt1.setInt(1, 9999);
       ResultSet rset = pstmt1.executeQuery();
       if (rset.next()) {
         System.out.println("The employee with empno 9999 already exists.");
         rset.close();
         }
        else
         {
         pstmt2.setInt(1, 9999);
         pstmt2.setString(2, "CHARLIE");
         pstmt2.setString(3, "ANALYST");
         pstmt2.setInt(4, 7566);
         pstmt2.setString(5, "01-JAN-01");
```

```
        pstmt2.setFloat(6, 12000);
        pstmt2.setFloat(7, (float)10.5);
        pstmt2.setInt(8, 10);
        pstmt2.executeUpdate(); }

        pstmt3.executeUpdate();
        pstmt1.close();
        pstmt2.close();
        pstmt3.close();
        // Commit the effect of all both the INSERT and UPDATE
        // statements together
        conn.commit();
        conn.close();
      } catch (SQLException e)
          { // Rollback all the changes so as to undo
            // the effect of both INSERT and UPDATE
            conn.rollback();
            ret_code = e.getErrorCode();
            System.err.println(ret_code + e.getMessage()); conn.close();
          }
  }
}
```

Based on the above example, the new row inserted into EMP table is visible to the application only when the operations of inserting into EMP table and incrementing of the emp_cnt in dept_audit table are both successful. If any one of these operations fails, the entire transaction is rolled back.

Oracle JDBC Extensions

Oracle has provided extensions to the JDBC standard by introducing in its drivers the support of Oracle data types and objects. It has provided implementation of these extensions in the form of packages and interfaces that let a greater flexibility in accessing and manipulating data inside Oracle 8i database. The Oracle extensions can be categorized into two types, namely, Oracle type extensions and Oracle performance extensions. The Oracle JDBC OCI, thin and server-side internal drivers support both these types of Oracle extensions.

This section discusses the Oracle Type extensions. Oracle performance extensions are discussed later in the section "JDBC Performance Extensions."

Features of Oracle Extensions

The Oracle extensions include features for standard Oracle data types and Oracle objects.

- Oracle Data Types

  Oracle JDBC extensions provide type support to all Oracle SQL data types through classes in the `oracle.sql.*` package. These classes map to all Oracle SQL data types that allow direct access to SQL data without first converting it to Java format. This direct access also results in more accurate mathematical calculations that would otherwise have had loss of precision. Once data access and manipulation is over, the `oracle.sql.*` package classes have methods to convert the results back to the appropriate Java format. Data type mappings are also provided for the advanced data types such as ROWID, REF CURSOR, LOBS, BFILES, object types, object REFS, and collections such as VARRAYS and NESTED TABLES.

- Oracle Objects

  Objects can be incorporated in the Oracle 8i database in various forms, namely, object types, object tables, object-relational tables, and collections. For example, an object type can be defined with specific attributes and then an object table can be created based on this object type.

Oracle Objects can be used in JDBC Java applications, provided the following have been taken care of:

- Proper mapping between Oracle object data types and Java classes
- Populating the respective Java objects with object attributes
- Transforming object attribute data between SQL and Java formats
- Proper access to Object data

Oracle provides two ways to implement the above procedures, namely, using Struct types or custom Java classes. The first method involves mapping objects to standard `java.sql.Struct` class or to `oracle.sql.STRUCT` class. The second method involves implementing interfaces, namely, `java.sql.SQLData` interface or the Oracle extension interface `oracle.sql.CustomDatum`. Either of the two interface implementations can be used. `java.sql.SQLData` interface is a more general one and uses type maps to define the correspondence between Oracle object data types and Java classes. Type maps and other implementation techniques of Oracle objects are discussed in Chapter 4, "Advanced JDBC Programming."

Oracle JDBC Packages and Classes

This section outlines the Oracle extension packages implemented to support Oracle Type extensions. The implementation packages are as follows:

- oracle.sql.*—This package provides classes to support all Oracle type extensions and supports both JDK 1.2.x and JDK.1.1.x (i.e., JDBC 2.0 and JDBC 1.22 standards).
- oracle.jdbc.driver.*—This package provides classes for DML support in Oracle Type formats and also supports both JDK 1.2.x and JDK 1.1.x.
- oracle.jdbc2.*—This package is for JDK1.1.x implementation only and provides classes that support JDBC 2.0 features. This has interfaces that simulate the JDBC 2.0 interfaces in the standard `java.sql.*` package.

The implementation details of each package can be found in the Oracle documentation "Oracle 8i JDBC Developer's Guide and Reference."

Oracle Type Extensions

This section highlights the details of the special Oracle Type extensions, namely, ROWID and REF CURSOR types.

Oracle ROWID Type

ROWID is a unique identifier for a row and gives the logical address of a row. It is 18 characters long and its value represents the physical location where the row is stored. Oracle ROWID can be used to select rows using the ROWID pseudo-column and provides a very fast row retrieval. It can also be used in the WHERE clause, for example to filter out duplicate rows existing in a table. Another use of a WHERE clause is for faster UPDATE and DELETE operations. An example of using ROWID in an UPDATE statement is given below.

```
SQL> select ROWID, ename, sal from emp where job='MANAGER';
ROWID              ENAME             SAL
------------------ ---------- ----------
AAAGDxAABAAAH9EAAD JONES            2975
AAAGDxAABAAAH9EAAF BLAKE            2850
AAAGDxAABAAAH9EAAG CLARK            2450

SQL> update emp set sal = sal + 1000 where rowid = 'AAAGDxAABAAAH9EAAD';
1 row updated.
```

```
SQL>  select ROWID, ename, sal from emp where job='MANAGER';
ROWID              ENAME            SAL
------------------ ---------- ----------
AAAGDxAABAAAH9EAAD JONES           3975
AAAGDxAABAAAH9EAAF BLAKE           2850
AAAGDxAABAAAH9EAAG CLARK           2450
```

ROWID is supported as a Java String. Oracle JDBC extensions provide the `oracle.sql.ROWID` class in the `oracle.sql.*` package for manipulating data using ROWIDs. This class acts as wrapper for the SQL ROWID data type. For Oracle–specific data types that are not part of the JDBC specification, an object is returned in the corresponding `oracle.sql.*` format. Since ROWID is one such data type, it is returned as an `oracle.sql.ROWID`.

ROWIDS

The ROWID pseudo-column can be included as part of a SELECT query just as any other table column. However, ROWIDs cannot be manually updated, it is updated by Oracle internally.

For querying purposes, when the ROWID pseudo-column is included as a column in a SELECT statement as part of a `Statement` object, its value can be retrieved by the `getROWID()` method of the corresponding `Resultset` object cast to `OracleResultSet`. Also, ROWID can be a part of a `PreparedStatement` as a bind parameter whose value can be set using the `setROWID()` method of the PreparedStatement object cast to `OraclePreparedStatement`.

The following example illustrates the use of ROWID. Specifically, for the purposes of this example, it increments the salary of each employee in a particular department by retrieving the rows based on individual ROWIDs.

```
import oracle.sql.*;
import java.sql.*;
import oracle.jdbc.driver.*;

public class RowidExample {
  public static void main(String[] args)
  throws SQLException {
int ret_code;
Connection conn = null;
  try {
      //Load and register Oracle driver
       DriverManager.registerDriver(new oracle.jdbc.driver.OracleDriver());
  //Establish a connection

    conn = DriverManager.getConnection("jdbc:oracle:thin:@training:1521:
    Oracle", "oratest", "oratest");
```

```
int i_deptno = 10;

   String sql1 = "SELECT ROWID, sal, comm FROM emp WHERE deptno = ?" ;
   String sql2 = "UPDATE emp SET sal = ? WHERE rowid = ?";

   PreparedStatement pstmt1 = conn.prepareStatement(sql1);
   PreparedStatement pstmt2 = conn.prepareStatement(sql2);

       pstmt1.setInt(1, i_deptno);
       ResultSet rset = pstmt1.executeQuery();
       while (rset.next()) {
         oracle.sql.ROWID i_rowid = ((OracleResultSet)rset).getROWID(1);
//         String i_rowid = "";
//         i_rowid = rset.getString(1);
         float i_sal =  rset.getFloat(2);
         float i_comm = rset.getFloat(3);
         pstmt2.setFloat(1, (float) (i_sal+(1.25*i_comm)));
         ((OraclePreparedStatement)pstmt2).setROWID (2, i_rowid);
//         pstmt2.setString(2, i_rowid);
         pstmt2.executeUpdate();
       }
   rset.close();
   pstmt1.close();
   pstmt2.close();
   conn.close();
       } catch (SQLException e) {ret_code = e.getErrorCode();
         System.err.println(ret_code + e.getMessage()); conn.close();}
   }
}
```

Oracle REF CURSOR

A REF CURSOR is a weakly typed cursor type that identifies a cursor variable. A variable can defined of the REF CURSOR type and then a query can be opened for it. The cursor variable then acts as a pointer to the query or SELECT thus opened. Stored procedures or functions as well as packaged procedures or functions can return cursor variables of type REF CURSOR. The output consists of a resultset that holds the rows returned by the REF CURSOR. This output can be captured in a JDBC ResultSet object.

For the purposes of this section, we will use the following table to demonstrate the Oracle REF CURSOR type.

```
CREATE TABLE emp_with_type
                (empno number(10) primary key,
                 ename varchar2(40) not null,
                 etype varchar2(10) not null,
                 job   varchar2(15) not null,
                 mgr   number(10) references emp(empno),
                 hiredate date not null,
                 sal   number(12,2) not null,
                 comm  number(4),
                 deptno number(4) references dept(deptno));
```

This table is populated with the following INSERT statements:

```
INSERT INTO emp_with_type
  SELECT empno, ename, 'SENIOR', job, mgr, hiredate, sal, comm,
         deptno
  FROM   emp
  WHERE  deptno in (10, 20)
  union
  SELECT empno, ename, 'JUNIOR', job, mgr, hiredate, sal, comm,
         deptno
  FROM   emp
  WHERE  deptno = 30;
```

Next we create a packaged function that returns a REF CURSOR. This is shown below:

```
CREATE OR REPLACE PACKAGE pkg_refcur IS

  TYPE bonus_refcur IS REF CURSOR;

  FUNCTION f_refcur(ip_etype VARCHAR2) RETURN pkg_refcur.bonus_refcur;

END pkg_refcur;
/

CREATE OR REPLACE PACKAGE BODY pkg_refcur IS

  FUNCTION f_refcur(ip_etype VARCHAR2) RETURN pkg_refcur.bonus_refcur
  IS
    v_bonus_refcur pkg_refcur.bonus_refcur;
  BEGIN
    IF ip_etype = 'JUNIOR' THEN
      OPEN v_bonus_refcur FOR
      SELECT etype, empno, ename, sal, 0.25*sal bonus, deptno
```

```
      FROM   emp_with_type
      WHERE  etype = ip_etype;
    ELSIF ip_etype = 'SENIOR' THEN
      OPEN v_bonus_refcur FOR
      SELECT etype, empno, ename, sal, 0.75*sal bonus, deptno
      FROM   emp_with_type
      WHERE  etype = ip_etype;
    END IF;
    RETURN (v_bonus_refcur);
  END f_refcur;

END pkg_refcur;
/
```

The next step is to write the JDBC program that calls the above packaged function and returns a resultset. The steps involved in this are as follows:

1. Call the packaged function using a JDBC `CallableStatement` object.
2. The return value of the function which is a REF CURSOR is registered as an OUT parameter using the typecode `OracleTypes.CURSOR`.
3. Execute the `CallableStatement` to obtain the REF CURSOR returned by the PL/SQL packaged function.
4. The `CallableStatement` object is cast to an `OracleCallableStatement` object to use the `getCursor()` method, which is an Oracle extension to the standard JDBC API, and returns the REF CURSOR into a `ResultSet` object.
5. Process the resultset as desired—for example, write to an O/S file, and so on.

The complete JDBC program is given below:

```
import java.sql.*;
import java.io.*;
import oracle.jdbc.driver.*;

public class RefCursorExample {
  public static void main(String[] args)
   throws SQLException, IOException {
  int ret_code;
  Connection conn = null;
  try {
      //Load and register Oracle driver
       DriverManager.registerDriver(new oracle.jdbc.driver.OracleDriver());
```

```
   //Establish a connection

     conn = DriverManager.getConnection("jdbc:oracle:thin:@training:1521:Oracle",
 "oratest", "oratest");

     String i_etype = "SENIOR";
     CallableStatement cstmt = conn.prepareCall("{? = call
 pkg_refcur.f_refcur(?)}");
     cstmt.registerOutParameter(1, OracleTypes.CURSOR);
     cstmt.setString(2, i_etype);
     cstmt.executeUpdate();

     ResultSet rset;
     rset = ((OracleCallableStatement)cstmt).getCursor(1);
     String str = "";
     while (rset.next())
       str += rset.getString(1)+" "+ rset.getInt(2)+" "+rset.getString(3)+"
 "+rset.getFloat(4)+" "+rset.getFloat(5)+" "+rset.getInt(6)+"\n";
     byte buf[] = str.getBytes();
     OutputStream fp = new FileOutputStream("senior.lst");
     fp.write(buf);
     fp.close();

     rset.close();
     cstmt.close();
     conn.close();
        } catch (SQLException e) {ret_code = e.getErrorCode();
System.err.println(ret_code + e.getMessage()); conn.close();}
          catch (IOException e) { System.err.println("Java File I/O Error:"+
e.getMessage()); }
   }
}
```

More on returning resultsets is detailed in the sub-section “Returning Resultsets” within the section “Handling Resultsets in JDBC,” later in this chapter.

Calling Stored Procedures in JDBC Programs

Stored procedures are part and parcel of any database application that enables a lot of business logic to be stored as application logic in the database in compiled form. Oracle 8i supports two types of stored procedures, namely, PL/SQL and Java. This section highlights the calling of both PL/SQL stored procedures and Java stored procedures from JDBC programs.

Calling PL/SQL Stored Procedures

PL/SQL stored procedures are called from within JDBC programs by means of the `prepareCall()` method of the `Connection` object created above. A call to this method takes variable bind parameters as input parameters as well as output variables and creates an object instance of the `CallableStatement` class.

The following line of code illustrates this:

```
CallableStatement stproc_stmt = conn.prepareCall("{call procname(?,?,?)}");
```

Here `conn` is an instance of the Connection class.

The input parameters are bound to this object instance using the `setXXX()` methods on the `CallableStatement` object. For each input bind parameter, a `setXXX()` method (e.g., setInt(), setString(),) is called. The following line of code illustrates this:

```
stproc_stmt.setXXX(…)
```

The output parameters are bound to this object instance using `registerOutParameter()` method on the `CallableStatement` object, as shown below:

```
stproc_stmt.registerOutParameter(2, OracleTypes.CHAR);
```

The above statement registers the second parameter passed to the stored procedure as an OUT parameter of type CHAR. For each OUT parameter, a `registerOutParameter()` method is called.

Once a `CallableStatement` object has been constructed, the next step is to execute the associated stored procedure or function. This is done by using the `executeUpdate()` method of the `CallableStatement` object. The following line of code illustrates this using the `stproc_stmt` object created above:

```
stproc_stmt.executeUpdate();
```

`prepareCall()` METHOD

The three different kinds of stored sub-programs, namely, stored procedures, stored functions, and packaged procedures and functions can be called using the `prepareCall()` method of the `CallableStatement` object.

The syntax for calling stored functions is as follows:

```
CallableStatement stproc_stmt = conn.prepareCall("{ ? = call
funcname(?,?,?)}");
```

The first ? refers to the return value of the function and is also to be registered as an OUT parameter.

PACKAGED PROCEDURES AND FUNCTIONS

Packaged procedures and functions can be called in the same manner as stored procedures or functions except that the name of the package followed a dot "." prefixes the name of the procedure or function.

Once the stored procedure or function has been executed, the values of the out parameters can be obtained using the `getXXX()` methods (for example, getInt() and getString()) on the `CallableStatement` object. This is shown below:

```
String op1 stproc_stmt.getString(2);
```

This retrieves the value returned by the second parameter (which is an OUT parameter of the corresponding PL/SQL stored procedure being called and has been registered as an OUT parameter in the JDBC program) into the Java `String` variable `op1`.

A complete example is shown below. Consider a procedure that returns the highest paid employee in a particular department. Specifically, this procedure takes a `deptno` as input and returns `empno`, `ename`, and `sal` in the form of three out parameters.

The procedure is created as follows:

```
CREATE OR REPLACE PROCEDURE p_highest_paid_emp
                           (ip_deptno NUMBER,
                            op_empno OUT NUMBER,
                            op_ename OUT VARCHAR2,
                            op_sal   OUT NUMBER)
IS
  v_empno NUMBER;
  v_ename VARCHAR2(20);
  v_sal   NUMBER;
BEGIN
   SELECT empno, ename, sal
   INTO   v_empno, v_ename, v_sal
   FROM   emp e1
   WHERE  sal = (SELECT MAX(e2.sal)
                 FROM   emp e2
                 WHERE  e2.deptno = e1.deptno
                   AND  e2.deptno = ip_deptno)
     AND deptno = ip_deptno;
   op_empno := v_empno;
   op_ename := v_ename;
```

```
   op_sal   := v_sal;
END;
/
```

Here we assume that there is only one highest paid employee in a particular department.

Next we write the JDBC program that calls this procedure. This is shown below:

```
import java.sql.*;

public class StProcExample {
  public static void main(String[] args)
  throws SQLException {
int ret_code;
Connection conn = null;
  try {
      //Load and register Oracle driver
       DriverManager.registerDriver(new oracle.jdbc.driver.OracleDriver());
  //Establish a connection

    conn = DriverManager.getConnection("jdbc:oracle:thin:@training:1521:
    Oracle", "oratest", "oratest");
    int i_deptno = 10;
    CallableStatement pstmt = conn.prepareCall("{call p_highest_
    paid_emp(?,?,?,?)}");
    pstmt.setInt(1, i_deptno);
    pstmt.registerOutParameter(2, Types.INTEGER);
    pstmt.registerOutParameter(3, Types.VARCHAR);
    pstmt.registerOutParameter(4, Types.FLOAT);
    pstmt.executeUpdate();

    int o_empno = pstmt.getInt(2);
    String o_ename = pstmt.getString(3);
    float o_sal = pstmt.getFloat(4);
    System.out.print("The highest paid employee in dept "
    +i_deptno+" is: "+o_empno+" "+o_ename+" "+o_sal);
    pstmt.close();
    conn.close();
       } catch (SQLException e) {ret_code = e.getErrorCode();
         System.err.println(ret_code + e.getMessage()); conn.close();}
    }
 }
```

Calling Java Stored Procedures

Java stored procedures can also be called from JDBC programs using the corresponding call specifications created to publish the Java methods into the Oracle 8i database. In other words, calling the published call specs executes the corresponding Java methods and the syntax for calling these is the same as calling PL/SQL stored procedures.

Here we will use the Java stored procedures created in Chapter 2, "Java Stored Procedures." The following JDBC program calls the packaged procedure `pkg_empmaster.fire_emp` (a Java stored procedure that corresponds to the Java method `empMaster.fireEmp()`). Specifically it deletes the record in `emp` table where `empno = 1002`.

Before executing the above Java stored procedure, the record corresponding to `empno` 1002 in `emp` table is as follows:

```
EMPNO ENAME      JOB               MGR HIREDATE         SAL       COMM
---------- ---------- --------- ---------- --------- ---------- ----------
    DEPTNO
----------
      1002 DAVID      ANALYST          1001 01-JAN-01        6000       1000
        10
```

The JDBC program to call the Java stored procedure is as follows:

```
import java.sql.*;
public class JavaProcExample {
  public static void main(String[] args)
  throws SQLException {
int ret_code;
Connection conn = null;
  try {
      //Load and register Oracle driver
       DriverManager.registerDriver(new oracle.jdbc.driver.OracleDriver());
  //Establish a connection

    conn = DriverManager.getConnection("jdbc:oracle:thin:@training:1521:
    Oracle", "oratest", "oratest");
    int i_empno = 1002;
    CallableStatement pstmt =
    conn.prepareCall("{call pkg_empmaster.fire_emp(?)}");
    pstmt.setInt(1, i_empno);
    pstmt.executeUpdate();
```

```
    pstmt.close();
    conn.close();
       } catch (SQLException e) {ret_code = e.getErrorCode();
         System.err.println(ret_code + e.getMessage()); conn.close();}
   }
}
```

The output of the above program can be verified as follows:

```
SQL> select * from emp where empno = 1002;

no rows selected

SQL>
```

Handling Resultsets in JDBC

We have seen how a query executed against a database returned a `ResultSet` that could be processed for obtaining the individual rows returned by the query. To do this, we used the `ResultSet` object obtained as return value of the `exceuteQuery()` method of `Statement` or `PreparedStatement` object. Also, we saw how a PL/SQL function returned a REF CURSOR using `prepareCall()` method of `CallableStatement` object and how this was captured in a JDBC resultset using `getCursor()` method cast to an `OracleCallableStatement`. The resultsets obtained in this way conform to JDBC 1.0 standards and are limited in scope. In this section we will elaborate on enhancements of resultsets in JDBC 2.0. We start with a discussion of PL/SQL procedures and/or functions returning resultsets.

Returning Resultsets

In the sub-section "Oracle Type Extensions," within the section "Oracle JDBC Extensions", a method of handling resultsets in the form of a REF CURSOR returned by a PL/SQL procedure or function was described. This is one way of handling returned resultsets in JDBC. In this sub-section, we describe a second way of handling returned resultsets. We use the same example as demonstrated earlier. The steps involved in this are as follows:

1. Call the packaged function using a JDBC `CallableStatement` object.
2. The return value of the function which is a REF CURSOR is registered as an OUT parameter using the typecode `OracleTypes.CURSOR`.
3. Execute the `CallableStatement` to obtain the REF CURSOR returned by the PL/SQL packaged function.

4. The `CallableStatement` object is cast to a `ResultSet` object (instead of an `OracleCallableStatement` object) to use the `getObject()` (instead of a `getCursor()` method), which is an Oracle extension to the standard JDBC API, and returns the REF CURSOR into a `ResultSet` object.
5. Process the resultset as desired, for example, write to an O/S file.

The complete JDBC program is given below:

```
import java.sql.*;
import java.io.*;
import oracle.jdbc.driver.*;

public class RefCursorExample2 {
  public static void main(String[] args)
   throws SQLException, IOException {
  int ret_code;
  Connection conn = null;
  try {
      //Load and register Oracle driver
       DriverManager.registerDriver(new oracle.jdbc.driver.OracleDriver());
  //Establish a connection

    conn = DriverManager.getConnection("jdbc:oracle:thin:
    @training:1521:Oracle", "oratest", "oratest");

    String i_etype = "SENIOR";
    CallableStatement cstmt = conn.prepareCall("{? =
    call pkg_refcur.f_refcur(?)}");

    // Register the OUT parameter of the PL/SQL function as
    // a OracleTypes.CURSOR datatype
    cstmt.registerOutParameter(1, OracleTypes.CURSOR);
    cstmt.setString(2, i_etype);
    cstmt.executeUpdate();

    ResultSet rset;

    // Obtain the cursor returned by the PL/SQL function using getObject()
    // and cast it to the ResultSet object.
    rset = (ResultSet) cstmt.getObject(1);
    String str = "";
```

```
    while (rset.next())
      str += rset.getString(1)+" "+ rset.getInt(2)+" "
      +rset.getString(3)+" "+rset.getFloat(4)+" "+rset.getFloat(5)+"
"+rset.getInt(6)+"\n";
    byte buf[] = str.getBytes();
    OutputStream fp = new FileOutputStream("senior.lst");
    fp.write(buf);
    fp.close();

    rset.close();
    cstmt.close();
    conn.close();
       } catch (SQLException e) {ret_code = e.getErrorCode();
       System.err.println(ret_code + e.getMessage()); conn.close();}
         catch (IOException e) { System.err.println
         ("Java File I/O Error:"+ e.getMessage()); }
   }
}
```

Scrollable Resultsets

In JDBC 1.0, the resultsets so defined were limited in scope in that the rows in the resultset could be accessed only in the forward-direction. This means there was no way of moving back and forth in a resultset or jumping to a particular row identified by a row number. Also, the resultsets were read-only in that there was no way for inserting new rows into the resultset, updating a particular row, or deleting a particular row. JDBC 2.0 made enhancements to resultsets by introducing scrollability, positioning, and concurrency capabilities. This sub-section discusses the first two enhancements of scrollability and positioning. The next sub-section discusses the enhanced feature of concurrency or updateable resultsets.

Scrollability refers to moving forwards or backwards through rows in a resultset. Positioning refers to moving the current row position to a different position by jumping to a specific row. These two features are provided by means of three additional method calls, one each for `createStatement()`, `prepareStatement()`, and `prepareCall()` methods. These new methods take two new parameters namely, the `resultSetType` and `resultSetConcurrency`. The definition of these new methods is as follows:

```
connection.createStatement(int resultSetType, int resultSetConcurrency);

connection.prepareStatement(String sql, int resultSetType, int
resultSetConcurrency);

connection.prepareCall(String sql, int resultSetType, int resultSetConcurrency);
```

The parameter `resultSetType` determines whether a resultset is scrollable or not. It can take one of the following three values only:

```
ResultSet.TYPE_FORWARD_ONLY

ResultSet.TYPE_SCROLL_INSENSITIVE

ResultSet.TYPE_SCROLL_SENSITIVE
```

`TYPE_FORWARD_ONLY` specifies that a resultset is not scrollable, that is, rows within it can be advanced only in the forward direction.

`TYPE_SCROLL_INSENSITIVE` specifies that a resultset is scrollable in either direction but is insensitive to changes committed by other transactions or other statements in the same transaction.

`TYPE_SCROLL_SENSITIVE` specifies that a resultset is scrollable in either direction and is affected by changes committed by other transactions or statements within the same transaction.

The second parameter `resultSetConcurrency` determines whether a resultset is updateable or not and can take one of the two values only:

```
ResultSet.CONCUR_READ_ONLY

ResultSet.CONCUR_UPDATABLE
```

With these resultset types and two concurrency types, there are six different kinds of resultsets that can be defined. These are

```
Type_Forward_Only/Concur_Read_Only

Type_Forward_only/Concur_Updateable

Type_Scroll_Insensitive/Concur_Read_Only

Type_Scroll_Insensitive/Concur_Updateable

Type_Scroll_Sensitive/Concur_Read_Only

Type_Scroll_Sensitive/Concur_Updateable
```

SPECIFY SCROLL SENSITIVITY

In a JDK1.1.x environment, the following have to be specified: `OracleResultSet.TYPE_SCROLL_SENSITIVE` and `OracleResultSet.TYPE_SCROLL_INSENSITIVE`. This is because the static constants are part of the `OracleResultSet` class included as an Oracle extension. To make this class available, import `oracle.jdbc.driver.*` package.

A scrollable resultset allows for random access to its rows. Random access in turn allows for accessing a particular row directly without having to advance row by row. This direct positioning of control at a specific row is termed positioning.

To enable scrollability and positioning, in JDBC 2.0, the `ResultSet` class provides a set of new methods in addition to the `next()` method available in JDBC 1.0. These methods are as follows:

- `boolean first()`—Positions the control at the first row in the resultset and returns true. If there are no rows in the resultset, it returns false.
- `boolean last()`—Positions the control at the last row in the resultset and returns true. If there are no rows in the resultset, it returns false.
- `boolean previous()`—Positions the control at the previous row in the resultset relative to the current row. This returns true if the previous row exists. It returns false, if it causes the resultset to be positioned before the first row.
- `boolean absolute(int row)`—Directly jumps to the row specified by the parameter. This is absolute positioning, meaning it jumps to the row specified starting from the beginning or end depending on whether the parameter is positive or negative. If control moves beyond the first or last row, the cursor is left before the first row or after the last row. This returns true if the row jumped to is valid. If a zero is passed, it throws an exception. `Remember that absolute(1)` is same as `first()` and `absolute(-1)` is same as `last()`.
- `boolean relative(int offset)`—directly jumps to the row starting from the current row by an offset specified by the parameter. This is relative positioning meaning, it jumps to the row specified starting from the current row. This returns true if the row jumped to is valid. If control moves beyond the first or last row, the cursor is left before the first row or after the last row.
- `void beforeFirst()`—Positions the resultset before the very first row.
- `void afterLast()`—Positions the resultset after the last row.
- `boolean isFirst()`—Returns true if the resultset is positioned at the first row.
- `boolean isLast()`—Returns true if the resultset is positioned at the last row.
- `boolean isBeforeFirst()`—Returns true if the resultset is positioned before the first row.

- `boolean isAfterLast()`—Returns true if the resultset is positioned after the last row.
- `int getRow()`—Returns the row number of the current row.

VALID FOR SCROLLABLE RESULTSETS

The above mentioned new methods are valid only for a scrollable resultset. A `SQLException` is thrown if the methods are used for Forward_only resultsets.

Updateable Resultsets

Updateable resultsets means the ability to update the contents of specific row(s) in the resultset and propagating these changes to the underlying database. This capability is supported in JDBC 2.0 only. Also the operations of INSERT and DELETE are possible. New rows can be inserted into the underlying table and existing rows can be deleted from both the resultset as well as the underlying table. The CLASSPATH has to include classes12.zip for using updateable resultsets.

We will first discuss the operation of UPDATE, followed by INSERT and DELETE.

UPDATE Operation Through a Resultset

The following are the steps involved in creating and using an updateable resultset:

1. To create an updateable resultset, the `resultSetConcurrency` parameter has to be specified as `ResulSet.CONCUR_UPDATABLE` while defining the `createStatement()`, `preparedStatement()`, or `prepareCall()` method on the `Connection` object. This is shown below:

```
Connection conn = null;

//Load and register Oracle driver
      DriverManager.registerDriver(new oracle.jdbc.driver.OracleDriver());
  //Establish a connection

    conn = DriverManager.getConnection("jdbc:oracle:thin:@training:1521:
    Oracle", "oratest", "oratest");

Statement stmt = conn.createStatement(Resultset.TYPE_SCROLL_SENSITIVE,
ResultSet.CONCUR_UPDATEABLE);

String sql = …
ResultSet rset =  stmt.executeQuery(sql);
… … … …
```

2. Use the `updateXXX()` (for example, updateInt() and updateString()) methods on the `ResultSet` object to set the values of the resultset columns. JDBC 2.0 has provided these methods for each of the Java primitive types as well for some SQL types that correspond to Java objects. The use of this method is as follows:

   ```
   rset.updateFloat(2, new_val);
   ```

   Here 2 refers to the second column in the resultset and new_val is a variable that holds a new value to which this column data is to be set to.

3. Use the `updateRow()` method on the `ResultSet` object to propagate the changes made to the resultset to the underlying database table and commit them. This has to be done once for each row in the resultset that is changed. This is shown below:

   ```
   rset.updateRow();
   ```

A complete example is shown below:

```
import java.sql.*;

public class UpdateableResultSetExample {
  public static void main(String[] args)
  throws SQLException {
int ret_code;
Connection conn = null;
  try {
      //Load and register Oracle driver
       DriverManager.registerDriver(new oracle.jdbc.driver.OracleDriver());
   //Establish a connection

     conn = DriverManager.getConnection("jdbc:oracle:thin:@training:1521:Oracle",
     "oratest", "oratest");
    int i_deptno = 10;
    String sql = "SELECT empno, sal, comm FROM emp_with_type WHERE deptno = ?" ;

    // Specify the resultset as Scroll Sensitive and Updateable
    PreparedStatement pstmt = conn.prepareStatement(sql, ResultSet.TYPE_
    SCROLL_SENSITIVE, ResultSet.CONCUR_UPDATABLE);
        pstmt.setInt(1, i_deptno);
        ResultSet rset = pstmt.executeQuery();
        while (rset.next()) {
          float i_sal = rset.getFloat(2);
          float i_comm = rset.getFloat(3);
```

```
            // Populate the resultset column using
            // the updateFloat() method on the ResultSet object
            rset.updateFloat(2, (float)(i_sal+(1.25*i_comm)));
            // Update the corresponding resultset row using the above value.
            rset.updateRow();
            }
    rset.close();
    pstmt.close();
    pstmt.close();
    conn.close();
        } catch (SQLException e) {ret_code = e.getErrorCode();
          System.err.println(ret_code + e.getMessage()); conn.close();}
    }
}
```

TIPS:

When using updateable resultsets, the columns in the resultset query have to be selected as table.* or by specifically listing the individual columns to be selected. Using SELECT * causes a `SQLException`.

The results of an UPDATE operation through a resultset are visible in the resultset immediately.

If auto-commit is enabled, the changes to the current row are committed immediately by calling `updateRow()`. If, auto-commit is disabled, changes can be committed or rolled back. Navigating to a different row cancels the current changes. Also, the changes to the current row can be cancelled by calling the method `cancelRowUpdates()` on the `ResultSet` object before calling the `updateRow()` method.

INSERT Operation Through a Resultset

A new row can be inserted into the underlying database table through a resultset. The steps involved are:

1. Navigate to the insert row. This is done by using the method `moveToInsertRow()` on the `ResultSet` object. The insert row is a special row in the resultset and is different from the existing rows in the resultset that have been returned by the query. After the insert, the control can be made to navigate to the current row (i.e., the row before moving to the new insert row) using the method `moveToCurrentRow()` on the `ResultSet` object.
2. Update the contents of this insert row by using the `updateXXX()` methods on the `ResultSet` object.
3. Apply the new row to the database by using `insertRow()` method on the `ResultSet` object.

TIPS:

Inserting a new row through a resultset only adds the row to the database, and not to the resultset. The new row is visible in the resultset only; it's selected as part of a new query that is executed again.

If auto-commit is enabled, the new row is committed immediately by calling `insertRow()`. If auto-commit is disabled, changes can be committed or rolled back. Navigating to a different row cancels the current changes.

DELETE Operation Through a Resultset

A row in a resultset can be deleted as follows:

1. Navigate to the specific row.
2. Delete the row using the `deleteRow()` method on the `ResultSet` object.

DELETING ROWS

Deleting a row from the resultset implicitly deletes the corresponding row from the database table. This is unlike updating or inserting rows through a resultset, when the changes made to the resultset have to be explicitly applied to the database using `updateRow()` or `insertRow()` methods.

Metadata

Metadata is data about data. Given a database table, the rows in the table constitute data whereas the type and name of the individual columns constitutes metadata. Oracle JDBC supports two types of metadata, namely,

1. Resultset metadata
2. Database metadata

Resultset Metadata

The resultset metadata can be obtained by calling the methods in the `ResultSetMetaData` class. To get the basic information about resultset metadata, the following methods can be used:

- getMetaData()—This method operates on a `ResultSet` object and returns a `ResultSetMetaData` object. This is shown below:

```
ResultSet rset;
ResultSetMetaData rsmd;
rset = pstmt.executeQuery();
rsmd = rset.getMetaData();
```

- getColumnName(int)—This method operates on a `ResultSetMetaData` object and returns the name of the column in the resultset whose position is specified by the `int` parameter. This is shown below:

```
String col_name = rsmd.getColumnName(i);
```

- getColumnType(int)—This method operates on a `ResultSetMetaData` object and returns the data type of the column in the resultset whose position is specified by the `int` parameter. It always returns an integer value. This return value corresponds to one of the variables in the `java.sql.Types` class. This is shown below:

```
int col_data_type = rsmd.getColumnType(i);
if (col_data_type = java.sql.Types.VARCHAR)
{
......
}
```

DEAL WITH ROWID CAREFULLY IN JDBC PROGRAMS

The usual way of dealing with bind variables in the case of a PreparedStatement is to use the getXXX() and setXXX() methods, where XXX stands for Int, String, Float, and so on. Using getString() and setString() might work with the ROWID column to retrieve the ROWID of any particular row into a String variable. However, I recommend that you use the oracle.sql.ROWID type to store the ROWID to avoid any loss of data during SQL-to-Java conversion and vice-versa. The obvious choice now is to use the getROWID() and setROWID methods in the oracle.sql.* package. I quickly change the declaration to oracle.sql.ROWID and then use the getROWID() method on the Resultset object. Similarly, I change the call to the PreparedStatement object to use the method setROWID(). This gives me compilation errors, "cannot resolve symbol symbol : method getROWID (int) location: interface java.sql.ResultSet" and "cannot resolve symbol symbol : method setROWID (int,oracle.sql.ROWID) location: interface java.sql.PreparedStatement."

What happened? After doing some research I found out that the getROWID() method works on an OracleResultSet object and the setROWID() method works on an OraclePreparedStatement object. In the above case the ResultSet object has to be cast to an OracleResultSet object and then have the getROWID method invoked on it. Similarly, the PreparedStatement object has to be cast to an OraclePreparedStatement object and then have the setROWID() method invoked on it.

Database Metadata

The database metadata can be obtained by calling the methods in the `DatabaseSetMetaData` class. Examples of database metadata include the type of JDBC drivers supported, the table names, constraints defined on tables in the database, and so on. To get the basic information about database metadata, the following method must be used:

- getMetaData()—This method operates on a `Connection` object and returns a `DatabaseMetaData` object. This is shown below:

```
Connection conn;
DatabaseMetaData dbmd;
dbmd = conn.getMetaData();
```

Summary

This chapter outlined the use of JDBC API for database access in Java. Essentially, the various methods of using JDBC starting from the querying and returning of resultsets to executing DML from the Oracle 8i database are described in detail. The Oracle JDBC extensions were discussed. Finally, details about handling resultsets in JDBC were presented.

4

ADVANCED JDBC PROGRAMMING

ESSENTIALS

- Advanced JDBC provides support for creation and manipulation of Objects in the Oracle8i database using Java programs. The use of Large Objects for unstructured data is also supported.
- To use objects such as Object Types along with DML on object tables(row objects) and object-relational tables(column objects), use either the JDBC STRUCT type and the corresponding methods or use custom Java classes that implement either the standard JDBC `java.sql.SQLData` interface or the Oracle extension `oracle.sql.customDatum` interface.
- To use object REFS, make use of the JDBC REF type (`oracle.sql.REF` or `java.sql.Ref`) to map to Oracle Objects, or use custom Java classes that implement the Oracle extension `oracle.sql.customDatum` interface. The `SQLData` interface is not supported for object REFS. Also, creation of object REFS is not supported in JDBC.
- For manipulating collections, use the JDBC ARRAY type (`oracle.sql.ARRAY` or `java.sql.Array`) to map to Oracle Collections, or use custom Java classes that implement the Oracle extension `oracle.sql.customDatum` interface. The `SQLData` interface is not supported for collections.
- Large Objects are supported in JDBC in form of BLOBS and CLOBS. BLOBS and CLOBS are handled by using the JDBC 1.2.x `Blob` and `Clob` objects (`java.sql.Blob` and `java.sql.Clob`) or the Oracle BLOB and CLOB objects (`oracle.sql.BLOB` and `oracle.sql.CLOB`) respectively. BFILES are handled by using the Oracle extension `oracle.sql.BFILE`.
- Use the JDBC performance enhancements such as disabling auto-commit mode, Oracle row pre-fetching, update batching, and using prepared statements and bind variables.

This chapter explains the use of advanced JDBC programming in Oracle. It highlights the methods to incorporate objects in the Oracle 8i database using JDBC, describing in detail the various methods of handling objects starting from object types to collections and large objects. The Oracle JDBC performance extensions are discussed. Finally, a discussion of using JDBC in the server-side is presented. A case study is presented to illustrate the concepts.

Overview

Oracle 8i provides the definition and manipulation of objects in the database. Specifically, it supports the following:

- Object types along with object tables (row objects) and object-relational tables (relational tables with column objects)
- Object references or REFS
- Collections such as VARRAYS and NESTED TABLES

Also Oracle 8i provides the inclusion of Large Objects (LOBS) in the database. JDBC also supports these features either through the standard JDBC implementation interface or through Oracle extension interface.

Case Study

We will use the schema `oratest/oratest@oracle` (where oracle is the tnsnames alias in tnsnames.ora). This is for tools such as SQL*Plus. As part of the case study we will use some of the schema objects as defined in the case studies in Chapters 2, "Java Stored Procedures," and 3, "Basic JDBC Programming." These are reproduced here for convenience:

Database objects (tables and object types):

```
CREATE TABLE emp (empno number(10) primary key,
                  ename varchar2(40) not null,
                  job   varchar2(15) not null,
                  mgr   number(10) references emp(empno),
                  hiredate date not null,
                  sal   number(12,2) not null,
                  comm  number(4),
                  deptno number(4) references dept(deptno));

CREATE OR REPLACE TYPE address AS OBJECT
                              (add_id number(10),
                               line1 varchar2(20),
```

```
                               line2 varchar2(20),
                               city  varchar2(15),
                               state varchar2(2),
                               zip   varchar2(11));
/
```

(This type is later changed to include member methods.)

```
CREATE TABLE addresses OF address;
```

In addition, the following schema objects are also used and should be defined in the above schema:

- Database tables and objects

```
CREATE TABLE emp_with_addr (empno number(10) primary key,
                 ename varchar2(40) not null,
                 job   varchar2(15) not null,
                 mgr   number(10) references emp(empno),
                 hiredate date not null,
                 sal   number(12,2) not null,
                 comm  number(4),
                 deptno number(4) references dept(deptno),
                 emp_addr REF address);
```

This is used for describing Object REFS later.

```
CREATE TYPE address_id_varray IS VARRAY(20) OF NUMBER;

CREATE TABLE address_id_list(address_id_list address_id_varray);
```

The type and table are used in describing collections later.

```
CREATE TABLE lob_tab
(id NUMBER PRIMARY KEY,
 blob_data BLOB,
 clob_data CLOB,
 bfile_data BFILE);
```

This table is used in describing large objects later.

```
CREATE TABLE tab1 (col1 NUMBER);
```

These schema objects are used to describe the ins and outs of using objects and performance extensions in JDBC programs.

Handling Object Types in JDBC

In this section, the method of defining and manipulating object types in JDBC is discussed. The next two sections describe the methods of handling Object REFS and Collections in JDBC.

JDBC implements objects (instances of object types) as instances of specific Java classes. A standard JDBC type can be used to map to Oracle objects, or custom Java classes can be used to do the mapping. The method of accessing Oracle objects consists of creating these Java classes and populating them. There are two methods available to do this:

- Use the JDBC `STRUCT` type to map to Oracle Objects.
- Use custom Java classes that implement either the standard JDBC `java.sql.SQLData` interface or the Oracle extension `oracle.sql.customDatum` interface.

Using JDBC STRUCT Type Handle Oracle Object Types

Basically, Oracle JDBC constructs an object type instance as an instance of the `oracle.sql.STRUCT` class. JDBC 2.0 provides a standard `java.sql.Struct` class for implementing object types. This functionality has been extended by Oracle in the `oracle.sql.STRUCT` class that implements the `java.sql.Struct` class. Either of these classes provides the following methods defined in them that can be used to access Object types from JDBC programs:

1. `getAttributes()`—Retrieves the values of the attributes that constitute the given object type.
2. `getSQLTypeName()`—Retrieves the fully qualified name of the SQL object type, (`schema.sql_type_name`) that the Struct or STRUCT represents, in the form of a Java String.

We will use the address object type and the addresses table based on this object type, created in the case study of Chapter 2 for describing the manipulation and access of object types in JDBC. The definitions of both are reproduced here for convenience.

DROP TABLE emp_with_addr;

DROP TABLE addresses;

```
CREATE OR REPLACE TYPE address AS OBJECT
                                (add_id number(10),
                                 line1 varchar2(20),
                                 line2 varchar2(20),
                                 city  varchar2(15),
```

```
                              state varchar2(2),
                              zip   varchar2(11));
/

CREATE TABLE addresses OF address;
```

The following are the steps involved to create STRUCT objects (`oracle.sql.STRUCT` objects) and perform INSERT or UPDATE into object tables:

1. Create a `StructDescriptor` object for the given object type. A `StructDescriptor` is an instance of the `oracle.sql.StructDescriptor` class that represents the `STRUCT` object.

   ```
   StructDescriptor address_sd =
      StructDescriptor.createDescriptor("ADDRESS", conn);
   ```

   Here `ADDRESS` is the object type created in SQL and `conn` is an instance of the `Connection` class.

2. Use the `StructDescriptor` to create the `STRUCT` object.

   Once a `StructDescriptor` is created, the next step is to create a `STRUCT` object by passing the `StructDescriptor`, the connection object, and an array of Java objects containing the attributes that the `STRUCT` will contain. Only one `StructDescriptor` should be created for each object type. This is shown below:

   ```
   Object[] address_attrib;
   address_attrib = new Object [6];
   STRUCT address_struct = new STRUCT(address_sd, conn, address_attrib);
   ```

3. Construct a `PreparedStatement` that executes an INSERT or UPDATE statement.

4. Use the `setObject()` method on the `PreparedStatement()` to set the values for the object type instance.

   A complete example is shown below:

   ```
   import oracle.sql.*;
   import java.sql.*;
   import java.math.*;

   public class ObjectTypeExample {
     public static void main(String[] args)
     throws SQLException {
   int ret_code;
   Connection conn = null;
     try {
   ```

```
    //Load and register Oracle driver
   DriverManager.registerDriver(new oracle.jdbc.driver.OracleDriver());
  //Establish a connection

    conn = DriverManager.getConnection(
      "jdbc:oracle:thin:@training:1521:Oracle", "oratest", "oratest");

    StructDescriptor address_sd =
      StructDescriptor.createDescriptor("ADDRESS", conn);
    Object[] address_attrib;
    address_attrib = new Object [6];
    address_attrib[0] = new BigDecimal(1001);
    address_attrib[1] = "50 Rockefeller Plaza";
    address_attrib[2] = "";
    address_attrib[3] = "New York";
    address_attrib[4] = "NY";
    address_attrib[5] = "10020";

    STRUCT address_struct = new STRUCT(address_sd, conn, address_attrib);

    String sql = "INSERT INTO addresses values (?)" ;

    PreparedStatement pstmt = conn.prepareStatement(sql);
    pstmt.setObject(1, address_struct);
    pstmt.executeUpdate();
   pstmt.close();
   conn.close();
       } catch (SQLException e) {ret_code = e.getErrorCode();
         System.err.println(ret_code + e.getMessage()); conn.close();}
   }
}
```

Querying an object table is also possible using the `oracle.sql.STRUCT` class. Unlike the INSERT operation, we do not need a `StructDescriptor`. The steps involved are as follows:

1. Create a `Statement` object and execute a SQL SELECT statement against the `Statement` object that returns the rows into a `ResultSet` object. Because we are querying an object table to retrieve objects as individual rows, the VALUE operator must be used as follows:

   ```
   SELECT VALUE FROM addresses a;
   ```

This is shown below:

```
Statement stmt = conn.createStatement();
 ResultSet rset = stmt.executeQuery("SELECT VALUE FROM addresses a");
```

2. Retrieve the object row having one column (that is, the object itself as a whole) into a `STRUCT` object by using `getObject()` method on the `ResultSet` object and casting it to `STRUCT` type, as shown here:

    ```
    STRUCT address_struct = (STRUCT) rset.getObject(1);
    ```

3. Create an array of Java objects that holds the attributes of each row object retrieved by `getObject()` method above. This is done using the `getAttributes()` method on the `STRUCT` object created in step 2:

    ```
    Object [] address_attrib = address_struct.getAttributes();
    ```

Once the object array is constructed, the individual attributes of the object correspond to the individual array elements:

```
System.out.println(((BigDecimal)address_attrib[0]).intValue());
System.out.println((String) address_attrib[1]);
System.out.println((String) address_attrib[2]);
```

A complete program is shown here:

```
import oracle.sql.*;
import java.sql.*;
import java.math.*;

public class ObjectTypeExample2 {
  public static void main(String[] args)
  throws SQLException {
int ret_code;
Connection conn = null;
  try {
      //Load and register Oracle driver
   DriverManager.registerDriver(new oracle.jdbc.driver.OracleDriver());
  //Establish a connection

    conn = DriverManager.getConnection(
         "jdbc:oracle:thin:@training:1521:Oracle", "oratest", "oratest");

    Statement stmt = conn.createStatement();
    ResultSet rset =
```

```
        stmt.executeQuery("SELECT VALUE FROM addresses a");
      System.out.println("The addresses are as follows:\n");
      while (rset.next())
      {
       STRUCT address_struct = (STRUCT) rset.getObject(1);
       Object [] address_attrib = address_struct.getAttributes();
       System.out.println(((BigDecimal)address_attrib[0]).intValue());
       System.out.println((String) address_attrib[1]);
       System.out.println((String) address_attrib[2]);
       System.out.println((String)address_attrib[3]+", "
        +(String)address_attrib[4]+" "+(String)address_attrib[5]);
      }
     stmt.close();
     conn.close();
         } catch (SQLException e) {ret_code = e.getErrorCode();
          System.err.println(ret_code + e.getMessage()); conn.close();}
     }
}
```

Using Custom Object Classes to Handle Oracle Object Types

A second method of accessing and manipulating object types in Java applications is to use custom Java classes, also known as custom object classes, that implement either the standard JDBC `java.sql.SQLData` interface or the Oracle extension `oracle.sql.customDatum` interface.

We will discuss the `SQLData` interface. The `SQLData` interface is for mapping SQL objects only. This interface can be used to read data from an Oracle object in the database into the Java program or write to an Oracle object from a Java application. First, the method of writing is described in detail followed by the method for the read operation.

The steps involved in the write operation are as follows:

1. Create the object type in SQL.

   We will use the address object type outlined in the earlier section. Also we will use the corresponding addresses object table based on the address object type for write and read operations on object types using `SQLData`.

2. Create the corresponding custom object class. This class should implement the `SQLData` class and should specify a `readSQL()` method and a `writeSQL()` method as defined in the `SQLData` interface. The `readSQL()` method is used to read a stream of data values from the database and populate an instance of the custom object class. The `writeSQL()` method is used to write data values from an instance of the custom object class to a stream that can be written to the database. The JDBC `SQLData` interface provides two

other interfaces SQLInput and SQLOutput that are passed as parameters to the readSQL() and writeSQL() methods respectively.

The method readSQL() is implemented as follows:

```
public void readSQL(SqLInput stream, String sql_type_name)
   throws SQLException {
......
}
```

The readSQL() method takes as input a SQLInput instance and a string that indicates the SQL object type name. It provides a readXXX() method (that is, readInt(), readString(), and so on) of the SQLInput stream that must be called for each Java type that maps to an attribute of the Oracle object type. This enables you to read and convert the data. Finally, the readSQL() method assigns this data to the object class attributes.

The method writeSQL() is implemented as follows:

```
public void writeSQL(SQLOutput stream) throws SQLException {
......
}
```

The writeSQL() method takes as input a SQLOutput instance. It provides a writeXXX() method (that is, writeInt(), writeString(), and so on) of the SQLOutput stream that must be called for each Java type that maps to an attribute of the Oracle object type and in the same order as in the Object type. This enables you to convert the data. Finally, the writeSQL() method writes this data to the SQLOutput stream. This in turn is written to the database when the prepared statement is executed.

An example using the address object type is shown here. The corresponding custom object class is AddressObj.

```
import java.sql.*;

public class AddressObj implements SQLData
{
  private String sql_type;
  public  int add_id;
  public  String line1;
  public  String line2;
  public  String city;
  public  String state;
  public  String zip;

  public AddressObj(String i_sql_type,
                    int    i_add_id,
```

```
                    String i_line1,
                    String i_line2,
                    String i_city,
                    String i_state,
                    String i_zip)
  {
   this.sql_type = i_sql_type;
   this.add_id = i_add_id;
   this.line1 = i_line1;
   this.line2 = i_line2;
   this.city = i_city;
   this.state = i_state;
   this.zip = i_zip;
  }

  public String getSQLTypeName() throws SQLException
  {
   return sql_type;
  }
  public void readSQL(SQLInput stream, String typeName)
     throws SQLException
  {
   sql_type = typeName;

   add_id = stream.readInt();
   line1 = stream.readString();
   line2 = stream.readString();
   city = stream.readString();
   state = stream.readString();
   zip = stream.readString();
  }
  public void writeSQL(SQLOutput stream)
    throws SQLException
  {
   stream.writeInt(add_id);
   stream.writeString(line1);
   stream.writeString(line2);
   stream.writeString(city);
   stream.writeString(state);
   stream.writeString(zip);
  }
 }
```

3. Define a type map to establish a mapping between the Oracle object and the custom object class. A type map should be created to specify the custom object class to use in mapping the SQL object type to Java. A default type map of the connection object can be used or a type map can be obtained by the `getObject()` method of the `ResultSet` object, as is shown here:

   ```
   Map map = (Map) conn.getTypeMap();
   map.put("ADDRESS", Class.forName("AddressObj"));
   ```

   Here, the default type map of the connection object is updated with the `AddressObj` class name for mapping the `ADDRESS` object type.

4. Create an instance of the custom object class that supplies the values for each attribute of the object type. This is for the new row to be inserted.

   ```
   AddressObj address1 = new AddressObj(
   "ORATEST.ADDRESS", 1002, "27 Thornall St.", "","Chicago", "IL", "23456");
   ```

   This uses the `AddressObj` custom object class created in Step 2.

5. Create a `PreparedStatement` instance that inserts an Oracle object of the Oracle object type into a table as part of a new record.

   ```
   PreparedStatement pstmt =
   conn.prepareStatement("insert into addresses values (?)");
   ```

6. Populate the bind parameter of the `PreparedStatement` with the value of the Java object (of the custom object class) using `setObject()` method.

   ```
   pstmt.setObject(1, address1);
   ```

7. Execute the `PreparedStatement` to insert the new row into the database.

   ```
   pstmt.executeUpdate();
   ```

TIP

The `setObject()` method triggers `writeSQL()`.

A complete program is shown here:

```
import oracle.sql.*;
import java.sql.*;
import java.math.*;
import java.util.Map;
```

```
public class ObjectTypeExample3 {
  public static void main(String[] args)
  throws SQLException, Exception {
int ret_code;
Connection conn = null;
  try {
      //Load and register Oracle driver
   DriverManager.registerDriver(new oracle.jdbc.driver.OracleDriver());
  //Establish a connection

    conn = DriverManager.getConnection(
        "jdbc:oracle:thin:@training:1521:Oracle", "oratest", "oratest");

    Map map = (Map) conn.getTypeMap();
    map.put("ADDRESS", Class.forName("AddressObj"));

   AddressObj address1 = new AddressObj(
"ORATEST.ADDRESS", 1002, "27 Thornall St.", "","Chicago", "IL", "23456");

   PreparedStatement pstmt =
    conn.prepareStatement("insert into addresses values (?)");
   pstmt.setObject(1, address1);
   pstmt.executeUpdate();
   pstmt.close();
       } catch (SQLException e) {ret_code = e.getErrorCode();
          System.err.println(ret_code + e.getMessage()); conn.close();}
         catch (Exception e)
         {System.err.println(e.getMessage()); conn.close();}
   }
}
```

Next we describe the steps involved in the read operation using `SQLData` interface. These are as follows:

1. Create the object type in SQL. (This should have been already in the database).
2. Create the corresponding custom object class. This class should specify a `readSQL()` method and a `writeSQL()` method as defined in the `SQLData` interface. The `readSQL()` and `writeSQL()` methods are implemented in the same manner as in the write operation.

   This is the same as in the case of write operation. We use the `AddressObj` class created in step 2 of the write operation.
3. Put an entry for the custom object class in the type map. This is also the same as in step 3 of the write operation.

4. Query the rows containing the Oracle objects into a `ResultSet` object:

    ```
    Statement stmt = conn.createStatement();
    ResultSet rset = stmt.executeQuery("SELECT VALUE FROM addresses a");
    ```

5. Create an instance of the custom object class that will hold the values for each attribute of the object type. This is for each queried row. Only one instance of the custom object class is sufficient. This is done by calling the empty `AddressObj()` constructor.

    ```
    AddressObj address1 = new AddressObj();
    ```

6. Populate the Java custom object with data from one row of the resultset using the `getObject()` method on the `ResultSet` object. The `getObject()` method returns an object of the custom object class (that is, the `SQLData` object) as per step 3, a type map exists:

    ```
    while (rset.next()) {
        address1 = (AddressObj) rset.getObject(1);
        System.out.println("Address Id = " +address1.add_id
                           +" and the corresponding address is:");
        System.out.println(address1.line1);
        System.out.println(address1.line2);
        System.out.println(address1.city+", "+address1.state+" "
                           +address1.zip);
      }
    ```

The `getObject()` method triggers `readSQL()`.

If there is no type map, the output of `getObject()` should be cast to type `STRUCT` as `getObject()` returns an `oracle.sql.STRUCT` instance in this case.

A complete example is shown here:

(This program should be compiled after compiling the class AddressObj, in a file named AddressObj.java and in the same working directory, written earlier).

```
import java.sql.*;
import java.util.Map;

public class ObjectTypeExample4 {
  public static void main(String[] args)
  throws SQLException, Exception {
int ret_code;
Connection conn = null;
  try {
      //Load and register Oracle driver
```

```
DriverManager.registerDriver(new oracle.jdbc.driver.OracleDriver());
//Establish a connection

 conn = DriverManager.getConnection(
     "jdbc:oracle:thin:@training:1521:Oracle", "oratest", "oratest");

 Map map = (Map) conn.getTypeMap();
 map.put("ORATEST.ADDRESS", Class.forName("AddressObj"));

 Statement stmt = conn.createStatement();

 ResultSet rset =
              stmt.executeQuery("SELECT VALUE FROM addresses a");
 System.out.println("The addresses are: ");
AddressObj address1 = new AddressObj();
while (rset.next()) {
 address1 = (AddressObj) rset.getObject(1);
 System.out.println("Address Id = " +address1.add_id
                   +" and the corresponding address is:");
 System.out.println(address1.line1);
 System.out.println(address1.line2);
 System.out.println(address1.city+", "+address1.state+" "
                   +address1.zip);
}
rset.close();
stmt.close();
    } catch (SQLException e) {ret_code = e.getErrorCode();
      System.err.println(ret_code + e.getMessage()); conn.close();}
      catch (Exception e)
      {System.err.println(e.getMessage()); conn.close();}
}
}
```

Handling Object REFS in JDBC

Objects REFS are supported in the Oracle 8i database as pointers to objects. JDBC also supports object REFS for the operation of SELECT and UPDATE only. Creation of object REFS is not allowed in JDBC. There are two methods available to do this:

1. Use the JDBC REF type (`oracle.sql.REF` or `java.sql.Ref`) to map to Oracle Objects.
2. Use custom Java classes that implement the Oracle extension `oracle.sql.customDatum` interface. The `SQLData` interface is not supported for object REFS.

Using JDBC REF Type to Handle Object REFS

Oracle JDBC constructs an object REF instance as an instance of the `oracle.sql.REF` class. JDBC 2.0 provides a standard `java.sql.Ref` class for implementing object types. This functionality has been extended by Oracle in the `oracle.sql.REF` class that implements the `java.sql.Ref` class. The advantage of using oracle.sql.REF is that it provides direct access to object REF data in SQL format. Hence no information is lost. Either of these classes provides the following methods defined in them that can be used to access Object REFS from JDBC programs:

1. getBaseTypeName()—Returns the fully qualified object type name of the object type to which the REF points to.
2. getValue()—This method is an Oracle extension and retrieves the corresponding referenced object to which the REF points to, from the database. Using this, the attributes of the retrieved object can be obtained.
3. setValue()—Sets the value of the referenced object in the database. Using this, the attributes of the object being updated can be set. An object type instance should be passed as input parameter to this method.

We will discuss the operations of SELECT and UPDATE of object REFS. We will describe the SELECT operation first.

Selection of object REFS can be done in two ways:

1. Using a `ResultSet` object instance.
2. Using a `CallableStatement` object instance. In this case, the REF is retrieved as an OUT parameter of a PL/SQL procedure or function.

JDBC provides a `getREF()` method on the `ResultSet` and `CallableStatement` objects to do this using either way.

We will use the `ADDRESS` object type and the `addresses` OBJECT TABLE for the purposes of this section.

The steps involved in retrieving an object REF using `ResultSet` are as follows:

1. Select the object REF from the database table using a SELECT statement. This is shown below:

   ```
   Statement stmt = conn.createStatement();
   ResultSet rset = stmt.executeQuery("SELECT REF FROM addresses a");
   ```

2. Retrieve the reference column value from the resultset into a REF object using `getREF()`.

   ```
   while (rset.next()){
   REF addr_ref = ((OracleResultSet)rset).getREF(1);
   ......
   }
   ```

   Instead of `getREF()`, `getObject()` can be used. In this case, the output of `getObject()` should be cast to `REF`.

   ```
   REF addr_ref = (REF) rset.getObject(1)
   ```

3. Retrieve the object value that the REF points to using the `getValue()` method of the `REF` object and cast it to a `STRUCT`.

   ```
   STRUCT address1 = (STRUCT) addr_ref.getValue();
   ```

4. Retrieve the values of the attributes of the object obtained in step 3 using the `getAttributes()` method.

   ```
   Object addr_attrib[] address1.getAttributes();
   ```

Combining steps 2–4 we have the following:

```
while (rset.next()){
REF addr_ref = rset.getREF(1);
STRUCT address1 = (STRUCT) addr_ref.getValue();
Object addr_attrib[] address1.getAttributes();
}
```

A complete program is shown here:

```
import java.sql.*;
import oracle.sql.*;
import java.math.*;
import oracle.jdbc.driver.*;
public class ObjectREFExample {
  public static void main(String[] args)
  throws SQLException, Exception {
int ret_code;
Connection conn = null;
  try {
      //Load and register Oracle driver
```

```
   DriverManager.registerDriver(new oracle.jdbc.driver.OracleDriver());
  //Establish a connection
    conn = DriverManager.getConnection(
           "jdbc:oracle:thin:@training:1521:Oracle", "oratest", "oratest");
Statement stmt = conn.createStatement();
    ResultSet rset = stmt.executeQuery("SELECT REF FROM addresses a");
    System.out.println("The addresses are: ");
   STRUCT address1;
   while (rset.next()){
//      REF addr_ref = (REF) rset.getObject(1);
        REF addr_ref = ((OracleResultSet)rset).getREF(1);
     address1 = (STRUCT) addr_ref.getValue();
     Object addr_attrib[] = address1.getAttributes();
    System.out.println("Address Id = " +((BigDecimal)addr_attrib[0]).intValue()
                      +" and the corresponding address is:");
    System.out.println(addr_attrib[1]);
    System.out.println(addr_attrib[2]);
    System.out.println(addr_attrib[3]+", "+addr_attrib[4]+" "+addr_attrib[5]);
}
   rset.close();
   stmt.close();
       } catch (SQLException e) {ret_code = e.getErrorCode();
         System.err.println(ret_code + e.getMessage()); conn.close();}
         catch (Exception e)
         {System.err.println(e.getMessage()); conn.close();}
   }
}
```

The steps for retrieving an object REF using a `CallableStatement` object instance are as follows:

1. Define a `CallableStatement` that calls the function or procedure returning REFS.

   ```
   OracleCallableStatement cstmt =
      (OracleCallableStatement) conn.prepareCall("{p_refs(?)}");
   ```

   Here we assume that `p_refs` is a PL/SQL procedure returning an object REF.

2. Register the OUT parameter that corresponds to the function return value or the OUT parameter of a procedure. This is shown below:

   ```
   csmt.registerOutParameter(1, OracleTypes.REF, "ADDRESS");
   ```

TIP

The SQL type code used should be `OracleTypes.REF`

The name of the SQL object type corresponding to the object REF should be passed an input parameter to `registerOutParameter()` method.

3. Execute the PL/SQL procedure or function. This is shown below:

```
csmt.executeUpdate();
```

The UPDATE operation involving object REFS has the following steps:

1. Define a `PreparedStatement` associated with a SQL UPDATE statement:

```
PreparedStatement pstmt = conn.prepareStatement(
"UPDATE emp_with_addr SET emp_add = ? WHERE empno = ?");
```

2. Set the value of the bind parameter corresponding to a REF value using `setREF()` method of the `PreparedStatement` object:

```
((OraclePreparedStatement)pstmt).setREF(1, addr_ref);
```

`setValue()` METHOD

Updating a REF column only updates the object reference to a new object reference. It does not update the attributes of the corresponding object pointed to by the REF. To update the actual object pointed to by the REF, the `setValue()` method on the REF object should be used.

We will use a new table `EMP_WITH_ADDR` for implementing the update operation. The structure of this table is shown below:

```
CREATE TABLE emp_with_addr (empno number(10) primary key,
                  ename varchar2(40) not null,
                  job   varchar2(15) not null,
                  mgr   number(10) references emp(empno),
                  hiredate date not null,
                  sal   number(12,2) not null,
                  comm  number(4),
                  deptno number(4) references dept(deptno),
                  emp_addr REF address);
```

We populate this table as follows:

```
DECLARE
  v_addr_ref REF address;
BEGIN
  SELECT REF
```

```
  INTO    v_addr_ref
  FROM    addresses a
  WHERE   add_id = 1001;
INSERT INTO emp_with_addr
   SELECT empno, ename, job, mgr, hiredate, sal, comm, deptno,
          v_addr_ref
   FROM   emp
   WHERE  deptno = 10;
  COMMIT;
END;
```

Next, the JDBC program for updating the `emp_addr` REF column of the `emp_with_addr` table is shown below. This program first retrieves the REF corresponding to `address id` 1002 and then updates the `emp_addr` REF column in `emp_with_addr` table with new REF so obtained. Originally, the `emp_addr` REF column was pointing to the object REF with `address id` 1001 as outlined in the INSERT statement above.

```
import java.sql.*;
import oracle.sql.*;
import oracle.jdbc.driver.*;

public class ObjectREFExample2 {
  public static void main(String[] args)
  throws SQLException, Exception {
int ret_code;
Connection conn = null;
  try {
      //Load and register Oracle driver
       DriverManager.registerDriver(new oracle.jdbc.driver.OracleDriver());
  //Establish a connection

    conn = DriverManager.getConnection(
           "jdbc:oracle:thin:@training:1521:Oracle", "oratest", "oratest");

String sql1 = "SELECT REF FROM addresses a WHERE add_id = ?";
   String sql2 = "UPDATE emp_with_addr SET emp_addr = ? WHERE deptno = ?";

   PreparedStatement pstmt1 = conn.prepareStatement(sql1);
   pstmt1.setInt(1, 1002);

    ResultSet rset = pstmt1.executeQuery();
```

```
    REF addr_ref = null;

   STRUCT address1;
   if (rset.next()){
//      REF addr_ref = (REF) rset.getObject(1);
        addr_ref = ((OracleResultSet)rset).getREF(1);
}
    PreparedStatement pstmt2 = conn.prepareStatement(sql2);
   ((OraclePreparedStatement)pstmt2).setREF(1, addr_ref);
    pstmt2.setInt(2, 10);
    pstmt2.executeUpdate();
   rset.close();
   pstmt1.close();
   pstmt2.close();
        } catch (SQLException e) {ret_code = e.getErrorCode();
          System.err.println(ret_code + e.getMessage()); conn.close();}
          catch (Exception e)
          {System.err.println(e.getMessage()); conn.close();}
   }
}
```

Handling Collections in JDBC

Collections are sets of elements that are stored as part of a single row. For example, an array of integers stored as part of a database table row forms a collection. Collections are supported in the Oracle 8i database as VARRAYS or nested tables. Oracle supports only named collections in the database—that is, a collection given a SQL type name. JDBC 2.0 supports collections by means of arrays. There are two methods available to do this:

1. Use the JDBC ARRAY type (`oracle.sql.ARRAY` or `java.sql.Array`) to map to Oracle Collections.
2. Use custom Java classes that implement the Oracle extension `oracle.sql.customDatum` interface. The `SQLData` interface is not supported for collections.

Using JDBC ARRAY Type to Handle Collections

Oracle JDBC constructs a collection instance as an instance of the `oracle.sql.ARRAY` class. JDBC 2.0 provides a standard `java.sql.Array` class for implementing arrays. This functionality has been extended by Oracle in the `oracle.sql.ARRAY` class that implements the `java.sql.Array` class. To use an ARRAY object an array descriptor should be created as an instance of the `oracle.sql.ArrayDescriptor` class to describe the array type. The `oracle.sql.ARRAY` class provides many methods defined in it that can be used to access collections from JDBC programs, the most important of which are:

1. `getArray()`—Retrieves the content of the array into JDBC java types.
2. `getDescriptor()`—Returns the `ArrayDescriptor` object that describes the array type.
3. `getBaseType()`—Returns the SQL Type Code for the array elements.
4. `getSQLTypeName()`—Returns the SQL type that the array is based on.
5. `length()`—Returns the number of elements in the array.

We will demonstrate the use of VARRAYS in this section. The following are the database objects created:

```
CREATE TYPE address_id_varray IS VARRAY(20) OF NUMBER;

create table address_id_list(address_id_list address_id_varray);
```

The following are the steps involved to create ARRAY objects (`oracle.sql.ARRAY` objects) and perform INSERT or UPDATE into database tables:

1. Create an `ArrayDescriptor` object for the given VARRAYS. An `ArrayDescriptor` is an instance of the `oracle.sql.ArrayDescriptor` class that must exist for the VARRAY type that represents the ARRAY object.

   ```
   ArrayDescriptor address_id_ad =
     ArrayDescriptor.createDescriptor("ADDRESS_ID_VARRAY", conn);
   ```

   Here `ADDRESS_ID_VARRAY` is the VARRAY created in SQL and conn is an instance of the `Connection` class.

2. Use the so created `ArrayDescriptor` to create the ARRAY object.

   Once a `ArrayDescriptor` is created, the next step is to create an ARRAY object by passing the `ArrayDescriptor`, the connection object and an element array in Java containing the elements that the ARRAY will contain. This element array can be an array of primitive Java types or an array of Java Objects. This is shown below:

   ```
   int  address_id_list[] = {1, 1001, 1002 };
   ARRAY address_id_array = new ARRAY(address_id_ad, conn, address_id_list);
   ```

TIP

Only one `ArrayDescriptor` should be created for any number of ARRAY objects of the same SQL type.

3. Construct a `PreparedStatement` that executes an INSERT or UPDATE statement.
4. Use the `setARRAY()` method on the `PreparedStatement` cast to an `OraclePreparedStatement`, to set the values for VARRAY instance.

```
PreparedStatement pstmt =
conn.prepareStatement("INSERT INTO address_id_list VALUES (?)");
((OraclePreparedStatement)pstmt).setARRAY(1, address_id_array);
pstmt.executeUpdate();
```

A complete program is shown below. It populates a Java array with `add_ids` retrieved from the `addresses` table and then inserts the resulting array into the `address_id_list` table.

```
import oracle.sql.*;
import java.sql.*;
import java.math.*;
import oracle.jdbc.driver.*;

public class CollectionExample {
  public static void main(String[] args)
  throws SQLException {
int ret_code;
Connection conn = null;
  try {
      //Load and register Oracle driver
       DriverManager.registerDriver(new oracle.jdbc.driver.OracleDriver());
  //Establish a connection

    conn = DriverManager.getConnection(
          "jdbc:oracle:thin:@training:1521:Oracle", "oratest", "oratest");

   ArrayDescriptor address_id_ad
            = ArrayDescriptor.createDescriptor("ADDRESS_ID_VARRAY", conn);

   Statement stmt = conn.createStatement();
   ResultSet rset = stmt.executeQuery("SELECT COUNT(add_id) from addresses");
   rset.next();
   int num_rows = rset.getInt(1);
   rset.close();
   rset = stmt.executeQuery("Select add_id from addresses");

   int  address_id_list[] = new int[num_rows];
   int i=0, val;
```

```
    while (rset.next())
    {
     val = rset.getInt(1);
     address_id_list[i] = val;
     i++;
    }
    rset.close();
    stmt.close();
    ARRAY address_id_array = new ARRAY(address_id_ad, conn, address_id_list);

    PreparedStatement pstmt
      = conn.prepareStatement("INSERT INTO address_id_list VALUES (?)");
    ((OraclePreparedStatement)pstmt).setARRAY(1, address_id_array);

    pstmt.executeUpdate();
    pstmt.close();
    conn.close();
        } catch (SQLException e) {ret_code = e.getErrorCode();
          System.err.println(ret_code + e.getMessage()); conn.close();}
    }
}
```

The output of the above program can be tested by querying the `address_id_list` table as follows:

```
SQL> select * from address_id_list;

ADDRESS_ID_LIST
------------------------------------------------------
ADDRESS_ID_VARRAY(1, 1001, 1002)

SQL>
```

Querying a table with collection columns is also possible using the `oracle.sql.ARRAY` class. Unlike the INSERT operation, we do not need an ARRAY descriptor.

Selection of object REFS can be done in two ways:

1. Using a `ResultSet` object instance.
2. Using a `CallableStatement` object instance. In this case, the collection is retrieved as an OUT parameter of a PL/SQL procedure or function.

JDBC provides a `getARRAY()` method on the `ResultSet` and `CallableStatement` objects to do this using either way.

The steps involved in retrieving a collection using `ResultSet` are as follows:

1. Create a Statement object and execute a SQL SELECT statement against the Statement object that returns the rows into a `ResultSet` object.

   ```
   SELECT * FROM address_id_list;
   ```

   This is shown below:

   ```
   Statement stmt = conn.createStatement();
   ResultSet rset = stmt.executeQuery("SELECT * FROM address_id_list");
   ```

2. Retrieve the array as a whole and then retrieve the elements of the array. Retrieving the array as a whole consists in retrieving the array into an ARRAY object by using `getARRAY()` method on the `ResultSet` object casting the resultset to an `OracleResultSet`. This is shown here:

   ```
       ARRAY address_id_array = ((OracleResultSet)rset).getARRAY(1);
   ```

   The method `getObject()` can also be used, and in this case, the output should be cast to an `oracle.sql.ARRAY` object:

   ```
   ARRAY address_id_array = (ARRAY) rset.getObject(1);
   ```

3. Retrieve the individual elements of the array obtained by using the `getArray()` method on the ARRAY object. For example, data in an integer array can be retrieved as follows:

   ```
   BigDecimal[] array_elements = (BigDecimal[]) address_id_array.getArray();
   ```

Here `BigDecimal` is used as Oracle `NUMBER` type and is mapped to Java `BigDecimal` by default in JDBC.

A complete example is shown here:

```
import oracle.sql.*;
import java.sql.*;
import java.math.*;
import oracle.jdbc.driver.*;

public class CollectionExample2 {
  public static void main(String[] args)
  throws SQLException {
int ret_code;
Connection conn = null;
```

```
  try {
      //Load and register Oracle driver
       DriverManager.registerDriver(new oracle.jdbc.driver.OracleDriver());
  //Establish a connection

    conn = DriverManager.getConnection(
           "jdbc:oracle:thin:@training:1521:Oracle", "oratest", "oratest");

    Statement stmt = conn.createStatement();
    ResultSet rset = stmt.executeQuery("SELECT * FROM address_id_list");

    while (rset.next())
    {
      ARRAY address_id_array = ((OracleResultSet)rset).getARRAY(1);
      BigDecimal[] array_elements = (BigDecimal[]) address_id_array.getArray();
      int idx = 0;
      int len = array_elements.length;
      System.out.println("The array is as follows :");
      for (idx=0;idx<len;idx++)
      {
        BigDecimal array_element = (BigDecimal) array_elements[idx];
        System.out.println(array_element.intValue());
      }
    }
    stmt.close();
    conn.close();
       } catch (SQLException e) {ret_code = e.getErrorCode();
         System.err.println(ret_code + e.getMessage()); conn.close();}
   }
}
```

There is no way to write to an array as there is no `setArray()` method on the ARRAY object.

The individual elements can also be retrieved using the methods `getOracleArray()` or `getResultSet()` methods on the ARRAY object instance.

When using the `getResultSet()` method, the resultset contains one row for each element of the array, with two columns in each row. The first column is the index of the array element and the second column is the value of the index element. These two column values can be obtained by using the `getInt()` and `getXXX()` methods (i.e., getString(), getObject() etc.) on the ResultSet object. The following shows an example using the `getResultSet()` method:

```
ResultSet rset = address_id_array.getResultSet();
while (rset.next()) {
```

```
int index = rset.getInt(1);
int value = rset.getInt(2);
......
}
```

getResultSet() METHOD

Oracle recommends using getResultSet() method while retrieving individual elements of a nested table.

To retrieve a subset of the array elements, use the getArray(index, count) or getResultSet(index, count) methods in this form. Here index indicates the starting element and count indicates the number of elements to be retrieved.

The steps for retrieving a collection using a CallableStatement object instance are as follows:

1. Define a CallableStatement that calls the function or procedure returning collections. This statement has to be cast to an OracleCallableStatement:

   ```
   OracleCallableStatement cstmt =
     (OracleCallableStatement) conn.prepareCall("{p_collections(?)}");
   ```

   Here p_collections is assumed to be PL/SQL procedure that returns a VARRAY.

2. Register the OUT parameter that corresponds to the function return value or the OUT parameter of a procedure. This is shown here:

   ```
   csmt.registerOutParameter(1, OracleTypes.ARRAY, "");
   ```

3. Execute the procedure call:

   ```
   csmt.executeUpdate();
   ```

4. Retrieve the entire array as a whole into an ARRAY object:

   ```
   ARRAY array = csmt.getARRAY(1);
   ```

Now that the entire array has been retrieved, the individual elements can be retrieved by using getArray() or getResultSet() methods as described earlier.

WHY DOESN'T IT COMMIT MY CHANGES?

Knowing that disabling the auto-commit mode of JDBC is faster, especially when handling objects, I cheerfully added the following line of code to my JDBC program:

```
conn.setAutoCommit(false);
```

where conn is the Connection object. I compiled my program and executed it. However, when I checked the results, the changes were not reflected.

After some thinking, it occurred to me that an explicit `commit()` on the connection object has to be invoked to commit any changes made to the database.

The moral of the lesson is, "Don't forget to commit the changes when setting auto-commit off."

Handling Large Objects in JDBC

Oracle 8i supports large objects (LOBS) in three major forms: BLOBS, CLOBS, and BFILES. A BLOB is a Binary Large Object that contains binary data such as binary stream, raw stream, images, and so on to a maximum length of 4GB. A CLOB is a Character Large Object that contains character data up to a maximum length of 4GB. A BFILE is an operating system file storing binary data external to the database having a pointer to it from a database table column. JDBC 2.0 supports BLOBS and CLOBS by means of Java stream. This means that BLOB and CLOB data is retrieved as a Java stream. JDBC 2.0 does not support BFILES. The support for BFILE is by means of an Oracle extension and BFILES data is also retrieved as a Java stream.

We will demonstrate the use of LOBS under the following headings:

1. Using BLOBS
2. Using CLOBS
3. Using BFILES

BLOBS and CLOBS are handled by using the JDBC 1.2.x `Blob` and `Clob` objects (`java.sql.Blob` and `java.sql.Clob`) or the Oracle BLOB and CLOB objects (`oracle.sql.BLOB` and `oracle.sql.CLOB`) respectively. BFILES are handled by using the Oracle extension `oracle.sql.BFILE`.

The following table (created earlier) demonstrates LOBS:

```
CREATE TABLE lob_tab
(id NUMBER PRIMARY KEY,
 blob_data BLOB,
 clob_data CLOB,
 bfile_data BFILE);
```

Next, a row is inserted into the lob_tab table as follows:

```
INSERT INTO lob_tab VALUES (1, empty_blob(), empty_clob(), null);
```

There are two steps in accessing and manipulating LOB data:

1. Reading the LOB locator.
2. Once the LOB locator is obtained, reading and writing the actual LOB data.

Using BLOBS

Oracle JDBC constructs a BLOB instance as an instance of the `oracle.sql.BLOB` class. JDBC 2.0 provides a standard `java.sql.Blob` class for implementing BLOBS. This functionality has been extended by Oracle in the `oracle.sql.BLOB` class that implements the `java.sql.Blob` class. To use a BLOB object a BLOB locator must be obtained first. A BLOB locator is a reference to the actual BLOB data that is stored. When a BLOB column is defined in a table, the values in the column store only the locators and not the actual bytes that make up the BLOB.

The following are the steps involved in obtaining the BLOB locator from the database table:

1. Cast the `ResultSet` object to `OracleResultSet`.

   ```
   Statement stmt = conn.createStatement();
   ResultSet rset =
   stmt.executeQuery("SElECT blob_data FROM lob_tab WHERE id = 1 FOR UPDATE");
   ```

2. Use the `getBLOB()` method to retrieve the BLOB locator into a `oracle.sql.BLOB` object.

   ```
   while (rset.next()) {
     BLOB blob_data = ((OracleResultSet)rset).getBLOB(1);
   ......
   }
   ```

Alternatively, use the `getBlob()` method of the `java.sql.Blob` class to retrieve the BLOB locator into a `java.sql.Blob` object. This is shown below:

```
Blob blob_data = rset.getBlob(1);
```

The `getObject()` method on the `ResultSet` object can also be used and in this case the output has to be cast to `java.sql.Blob` or `oracle.sql.BLOB`. This is shown below:

```
Blob blob_data = (java.sql.Blob) rset.getObject(1);
```

or

```
BLOB blob_data = (oracle.sql.BLOB) rset.getObject(1);
```

Once a BLOB locator is obtained, the BLOB can be read into an input stream or can be written into from an output stream with actual byte data.

TIPS:

Writing LOB data requires a lock to be acquired on the LOB.

The AUTO COMMIT must be set to FALSE.

JDBC 2.0 does not support writing to BLOB. Use the Oracle extension to `oracle.sql.BLOB` to do this.

The steps involved in writing to a BLOB are as follows:

1. Use the `getBinaryOutputStream()` method on an instance of `oracle.sql.BLOB` object. This method returns a `java.out.OutputStream` object.
2. Use the `write()` method on the resulting `OutputStream` object to write to the BLOB.
3. Use the `close()` method to close the write operation.

The steps involved in writing to a CLOB are as follows:

1. Use the `getCharacterOutputStream()` method on an instance of `oracle.sql.CLOB` object. This method returns a Unicode output stream in the form of a `java.io.Writer` object.

   Alternatively, the `getAsciiOutputStream()` method can be used on an instance of `oracle.sql.CLOB` object. This method returns a `java.io.OutputStream` object.
2. Use the `write()` method on the resulting writer or `OutputStream` object to write to the CLOB.
3. Use the `flush()` and `close()` methods to close the write operation.

`write()` TO A BLOB

Writing to a BLOB using the `write()` writes the data to the database automatically. Hence, an explicit COMMIT or UPDATE is not required.

The following complete program obtains a BLOB locator from the `lob_tab` table and then populates the BLOB obtained from an input file:

```
import java.sql.*;
import oracle.sql.*;
import java.io.*;
import oracle.jdbc.driver.*;

public class BLOBExample {
  public static void main(String[] args)
  throws SQLException {
int ret_code;
Connection conn = null;
BufferedInputStream inStream = null;
FileInputStream fileStream = null;
  try {
      //Load and register Oracle driver
       DriverManager.registerDriver(new oracle.jdbc.driver.OracleDriver());
  //Establish a connection
```

```
        conn = DriverManager.getConnection(
               "jdbc:oracle:thin:@training:1521:Oracle", "oratest", "oratest");

        conn.setAutoCommit(false);

        Statement stmt = conn.createStatement();
        ResultSet rset =
        stmt.executeQuery("SELECT blob_data from lob_tab WHERE id = 1 FOR UPDATE");

        if (rset.next()) {
          BLOB blob_data = ((OracleResultSet)rset).getBLOB(1);

          OutputStream outStream = blob_data.getBinaryOutputStream();
          //compute buffer size for writing to BLOB.
           int buffSize = blob_data.getBufferSize();
           fileStream = new FileInputStream("test.bmp");
           inStream = new BufferedInputStream(fileStream, buffSize);

           byte[] nextChunk = new byte[buffSize];
           //read the first chunk of data from the file
           int numOfBytes = inStream.read(nextChunk,0, buffSize);

           //write the chunk read to the BLOB
           while (numOfBytes != -1) {
             outStream.write(nextChunk, 0, numOfBytes);
             numOfBytes = inStream.read(nextChunk, 0, buffSize);
           }
           outStream.close();
           inStream.close();
           conn.commit();
       }
       conn.close();
          } catch (SQLException e) {ret_code = e.getErrorCode();
            System.err.println(ret_code + e.getMessage()); conn.close();}
            catch (Exception e) {System.out.println(e.getMessage());}
     }
}
```

There is no way to create a BLOB locator in JDBC. This has to be done using SQL only.

The steps for reading from a BLOB are as follows:

1. Use the `getBinaryStream()` method on an instance of `oracle.sql.BLOB` object. This method returns a `java.in.InputStream` object.
2. Use the `read()` method on the resulting `InputStream` object to read from the BLOB.
3. Use the `close()` method to close the read operation.

The following complete program retrieves the BLOB from a row in the `lob_tab` table and then writes the contents of the BLOB to an output file:

```
import java.sql.*;
import oracle.sql.*;
import java.io.*;
import oracle.jdbc.driver.*;

public class BLOBExample2 {
  public static void main(String[] args)
  throws SQLException {
int ret_code;
Connection conn = null;
BufferedOutputStream outStream = null;
FileOutputStream fileStream = null;
int buffSize;
  try {
      //Load and register Oracle driver
       DriverManager.registerDriver(new oracle.jdbc.driver.OracleDriver());
  //Establish a connection

    conn = DriverManager.getConnection(
          "jdbc:oracle:thin:@training:1521:Oracle", "oratest", "oratest");

    conn.setAutoCommit(false);

    Statement stmt = conn.createStatement();
    ResultSet rset
      = stmt.executeQuery("SELECT blob_data from lob_tab WHERE id = 1");

    if (rset.next()) {
      BLOB blob_data = ((OracleResultSet)rset).getBLOB(1);

      InputStream inStream = blob_data.getBinaryStream();
      buffSize = blob_data.getBufferSize();
```

```
        // Open the output file for writing
        fileStream = new FileOutputStream("out.bmp");
        outStream = new BufferedOutputStream(fileStream, buffSize);

        byte[] nextChunk = new byte[buffSize];

       //read the first chunk of data from the BLOB

       int numOfBytes = inStream.read(nextChunk, 0, buffSize);

      // write the chunk read into the output file,
     //  read nextChunk from the BLOB in a loop
       while (numOfBytes != -1) {
         outStream.write(nextChunk, 0, buffSize);
         numOfBytes = inStream.read(nextChunk, 0, buffSize);
        }
        outStream.close();
        inStream.close();
      }
      conn.close();
         } catch (SQLException e) {ret_code = e.getErrorCode();
           System.err.println(ret_code + e.getMessage()); conn.close();}
           catch (Exception e) {System.out.println(e.getMessage());}
     }
  }
```

Using CLOBS

Oracle JDBC constructs a CLOB instance as an instance of the `oracle.sql.CLOB` class. JDBC 2.0 provides a standard `java.sql.Clob` class for implementing CLOBS. This functionality has been extended by Oracle in the `oracle.sql.CLOB` class that implements the `java.sql.Clob` class. Like in case of a BLOB, to use a CLOB object, a CLOB locator must be obtained first.

The following are the steps involved in obtaining the BLOB locator from the database table:

1. Cast the `ResultSet` object to `OracleResultSet`.
2. Use the getCLOB() method to retrieve the CLOB locator into a oracle.sql.CLOB object, as shown here:

```
Statement stmt = conn.createStatement();
ResultSet rset
= stmt.executeQuery("SElECT clob_data FROM lob_tab WHERE id = 1 FOR
UPDATE");
```

```
while (rset.next()) {
  CLOB clob_data = ((OracleResultSet)rset).getCLOB(1);
......
}
```

Alternatively, use the `getClob()` method of the `java.sql.Clob` class to retrieve the CLOB locator into a `java.sql.Clob` object. This is shown here:

```
Blob clob_data = rset.getClob(1);
```

The `getObject()` method on the `ResultSet` object can also be used and in this case the output has to be cast to `java.sql.Clob` or `oracle.sql.CLOB`:

```
Clob Clob_data = (java.sql.Clob) rset.getObject(1);
```

or

```
CLOB Clob_data = (oracle.sql.CLOB) rset.getObject(1);
```

Once a CLOB locator is obtained, the CLOB can be read into an input stream or can be written into from an output stream with actual byte data.

TIPS:

Writing CLOB data requires a lock to be acquired on the CLOB.

The AUTO COMMIT must be set to FALSE.

JDBC 2.0 does not support writing to CLOB. Use the Oracle extension to `oracle.sql.CLOB` to do this.

The steps involved in writing to a CLOB are as follows:

1. Use the `getCharacterOutputStream()` method on an instance of `oracle.sql.CLOB` object. This method returns a Unicode output stream in the form of an `java.io.Writer` object.

   Alternatively, the `getAsciiOutputStream()` method can be used on an instance of `oracle.sql.CLOB` object. This method returns a `java.io.OutputStream` object.

2. Use the `write()` method on the resulting `Writer` or `OutputStream` object to write to the CLOB.

3. Use the `flush()` and `close()` methods to close the write operation.

`write()` TO A CLOB

Writing to a CLOB using the `write()` writes the data to the database automatically. Hence, an explicit COMMIT or UPDATE is not required.

The following complete program obtains a CLOB locator from the `lob_tab` table and then populates the CLOB obtained from an input file:

```
import java.sql.*;
import oracle.sql.*;
import java.io.*;
import oracle.jdbc.driver.*;

public class CLOBExample {
  public static void main(String[] args)
  throws SQLException {
int ret_code;
Connection conn = null;
BufferedReader bufReader = null;
FileReader fileReader = null;
  try {
      //Load and register Oracle driver
       DriverManager.registerDriver(new oracle.jdbc.driver.OracleDriver());
  //Establish a connection

    conn = DriverManager.getConnection(
           "jdbc:oracle:thin:@training:1521:Oracle", "oratest", "oratest");

    conn.setAutoCommit(false);

    Statement stmt = conn.createStatement();
    ResultSet rset
  = stmt.executeQuery("SELECT clob_data from lob_tab WHERE id = 1 FOR UPDATE");

    if (rset.next()) {
      CLOB clob_data = ((OracleResultSet)rset).getCLOB(1);

      Writer outStream = clob_data.getCharacterOutputStream();
      //compute buffer size for writing to CLOB.
       int buffSize = clob_data.getBufferSize();
       fileReader = new FileReader("test.dat");
       bufReader = new BufferedReader(fileReader, buffSize);

       char[] nextChunk = new char[buffSize];
       //read the first chunk of data from the file
       int numOfBytes = bufReader.read(nextChunk,0, buffSize);
```

```
        //write the chunk read to the BLOB
        while (numOfBytes != -1) {
          outStream.write(nextChunk, 0, numOfBytes);
          numOfBytes = bufReader.read(nextChunk, 0, buffSize);
        }
        outStream.close();
        bufReader.close();
//        conn.commit();
      }
      conn.close();
        } catch (SQLException e) {ret_code = e.getErrorCode();
          System.err.println(ret_code + e.getMessage()); conn.close();}
          catch (Exception e) {System.out.println(e.getMessage());}
    }
}
```

There is no way to create a CLOB locator in JDBC. This has to be done using SQL only.

The steps for reading from a CLOB are as follows:

1. Use the `getCharacterStream()` method on an instance of `oracle.sql.CLOB` object. This method reads a Unicode output stream in the form of a `java.io.Reader` object.

   Alternatively, the `getAsciiStream()` method can be used on an instance of `oracle.sql.CLOB` object. This method returns a `java.io.InputStream` object.

2. Use the `read()` method on the resulting `Reader` or `InputStream` object to read from the BLOB.

3. Use the `close()` method to close the read operation.

The following program reads CLOB data from the `clob_data` column in the `lob_tab` table and writes it to an output file:

```
import java.sql.*;
import oracle.sql.*;
import java.io.*;
import oracle.jdbc.driver.*;

public class CLOBExample1 {
  public static void main(String[] args)
  throws SQLException {
int ret_code;
Connection conn = null;
BufferedWriter bufWriter = null;
```

```
    FileWriter fileWriter = null;
      try {
          //Load and register Oracle driver
           DriverManager.registerDriver(new oracle.jdbc.driver.OracleDriver());
      //Establish a connection

        conn = DriverManager.getConnection(
               "jdbc:oracle:thin:@training:1521:Oracle", "oratest", "oratest");

        conn.setAutoCommit(false);

        Statement stmt = conn.createStatement();
        ResultSet rset
          = stmt.executeQuery("SELECT clob_data from lob_tab WHERE id = 1");

        if (rset.next()) {
          CLOB clob_data = ((OracleResultSet)rset).getCLOB(1);

          Reader inStream = clob_data.getCharacterStream();
          //compute buffer size for writing to CLOB.
           int buffSize = clob_data.getBufferSize();
           fileWriter = new FileWriter("out.dat");
           bufWriter = new BufferedWriter(fileWriter, buffSize);

           char[] nextChunk = new char[buffSize];
           //read the first chunk of data from the CLOB
           int numOfBytes = inStream.read(nextChunk,0, buffSize);

           //write the chunk read to the File
           while (numOfBytes != -1) {
             bufWriter.write(nextChunk, 0, numOfBytes);
             numOfBytes = inStream.read(nextChunk, 0, buffSize);
           }
           inStream.close();
           bufWriter.close();
//           conn.commit();
       }
       conn.close();
          } catch (SQLException e) {ret_code = e.getErrorCode();
            System.err.println(ret_code + e.getMessage()); conn.close();}
            catch (Exception e) {System.out.println(e.getMessage());}
     }
}
```

Using BFILES

Oracle 8i supports BFILES. Unlike BLOBS and CLOBS, BFILES are external large objects stored in O/S files. Only the BFILE locator is stored in a table column of data type BFILE. The use of BFILES comes into picture when data larger than 4GB is to be stored in the database. Oracle JDBC constructs a BFILE instance as an instance of the `oracle.sql.BFILE` class. JDBC 2.0 has no features to support BFILES. This functionality has been extended by Oracle in the `oracle.sql.BFILE` class.

The following are the steps involved in obtaining the BFILE locator from the database table:

1. Cast the `ResultSet` object to `OracleResultSet`.
2. Use the `getBFILE()` method to retrieve the BFILE locator into a `oracle.sql.BFILE` object.

```
Statement stmt = conn.createStatement();
ResultSet rset =
  stmt.executeQuery("SElECT bfile_data FROM lob_tab WHERE id = 1");
while (rset.next()) {
  BFILE bfile_data = ((OracleResultSet)rset).getBFILE(1);
......
}
```

The `getObject()` method on the `ResultSet` object can also be used and in this case the output has to be cast to `oracle.sql.BFILE`. This is shown below:

```
BFILE bfile_data = (oracle.sql.BFILE) rset.getObject(1);
```

Once a BFILE locator is obtained, its contents can be read into an input stream.

TIPS:

There is no way to write to a BFILE.

The AUTO COMMIT must be set to FALSE.

There is no way to create a BFILE locator in JDBC. This has to be done using SQL only.

The steps for reading from a BFILE are as follows:

1. Use the `getBinaryStream()` method on an instance of `oracle.sql.BFILE` object. This method returns a `java.in.InputStream` object.
2. Use the `read()` method on the resulting `InputStream` object to read from the BFILE.
3. Use the `close()` method to close the read operation.

Also, other methods of the BFILE class such as `fileExists()`, `isFileOpen()` and `OpenFile()` and `closeFile()` can be used to perform functions as follows:

1. fileExists()—Checks whether the actual O/S file pointed to by the bfile locator exists.
2. IsFileOpen()—Checks whether the actual O/S file pointed to by the bfile locator is open.
3. openFile()—Opens the file pointed to by bfile locator.
4. closeFile()—Closes the file pointed to by bfile locator.
5. getDirAlias()—Returns the directory alias corresponding to the physical directory where the bfiles are existing.

We will use the `lob_tab` table created earlier to insert BFILE data into the table. Additionally, a directory has to be created to specify the location of the bfiles residing on the O/S. This is done in SQL as follows:

```
create directory bfile_dir as 'c:\oratest\bfiles';
```

Initially, we update the `bfile_data` column in the `lob_tab` table as follows:

```
update lob_tab
set bfile_data = BFILENAME('bfile_dir', 'test.dat') where id = 1;
```

A complete program is shown below:

```
import java.sql.*;
import oracle.sql.*;
import java.io.*;
import oracle.jdbc.driver.*;

public class BFILEExample {
  public static void main(String[] args)
  throws SQLException {
int ret_code;
Connection conn = null;
BufferedOutputStream outStream = null;
FileOutputStream fileStream = null;
int buffSize = 10;
  try {
      //Load and register Oracle driver
       DriverManager.registerDriver(new oracle.jdbc.driver.OracleDriver());
  //Establish a connection
```

```
    conn = DriverManager.getConnection(
           "jdbc:oracle:thin:@training:1521:Oracle", "oratest", "oratest");

    conn.setAutoCommit(false);

    Statement stmt = conn.createStatement();
    ResultSet rset
      = stmt.executeQuery("SELECT bfile_data from lob_tab WHERE id = 1");

    if (rset.next()) {
      BFILE bfile_data = ((OracleResultSet)rset).getBFILE(1);

      if (bfile_data.fileExists()) {
        bfile_data.openFile();

      InputStream inStream = bfile_data.getBinaryStream();

      // Open the output file for writing
      fileStream = new FileOutputStream("bfile.dat");
      outStream = new BufferedOutputStream(fileStream, buffSize);

      byte[] nextChunk = new byte[buffSize];

     //read the first chunk of data from the BFILE

     int numOfBytes = inStream.read(nextChunk, 0, buffSize);

    // write the chunk read into the output file,
    // read nextChunk from the BLOB in a loop
     while (numOfBytes != -1) {
       outStream.write(nextChunk, 0, buffSize);
       numOfBytes = inStream.read(nextChunk, 0, buffSize);
      }
      outStream.close();
      inStream.close();
     } // if fileExists()
    } // if rset.next()
    conn.close();
       } catch (SQLException e) {ret_code = e.getErrorCode();
         System.err.println(ret_code + e.getMessage()); conn.close();}
         catch (Exception e) {System.out.println(e.getMessage());}
    }
}
```

The steps for creating and populating a BFILE column are as follows:

We perform an INSERT into the lob_tab table using the following SQL:

```
INSERT INTO lob_tab VALUES (2, empty_blob(), empty_clob(), null);
```

After doing this, the JDBC steps involved are as follows:

1. Query the bfile column to obtain a valid BFILE locator. This is shown below:

   ```
   ResultSet rset
     = stmt.executeQuery("SELECT bfile_data FROM lob_tab WHERE id = 1");
   rset.next();
   BFILE bfile_data = ((OracleResultSet)rset).getBFILE(1);
   ```

2. Create a `PreparedStatement` cast to an `OraclePreparedStatement` that updates the `bfile_data` column in the `lob_tab` table for the new row with `id` 2 inserted above.

   ```
   OraclePreparedStatement pstmt
   = (OraclePreparedStatement) conn.prepapreStatement(
     "UPDATE lob_tab SET bfile_data = ? WHERE id = ?");
   ```

3. Use the `setBFILE()` method on the `OraclePreparedStatement` object to set the BFILE locator of the new row to the value of the locator obtained in Step 1 above.

   ```
   pstmt.setBFILE(1, bfile_data);
   pstmt.setInt(2, 2);
   ```

   Alternatively, `setOracleObject()` can be used as shown below:

   ```
   pstmt.setOracleObject(1, bfile_data);
   ```

4. Execute the prepared statement.

   ```
   pstmt.executeUpdate();
   ```

Alternatively, the `setObject()` or `setOracleObject()` methods on the `PreparedStatement` object can be used to set the value of the BFILE locator. In this case, there is no need to cast the output to `OraclePreparedStatement`. This is shown below:

```
PreparedStatement pstmt
  = conn.prepapreStatement("UPDATE lob_tab SET bfile_data = ? WHERE id = ?");
pstmt.setObject(1, bfile_data);
pstmt.setInt(2, 2);
pstmt.executeUpdate();
```

JDBC Performance Extensions

Disabling Auto-Commit Mode

Disabling auto-commit mode of JDBC is faster, especially when handling large objects and objects such as object types, object references, and collections. The default auto-commit mode can be turned off using the method `setAutoCommit()` on the connection object as follows:

```
conn.setAutoCommit(false);
```

However, the `commit()` on the connection object has to be invoked to commit any changes made to the database.

```
conn.commit();
```

Oracle Row Prefetching

Oracle row prefetching is a process of fetching multiple rows of data whenever a resultset is populated with a query. The additional rows are stored on the client-side buffer. Standard JDBC fetches one row at a time making a round-trip for each row fetched. With row prefetching, the prefetch size can be set to an integer value, *n*, so that *n* rows are fetched each time a fetch is executed. The steps involved are as follows:

1. Cast the JDBC statement to an `OracleStatement`, `OraclePreparedStatement`, or `OracleCallableStatement` depending on whether the JDBC statement is a `Statement`, a `PreparedStatement`, or `CallableStatement` respectively.
2. Invoke the `setRowPrefetch()` method on the JDBC statement object, passing the number of rows to prefetch as an integer value.

To obtain the current prefetch value, invoke the `getRowPrefetch()` method on one of the casted statements above.

TIP

To set the default prefetch size for all statements in a connection:

Cast the connection object to an `OracleConnection` object.

Invoke the `setDefaultRowPrefetch()` method on the above casted connection object passing the number of rows to prefetch as an integer value.

To obtain the current default prefetch value, invoke the `getDefaultRowPrefetch()` method on `OracleConnection` object.

Update Batching

JDBC 1.0 supports transactions for executing SQL statements. When the auto-commit mode is disabled, JDBC executes a sequence of SQL statements as a transaction and commits or rolls back all of these SQL statements. JDBC 2.0 supports a new feature called update batching, where a sequence of SQL statements on a particular Statement object can be sent to the database as a batch and then the batch is executed as a whole. Any set of non-query SQL statements that return an update count can be executed as a whole when defined as a batch. The advantages of batching are as follows:

- It reduces the number of trips to the database, thereby improving the performance. This is because multiple INSERT, UPDATE, or DELETE statements are grouped into a single batch and that whole batch is sent to the database. Thus the set of statements is processed in one trip.
- Prepared statements execute faster when repeating the same statements with different bind variables.

Oracle 8i JDBC drivers support two types of batching:

1. Oracle style of batching
2. JDBC 2.0 style of batching

The following table illustrates update batching:

```
CREATE TABLE tab1 (col1 NUMBER);
```

These two styles of batching are discussed below:

1. Oracle style of batching.

   This is an implicit batching with SQL statements being automatically accumulated into a batch and queued for execution. This only works on instances of `OraclePreparedStatement` object. The steps involved are as follows:

   1. Turn auto-commit off:

      ```
      conn.setAutoCommit(false);
      ```

   2. Use the `setExecuteBatch()` of the `OraclePreparedStatement` object to set the batch size. The batch size is to be passed to this method as an integer.
   3. Use the `executeUpdate()` method on the above statement object to queue the corresponding SQL statement into a batch. The SQL statements are queued until the number of statements queued becomes equal to the batch size specified in step 1.

4. After the queuing is done, all the queued SQL statements are sent to the database and executed, as shown here:

```
conn.setAutoCommit(false);
OraclePreparedStatement opstmt
  = (OraclePreparedStatement) opstmt.prepareStatement(
     "INSERT INTO tab1 values (?)");
opstmt.setExecuteBatch(5);
opstmt.setInt(1, 10);
opstmt.executeUpdate();

opstmt.setInt(1, 20);
opstmt.executeUpdate();

opstmt.setInt(1, 30);
opstmt.executeUpdate();

opstmt.setInt(1, 40);
opstmt.executeUpdate();

opstmt.setInt(1, 50);
opstmt.executeUpdate();

conn.commit();
opstmt.close();
```

TIP

As an alternative to `setExecuteBatch()` method, the `setDefaultExecuteBatch()` method on an `OracleConnection` object can be used to set the default batch size. The batch size has to be passed to this method an integer.

The Oracle style of batching waits till the queue size equals the batch size. Only then does it send the set of SQL statements to the database for execution. To send the current set of SQL statements to the database without waiting, the `sendBatch()` on the `OraclePreparedStatement` object can be used.

2. JDBC 2.0 style of batching.

   This is an explicit batching with SQL statements being accumulated into a batch on a specific `addBatch()` method call. The steps involved are as follows:

   1. Turn auto-commit off

      ```
      conn.setAutoCommit(false);
      ```

2. Use the `addBatch()` of the `Statement`, `PreparedStatement`, or `CallableStatement` objects to send the SQL statement to a batch:

```
PreparedStatement pstmt
  = conn.prepareStatement("INSERT INTO tab1 values (?)");
pstmt.setInt(1, 10);
pstmt.aaddBatch();
```

`CallableStatement`

In case of `CallableStatement`, only stored procedures without OUT or IN OUT parameters can be called. Also, the procedure must return an update count.

3. Use the `executeBatch()` method on the above statement object to send the batch of corresponding SQL statements to the database for execution, as shown here:

```
conn.setAutoCommit(false);
PreparedStatement opstmt
  = pstmt.prepareStatement("INSERT INTO tab1 values (?)");

pstmt.setInt(1, 10);
pstmt.addBatch();

pstmt.setInt(1, 20);
pstmt.addBatch();

pstmt.setInt(1, 30);
pstmt.addBatch();

pstmt.setInt(1, 40);
pstmt.addBatch();

pstmt.setInt(1, 50);
pstmt.addBatch();

int num_rows[] = pstmt.executeBatch();

conn.commit();
pstmt.close();
```

TIPS

JDBC 2.0 batching also executes the SQL statements as a batch of the batch size, but adding to the batch is done by an explicit call to `addBatch()`.

The two types of batching cannot be mixed on a single connection.

Using Prepared Statements and Bind Variables

Using `PreparedStatement` object instances makes the JDBC program faster because the resulting SQL statement is stored as parsed SQL and can be reused. When using `PreparedStatement`, bind variables are used. Bind variables allow the reuse of the SQL statement with different values at runtime thus eliminating the recompilation of the SQL statement for a different set of input values. These have been discussed in various earlier sections.

JDBC in the Server

JDBC in the server involves the execution of a Java Stored Procedure or Enterprise Java Bean or any other Java program inside the Oracle8i database. These Java programs must use the server-side internal JDBC driver. The server-side internal driver provides the same features and Oracle extensions as the client-side JDBC driver. When using the server-side internal driver, there are four issues to take care of:

1. Default connection

   Using the server-side JDBC internal driver establishes a default connection to the database. The Java program runs in the same session as the database session using the database connection as the default connection for the Java program.

   A default connection can be obtained using the `DriverManager.getConnection()` method with the connect string `"jdbc:default:connection"` being passed as a parameter. This is shown here:

   ```
   Connection conn =  DriverManager.getConnection("jdbc:default:connection");
   ```

   Alternatively, the `defaultConnection()` method of `oracle.jdbc.driver.OracleDriver()` class can be used to establish a default connection, as shown here:

   ```
   Connection conn = new OracleDriver().defaultConnection();
   ```

   There is no need to call `conn.close()` method as the connection should remain open. Even if the connection object is closed, the implicit connection to the database is not closed.

2. Transaction control

   Unlike client-side JDBC, server-side JDBC has the auto-commit feature disabled by default. Transaction commit and rollback is by explicitly calling `conn.commit()` or `conn.rollback()` methods to COMMIT or ROLLBACK the transaction respectively. The default JDBC connection inherits the default session and transaction contexts of the database session in which the JVM was invoked.

3. Exception handling

   SQLException is supported in the server-side internal driver. This means the methods `getErrorCode()`, `getMessage()`, and `getSQLState()` can be used. There is a fourth method that returns the next exception in an error stack:

   ```
   SQLException getNextException()
   ```

   In addition, the server-side internal driver supports an extension class named `OracleSQLException` that includes two new methods, namely, `getNumParameters()` that returns an `int` and `getParameters()` that returns an array of Java objects containing the parameters listed out with the exception.

4. Loading Java source and class files

   This is done using the `loadjava` utility from the command-line. When loading source files, `loadjava` loads the particular .java file and compiles it to obtain a database object of type JAVA CLASS. The `loadjava` utility has been discussed in detail in Chapter 2.

Summary

This chapter outlined the use of advanced JDBC programming in Oracle. The use of JDBC in accessing and manipulating objects in the database was presented. The JDBC performance enhancements in JDBC were discussed. Finally, details about JDBC in the Oracle database server was presented.

BASIC SQLJ PROGRAMMING

ESSENTIALS

- SQLJ is a second method of Java calling SQL and PL/SQL, the first one being JDBC. The DML operations of SELECT, INSERT, UPDATE, and DELETE as well calling PL/SQL procedures and returning of resultsets can be done using SQLJ.
- SQLJ programs can call SQL and PL/SQL using the classes Oracle supplied package oracle.sqlj.runtime.* in conjunction with the JDBC packages java.sql.*, oracle.sql.*, and oracle.jdbc.driver.*.
- SQLJ consists of a translator and a runtime component. Use the sqlj.exe utility to invoke the translator to produce the Java source and compile it. The sqlj runtime is invoked automatically while executing the sqlj application using the `java` utility.
- The basic steps in creating an SQLJ application involve load a JDBC driver if using a non-Oracle driver, establish a database connection which implicitly registers the Oracle JDBC driver, define static declaration statements or static SQL statements that can be executed, process the results in the Java application, catch exceptions, and finally close the connection.
- Establish an SQLJ connection using Oracle.connect() method. Define SQL and PL/SQL statements using the #sql syntax. Use iterators for processing multi-row queries.
- Transaction processing involving COMMIT and ROLLBACK is done by using default the auto-commit mode set to OFF and then using the #sql {COMMIT} and #sql {ROLLBACK} statements.
- To manipulate ROWIDS use the ROWID class in the Oracle Extensions package oracle.sql.*. To process REF CURSORS use an iterator.

This chapter explains the use of SQLJ for database access in Java. It highlights the methods to incorporate Java in the Oracle8i database using SQLJ. The various methods of creating SQLJ programs starting from writing the Java class using SQLJ syntax to manipulating the Oracle8i database using DML operations with embedded SQL in Java are described in detail. A case study is presented to illustrate the concepts.

Overview of SQLJ—Java Calling SQL and PL/SQL

About SQLJ

SQLJ provides an embedded SQL interface for accessing a relational database from a Java application. From an Oracle8i perspective, it provides one way for Java applications to call SQL and PL/SQL. However, the SQLJ interface consists in embedding static SQL in Java code. All the SQL statements are known completely (syntactically and semantically) at compile time.

Figure 5.1 shows a typical implementation of an SQLJ application.

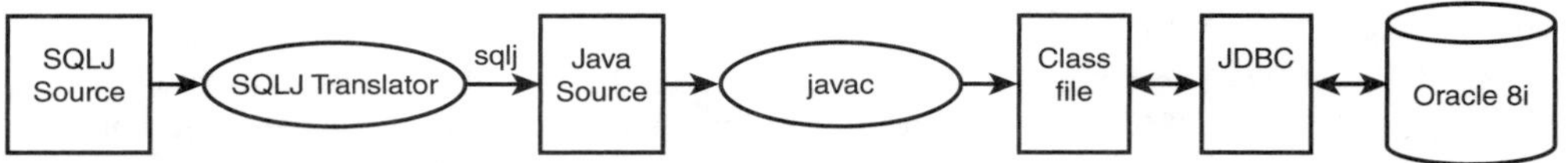

FIGURE 5.1
An outline of SQLJ processing.

Basically a Java program implementing SQLJ performs the following functions:

- Load a JDBC driver if using a non-Oracle Driver
- Establish a database connection which implicitly registers the Oracle JDBC driver
- Define static declaration statements or static SQL statements that can be executed
- Process the results in the Java application
- Catch exceptions
- Close the connection

An SQLJ source program should be saved with extension `.sqlj`. After writing the SQLJ source program, use the SQLJ translator to convert the SQLJ program into a Java program. This can be done using the `sqlj.exe` executable from the command line. This results in a `.java` program and one or more SQLJ profiles with .ser extension. This `.java` program has to be compiled using the Java compiler and then executed. When `.sqlj` executable is run from the command line, after generating the `.java` files, SQLJ then automatically invokes the Java compiler to produce .class files from the so obtained .java files.

A second component of SQLJ is the SQLJ runtime. It consists of an SQLJ runtime library that is implemented in pure Java. This library uses JDBC and hence retains the features of vendor independence and portability. However, the Oracle-SQLJ runtime library is a thin layer of pure Java code that runs above the JDBC driver. The SQLJ runtime library is automatically invoked when executing the SQLJ program.

The SQLJ translator is provided by the `sqlj.exe` utility supplied by Oracle. This is automatically installed when installing Oracle8i and is located in the `[Oracle Home]\bin` directory. The bin directory is created under the `[Oracle Home]` directory while installing Oracle8i. In addition, a `sqlj` directory is created under `[Oracle Home]` with three subdirectories named `demo`, `doc`, and `lib` are created. The `lib` directory contains the class files for SQLJ. The SQLJ translator-related class files are contained in the archive `translator.zip` located in this subdirectory. The SQLJ translator takes care of translation, compilation, and profile customization.

The following shows the `sqlj` command-line usage with options:

```
sqlj [options] file1.sqlj [file2.java] ...
```

or

```
sqlj [options] file1.ser  [file2.jar]  ...
```

where options include:

`-d=<directory>`	root directory for generated binary files
`-encoding=<encoding>`	Java encoding for source files
`-user=<user>/<password>`	enables online checking
`-url=<url>`	specify URL for online checking
`-status`	print status during translation
`-compile=false`	do not compile generated Java files
`-linemap`	instrument compiled class files from `sqlj` source
`-profile=false`	do not customize generated `*.ser` profile files
`-ser2class`	convert generated `*.ser` files to `*.class` files
`-P-<option>  -C-<option>`	pass `-<option>` to profile customizer or compiler
`-P-help  -C-help`	get help on profile customizer or compiler
`-J-<option>`	pass -<option> to the JavaVM running SQLJ
`-version`	get SQLJ version
`-help-alias`	get help on command-line aliases
`-help-long`	get full help on all front-end options

The SQLJ runtime is provided by Oracle as class archive contained in the file `runtime.zip` and automatically installed in the `[Oracle Home]\sqlj\lib` directory when Oracle8i is installed.

Oracle SQLJ requires the following for its functioning:

- A JDBC driver implementing the standard `java.sql` JDBC interfaces from Sun Microsystems. These are installed in the `[Oracle Home]\jdbc\lib` directory as an archived file named `classes12.zip` or `classes111.zip`
- An Oracle8i database that can be accessed using the JDBC driver
- Class files for SQLJ translator and SQLJ profile customizer. These are installed in the `[Oracle Home]\sqlj\lib` directory as mentioned above.
- Class files for the SQLJ runtime. These are also installed in the `[Oracle Home]\sqlj\lib` directory as mentioned above.

The environment setup for Oracle SQLJ should be done before translating and running the SQLJ application. The following are the setup steps:

1. Set the `CLASSPATH` environment variable for using JDBC to include `[Oracle Home]\jdbc\lib\classes12.zip` if using JDK 1.2.x or `[Oracle Home]\jdbc\lib\classes111.zip` if using JDK 1.1.x.
2. Set the `PATH` environment variable to include `[Oracle Home]\bin`. This is to invoke the `sqlj.exe` utility.
3. Set the `CLASSPATH` variable to include the current working directory where the `.sqlj` source files reside.
4. Set the CLASSPATH environment variable to include [Oracle Home]\sqlj\lib\translator.zip and [Oracle Home]\sqlj\lib\runtime.zip.

Here a Windows environment is assumed. For a UNIX environment, the back slashes should be replaced by forward slashes.

Advantages of Using SQLJ

With its static SQL interface, SQLJ offers a number of advantages, the primary ones being the following:

- SQL statements are checked at compile time rather than at runtime. Also, optimization of the SQL statements is done at compile time. This provides a significant speed improvement.
- SQLJ provides strong type-checking of queries and other return parameters.

- It offers more efficient runtime execution using SQL precompilation techniques.
- SQLJ is at a higher level than JDBC. In SQLJ programs, SQL statements are not hidden in method calls.
- SQLJ gives you flexible deployment configurations. An SQLJ program can be deployed on the client side, middle-tier, or as a server-side application. Also, SQLJ applications can be deployed on a thick client, on a thin-client such as a Web browser, or as a Java applet.
- SQLJ conforms to ANSI standards and is vendor-neutral and portable.

Comparison of SQLJ and JDBC

A comparison of SQLJ and JDBC is worth mentioning at this point. The following points outline the subtle differences between SQLJ and JDBC:

- SQLJ is a static SQL interface for Java, whereas JDBC is a dynamic SQL interface for Java. The details of database objects such as table names, column names, and so on are known at compile time in SQLJ programs whereas such details become available to JDBC applications only at runtime. This results in faster execution of SQLJ programs.
- Syntactic and semantic checking on the code is done at compile time, whereas this is done at runtime in JDBC programs.
- In SQLJ the SQL statements are visible in that they are not hidden within method calls as in JDBC.
- SQLJ implements an easier method of writing code than JDBC. For example, to perform a SELECT INTO in SQLJ requires only two steps: defining the host variables and executing a SELECT. In JDBC, this requires an additional step of writing a separate method call for each input and output bind parameter.
- To simulate dynamic SQL, SQLJ provides the use of anonymous PL/SQL blocks in SQLJ statements. Dynamic SQL is directly supported in JDBC.

Comparison of Java and PL/SQL

PL/SQL is best suited for SQL-intensive applications. PL/SQL has an optimized interface for SQL and hence SQL in PL/SQL is faster than SQL in Java. On the other hand, Java with its robustness and security features is best suited for non-SQL logic-intensive applications. Oracle8i provides interoperability of both Java and PL/SQL in the database. Java can call SQL and PL/SQL using SQLJ or JDBC. PL/SQL can call Java using Java stored procedures or SQLJ stored procedures.

SQLJ Declarations

SQLJ declarations can be of two types:

- Pure SQLJ declarations
- Declaration of Java host variables

Pure SQLJ declarations consist of iterator or connection context declarations. These declaration statements start with `#sql` followed by declaration of a class. An iterator is similar to a cursor in PL/SQL or a resultset in JDBC. The syntax for declaring iterators is

```
#sql <modifier> iterator iterator_classname (datatype declarations);
```

For example, an iterator can be declared as follows:

```
#sql public iterator EmpIter (int empno, int ename, int sal);
```

Iterators are discussed in detail in later sections that follow.

A connection context is declared to establish connections to particular database schemas. The syntax for declaring connection context is as follows:

```
#sql <modifier> context Context_classname;
```

For example, a context can be declared as follows:

```
#sql public context myConnCtxt;
```

In addition to iterator and connection contexts, host variables can be declared in SQLJ programs. This is outlined in the next subsection.

SQLJ Expressions

SQLJ expressions fall into three categories, namely, host expressions, result expressions, and context expressions.

- Host expressions—A host expression consists of Java host variables for input or Java expressions for calculation. A Java host variable can represent one of the following:
    - Java local variables. For example, a host variable declared as

      ```
      int i_deptno;
      ```

      is used as a host variable in the following way:

      ```
      #sql {UPDATE emp set sal = sal + 1.25*comm WHERE deptno = :i_deptno};
      ```

Optionally the mode of the host variable can precede its usage as shown here:

```
:IN i_deptno
```

A second example involving host expressions is given here:

```
int i_deptno = 10;
float i_sal = 10000;
float i_comm = 1250;
#sql {UPDATE emp set sal = :(i_sal + 1.25*i_comm) WHERE deptno =
:i_deptno};
```

- Declared parameters
- Java class attributes
- Static or instance method calls

```
int i_empno = 7788;
#sql {UPDATE sal = :(hikeSal(i_empno)) where ename = 'SMITH'};
```

- Array elements

```
int[] deptno_list = new int[10];
int index = 1;
#sql {SET :(deptno_list[index]) = 10 };
```

- Result expressions—A result expression is an output host expression used for query results or a function return.

  For example, a function return value can be captured in a result variable as follows:

```
int out_sal ;
#sql outsal = { VALUES (hikeSal(7788)) };
```

- Context expressions—A context expression specifies the name of a connection context instance or execution context instance that is used in an SQLJ executable statement.

There are certain rules for expression evaluation:

1. Connection context expressions are evaluated first followed by execution context expressions.
2. Result expressions are evaluated after context expressions but before host expressions.
3. After evaluation of any context or result expressions, host expressions are evaluated from left to right in the order they appear in the SQLJ statement.

4. IN and INOUT host expressions are passed to SQL, and the SQL is executed.
5. After execution of SQL, Java OUT and INOUT expressions are assigned values in order from left to right as they appear in the SQLJ statement.
6. The result expression is assigned output last.

Case Study

We will use the schema `oratest/oratest@oracle` (where oratest/oratest refer to the oracle schema username and password and oracle is the tnsnames alias in tnsnames.ora). As part of the case study we will use the same schema objects as defined in the case studies of Chapter 2, "Java Stored Procedures," 3, "Basic JDBC Programming," and 4, "Advanced JDBC Programming." These should already have been created and are reproduced here for convenience:

Database objects (tables and object types):

```
CREATE TABLE dept (deptno number(4) primary key,
                   dname  varchar2(20) not null,
                   loc    varchar2(15) not null);

CREATE TABLE emp (empno number(10) primary key,
                  ename varchar2(40) not null,
                  job   varchar2(15) not null,
                  mgr   number(10) references emp(empno),
                  hiredate date not null,
                  sal   number(12,2) not null,
                  comm  number(4),
                  deptno number(4) references dept(deptno));

CREATE TABLE dept_audit (deptno number(4) primary key references dept(deptno),
                         cnt_emp number(10) not null);

CREATE OR REPLACE TYPE address AS OBJECT
                              (add_id number(10),
                               line1 varchar2(20),
                               line2 varchar2(20),
                               city  varchar2(15),
                               state varchar2(2),
                               zip   varchar2(11));
/
```

(This type is changed in Chapter 6, "Advanced SQLJ Programming," to include member methods.)

```
CREATE TABLE addresses OF address;
```

In addition, the following schema objects are also used and should be defined in the above schema:

- Database tables and objects:

```
CREATE TABLE emp_with_type
                 (empno number(10) primary key,
                  ename varchar2(40) not null,
                  etype varchar2(10) not null,
                  job   varchar2(15) not null,
                  mgr   number(10) references emp(empno),
                  hiredate date not null,
                  sal   number(12,2) not null,
                  comm  number(4),
                  deptno number(4) references dept(deptno));

CREATE TABLE emp_with_addr (empno number(10) primary key,
                  ename varchar2(40) not null,
                  job   varchar2(15) not null,
                  mgr   number(10) references emp(empno),
                  hiredate date not null,
                  sal   number(12,2) not null,
                  comm  number(4),
                  deptno number(4) references dept(deptno),
                  emp_addr REF address);
```

  This is used for describing Object REFS in Chapter 6.

```
CREATE TYPE address_id_varray IS VARRAY(20) OF NUMBER;
CREATE TABLE address_id_list(address_id_list address_id_varray);
```

  The above created type and table are used in describing collections in Chapter 6.

```
CREATE TABLE tab1 (col1 NUMBER);
```

- PLSQL packages and procedures:

```
CREATE OR REPLACE PACKAGE pkg_refcur IS

  TYPE bonus_refcur IS REF CURSOR;
```

```
    FUNCTION f_refcur(ip_etype VARCHAR2) RETURN pkg_refcur.bonus_refcur;

END pkg_refcur;
/
```

This package is used in describing Oracle REF CURSOR in the section Oracle Extensions.

The above schema objects are used to describe the ins and outs of SQLJ programs.

Connecting to a Database

Establishing a Connection

Opening a connection to a database can involve a single connection or multiple connections. A connection context instance should be created for a database connection. This can be an instance of `DefaultContext` class or of a declared connection context class.

A single connection is opened by using the `connect()` method of the `oracle.sqlj.runtime.Oracle` class.

Establishing a connection involves the following steps:

1. Load and register the JDBC driver.

   This is for establishing a communication between the SQLJ program and the Oracle database. This is done by using the static `registerDriver()` method of the `DriverManager` class of the JDBC API. The `Oracle.connect()` method automatically registers the `oracle.jdbc.driver.OracleDriver` class. When using an Oracle JDBC driver and not using the `Oracle.connect()` method, the JDBC driver has to registered explicitly.

   The following line of code does this job:

   ```
   DriverManager.registerDriver(new oracle.jdbc.driver.OracleDriver());
   ```

2. Set the connection URL, username, and password.

   This is to specify the required schema to connect to. This can be done by specifying username and password directly:

   ```
   Oracle.connect("jdbc:oracle:thin:@training:1521:Oracle",
      "oratest","oratest");
   ```

In this explicit method, a connection is opened to a database on host training that has a TCP/IP listener on port 1521 and the SID for the database instance is Oracle and username and password are both oratest.

Alternatively, a properties file named connect.properties can be used to set the URL, username, and password:

```
Oracle.connect(ClassName.class, "connect.properties");
```

Here `ClassName` is the name of the class defining the connection process.

Also, the `getClass()` method to obtain the said class:

```
Oracle.connect(getClass(), "connect.properties");
```

The `connect.properties` file contains the connection parameters such as url, username, and password. Its content is similar to the following:

```
# Users should uncomment one of the following URLs or add their own.
# (If using Thin, edit as appropriate.)
sqlj.url=jdbc:oracle:thin:@training:1521:Oracle
#sqlj.url=jdbc:oracle:oci8:@
#sqlj.url=jdbc:oracle:oci7:@
# User name and password here (edit to use different user/password)
sqlj.user=oratest
sqlj.password=oratest
```

Using the `Oracle.connect()` method creates an instance of `DefaultContext` class and sets it as the default connection.

TIP

Import the `oracle.sqlj.runtime.Oracle` class to use the `Oracle.connect()` method.

Setting the Default Connection Context

Multiple connections may be requirement when there is a need to connect to multiple schemas or to the same schema executing multiple sessions or transactions.

In case of multiple connections to the same schema or to different schemas, multiple instances of the `DefaultContext` class can be created and used in the SQLJ connection. This is done by invoking the `Oracle.getConnection()` method. This method returns an instance of the `DefaultContext` class:

```
DefaultContext defcontext =
Oracle.getConnection("jdbc:oracle:thin:@training:1521:Oracle",
 "oratest1","oratest1");
```

Once multiple connections contexts have been created, SQLJ statements can use either the default connection context or the new connection contexts. This is done by setting the default context using the `setDefaultContext()` method of the DefaultContext class. This method takes an input parameter, an instance of the `DefaultContext` class:

```
#sql {INSERT...}
#sql {INSERT ...}
DefaultContext.setDefaultContext(defcontext);
#sql {INSERT ... }
#sql {SELECT ... }
```

In the above code, the first two statements use the default connection context specified by the `Oracle.connect()` method and the last two statements use the connection context defined by `defcontext`.

Alternatively, the context instance can be specified as part of each `#sql` statement as follows:

```
#sql {INSERT ... }
#sql {INSERT ... }
#sql [defcontext] {INSERT ... }
#sql [defcontext] {SELECT ...}
```

SQLJ Query Processing

Writing a Query in SQLJ

SQLJ allows the processing of queries by means of the SQL SELECT statement included in an SQLJ program as part of `#sql` statement. This is shown here:

```
#sql {SELECT statement};
```

Queries that return a single row as well as queries that return multiple rows or resultsets can be specified in this manner.

In case of single row-queries, selected columns are assigned directly to Java host variables inside SQL syntax; that is, as part of the `#sql` {SELECT statement}. This is shown here:

```
#sql {SELECT column1, column2, … INTO :host_var1, host_var2, …
FROM table_name <optional_clauses>};
```

Here any number of columns can be selected into the corresponding number of host variables provided the column and host variables match one-to-one in position and data type.

In case of queries involving multiple rows, iterators should be used. This is discussed in the section "Processing the Results—Multi-Row Query," later in this chapter.

Executing a Query

A SELECT INTO statement as part of a #sql statement is executed automatically and data fetched into the host variables. In case of multi-row queries also, the SELECT statement specified is executed and an instance of the iterator is used to fetch the rows one by one.

Processing the Results—Single-Row Query

The results of a SELECT INTO statement are automatically fetched into the host variables once the SELECT INTO is specified as a #sql statement. Once the data is in Java host variables, it can be used as desired. The fundamental steps in processing the results of a single-row query are as follow:

1. Import the necessary classes such as JDBC or SQLJ classes. For example, the `oracle.sqlj.runtime.*` package is needed to use the `DefaultContext` class and establish a default connection using `Oracle.connect()` method. Also, `java.sql.*` class might be needed to use any JDBC classes.

   ```
   import java.sql.*;
   import oracle.sqlj.runtime.*;
   ```

2. Open a database connection using the `Oracle.connect()` method. This automatically registers the Oracle JDBC driver. If using `Oracle.getConnection()` method, the driver has to be registered explicitly.

   ```
   Oracle.connect("jdbc:oracle:thin:@training:1521:Oracle",
   "oratest","oratest");
   ```

3. Declare host variables, one for each column in the SELECT column list of the query.

   ```
   int o_empno=0;
   String o_ename="";
   float o_sal=0.0f;
   int o_deptno=0;
   ```

4. Write the #sql SELECT INTO statement that binds the Java host variables into an embedded SELECT statement, executes the SELECT and fetches the data into host variables.

   ```
   #sql { SELECT empno, ename, sal, deptno INTOFROM emp WHERE ROWNUM = 1 };
   ```

5. Process the fetched data.

   ```
   System.out.println("The employee data is:");
   System.out.println("EmpNo: = " + o_empno);
   System.out.println("EmpName: is " + o_empname);
   ```

```
System.out.println("Salary: = " + o_sal);
System.out.println("DeptNo: = " + o_deptno);
```

6. Close the Oracle connection using `Oracle.close()` method.

```
Oracle.close();
```

A complete example is shown here:

```
import java.sql.*;
import oracle.sqlj.runtime.*;

public class SQLJQueryExample {
public static void main (String [] args) throws SQLException {
Oracle.connect("jdbc:oracle:thin:@training:1521:oracle","oratest","oratest");
//Oracle.connect(SQLJQueryExample.class, "connect.properties");
int o_empno=0;
String o_ename="";
float o_sal=0.0f;
int o_deptno=0;

#sql { SELECT empno, ename, sal, deptno INTO :o_empno, :o_ename, :o_sal,
 :o_deptno FROM emp WHERE ROWNUM = 1 };

System.out.println("The employee data is:");
System.out.println("EmpNo: = " + o_empno);
System.out.println("EmpName: is " + o_ename);
System.out.println("Salary: = " + o_sal);
System.out.println("DeptNo: = " + o_deptno);

Oracle.close();

  }
}
```

This program should be stored in a file named `SQLJQueryExample.sqlj`. Next the pre-processor command is issued by invoking the `sqlj.exe` utility as follows:

```
sqlj SQLJQueryExample.sqlj
```

This produces the following files as output:

SQLJQueryExample.java—Translated Java file

SQLJQueryExample.class—Compiled Java class file

SQLJQueryExample_SJProfile0.ser—The serialized application profile file corresponding to the connection class used in the application

SQLJQueryExample_SJProfilKeys.class—The profile-keys class file used by the translator along with the profiles to implement SQL operations

The post-processed `.java` file for the above example is shown below. This is just to show what the translated file looks like.

```
/*@lineinfo:filename=SQLJQueryExample*//*@lineinfo:user-code*//
*@lineinfo:1^1*/import java.sql.*;
import oracle.sqlj.runtime.*;

public class SQLJQueryExample {
public static void main (String [] args) throws SQLException {
Oracle.connect("jdbc:oracle:thin:@training:1521:oracle","oratest","oratest");
//Oracle.connect(SQLJQueryExample.class, "connect.properties");
int o_empno=0;
String o_ename="";
float o_sal=0.0f;
int o_deptno=0;

/*@lineinfo:generated-code*//*@lineinfo:13^3*/

//  ************************************************************
//  #sql { SELECT empno, ename, sal, deptno  FROM emp WHERE ROWNUM = 1  };
//  ************************************************************

{
  sqlj.runtime.profile.RTResultSet __sJT_rtRs;
  sqlj.runtime.ConnectionContext __sJT_connCtx =
  sqlj.runtime.ref.DefaultContext.getDefaultContext();
  if (__sJT_connCtx == null) sqlj.runtime.error.RuntimeRefErrors.
  raise_NULL_CONN_CTX();
  sqlj.runtime.ExecutionContext __sJT_execCtx = __
  sJT_connCtx.getExecutionContext();
  if (__sJT_execCtx == null) sqlj.runtime.error.RuntimeRefErrors.
  raise_NULL_EXEC_CTX();
  synchronized (__sJT_execCtx) {
    sqlj.runtime.profile.RTStatement __sJT_stmt = __
    sJT_execCtx.registerStatement(__sJT_connCtx,
```

```
SQLJQueryExample_SJProfileKeys.getKey(0), 0);
      try
      {
        sqlj.runtime.profile.RTResultSet __sJT_result = __
        sJT_execCtx.executeQuery();
        __sJT_rtRs = __sJT_result;
      }
      finally
      {
        __sJT_execCtx.releaseStatement();
      }
    }
    try
    {
      sqlj.runtime.ref.ResultSetIterImpl.checkColumns(__sJT_rtRs, 4);
      if (!__sJT_rtRs.next())
      {
        sqlj.runtime.error.RuntimeRefErrors.raise_NO_ROW_SELECT_INTO();
      }
      o_empno = __sJT_rtRs.getIntNoNull(1);
      o_ename = __sJT_rtRs.getString(2);
      o_sal = __sJT_rtRs.getFloatNoNull(3);
      o_deptno = __sJT_rtRs.getIntNoNull(4);
      if (__sJT_rtRs.next())
      {
        sqlj.runtime.error.RuntimeRefErrors.raise_MULTI_ROW_SELECT_INTO();
      }
    }
    finally
    {
      __sJT_rtRs.close();
    }
  }


//  ***********************************************************

/*@lineinfo:user-code*//*@lineinfo:13^110*/

System.out.println("The employee data is:");
System.out.println("EmpNo: = " + o_empno);
System.out.println("EmpName: is " + o_ename);
```

```
System.out.println("Salary: = " + o_sal);
System.out.println("DeptNo: = " + o_deptno);

Oracle.close();

  }
}/*@lineinfo:generated-code*/class SQLJQueryExample_SJProfileKeys
{
  private static SQLJQueryExample_SJProfileKeys inst = null;
  public static java.lang.Object getKey(int keyNum)
    throws java.sql.SQLException
  {
    if (inst == null)
    {
      inst = new SQLJQueryExample_SJProfileKeys();
    }
    return inst.keys[keyNum];
  }
  private final sqlj.runtime.profile.Loader loader =
sqlj.runtime.RuntimeContext.getRuntime().getLoaderForClass(getClass());
  private java.lang.Object[] keys;
  private SQLJQueryExample_SJProfileKeys()
    throws java.sql.SQLException
  {
    keys = new java.lang.Object[1];
    keys[0] = sqlj.runtime.ref.DefaultContext.getProfileKey(loader,
    "SQLJQueryExample_SJProfile0");
  }
}
```

Processing the Results—Multi-Row Query

Multi-row queries are specified as a SELECT statement without an INTO clause as shown here:

```
#sql {SELECT statement};
```

The SELECT statement is executed and the resulting rows are stored in an instance of an SQLJ iterator defined for the purpose. An iterator corresponds to a JDBC resultset and has to be declared after the import statements in the SQLJ program. Subsequently, an instance of this iterator so declared is used to hold the resultset returned by the multi-row query. Rows are fetched by using either `FETCH INTO` or the `next()` method (depending on the type of iterator) in a loop. We will first discuss iterators and then outline the steps needed to process a multi-row query.

Iterators

An iterator defines a Java class created by SQLJ with the class attributes predefined. Each attribute in the iterator class corresponds to the data types and optionally the names of data that the iterator will hold. This in turn corresponds to the types and names of the SQL SELECT statement columns, one-to-one.

Once an iterator class is declared, an iterator object of that class is instantiated. Unlike a JDBC `java.sql.ResultSet` object that has any number of columns as defined by the query SELECT, this object has a fixed set of columns of the predefined data types as in the iterator.

Iterators are of two types:

1. Positional iterators
2. Named iterators

Positional iterators are defined by specifying just the data types of the data columns in the Iterator class. In this case, the data types of each iterator column must match the data type of the corresponding `SELECT` column, in that order. Rows are fetched by using `FETCH INTO` into host Java variables, in a loop. The advantage of positional iterators is that the names of the SELECT columns are irrelevant as long as the corresponding data types match. However, they offer less flexibility because the data is selected into the iterator columns by position. Also, there is a chance that data gets written into the wrong iterator column as long as the data type matches. Access to individual columns is by means of fetching into Java host variables that must be defined one-to-one with the iterator column. Finally, when the `SELECT *` syntax is used in populating the iterator, the number of columns in the table should be equal to the number of columns in the iterator.

Named iterators are defined by specifying the names and data types of the data columns in the Iterator class. In this case, the names and data types of each iterator column must match the names and data types of the corresponding `SELECT` column, but the iterator columns can appear in any order. Rows are fetched by using `next()` method in a loop. Using accessor methods for each column accesses individual iterator columns. The accessor method names are same as the individual column names in the iterator. One advantage of named iterators is that the order of the SELECT columns is irrelevant as long as their names and corresponding data types match. This offers greater flexibility and is less error prone as it prevents data to be placed in the wrong column. Also, access to each iterator column is convenient using a method name that matches the column name. However, when populating the iterator using the `SELECT *` syntax, the number of columns in the table can be greater than or equal to the number of columns in the iterator.

TIPS

Using an SQLJ iterator requires its class to be declared as `public`.

If an iterator is declared as `public`, its declaration should be placed in a separate `.sqlj` file having the same name as the iterator name.

Next we demonstrate the steps involved in processing multi-row queries using named iterators. The steps are as follows:

1. Import the necessary classes such as JDBC or SQLJ classes. For example, the `oracle.sqlj.runtime.*` package is needed to use the DefaultContext class and establish a default connection using `Oracle.connect()` method. Also, `java.sql.*` class might be needed to use JDBC classes.

   ```
   import java.sql.*;
   import oracle.sqlj.runtime.*;
   ```

2. Open a database connection using the `Oracle.connect()` method. This automatically registers the Oracle JDBC driver. If using `Oracle.getConnection()` method, the driver has to be registered explicitly.

   ```
   Oracle.connect("jdbc:oracle:thin:@training:1521:Oracle",
   "oratest","oratest");
   ```

3. Define an Iterator class using a `#sqlj` declaration.

   ```
   #sql iterator EmpIter (int empno, String ename, float  sal);
   ```

   This automatically makes available the following iterator methods to access the individual columns of the iterator:

   ```
   empno(), ename(), sal().
   ```

TIP

Accessor methods are created with the same case as in the declaration in the iterator.

4. Instantiate an object of the iterator class:

   ```
   EmpIter emprow = null;
   ```

5. Populate this iterator object with a resultset returned by a SQL SELECT statement.

   ```
   #sql emprow = {SELECT empno, ename, sal FROM emp WHERE deptno = 10};
   ```

6. Access the individual columns from the iterator using the accessor methods.

```
System.out.println("The employees in dept 10 are:");
while (emprow.next()) {
System.out.println("EmpNo: = " + emprow.empno());
System.out.println("EmpName: is " + emprow.ename());
System.out.println("Salary: = " + emprow.sal());
}
```

7. Close the iterator after processing the results of the query.

```
emprow.close();
```

8. Close the Oracle connection using `Oracle.close()` method.

```
Oracle.close();
```

A complete example is shown here:

```
import java.sql.*;
import oracle.sqlj.runtime.*;

#sql iterator EmpIter (int empno, String ename, float  sal);
public class SQLJQueryExample2 {
public static void main (String [] args) throws SQLException {
Oracle.connect("jdbc:oracle:thin:@training:1521:Oracle","oratest","oratest");
EmpIter emprow = null;
#sql emprow = {SELECT empno, ename, sal FROM emp WHERE deptno = 10};
System.out.println("The employees in dept 10 are:");
while (emprow.next()) {
System.out.println("EmpNo: = " + emprow.empno());
System.out.println("EmpName: is " + emprow.ename());
System.out.println("Salary: = " + emprow.sal());
     }
emprow.close();
Oracle.close();

  }
}
```

The steps involved in using a positional iterator are as follows:

1. Import the necessary classes such as JDBC or SQLJ classes. For example, the `oracle.sqlj.runtime.*` package is needed to use the DefaultContext class and establish a default connection using `Oracle.connect()` method. Also, `java.sql.*` class might be needed to use JDBC classes.

```
import java.sql.*;
import oracle.sqlj.runtime.*;
```

2. Open a database connection using the `Oracle.connect()` method. This automatically registers the Oracle JDBC driver. If using `Oracle.getConnection()` method, the driver has to be registered explicitly.

```
Oracle.connect("jdbc:oracle:thin:@training:1521:Oracle",
"oratest","oratest");
```

3. Define a positional Iterator class using a `#sqlj` declaration.

```
#sql iterator EmpIter (int, String, float);
```

4. Instantiate an object of the iterator class. This is shown here:

```
EmpIter emprow = null;
```

5. Declare host variables corresponding to each of the iterator columns.

```
int o_empno=0;
String o_ename=null;
float o_sal=0.0f;
```

6. Populate this iterator object with a resultset returned by a SQL SELECT statement.

```
#sql emprow = {SELECT empno, ename, sal FROM emp WHERE deptno = 10};
```

7. Fetch the rows contained in the iterator using a FETCH INTO in a loop and process the returned rows.

```
System.out.println("The employees in dept 10 are:");
while (true) {
#sql  {FETCH :emprow INTO :o_empno, :o_ename, :o_sal};
if (emprow.endFetch()) break;
System.out.println("EmpNo: = " + o_empno);
System.out.println("EmpName: is " + o_ename);
System.out.println("Salary: = " + o_sal);
     }
```

8. Close the iterator after processing the results of the query.

   ```
   emprow.close();
   ```

9. Close the Oracle connection using `Oracle.close()` method.

   ```
   Oracle.close();
   ```

A complete example is shown here:

```
import java.sql.*;
import oracle.sqlj.runtime.*;

#sql iterator EmpIter (int, String, float);
public class SQLJQueryExample3 {
public static void main (String [] args) throws SQLException {
Oracle.connect("jdbc:oracle:thin:@training:1521:Oracle","oratest","oratest");
EmpIter emprow = null;
int o_empno=0;
String o_ename=null;
float o_sal=0.0f;

#sql emprow = {SELECT empno, ename, sal FROM emp WHERE deptno = 10};
System.out.println("The employees in dept 10 are:");
while (true) {
#sql  {FETCH :emprow INTO :o_empno, :o_ename, :o_sal};
if (emprow.endFetch()) break;
System.out.println("EmpNo: = " + o_empno);
System.out.println("EmpName: is " + o_ename);
System.out.println("Salary: = " + o_sal);
     }
emprow.close();
Oracle.close();

  }
}
```

Exception Handling in SQLJ

Just as in JDBC programs, SQLJ programs also require exception handling. Any statement beginning with `#sql` is an SQLJ executable statement and results in JDBC calls internally. Hence, any method containing `#sql` statements must throw or catch SQL exceptions. SQL exceptions are captured using the `java.sql.SQLException` class which is part of the `java.sql.*` package. Hence, this package has to be imported in any SQLJ program handling SQL exceptions. The source code when compiled without proper exception handling generates errors.

Exceptions in SQLJ are usually of three types:

1. Exceptions occurring in SQLJ runtime
2. Exceptions occurring in the JDBC driver
3. Exceptions occurring in the Oracle8i database itself

Oracle SQLJ programs can use a `throw` statement that is used to inform that SQLJ/JDBC calls throw the SQL exceptions. This is shown here:

```
throws SQLException
```

This creates instances of the class `java.sql.SQLException`.

Like in JDBC, SQL exceptions in SQLJ have to be handled explicitly. Basic exception handling can be done with the try/catch block as follows:

```
try {
......
} catch (SQLException e) {System.err.println("Error occurred: " + e);}
```

Handling an exception can basically include printing error text, retrieving the error code, error text, and the SQL state, or using exception subclasses. These are described here:

1. Printing error text

   ```
   try { <SQLJ code> }
   catch (SQLException e) { System.err.println("Error occurred: "+ e);}
   ```

   This prints the error message with some additional text such as "SQLException."

2. Retrieving the error code, error text, and the SQL state. The `SQLException` class provides methods for obtaining all of this information in case of error conditions.

There are the methods `getErrorCode()` and `getMessage()` similar to the functions `SQLCODE` and `SQLERRM` in PL/SQL. To retrieve the SQL state, there is the method `getSQLState()`. A brief description of these methods is given here:

1. `getErrorCode()`

   This function returns the five-digit ORA number of the error in case of exceptions occurring in the JDBC driver as well in the database. For error messages occurring in SQLJ runtime this returns no meaningful information.

2. `getMessage()`

   This function returns the error message text in case of exceptions occurring in SQLJ runtime or in the JDBC driver. For exceptions occurring in the database, this function returns the error message text prefixed with the ORA number.

3. `getSQLState()`

   This function returns the five-digit code indicating the SQL state only for exceptions occurring SQLJ runtime or in the database.

   We now show the `SQLJQueryExample` class of the earlier section with complete exception handlers built in it. The code is as follows:

```
import java.sql.*;
import oracle.sqlj.runtime.*;

public class SQLJQueryExampleExcep {
public static void main (String [] args) throws SQLException {
try {
Oracle.connect("jdbc:oracle:thin:@training:1521:Oracle",
"oratest","oratest");
int o_empno=0;
String o_ename="";
float o_sal=0.0f;
int o_deptno=0;

#sql { SELECT empno, ename, sal, deptno INTO :o_empno, :o_ename, :o_sal,
 :o_deptno FROM emp WHERE ROWNUM = 1 };

System.out.println("The employee data is:");
System.out.println("EmpNo: = " + o_empno);
System.out.println("EmpName: is " + o_ename);
System.out.println("Salary: = " + o_sal);
System.out.println("DeptNo: = " + o_deptno);

Oracle.close();
} catch (SQLException e)              { System.err.println("Error occurred:
" + e.getErrorCode()
                 + e.getMessage()); }
}
}
```

4. `SQLException` subclasses

   These are subclasses of the `SQLException` class. A good example of one such class is for handling null values, namely, the `sqlj.runtime.SQLNullException` class. This can be used to catch null values returned into Java primitive host variables.

TIPS:

The subclass `SQLNullException` exception is to be caught first before the `SQLException` class.

The `sqlj.runtime.*` package must be imported to use the `SQLNullException` class.

A complete program using the `SQLNullException` is shown here:

```
import java.sql.*;
import oracle.sqlj.runtime.*;
import sqlj.runtime.*;

public class SQLJQueryExampleExcep1 {
public static void main (String [] args) throws SQLException {
try {
Oracle.connect("jdbc:oracle:thin:@training:1521:Oracle","oratest","oratest");
int o_empno=0;
String o_ename="";
float o_sal=0.0f;
int o_deptno=0;
float o_comm;

#sql { SELECT empno, ename, sal, comm, deptno INTO :o_empno, :o_ename,
 :o_sal, :o_comm, :o_deptno FROM emp WHERE ROWNUM = 1 };

System.out.println("The employee data is:");
System.out.println("EmpNo: = " + o_empno);
System.out.println("EmpName: is " + o_ename);
System.out.println("Salary: = " + o_sal);
System.out.println("Commission: = " + o_comm);
System.out.println("DeptNo: = " + o_deptno);

Oracle.close();
} catch (SQLNullException ne) { System.err.println(
"Null values returned: " + ne); }
  catch (SQLException e) { System.err.println("Error occurred: " + e); }
  }
}
```

The output of this program is as follows:

```
Null values returned: sqlj.runtime.SQLNullException:
cannot fetch null into primitive data type
```

This is because it raises a `SQLNullException` exception when a null value for `comm` column is fetched into `o_comm` host variable that is of Java primitive type (`float` type). To avoid this, `o_comm` should be declared as of `Float` type. Here `Float` is a wrapper of the primitive `float` type. The value of `o_comm` is obtained using the `floatValue()` method on it, if it is not null. There is no need to catch the `SQLNullException` in this case. With these changes, the above program looks as follows:

```
import java.lang.*;
import java.sql.*;
import oracle.sqlj.runtime.*;
import sqlj.runtime.*;

public class SQLJQueryExampleExcep2 {
public static void main (String [] args) throws SQLException {
try {
Oracle.connect("jdbc:oracle:thin:@training:1521:Oracle","oratest","oratest");
int o_empno=0;
String o_ename="";
float o_sal=0.0f;
int o_deptno=0;
Float o_comm;

#sql { SELECT empno, ename, sal, comm, deptno INTO :o_empno, :o_ename,
:o_sal, :o_comm, :o_deptno FROM emp WHERE ROWNUM = 1 };

System.out.println("The employee data is:");
System.out.println("EmpNo: = " + o_empno);
System.out.println("EmpName: is " + o_ename);
System.out.println("Salary: = " + o_sal);
if (o_comm != null)
System.out.println("Commission: = " + o_comm.floatValue());
System.out.println("DeptNo: = " + o_deptno);

Oracle.close();
} catch (SQLException e) { System.err.println("Error occurred: " + e); }
  }
}
```

INSERT, UPDATE, DELETE, and COMMIT Operations in SQLJ

INSERT, UPDATE, DELETE Operations

Non-query DML operations such as INSERT, UPDATE, and DELETE are carried out using `#sql` statements. The `#sql` statements can involve host expressions similar to SELECT statements.

For example, in an INSERT statement, a host expression can appear in the VALUES clause. If the INSERT is an INSERT SELECT statement, a host expression can appear in the SELECT list and anywhere in the WHERE clause that can an expression can appear. In the case of an UPDATE statement, a host expression can appear in the SET clause and in the WHERE clause anywhere that an expression can appear. In case of a DELETE statement, a host expression can appear anywhere in the WHERE clause that an expression can appear.

Non-query DML statements are defined as follows:

```
#sql {INSERT statement};
```

or

```
#sql {UPDATE statement};
```

or

```
#sql {DELETE statement};
```

These statements must be followed by an SQLJ COMMIT statement as follows:

```
#sql {COMMIT};
```

An example for the INSERT operation is shown here:

```
import java.sql.*;
import oracle.sqlj.runtime.*;
public class SQLJInsertExample {
public static void main (String [] args) throws SQLException {
try {
Oracle.connect("jdbc:oracle:thin:@training:1521:Oracle","oratest","oratest");

        int cnt=0;
        int i_empno[] = {1101, 1102, 7788};
        String i_ename[] = {"JONNY","DAVE","SCOTT"};
        String i_job[] = {"MANAGER","ANALYST","ANALYST"};
        int i_mgr[] = {7839, 1101, 1102};
```

```
        String i_hiredate = "01-JAN-01";
        float i_sal[] = {10000,6000, 3000};
        float i_comm[] = {2000,1000,500};
        int i_deptno = 10;
    for (int idx=0;idx<3;idx++)
    {
     #sql {SELECT count(*) INTO :cnt FROM emp WHERE empno = :(i_empno[idx])};
      if (cnt == 0)
      {  #sql {INSERT INTO emp VALUES (:(i_empno[idx]), :(i_ename[idx]),
                                         :(i_job[idx]),
                                        :(i_mgr[idx]), :i_hiredate, :(i_sal[idx]),
                                        :(i_comm[idx]), :i_deptno ) };
      }
    }
     #sql {COMMIT};

Oracle.close();
     } catch (SQLException e) { System.err.println("Error occurred: " + e); }
  }
}
```

Similar to the INSERT operation above, UPDATE and DELETE operations can be defined.

WHAT WENT WRONG WITH PUBLIC ITERATORS?

When I first used iterators I had a good learning experience about public iterators. I was using a public iterator declared in the same .sqlj file as the SQLJ program. I tried to compile it and it bounced back with an error. This got on my nerves and I couldn't figure out the cause of the error.

After a careful reading, I figured out that the public iterator was in the wrong place and it had to be placed in a separate .sqlj file. I heaved a big sigh and learned a very useful lesson. The moral of this lesson is, "Place the declarations of all public iterators in a separate .sqlj file. This file has to be in the same working directory as the source SLQJ program."

Transaction Control

A transaction is a collection of DML statements that are executed as if they are a single operation. AN SQLJ application that needs to execute multiple SQL statements targeted towards a specific function, can make use of transaction services.

Transaction services basically includes beginning the transaction, executing the SQL statements that make up the transaction, and either perform a commit on overall success of each SQL statement or roll back the transaction as a whole if one of the SQL statements fails.

A second issue with transactions occurs when changes to the database become visible to the rest of the application system. This is called *isolation level*. For example, in a multi-user system, when do changes performed by one user become visible to the remaining users? Transactions can operate at various isolation levels. At the highest isolation level, the changes to the database become visible only when the transaction is committed.

Transaction management in SQLJ is handled to some extent when a connection is defined. Whenever a new Connection is opened, the transaction auto-commit mode is turned off by default. In this case, every SQL statement is executed as a part of a transaction that is committed to the database upon execution of an SQLJ `COMMIT` statement. To execute each SQL statement as a single transaction, the auto-commit is to be enabled. This can be done in two ways:

- Using the signatures of `Oracle.connect()` or `Oracle.getConnection()` methods by passing a value of true as an argument to either of these methods. This is shown here:

  ```
  Oracle.connect("jdbc:oracle:thin:@training:1521:Oracle",
  "oratest","oratest");
  ```

  This sets the auto-commit to false by default. It can be turned on as follows:

  ```
  Oracle.connect("jdbc:oracle:thin:@training:1521:Oracle",
  "oratest","oratest", true);
  ```

  Also, the `getConnection()` method can be used to specify auto-commit mode as follows:

  ```
  DefaultContext defcontext =
  Oracle.getConnection("jdbc:oracle:thin:@training:1521:Oracle",
  "oratest1","oratest1", true);
  ```

- Calling the `setAutoCommit()` of the underlying connection object. The auto-commit flag setting for an existing connection can be changed using the `setAutoCommit()` method of the underlying connection object. This has two steps:

  1. Use the `getConnection()` method of the SQLJ connection context instance to obtain the underlying JDBC connection.
  2. Invoke the `setAutoCommit()` method with true or false as desired on the connection obtained above.

  The code of these two steps can be written in a single line as follows:

  ```
  defcontext.getConnection().setAutoCommit(true);
  ```

Once the auto-commit mode is turned off, an explicit `COMMIT` or `ROLLBACK` should be done to commit any unsaved database changes. Using the SQLJ COMMIT or ROLLBACK statements as shown here can do COMMIT or ROLLBACK:

```
#sql {COMMIT};
```

or

```
#sql {ROLLBACK};
```

TIPS:

Explicit COMMIT or ROLLBACK is done for a transaction and not for individual DML statements.

Explicit COMMIT or ROLLBACK is to be done only when auto-commit is set to false.

Closing a connection context instance before an explicit commit automatically rolls back the transaction, if auto-commit mode is turned off.

Executing a DDL statement automatically commits the transaction even if auto-commit mode is turned off.

Committing either manually or automatically and using rollback in an SQLJ program do not affect open resultsets and iterators. So any INSERT, UPDATE, or DELETE operations done after the iterator or resultset SELECT is executed do not affect the contents of the iterator or resultset.

The following example program illustrates transaction management:

```
import java.sql.*;
import oracle.sqlj.runtime.*;
public class SQLJTransactionExample {
public static void main (String [] args) throws SQLException {
try {

int cnt;
// Here auto-commit is set to false, the default.
Oracle.connect("jdbc:oracle:thin:@training:1521:Oracle","oratest","oratest");

     #sql {SELECT count(*) INTO :cnt FROM emp WHERE empno = 9998};
     if (cnt == 0)
     {  #sql {INSERT INTO emp VALUES (9998, 'ROCKFELLER', 'ANALYST',
                                       7566, '01-JAN-01', 6000,
                                      1000, 10 ) };
        #sql {UPDATE dept_audit SET cnt_emp = nvl(cnt_emp,0) + 1
        WHERE deptno = 10 };
        #sql {COMMIT};
     }
```

```
    else
      { System.out.println("The employee with empno 9998 already exists."); }
        #sql {ROLLBACK};Oracle.close();
    } catch (SQLException e) { System.err.println("Error occurred: " + e); }
  }
}
```

Based on the above example, the new row inserted into EMP table is visible to the application only when the operations of inserting into EMP table and incrementing the emp_cnt in dept_audit table are both successful. If any one these operations fails, the entire transaction is rolled back.

Handling Types and Large Objects in SQLJ

Handling Types

Oracle SQLJ supports many different data types of Oracle8i including support for the JDBC 2.0 types. Java types can be used in host expressions in SQLJ programs. The SQL data output to a Java variable is converted into a corresponding Java type and Java variable input to SQL is converted to the corresponding Oracle8i data type. Table 5.1 details the correlation between Java types, Oracle Types definitions (SQL type codes) and Oracle8i data types.

Table 5.1 Correlation Between Java Types, Oracle Type Codes, and Oracle8i Data Types

Java Type	OracleTypes Definition	Oracle Data Type
Standard JDBC 1.x Types		
Boolean	BIT	NUMBER
byte	TINYINT	NUMBER
short	SMALLINT	NUMBER
int	INTEGER	NUMBER
long	BIGINT	NUMBER
float	REAL	NUMBER
double	FLOAT, DOUBLE	NUMBER
java.lang.String	CHAR	CHAR
java.lang.String	VARCHAR	VARCHAR2
java.lang.String	LONGVARCHAR	LONG
byte[]	BINARY	RAW
byte[]	VARBINARY	RAW
byte[]	LONGVARBINARY	LONGRAW
java.sql.Date	DATE	DATE

Table 5.1 Continued

Java Type	OracleTypes Definition	Oracle Data Type
java.sql.Time	TIME	DATE
java.sql.Timestamp	TIMESTAMP	DATE
java.math.BigDecimal	NUMERIC	NUMBER
java.math.BigDecimal	DECIMAL	NUMBER
Standard JDBC 2.0 Types		
java.sql.Blob	BLOB	BLOB
java.sql.Clob	CLOB	CLOB
java.sql.Struct	STRUCT	STRUCT
java.sql.Ref	REF	REF
java.sql.Array	ARRAY	ARRAY
custom object classes implementing java.sql.SQLData	STRUCT	STRUCT
Java Wrapper Classes		
java.lang.Boolean	BIT	NUMBER
java.lang.Byte	TINYINT	NUMBER
java.lang.Short	SMALLINT	NUMBER
java.lang.Integer	INTEGER	NUMBER
java.lang.Long	BIGINT	NUMBER
java.lang.Float	REAL	NUMBER
java.lang.Double	FLOAT, DOUBLE	NUMBER
SQLJ Stream Classes		
sqlj.runtime.BinaryStream	LONGVARBINARY	LONG RAW
sqlj.runtime.AsciiStream	LONGVARCHAR	LONG
sqlj.runtime.UnicodeStream	LONGVARCHAR	LONG
Oracle Extensions		
oracle.sql.NUMBER	NUMBER	NUMBER
oracle.sql.CHAR	CHAR	CHAR
oracle.sql.RAW	RAW	RAW
oracle.sql.DATE	DATE	DATE
oracle.sql.ROWID	ROWID	ROWID
oracle.sql.BLOB	BLOB	BLOB
oracle.sql.CLOB	CLOB	CLOB
oracle.sql.BFILE	BFILE	BFILE
oracle.sql.STRUCT	STRUCT	STRUCT
oracle.sql.REF	REF	REF
oracle.sql.ARRAY	ARRAY	ARRAY

Table 5.1 Continued

Java Type	OracleTypes Definition	Oracle Data Type
custom object classes implementing oracle.sql.CustomDatum	STRUCT	STRUCT
custom reference classes implementing oracle.sql.CustomDatum	REF	REF
custom collection classes implementing oracle.sql. CustomDatum	ARRAY	ARRAY
any other custom Java classes implementing oracle.sql.CustomDatum (to wrap any oracle.sql type)	any	any
Query Result Objects		
java.sql.ResultSet	CURSOR	CURSOR
SQLJ iterator objects	CURSOR	CURSOR

TIP

The Java wrapper classes Integer and Float are for outputting NULL values into Java host variables. The Java primitive types int and float cannot contain null values.

Oracle SQLJ supports JDBC 2.0 types in the `java.sql.*` package. The JDBC 2.0 types supported are detailed in Table 5.2 along with their Oracle extension counterpart.

Table 5.2 Correlation Between JDBC2.0 Types and Corresponding Oracle Extensions

JDBC 2.0 Type	Oracle Extension
java.sql.Blob	oracle.sql.BLOB
java.sql.Clob	oracle.sql.CLOB
java.sql.Struct	oracle.sql.STRUCT
java.sql.Ref	oracle.sql.REF
java.sql.Array	oracle.sql.ARRAY
java.sql.SQLData (where _SQL_TYPECODE = OracleTypes.STRUCT)	oracle.sql.CustomDatum

TIP

Any implementation of the `oracle.sql.CustomDatum` class requires the `public static _SQL_TYPECODE` set to the corresponding values in the `oracle.jdbc.OracleTypes` class. In case of objects and object references, an additional parameter `_SQL_NAME` and `_SQL_BASETYPE` respectively, must be set.

Oracle.sql Package

The `oracle.sql` package contains classes to map all Oracle8i data types. The classes are defined as `oracle.sql.NUMBER`, `oracle.sql.ROWID`, `oracle.sql.BLOB`, and so on corresponding to the data type. However, there is no `oracle.sql` class for a REF CURSOR. The oracle.sql classes act as wrappers to SQL data and provide mappings to Java formats. To use these classes, the following import should be defined in SQLJ programs:

```
import oracle.sql.*;
```

Oracle SQLJ Type Extensions

Oracle SQLJ has provided extensions to the JDBC 2.0 standard by introducing the support of JDBC 2.0 and Oracle-specific data types and objects. It has provided implementation of these extensions in the form of `oracle.sql.*` package and interfaces that let a greater flexibility in accessing and manipulating data inside Oracle8i database. The Oracle SQLJ extensions can be categorized into two types, namely, Oracle SQLJ type extensions and Oracle SQLJ performance extensions. This section discusses the Oracle SQLJ Type extensions. Oracle performance extensions are discussed later in the section "SQLJ Performance Extensions".

The Oracle SQLJ type extensions include features for standard Oracle data types as well as JDBC 2.0 data types which are the following:

- LOB and CLOB data types (supported by JDBC 2.0)
- Oracle BFILE data type
- Oracle ROWID data type
- Oracle REF CURSOR data type

TIP

The package `oracle.sql.*` must be imported to use oracle type extensions.

LOB, CLOB, and BFILE data types are discussed in the section "Handling Large Objects," later in the chapter. This section discusses the ROWID and REF CURSOR data types.

Oracle ROWID

Oracle ROWID is supported in the `oracle.sql.ROWID` class of the `oracle.sql` package. This class acts as wrapper for the SQL ROWID data type. Variables of type `oracle.sql.ROWID` can be defined in SQLJ programs in the following contexts:

- As IN, INOUT, or OUT host variables as in SELECT INTO lists
- As a stored function return value
- As an iterator column type (both named and positional)

The following example illustrates the use of ROWID. Specifically, for the purposes of this example, it increments the salary of each employee in a particular department by retrieving the rows based on individual ROWIDs.

```
import oracle.sql.*;
import java.sql.*;
import oracle.sqlj.runtime.*;

#sql iterator EmpIter (ROWID rowid, float sal, Float comm);

public class SQLJRowidExample {
  public static void main(String[] args)
  throws SQLException {

try {
 Oracle.connect("jdbc:oracle:thin:@training:1521:
  Oracle","oratest","oratest");

int i_deptno = 10;
EmpIter emprow;

#sql emprow = { SELECT ROWID, sal, comm FROM emp WHERE deptno = :i_deptno};

ROWID o_rowid;
float  o_sal;
Float  o_comm;

while (emprow.next()) {
      o_rowid = emprow.rowid();
      o_sal   = emprow.sal();
      o_comm  = emprow.comm();
```

```
        if (o_comm != null)
          #sql {UPDATE emp SET sal = :(o_sal+(1.25*o_comm.floatValue()))
          WHERE rowid = :o_rowid};
    }
      #sql {COMMIT};
       emprow.close();
     Oracle.close();
      } catch (SQLException e) { System.err.println("Error occurred: " + e); }
     }
    }
```

Oracle REF CURSOR

Oracle SQLJ supports REF CURSORs by mapping them to iterator columns or host variables of an iterator class or to host variables of type `java.sql.ResultSet`. The iterator instance can be one of the following:

- A result expression corresponding to the return value of a function
- An argument corresponding to an OUT parameter of a procedure or function
- An OUT host variable in a PL/SQL block
- An OUT host variable in an SQLJ SELECT INTO list

TIP

There is no oracle.sql class corresponding to a REF CURSOR.

For the purposes of this section, we will use the following table to demonstrate the Oracle REF CURSOR type. This section uses the same database objects as demonstrated in the discussion of REF CURSORS in Chapter 3, "Basic JDBC Programming". For convenience they are reproduced here again.

```
CREATE TABLE emp_with_type
                  (empno number(10) primary key,
                   ename varchar2(40) not null,
                   etype varchar2(10) not null,
                   job   varchar2(15) not null,
                   mgr   number(10) references emp(empno),
                   hiredate date not null,
                   sal   number(12,2) not null,
                   comm  number(4),
                   deptno number(4) references dept(deptno));
```

This table is populated with the following INSERT statements:

```
INSERT INTO emp_with_type
  SELECT empno, ename, 'SENIOR', job, mgr, hiredate, sal, comm,
         deptno
  FROM   emp
  WHERE  deptno in (10, 20)
  union
  SELECT empno, ename, 'JUNIOR', job, mgr, hiredate, sal, comm,
         deptno
  FROM   emp
  WHERE  deptno = 30;
```

Next we create a packaged function that returns a REF CURSOR. This is shown here:

```
CREATE OR REPLACE PACKAGE pkg_refcur IS

  TYPE bonus_refcur IS REF CURSOR;

  FUNCTION f_refcur(ip_etype VARCHAR2) RETURN pkg_refcur.bonus_refcur;

END pkg_refcur;
/

CREATE OR REPLACE PACKAGE BODY pkg_refcur IS

  FUNCTION f_refcur(ip_etype VARCHAR2) RETURN pkg_refcur.bonus_refcur
  IS
    v_bonus_refcur pkg_refcur.bonus_refcur;
  BEGIN
    IF ip_etype = 'JUNIOR' THEN
      OPEN v_bonus_refcur FOR
      SELECT etype, empno, ename, sal, 0.25*sal bonus, deptno
      FROM   emp_with_type
      WHERE  etype = ip_etype;
    ELSIF ip_etype = 'SENIOR' THEN
      OPEN v_bonus_refcur FOR
      SELECT etype, empno, ename, sal, 0.75*sal bonus, deptno
      FROM   emp_with_type
      WHERE  etype = ip_etype;
    END IF;
    RETURN (v_bonus_refcur);
  END f_refcur;
```

```
END pkg_refcur;
/
```

The next step is to write the SQLJ program that calls the above packaged function and returns a resultset. The steps involved in this are as follows:

1. Define an iterator with columns corresponding to the resultset columns returned by the REF CURSOR. This should be done is a separate `.sqlj` file and compiled as a stand-alone program.

```
#sql public iterator RefCurIter (String etype, int empno, String ename,
float sal, float bonus, int deptno);
```

TIP

An iterator should be declared as public if an instance of it is used in a result expression or a host expression.

2. Declare an instance of this iterator.

```
RefCurIter refCurIns;
```

3. Define an SQLJ statement that execute the packaged function `pkg_refcur.f_refcur` and populate the iterator instance with the resultset returned by this function.

```
String i_etype = "SENIOR";
#sql refCurIns = {VALUES (pkg_refcur.f_refcur(:i_etype))};
```

4. Process the iterator resultset as desired.

```
while (refCurIns.next()) {
  String o_etype = refCurIns.etype();
  int o_empno = refCurIns.empno();
  String o_ename = refCurIns.ename();
  float o_sal = refCurIns.sal();
  float o_bonus = refCurIns.bonus();
  int o_deptno = refCurIns.deptno();
}
```

5. Close the iterator instance.

```
refCurIns.close();
```

A complete program is given here:

```
//File name: RefCurIter.sqlj
#sql public iterator RefCurIter (String etype, int empno, String ename,
float sal, float bonus, int deptno);

//File name: SQLJRefCursorExample.sqlj
import oracle.sql.*;
import java.sql.*;
import oracle.sqlj.runtime.*;

public class SQLJRefCursorExample {
  public static void main(String[] args)
  throws SQLException {

try {
 Oracle.connect("jdbc:oracle:thin:@training:1521:Oracle",
"oratest","oratest");

RefCurIter refCurIns;
String i_etype = "SENIOR";
#sql refCurIns = {VALUES (pkg_refcur.f_refcur(:i_etype))};
while (refCurIns.next()) {
  String o_etype = refCurIns.etype();
  int o_empno = refCurIns.empno();
  String o_ename = refCurIns.ename();
  float o_sal = refCurIns.sal();
  float o_bonus = refCurIns.bonus();
  int o_deptno = refCurIns.deptno();
}
refCurIns.close();
Oracle.close();
  } catch (SQLException e) { System.err.println("Error occurred: " + e); }
 }
}
```

Summary

This chapter outlined the use of SQLJ for database access in Java. Essentially, the various methods of using SQLJ starting from establishing a connection to the querying and returning of resultsets to executing DML from the Oracle8i database are described in detail. The use of SQLJ in handling types was presented. Finally, the Oracle SQLJ extensions was presented.

ADVANCED SQLJ PROGRAMMING

ESSENTIALS

- Advanced SQLJ provides various methods for storing and querying objects in the Oracle8i database using SQLJ programs. The use of Large Objects for unstructured data is also supported.
- BLOBS, CLOBS, and BFILES are handled by using the Oracle BLOB, CLOB, and BFILE classes in the oracle.sql package, namely, `oracle.sql.BLOB`, `oracle.sql.CLOB`, and `oracle.sql.BFILE` respectively. Retrieve the BLOB, CLOB, or BFILE locator using a #sql SELECT statement.
- To handle the query and manipulation of object types and object references, create custom Java classes for each object type and object reference used that implement the `oracle.sql.customDatum` interface. Use the utility jpub.exe for this. Then use the methods of the above-created custom Java classes to access (get) and manipulate (set) SQL object types and REF types.
- For collections, use jpub.exe utility to create custom Java classes that implement the oracle.sql.customDatum interface. Then use the methods getArray(), getElement(), setArray(), and setElement() of the above-created custom Java classes to access and manipulate the collection.
- Use the SQLJ performance enhancements such as using the default OFF commit mode, Oracle row pre-fetching, update batching, and using Oracle optimizer.

This chapter describes the use of SQLJ in object-relational processing in Oracle. The various methods of storing and querying objects from SQLJ applications are highlighted in detail. The chapter starts with large objects and then goes on to discuss object types and collections from an SQLJ perspective. The Oracle SQLJ performance extensions are then outlined. Finally, a discussion of using SQLJ in the Oracle8i database server is presented. A case study is presented to illustrate the concepts.

Overview

As outlined in Chapter 4, "Advanced JDBC Programming," Oracle8i supports the definition and manipulation of objects in the database. Basically the following can be defined:

- Object types along with object tables (row objects) and object-relational tables (relational tables with column objects)
- Object references or REFS
- Collections such as VARRAYS and NESTED TABLES
- Large objects in the form of BLOBS, CLOBS, and BFILES.

SQLJ supports these features in various ways. We begin by discussing the implementation of large objects in SQLJ and then proceed to describe the implementation of objects in SQLJ.

Case Study

We will use the schema oratest/oratest@oracle (where oratest/oratest refer to the schema username and password and oracle is the tnsnames alias in tnsnames.ora). As part of the case study we will use some of the schema objects as defined in case study of Chapters 2, "Java Stored Procedures," 3, "Basic JDBC Programming," 4, "Advanced JDBC Programming," and 5, "Basic SQLJ Programming." These are reproduced here for convenience:

Database objects (tables and object types):

```
CREATE TABLE emp (empno number(10) primary key,
                  ename varchar2(40) not null,
                  job   varchar2(15) not null,
                  mgr   number(10) references emp(empno),
                  hiredate date not null,
                  sal   number(12,2) not null,
                  comm  number(4),
                  deptno number(4) references dept(deptno));
```

```
CREATE OR REPLACE TYPE address AS OBJECT
                              (add_id number(10),
                               line1 varchar2(20),
                               line2 varchar2(20),
                               city  varchar2(15),
                               state varchar2(2),
                               zip   varchar2(11));
/
```

(This type is later changed to include member methods.)

```
CREATE TABLE addresses OF address;
```

In addition, the following schema objects are also used and should be defined in the above schema:

- Database tables and objects

```
CREATE TABLE emp_with_addr (empno number(10) primary key,
                  ename varchar2(40) not null,
                  job   varchar2(15) not null,
                  mgr   number(10) references emp(empno),
                  hiredate date not null,
                  sal   number(12,2) not null,
                  comm  number(4),
                  deptno number(4) references dept(deptno),
                  emp_addr REF address);
```

This is used for describing Object REFS later.

```
CREATE TYPE address_id_varray IS VARRAY(20) OF NUMBER;
CREATE TABLE address_id_list(address_id_list address_id_varray);
```

The type and table are used in describing collections later.

```
CREATE TABLE lob_tab
(id NUMBER PRIMARY KEY,
 blob_data BLOB,
 clob_data CLOB,
 bfile_data BFILE);
```

This table is used in describing large objects in the next section.

```
CREATE TABLE tab1 (col1 NUMBER);
```

The above schema objects are used to describe the ins and outs of using objects and performance extensions in JDBC programs.

Handling Large Objects

Oracle8i supports large objects (LOBS) in three major forms: BLOBS, CLOBS, and BFILES. SQLJ supports BLOBS, CLOBS, and BFILES by means of Java stream. This means that BLOB, CLOB, and BFILE data is retrieved as a Java stream.

We will demonstrate the use of LOBS under the following headings:

1. Using BLOBS
2. Using BFILES

BLOBS, CLOBS, and BFILES are handled by using the Oracle BLOB, CLOB, and BFILE classes in the oracle.sql package, namely, `oracle.sql.BLOB`, `oracle.sql.CLOB`, and `oracle.sql.BFILE` respectively.

The following table created earlier is used to demonstrate LOBS:

```
CREATE TABLE lob_tab
(id NUMBER PRIMARY KEY,
 blob_data BLOB,
 clob_data CLOB,
 bfile_data BFILE);
```

Next, a row is inserted into the lob_tab table as follows:

```
INSERT INTO lob_tab VALUES (1, empty_blob(), empty_clob(), null);
```

There are two steps in accessing and manipulating LOB data:

1. Reading the LOB locator
2. Once the LOB locator is obtained, reading and writing the actual LOB data

Using BLOBS

Oracle SQLJ constructs a BLOB instance as an instance of the `oracle.sql.BLOB` class. To use a BLOB object, a BLOB locator must be obtained first. A BLOB locator is a reference to where the actual BLOB data is stored. When a BLOB column is defined in a table, the values in the column store only the locators and not the actual bytes that make up the BLOB.

The following are the steps involved in obtaining the BLOB locator from the database table:

1. Declare an instance of the oracle.sql.BLOB class.

```
BLOB blobins;
```

2. Retrieve the BLOB locator into this BLOB host variable using a SQLJ SELECT statement.

```
#sql { SELECT blob_data INTO :blobins FROM lob_tab WHERE id = 1 FOR
UPDATE};
```

Once a BLOB locator is obtained, the BLOB can be read into an input stream or can be written into from an output stream with actual byte data.

TIP

Writing LOB data requires a lock to be acquired on the LOB.

The AUTO COMMIT must be set to FALSE.

The steps involved in writing to a BLOB are as follows:

1. Select a BLOB locator from the database BLOB column into a BLOB host variable.
2. Use the `putBytes()` method of the `oracle.sql.BLOB` class on the BLOB host variable to write binary data into the BLOB column.
3. Commit the changes.

The following complete program obtains a BLOB locator from the `lob_tab` table and then populates the BLOB obtained from an input file.

```
import java.sql.*;
import oracle.sql.*;
import java.io.*;
import oracle.sqlj.runtime.*;

public class SQLJBLOBExample {
  public static void main(String[] args)
  throws SQLException,IOException {

BufferedInputStream inStream = null;
FileInputStream fileStream = null;
  try { Oracle.connect("jdbc:oracle:thin:@training:1521:Oracle",
        "oratest","oratest");
    BLOB blobins;
#sql {SELECT blob_data INTO :blobins from lob_tab WHERE id = 1 FOR UPDATE};
```

```
//compute buffer size for writing to BLOB.
       int buffSize = blobins.getBufferSize();
       fileStream = new FileInputStream("test.bmp");
       inStream = new BufferedInputStream(fileStream, buffSize);

       byte[] nextChunk = new byte[buffSize];
       //read the first chunk of data from the file
       int numOfBytes = inStream.read(nextChunk,0, buffSize);
        long offset = 1;
       //write the chunk read to the BLOB
       while (numOfBytes != -1) {
         //outStream.write(nextChunk, 0, numOfBytes);
         blobins.putBytes(offset, nextChunk);
         numOfBytes = inStream.read(nextChunk, 0, buffSize);
         offset += numOfBytes;
       }

       inStream.close();
       #sql {COMMIT};

    Oracle.close();
    } catch (SQLException e) { System.err.println("Error occurred: " + e); }
  }
}
```

There is no way to create a BLOB locator in SQLJ. This has to be done using SQL only.

The steps for reading from a BLOB are as follows:

1. Select a BLOB locator from the database BLOB column into a BLOB host variable.
2. Use the `getBytes()` method of the `oracle.sql.BLOB` class on the BLOB host variable to read binary data from the BLOB column.

The following complete program retrieves the BLOB from a row in the `lob_tab` table and then writes the contents of the BLOB to an output file.

```
import java.sql.*;
import oracle.sql.*;
import java.io.*;
import oracle.sqlj.runtime.*;

public class SQLJBLOBExample2 {
  public static void main(String[] args)
```

```
  throws SQLException, IOException {
BufferedOutputStream outStream = null;
FileOutputStream fileStream = null;
int buffSize;
  try {
Oracle.connect("jdbc:oracle:thin:@training:1521:Oracle","oratest","oratest");
    BLOB blobins;
#sql {SELECT blob_data INTO :blobins from lob_tab WHERE id = 1};

      buffSize = blobins.getBufferSize();
      // Open the output file for writing
      fileStream = new FileOutputStream("out.bmp");
      outStream = new BufferedOutputStream(fileStream, buffSize);

      byte[] nextChunk = new byte[buffSize];

     //read the first chunk of data from the BLOB
      int numOfBytes = blobins.getBytes(1, buffSize, nextChunk);
      long len = blobins.length();
    // write the chunk read into the output file,
   // read nextChunk from the BLOB in a loop
   long offset = 1;
   while (offset < len) {
       outStream.write(nextChunk, 0, buffSize);
       offset += numOfBytes;
       numOfBytes = blobins.getBytes(offset, buffSize, nextChunk);
      }
    outStream.close();
    Oracle.close();
    } catch (SQLException e) { System.err.println("Error occurred: " + e); }
  }
}
```

Using BFILES

Oracle8i supports BFILES. Unlike BLOBS and CLOBS, BFILES are external large objects stored in operating system files. Only the BFILE locator is stored in a table column of data type BFILE. The use of BFILES comes into picture when data larger than 4GB is to be stored in the database. Oracle SQLJ constructs a BFILE instance as an instance of the `oracle.sql.BFILE` class.

The following steps are involved in reading from a BFILE column:

1. Select a BFILE locator from the database BFILE column into a BFILE host variable.
2. Use the `getBytes()` method of the `oracle.sql.BFILE` class on a BFILE host variable to read binary data from the BFILE column.

Once a BFILE locator is obtained, its contents can be read into an input stream.

TIP

There is no way to write to a bfile.

The AUTO COMMIT must be set to FALSE.

There is no way to create a BFILE locator in SQLJ. This has to be done using SQL only.

The steps for reading from a BFILE are as follows:

We will use the `lob_tab` table created earlier to insert BFILE data into the table. Additionally, a directory has to be created to specify the location of the bfiles residing on the O/S. This is done in SQL as follows:

```
create directory bfile_dir as 'c:\oratest\bfiles';
```

Initially, we update the `bfile_data` column in the `lob_tab` table as follows:

```
update lob_tab
set bfile_data = BFILENAME('bfile_dir', 'test.dat') where id = 1;
```

A complete program is shown here:

```
import java.sql.*;
import oracle.sql.*;
import java.io.*;
import oracle.sqlj.runtime.*;

public class SQLJBFILEExample {
  public static void main(String[] args)
  throws SQLException, IOException {
BufferedOutputStream outStream = null;
FileOutputStream fileStream = null;
int buffSize = 10;
  try {
Oracle.connect("jdbc:oracle:thin:@training:1521:Oracle","oratest","oratest");
    BFILE bfileins;
```

```
#sql {SELECT bfile_data INTO :bfileins from lob_tab WHERE id = 1};

     if (bfileins.fileExists()) {
        bfileins.openFile();

// Open the output file for writing
       fileStream = new FileOutputStream("bfile.dat");
       outStream = new BufferedOutputStream(fileStream, buffSize);

       byte[] nextChunk = new byte[buffSize];

      //read the first chunk of data from the BFILE
       int numOfBytes = bfileins.getBytes(1, buffSize, nextChunk);
       long len = bfileins.length();
     // write the chunk read into the output file,
    // read nextChunk from the BFILE in a loop
    long offset = 1;
    while (offset < len) {
        outStream.write(nextChunk, 0, buffSize);
        offset += numOfBytes;
        numOfBytes = bfileins.getBytes(offset, buffSize, nextChunk);
       }
      } // if fileExists()

       outStream.close();
     Oracle.close();
     } catch (SQLException e) { System.err.println("Error occurred: " + e); }
  }
}
```

Handling Objects and Collections in SQLJ

Oracle8i is an object-relational database and thus supports the definition and manipulation of objects in the database. Objects in the database can be one of the following:

- Object types along with object tables (row objects) and object-relational tables (relational tables with column objects)
- Object references or REFS
- Collections such as VARRAYS and NESTED TABLES

SQLJ also supports these features in three forms, namely, as host variables, as a return variable, or as an iterator attribute. Selection and manipulation of object data in SQLJ can be done in two ways:

1. Using custom Java classes that correspond to an object or collection. This is for strongly typed objects. Use custom Java classes that implement either the standard JDBC `java.sql.SQLData` interface (for object types only) or the Oracle extension `oracle.sql.customDatum` interface.
2. Using the Oracle extensions provided in the oracle.sql.* classes, namely, `oracle.sql.STRUCT` (for object types), `oracle.sql.REF` for object references and `oracle.sql.ARRAY` for collections. This is for weakly typed objects. We will discuss the SQLJ implementation of object types and object references in the following subsection and then describe the SQLJ implementation of collections in the subsequent subsection.

Handling Objects

This section highlights the use of custom Java classes for strongly typed object types and object references. We will use the address object type, the addresses table based on this object type, and the emp_with_addr table having the REF column emp_addr created in the case study of Chapter 3 for describing the manipulation and access of object types in SQLJ. The definitions of these are reproduced here for convenience:

```
CREATE OR REPLACE TYPE address AS OBJECT
                               (add_id number(10),
                                line1 varchar2(20),
                                line2 varchar2(20),
                                city  varchar2(15),
                                state varchar2(2),
                                zip   varchar2(11));
/
CREATE TABLE addresses OF address;

CREATE TABLE emp_with_addr (empno number(10) primary key,
                  ename varchar2(40) not null,
                  job   varchar2(15) not null,
                  mgr   number(10) references emp(empno),
                  hiredate date not null,
                  sal   number(12,2) not null,
                  comm  number(4),
                  deptno number(4) references dept(deptno),
                  emp_addr REF address);
```

This is used for describing Object REFS.

```
CREATE TYPE address_id_varray IS VARRAY(20) OF NUMBER;
CREATE TABLE address_id_list(address_id_list address_id_varray);
```

Handling the query and manipulation of object types and object references involves

1. The creation of custom Java classes for each object type and object reference used. This class should implement the `oracle.sql.customDatum` interface.
2. Using the methods of the above-created custom Java classes to access (get) and manipulate (set) SQL object types and REF types.

For step 1, using JPublisher is the easy way; it automatically generates the custom Java classes, including the get and set methods for access and manipulation of the object attributes.

JPublisher can be invoked from the command line using the executable jpub.exe. This executable is provided by Oracle and is automatically installed in the [Oracle Home]\bin directory when Oracle8i is installed. The `PATH` environment variable should be set to include the `[Oracle Home]\bin` directory. `jpub.exe` should be invoked with the `sql` and `user` parameters specified. This is shown here:

```
jpub -sql=Address -user=oratest/oratest
```

Here `Address` corresponds to the address object type. The *A* is in uppercase to specify a Java class filename and classname as per standard Java conventions.

This creates the following files:

1. Address.java, having an `Address` class corresponding to the address object type. The `Address` class is the custom Java class that implements the `oracle.sql.customDatum` interface and is used in the communication between Java and SQLJ.
2. AddressRef.java, having an `AddressRef` class corresponding to the emp_addr REF column. `jpub` creates custom Java classes, one for each object type and also one for each reference to that object type. Each .java file generated should be compiled using javac or sqlj.

In addition, the individual .java files contain methods to `get` and `set` object attributes for the object type and the methods `getValue()` and `setValue()` for the object REF. The method `getValue()` returns the object that is being referenced. The get and set methods for the `Address` class generated are as follows:

```
public java.math.BigDecimal getAddId() throws SQLException
public void setAddId(java.math.BigDecimal x) throws SQLException
public String getLine1() throws SQLException
public void setLine1(String x) throws SQLException
```

```
public String getLine2() throws SQLException
public void setLine2(String x) throws SQLException
public String getCity() throws SQLException
public void setCity(String x) throws SQLException
public String getState() throws SQLException
public void setState(String x) throws SQLException
public String getZip() throws SQLException
public void setZip(String x) throws SQLException
```

The `getValue()` and `setValue()` methods for the generated `AddressRef` class are as follows:

```
public Address getValue() throws SQLException
public void setValue(Address x) throws SQLException
```

We first describe the operations of INSERT and SELECT on the `addresses` object table. The steps involved in the creation of objects and perform INSERT operation into the `addresses` table is quite straightforward and doesn't involve the use of the above created custom Java classes. Using a single SQLJ INSERT statement as follows can do it:

```
#sql {INSERT INTO addresses VALUES (address(:i_add_id,
:i_line1, :i_line2, :i_city, :i_state, :i_zip))};
```

Here the variables with prefix ":" are host variables.

However, the process of querying the object table to retrieve whole objects involves custom classes and involves the following steps:

1. Define a SQLJ iterator that corresponds to the `address` object. This involves the `Address` custom class generated earlier, as shown here:

   ```
   #sql iterator AddIter (Address a);
   ```

2. Declare an instance of this iterator.

   ```
   AddIter addrow=null;
   ```

3. Populate this iterator object with the resultset returned by a SQLJ SELECT statement.

   ```
   #sql addrow = {SELECT VALUE(addr) AS a FROM addresses addr};
   ```

4. Declare an instance of the `Address` class to output each row of the object table `addresses`.

   ```
   Address o_address;
   ```

5. Fetch the data contained in the iterator into the host variable `o_address` and use the get methods of the custom Java class `Address` to retrieve the individual attributes of each `address` row object.

```
System.out.println("The addresses are: ");
while (addrow.next()) {
  o_address = addrow.a();
  System.out.println("ID: "+ o_address.getAddId() );
  System.out.println(o_address.getLine1());
  System.out.println(o_address.getLine2());
  System.out.println(o_address.getCity()+", "+o_address.getState()+" "
                    +o_address.getZip());
}
Close the iterator.
addrow.close();
```

6. Close the connection using `Oracle.close()` method.

```
Oracle.close();
```

A complete program is given below:

```
import java.sql.*;
import oracle.sqlj.runtime.*;

#sql iterator AddIter (Address a);
public class SQLJObjectExample1 {
public static void main (String [] args) throws SQLException {
try {
Oracle.connect("jdbc:oracle:thin:@training:1521:Oracle","oratest","oratest");

int i_add_id=9999;
String i_line1="101 Welligton Rd";
String i_line2="";
String i_city="Freemont";
String i_state="CA";
String i_zip="94875";
#sql {INSERT INTO addresses VALUES (address(:i_add_id,
:i_line1, :i_line2, :i_city,
:i_state, :i_zip))};
#sql {COMMIT};
AddIter addrow=null;
#sql addrow = {SELECT VALUE(addr) AS a FROM addresses addr};
```

```
Address o_address;
System.out.println("The addresses are:");
while (addrow.next()) {
  o_address = addrow.a();
  System.out.println("ID: "+ o_address.getAddId() );
  System.out.println(o_address.getLine1());
  System.out.println(o_address.getLine2());
  System.out.println(o_address.getCity()+", "+o_address.getState()+" "
                    +o_address.getZip());
}
addrow.close();
Oracle.close();
    } catch (SQLException e){System.out.println("ERR: "+ e);}
  }
}
```

The table `emp_with_addr` is populated using PL/SQL as follows:

```
DECLARE
  v_addr_ref REF address;
BEGIN
  SELECT REF(a)
  INTO   v_addr_ref
  FROM   addresses a
  WHERE  add_id = 9999;
INSERT INTO emp_with_addr
   SELECT empno, ename, job, mgr, hiredate, sal, comm, deptno,
          v_addr_ref
   FROM   emp
   WHERE  deptno = 10;
  COMMIT;
END;
/
```

Next, we describe the query of object references on the `emp_with_addr` table using custom Java classes. The steps involved are as follows:

1. Define a SQLJ iterator that corresponds to the `ename` column and `emp_addr` REF column. This involves the `AddressRef` custom class generated earlier, as shown here:

   ```
   #sql iterator AddRefIter (String ename, AddressRef aref);
   ```

2. Declare an instance of this iterator.

   ```
   AddRefIter addrowref;
   ```

3. Populate this iterator object with the resultset returned by a SQLJ SELECT statement.

   ```
   #sql addrowref = {SELECT empno, emp_addr AS aref FROM emp_with_addr where
   deptno = 10};
   ```

4. Define an instance of the class `AddressRef` generated by JPublisher corresponding to the object REF column `emp_addr` in the `emp_with_addr` column. Also declare a second host variable `o_ename` to hold the `ename` contained in the `addrowref` iterator.

   ```
   AddressRef o_addressref;
   String o_ename;
   ```

5. Fetch the data contained in the iterator into the host variables `ename` and `o_addressref`. To access the `address` object pointed to by `o_addressref`, use the `getValue()` method on it and assign the return value to an instance of type `Address`. Then use the `get()` methods on this `Address` instance to obtain the individual attributes of the `Address` instance, as shown here:

   ```
   System.out.println("The employees and their addresses
   in department 10 are: ");
   while (addrowref.next()) {
     o_ename = addrowref.ename();
     o_addressref = addrowref.aref();
     Address a = o_addressref.getValue();
     System.out.println("Employee: "+ o_ename);
     System.out.println(a.getLine1());
     System.out.println(a.getLine2());
     System.out.println(a.getCity()+", "+a.getState()+" "+a.getZip());
     System.out.println("\n");
   }
   ```

6. Close the iterator:

   ```
   addrowref.close();
   ```

7. Close the connection using `Oracle.close()` method:

   ```
   Oracle.close();
   ```

A complete program is shown here:

```
import java.sql.*;
import oracle.sqlj.runtime.*;

#sql iterator AddRefIter (String ename, AddressRef aref);
```

```
public class SQLJObjectRefExample {
public static void main (String [] args) throws SQLException {
try {
Oracle.connect("jdbc:oracle:thin:@training:1521:Oracle","oratest","oratest");

AddRefIter addrowref;
#sql addrowref = {SELECT ename, emp_addr AS aref FROM emp_with_
addr where deptno = 10};
AddressRef o_addressref;
String o_ename;
System.out.println("The employees and their addresses
in department 10 are: ");
while (addrowref.next()) {
  o_ename = addrowref.ename();
  o_addressref = addrowref.aref();
  Address a = o_addressref.getValue();
  System.out.println("Employee: "+ o_ename);
  System.out.println(a.getLine1());
  System.out.println(a.getLine2());
  System.out.println(a.getCity()+", "+a.getState()+" "+a.getZip());
  System.out.println("\n");
}
addrowref.close();
Oracle.close();
} catch (SQLException e){System.out.println("ERR: "+ e);}
  }
}
```

Handling Collections

This section highlights the use of custom Java classes for strongly typed collections. Specifically, it discusses the processing of VARRAYS in SQLJ. We will use the `address_id_varray` VARRAY and the `address_id_list` table based on this VARRAY created in the case study of Chapter 3 for describing the manipulation and access of VARRAYS in SQLJ. The definitions of these are reproduced here for convenience.

```
CREATE TYPE address_id_varray IS VARRAY(20) OF NUMBER;

CREATE TABLE address_id_list(address_id_list address_id_varray);
```

Handling the query and manipulation of VARRAYS involves

1. The creation of custom java classes for each VARRAY used. This class should implement the `oracle.sql.customDatum` interface.
2. Using the methods of the above created custom Java classes to access (`getArray()` and `getElement()`) and manipulate (`setArray()` and `setElement()`) SQL VARRAYS. Other methods, such as a constructor method and `length()`, method are also generated. The methods generated are described later.

For step 1, using JPublisher is the easy way that automatically generates the custom Java classes, including the methods for access and manipulation of the VARRAY.

JPublisher can be invoked from the command line using the executable `jpub` with the `sql` and `user` parameter specified. This is shown below:

```
jpub -sql=Address_Id_Varray -user=oratest/oratest
```

Here `Address_Id_Varray` corresponds to the `address_id_varray` VARRAY. The *A*, *I*, and *V* are in uppercase to specify a Java class filename and classname as per standard Java conventions.

This creates the following files:

1. Address_Id_Varray.java, having an `Address_Id_Varray` class corresponding to the `address_id_varray` varray. The `Address_Id_Varray` class is the custom Java class that implements the `oracle.sql.customDatum` interface and is used in the communication between Java and SQLJ. jpub creates custom Java classes, one for each VARRAY and also one for each object type and object reference if the VARRAY is an array of objects. Each .java file generated should be compiled using javac or sqlj.

In addition, the individual .java files contain methods to get and set the collection as whole as well as its individual elements. Also, a constructor method and a `length()` method are generated. The methods for the `Address_Id_Varray` class generated are as follows:

```
public Address_Id_Varray () throws SQLException
```

This is the constructor method that initializes the new custom class instance with a numeric array that is passed in as an argument.

```
public java.math.BigDecimal[] getArray() throws SQLException
```

This method returns as an array the collection represented by the custom Java class instance.

```
public void setArray(java.math.BigDecimal[] ) throws SQLException
```

This method then sets the array represented by the custom Java class instance to the array passed as an argument to it.

```
public int length() throws SQLException
```

This method returns the number of elements in the VARRAY represented by custom Java class instance.

```
public java.math.BigDecimal getElement(long index) throws SQLException
```

This method returns an individual element at a position given by index in the VARRAY represented by custom Java class instance.

```
public void setElement(java.math.BigDecimal, long index) throws SQLException
```

This method sets the value of an individual element at position index in the VARRAY represented by custom Java class instance.

We first describe the operation of INSERT on the `address_id_list` table. This example queries `add_ids` from `addresses` table and populates an array with the `add_ids` so obtained. It then inserts this array into the `address_id_list` table. It makes use of custom Java classes in the process. The steps involved are as follows:

1. Define a SQLJ SELECT statement to get the count of add_ids in addresses table:

   ```
   int cnt;
   #sql {SELECT count(add_id) INTO :cnt FROM addresses};
   ```

2. Define an iterator to select `add_ids` from `addresses` table:

   ```
   #sql iterator AddIdIter (int add_id);
   ```

3. Declare an instance of this iterator:

   ```
   AddIdIter addids=null;
   ```

4. Populate this iterator instance with the resultset obtained from a SQLJ SELECT statement that queries address ids:

   ```
   #sql addids = {SELECT add_id from addresses};
   ```

5. Declare a `BigDecimal` array and populate it with the queried `add_ids`:

   ```
   int i=0;
   BigDecimal[] add_id_array = new BigDecimal[cnt];
   while (addids.next()){
      BigDecimal v_x = new BigDecimal(addids.add_id());
   ```

```
        add_id_array[i] = v_x;
        i++;
    }
```

6. Declare an array instance of `AddressIdVarray` custom Java class using the constructor method and initialize this instance with the `add_id_array` created above:

```
Address_Id_Varray addidvarray = new AddressIdVarray(add_id_array);
```

7. Insert into `address_id_list` table the VARRAY represented by `addidvarray`:

```
#sql {INSERT INTO address_id_list VALUES (:addidvarray)};
```

8. Commit the changes:

```
#sql {COMMIT};
```

9. Close the iterator:

```
addids.close();
```

10. Close the connection:

```
Oracle.close();
```

A complete program is given here:

```
import java.sql.*;
import oracle.sqlj.runtime.*;
import java.math.*;

#sql iterator AddIdIter (int add_id);
public class SQLJVARRAYExample {
public static void main (String [] args) throws SQLException {
try {
Oracle.connect("jdbc:oracle:thin:@training:1521:Oracle",
"oratest","oratest");

int cnt;
#sql {SELECT count(add_id) INTO :cnt FROM addresses};

AddIdIter addids=null;
#sql addids = {SELECT add_id from addresses};
int i=0;
```

```
BigDecimal[] add_id_array = new BigDecimal[cnt];
while (addids.next()){
   BigDecimal v_x = new BigDecimal(addids.add_id());
   add_id_array[i] = v_x;
   i++;
}
Address_Id_Varray addidvarray = new Address_Id_Varray(add_id_array);
#sql {INSERT INTO address_id_list VALUES (:addidvarray)};
#sql {COMMIT};

addids.close();

Oracle.close();
} catch (SQLException e){System.out.println("ERR: "+ e);}
  }
}
```

Next, the process of querying VARRAY columns is detailed. Here the `getArray()` method of the `Address_Id_Varray` custom Java class is used. The steps involved are as follows:

1. Define an iterator corresponding to the `Address_Id_Varray` class:

   ```
   #sql iterator varrayIter (Address_Id_Varray address_id_list);
   ```

2. Declare an instance of the above iterator class:

   ```
   varrayIter arr;
   ```

3. Populate the iterator instance with a SQLJ SELECT querying the `address_id_list` table:

   ```
   #sql arr = {SELECT address_id_list FROM address_id_list};
   ```

4. Declare an instance of the `Address_Id_Varray` class to hold the array rows retrieved by the above query. Use the `getArray()` method to obtain the array rows one by one:

   ```
   while (arr.next()) {
     Address_Id_Varray o_array = arr.address_id_list();
     BigDecimal[] o_arr = o_array.getArray();
     String str="";
     int i=0;
     for(i=0;i<o_arr.length;i++) {
       str = str + o_arr[i];
       if (i != o_arr.length-1) str = str + ",";
   ```

```
    }
    System.out.println("The individual array is: "+str);
   }
```

5. Close the iterator:

```
arr.close();
```

6. Close the connection:

```
Oracle.close();
```

A complete program is shown here:

```
import java.sql.*;
import oracle.sqlj.runtime.*;
import java.math.*;

#sql iterator varrayIter (Address_Id_Varray address_id_list);
public class SQLJVARRAYExample1 {
public static void main (String [] args) throws SQLException {
try {
Oracle.connect("jdbc:oracle:thin:@training:1521:Oracle",
   "oratest","oratest");
varrayIter arr;
#sql arr = {SELECT address_id_list FROM address_id_list};

while (arr.next()) {
  Address_Id_Varray o_array = arr.address_id_list();
  BigDecimal[] o_arr = o_array.getArray();
  String str="";
  int i=0;
  for(i=0;i<o_arr.length;i++) {
    str = str + o_arr[i];
    if (i != o_arr.length-1) str = str + ",";
  }
  System.out.println("The individual array is: "+str);
 }
  arr.close();
  Oracle.close();
} catch (SQLException e){System.out.println("ERR: "+ e);}
  }
}
```

SQLJ Performance Extensions

Disabling Auto-Commit Mode

Disabling the auto-commit mode of SQLJ is faster, especially when handling large objects and objects such as object types, object references, and collections. The default auto-commit mode is false. The auto-commit flag setting for an existing connection can be changed using the `setAutoCommit()` method of the underlying connection object. This has two steps:

1. Use the `getConnection()` method of the SQLJ connection context instance to obtain the underlying JDBC connection.
2. Invoke the `setAutoCommit()` method with true or false as desired on the connection obtained above.

The code of these two steps can be written in a single line as follows:

```
defcontext.getConnection().setAutoCommit(true);
```

However, the SQLJ COMMIT statement has to be executed to commit any changes made to the database. Tip: Auto-commit cannot be enabled in Oracle8i database server-side SQLJ.

```
#sql {COMMIT};
```

Oracle Row Prefetching

Oracle row prefetching is a process of fetching multiple rows of data whenever a resultset is populated with a query. The additional rows are stored on the client-side buffer. Standard JDBC fetches one row at a time, making a round-trip for each row fetched. With row prefetching, the prefetch size can be set to an integer value, *n*, so that n rows are fetched each time a fetch is executed. The steps involved are as follows:

1. Convert the SQLJ `DefaultContext` connection to a `java.sql.Connection` object. This can be done in two ways:

    a. First, declare a `DefaultContext` instance and use the `Oracle.getConnection()` method to establish a database connection in SQLJ:

    ```
    DefaultContext defcontext =
    Oracle.getConnection("jdbc:oracle:thin:@training:1521:Oracle",
    "oratest","oratest");
    ```

    Then, declare a `Connection` object and use the `getConnection()` method on the `DefaultContext` object to get the underlying `Connection` instance:

    ```
    Connection conn = defcontext.getConnection();
    ```

   b. Invoke the `getDefaultContext()` method of the `DefaultContext` class on the DefaultContext instance and then get its underlying Connection instance with the `getConnection()` method:

```
Connection conn = DefaultContext.getDefaultContext().getConnection();
```

2. Cast the so-obtained `Connection` object to an `OracleConnection` object:
3. Invoke the `setDefaultRowPrefetch()` method on the above cast object passing the number of rows to prefetch as an integer value:

The code for steps 2 and 3 is as follows:

```
((OracleConnection) conn).setDefaultRowPrefetch(10);
```

To obtain the current default prefetch value, invoke the `getDefaultRowPrefetch()` method on the casted object above. Invoking `setDefaultRowPrefetch()` method sets the default prefetch size for all statements in a connection.

Update Batching

JDBC 2.0 supports new feature called *update batching* where a sequence of SQL statements on a particular `Statement` object can be sent to the database as a batch and then the batch is executed as a whole. Any set of non-query SQL statements that return an update count can be executed as a whole when defined as a batch. Oracle SQLJ supports update batching as of Oracle8i Release 2. In SQLJ, update batching is in reference to an execution context. For a statement to be executed as part of batch, it should be an INSERT, UPDATE, or DELETE statement (batchable) and it should be executed in a loop (compatible). Update batching is disabled by default in SQLJ.

We will assume the following table to illustrate update batching:

```
CREATE TABLE tab1 (col1 NUMBER);
```

This is an implicit batching with SQL statements being automatically accumulated into a batch and queued for execution. This only works on instances of OraclePreparedStatement object. The steps involved are as follows:

1. Turn auto-commit off.
2. Turn on update batching feature using the `setBatching()` method with a Boolean true as an argument:

```
ExecutionContext ecins = new ExecutionContext();
ecins.setBatching(true);
```

3. Set the batch limit by invoking the `setBatchLimit()` method with a numeric value indicating the batch limit:

   ```
   ecins.setBatchLimit(10);
   ```

4. Use the `executeBatch()` of the Execution Context object to set the batch size. This method returns an integer array of update counts:

   ```
   for (int i=0;i<10;i++) {
   #sql [ecins] {INSERT INTO tab1 VALUES (:i)};
   }
   int[] updateCounts = ecins.executeBatch();
   ```

The `updateCounts` array contains whether each statement in the batch was successful or not. As per JDBC 2.0, a value of -2 for an array element indicates that the corresponding batch statement was successful.

Oracle Optimizer

The Oracle SQL optimizer uses either the rule-based approach or the cost-based approach to select an access path to execute SQL statements. Oracle SQLJ allows to specify hints to in SQLJ SELECT, INSERT, or UPDATE statements so that the Oracle optimizer can use them for efficient processing at runtime. The syntax for placing the hints is as follows:

```
#sql public iterator EmpIter (int empno, String ename, float sal);
EmpIter emprow;
#sql emprow = {SELECT /*+ FIRST_ROWS */ empno, ename, sal FROM emp
WHERE deptno = 10};
...
...
```

The ability to specify hints is an advantage of SQLJ over JDBC especially for large databases such as data warehouses where processing of records is in millions.

DON'T CONFUSE AUTO-COMMIT MODES OF SQLJ AND JDBC

An interesting point to note for the SQLJ and JDBC programmer is to know the default settings of auto-commit mode. The default setting of auto-commit mode in SQLJ is false and in JDBC it is true. Disabling auto-commit mode is faster in both SQLJ and JDBC, especially when handling objects. Because of the default false setting in SQLJ (as no code needs to be written to disable it), programmers might be led to a point where they forget to do an explicit commit in SQLJ programs requiring writing of changes to the database.

The moral of the lesson is, "Don't forget to commit the changes in SQLJ by using the following line of code:

```
#sql {COMMIT};
```

Also, auto-commit mode is set to true and cannot be disabled in Oracle 8i database server-side SQLJ."

SQLJ in the Server

SQLJ in the server involves the execution of a Java stored procedure, Enterprise Java bean, or CORBA object inside the Oracle8i database. These Java programs must use the server-side internal driver. There are four issues to take care of:

1. Default connection

   Using SQLJ in the server-side implicitly establishes a default connection to the database. The Java program runs in the same session as the database session using the database connection as the default connection for the Java program. There is no need to register a driver, create a connection instance, or specify a default connection context. There is no need to call `Oracle.close()` method as the connection should remain open.

2. Transaction control

   Unlike client-side SQLJ, server-side JDBC has the auto-commit feature ignored by default. Transaction commit and rollback is by explicitly calling `#sql {commit};` or `#sql {rollback};` methods to COMMIT or ROLLBACK the transaction respectively.

3. Loading Java source and class files.

   This is done using the `loadjava` utility from the command-line. When loading source files, loadjava loads the particular .java file and compiles it to obtain a database object of type JAVA CLASS. The loadjava utility has been discussed in detail in Chapter 2. Either .sqlj files can be first be translated into .java or .class files on the client-side and then loaded into Oracle`8i` or .sqlj can be directly loaded into the database and then translated in the server using the embedded SQLJ translator in the Oracle`8i` JVM.

On the client-side, SQLJ profiles can be converted into class files by specifying `-ser2class` option of the client-side SQLJ translator. However, on the server side, SQLJ profiles are translated as resource files as there is no `-ser2class` option in the server-side. One Java class object is created per class file and one Java resource object is created per profile (.ser) file.

Summary

This chapter outlined the use of advanced SQLJ for database access in Java. Essentially, the use of SQLJ in accessing and manipulating objects in the database including large objects was presented. The performance enhancements in SQLJ were discussed. Finally, details about SQLJ in the server were presented.

USING JAVABEANS

7

ESSENTIALS

- Use JavaBeans to build reusable components. Create a JavaBean and add properties, methods, and events to the Bean.
- Add properties by means of private declarations.
- Add methods by defining public getter and setter methods using getProperty() and setProperty() signatures.
- JavaBeans allow the use of JDBC statements, classes, and class methods in the body of the Bean methods.
- Execute a JavaBean from a container program.
- Use the BeanInfo class for introspection and use its various methods to get the properties, methods, and events for a specific Bean class.

This chapter explains the use of JavaBeans in Oracle Server 8i. The method of creating a JavaBean and the various ways to add properties and events to a JavaBean are discussed.

Overview of JavaBeans

One of the major goals of object-oriented software is the ability to reuse software components of one application in developing another. JavaBeans is the implementation of Java's component model. As per the JavaBeans white paper, "a Java Bean is a reusable software component that can be manipulated visually in a builder tool." However, all JavaBeans need not have a visual component. The JavaBeans framework allows you to assemble together software components either programmatically or visually or both. Programmatically, to refer to a JavaBean is to refer to a class or a set of classes that has extra characteristics. Any Java class can be a JavaBean as long as it has these characteristics. These classes are written once and used everywhere they are required. No special classes or libraries are required to use the JavaBean components. Here is a sample Java class implemented as a JavaBean.

```
import java.io.*;
public class Bean1 implements Serializable
{
  private int Var1;
  private String Var2;

  public Bean1()
  {
  }

  public int getVar1()
  {
    return Var1;
  }

  public void setVar1(int value)
  {
    Var1 = value;
  }

  public String getVar2()
  {
    return Var2;
  }
```

```
  public void setVar2(String value)
  {
    Var2 = value;
  }
}
```

Here `Bean1` is a JavaBean that has a state represented by the variables `Var1` and `Var2`. The state is automatically saved and restored by the JavaBeans persistence mechanism. This Bean also has two properties `Var1` and `Var2` that can be used by any visual programming environment. Note that the `bean1` Bean doesn't itself have any visual representation.

A JavaBean has the following characteristics associated with it:

1. Properties, methods, and events
2. Persistence
3. Introspection
4. Customization
5. Design-time and runtime operation
6. Visibility
7. Multithreading
8. Security
9. Visual presentation

The advantages of JavaBeans are manifold, as follows:

1. They are a simple and easy way to construct programs. They support software reuse and enable you to use a predesigned JavaBean that does part of the work already.
2. JavaBeans are built purely in Java and hence are portable to any platform that has the Java runtime environment.
3. JavaBeans are built on and extend the existing Java platform. There is no other complex mechanism required to implement JavaBeans.

MATCH GET AND SET ACCESSOR METHODS CORRECTLY

Writing a JavaBean consists of defining properties and accessor methods. The important thing to remember here is that the get and set methods must match exactly with the property defined. This means that there should be `public` accessor "get" and "set" methods for each property of a Bean.

Ignoring this fact can lead to errors while accessing the Bean. The errors might not be conspicuous and might not directly lead to the fact that an accessor method is missing.

JavaBean Naming Conventions

For a Java class to be a JavaBean, it should provide the following features:

1. Methods that allow the JavaBean to be manipulated by any container. These correspond to event methods.
2. Properties that modify the state or behavior of the JavaBean. There should be `public` accessor "get" and "set" methods for each property. The get method enables the property value to be queried and the set method modifies the value of the property. The properties can be manipulated either at design time by a builder tool or at runtime by a program. The properties are generally defined as instance variables and are usually declared as `protected` or `private` to prevent direct manipulation. The convention is as follows:

   ```
   private TYPE MyProperty;
   public TYPE getMyProperty() ...
   public void setMyProperty(TYPE arg) ...
   ```

   This specifies `MyProperty` as a property of the JavaBean whose value can be manipulated using the public accessor methods `getMyProperty()` and `setMyProperty()`.
3. The class should implement the `java.io.Serializable` interface so that the added component can "talk" to the Bean using the `get()` and `set()` methods.
4. A no-arg constructor that allows an instance of the Bean to be created automatically when a component is added to a program.

Adding Properties to the JavaBean

As stated earlier, the properties of a JavaBean define its state or behavior. Also properties are defined as instance variables of the bean class and declared usually as `private` or `protected`. In the JavaBean bean1 defined earlier, the private variables `Var1` and `Var2` define two properties of it and they represent the state of the bean1 component. A property is accessed by calling methods that are defined for setting and getting the property value. These methods are declared as public methods to enable access by other components that access the Bean. As per the JavaBean convention, a property is defined as follows:

```
private TYPE MyProperty;
```

The getter and setter methods for this property have the following signatures:

```
public TYPE getMyProperty() ...

public void setMyProperty(TYPE arg) ...
```

JAVABEAN PROPERTIES

Properties of a JavaBean can be read-write, read-only or write-only. If both the `get()` and `set()` methods exist, the property is read-write. If only the `get()` method exists, the property is read-only. If only the `set()` method exists, the property is write-only.

Also the properties of a Bean can be `boolean`. As per the JavaBeans convention, Boolean properties have a slightly different signature for the get method. The following code shows how a Boolean property is defined along with its `get()` and `set()` methods:

```
private boolean MyProperty;

public boolean isMyProperty()...

public void setMyProperty(boolean value)...
```

PROPERTY ACCESSORS

The Property accessor methods is just like any other `public` methods and can be called from a container program to alter the runtime state of the JavaBean.

Types of Properties

There are different types of properties that can govern the state of a JavaBean. They are as follows:

- Single-valued properties

  So far the properties described have a single-value. This means only one value is associated with each named property.

- Indexed properties

  A property can also be multi-valued. Multi-valued properties have an ordered collection of values associated with a single name. These are termed *indexed properties* as the individual values are accessed by using an integer index similar to accessing an array. An indexed property can be defined as follows:

  ```
  private TYPE[] MyProperty;
  ```

  The `get()` and `set()` methods for indexed properties have the following signatures:

  ```
  public TYPE[] getMyProperty() ...
  public void setMyProperty(TYPE[] arg) ...
  ```

These methods are used to access the whole array of property values. To access the individual elements in the property array, two additional methods can be defined with the following signatures:

```
public TYPE getMyProperty(int index) ...
public void setMyProperty(int index, TYPE arg) ...
```

- Bound properties

  A JavaBean allows users to modify its properties either through the `set()` method or visually in a builder tool. This kind of change can be notified to other users of the Bean in the form of an associated event. Properties that enable such change notifications are known as *bound* properties.

- Constrained properties

  These are properties whose values when set are not acceptable by the owner object and therefore rejected. These properties are characterized by the corresponding `set()` method throwing the `java.beans.PropertyVetoException`. The signatures of the `get()` and `set()` methods for a constrained property assume the following form:

```
public TYPE getMyProperty() ...

public void setMyProperty(TYPE arg)
        throws java.beans.PropertyVetoException ...
```

Adding Events to the JavaBean

As mentioned earlier, one of the properties of a JavaBean is that it generates events notifying listeners that an associated action has happened. A JavaBean can use existing event types defined in the Bean component or define new custom event types. Examples of events are an `ActionEvent`, when a button is pressed, or an `ItemEvent`, when an item is selected from a drop-down list. JavaBean components follow the standard Java 1.1 event model to generate events and notify listeners. This model consists of event objects, event listeners, and event sources. These interoperate in a standard way using method invocation as part of firing and handling events. The procedure is as follows:

1. The event source creates an event object as part of the event process. This object is inherited from the `java.util.EventObject` class. In fact, all event classes are inherited from this `EventObject` class. This is shown below:

```
public class MyEvent extends java.util.EventObject
{
  // constructor
  public MyEvent(Object source)
```

```
    {
     super(source);
    }
  }
```

2. The event listener registers its interest in specific events from the Event Source. First, the listener object has to implement a specific interface for the event type. This is called Event Listener interface and should inherit from the base `java.util.EventListener` interface. It takes the following form:

   ```
   public interface <Event>Listener extends java.util.EventListener
   ```

   Event dispatch is done by calling methods on the listening object with the event object passed as a parameter. These methods are the handler methods and are also defined in this Event Listener interface. These methods have the following signature:

   ```
   void <eventMethodName>(<EventObjectType> e);
   ```

   The Event source implements add and remove methods. The add method that allows the listener object to register itself for a specific event. When event notification is no longer necessary, the remove method is called. These method signatures are as follows:

   ```
   public void add<ListenerType>(<ListenerType> listener);
   ```

   `<ListenerType>` corresponds to the Event Listener interface name defined above.

   ```
   public void remove<ListenerType>(<ListenerType> listener);
   ```

   The JavaBean keeps a list of all objects listening for the event. On the occurrence of the event, it loops through this list and invokes the handler method on each listener object.

3. The Event Source fires an event and the event listener handles the event.

Steps to Create a JavaBean

A JavaBean is a class that follows a standard format. This format was mentioned earlier in the section "JavaBean naming conventions". This section will demonstrate the use of JavaBeans from an Oracle 8i perspective. For the purposes of this section we shall use the `DEPT` table created in Chapter 3, "Basic JDBC Programming," and define a JavaBean named `DeptBean` that provides methods for the standard DML operations on the `DEPT` table. The steps to create the `DeptBean` follow.

Writing the JavaBean Class

This involves defining a public class named `DeptBean` that implements `java.io.Serializable` interface and has

- A no-arg default constructor for the class
- Properties defined as instance variables
- `public get()` and `set()` methods to access these properties
- `public` methods to describe the operations of `INSERT`, `UPDATE`, `DELETE`, and `SELECT` on the `DEPT` table

Initially, the `DeptBean` class looks as follows:

```
import java.io.*;
public class DeptBean implements Serializable {
  // default constructor
  public DeptBean()
  {
  }
}
```

Set Properties for JavaBeans

Once the `DeptBean` class is defined, properties can be added to it. Adding properties corresponds to declaring `private` variables in the bean class. The `DeptBean` class defines three private variables that correspond to the columns in the `DEPT` table:

```
private int dbDeptNo;

private String dbDname;

private String dbLoc;
```

Define Methods

Similar to any Java class, a JavaBean can define public methods that constitute the "public interface" of the Bean. These methods can be accessed by container programs that use the Bean and defined and invoked in the same way as methods in any Java class. A sample container program in the form of a servlet that invokes the Bean methods is given at the end of this section. Basically, a JavaBean can have two sets of public methods:

1. Accessor methods that allow access and modification to the properties of the Bean.
2. Methods that perform particular actions and relate to the functionality of the JavaBean. It is not necessary that a JavaBean have both the sets of methods. In fact, a JavaBean can have only the accessor methods defined in it.

The `DeptBean` has the following accessor methods defined:

```
public int getdbDeptNo()
{
return this.dbDeptNo;
}

public void setdbDeptNo(int valDeptNo)
{
  this.dbDeptNo = valDeptNo;
}

public String getdbDname()
{
return this.dbDname;
}

public void setdbDname(String valDname)
{
  this.dbDname = valDname;
}

public String getdbLoc()
{
return this.dbLoc;
}

public void setdbLoc(String valLoc)
{
  this.dbLoc = valLoc;
}
```

With this set of methods defined, the `DeptBean` class looks as follows:

```
import java.io.*;
public class DeptBean implements Serializable {
  private int dbDeptNo;
  private String dbDname;
```

```
    private String dbLoc;
    // default constructor
    public DeptBean()
    {
    }
    public int getdbDeptNo()
    {
      return this.dbDeptNo;
    }

    public void setdbDeptNo(int valDeptNo)
    {
      this.dbDeptNo = valDeptNo;
    }

    public String getdbDname()
    {
      return this.dbDname;
    }

    public void setdbDname(String valDname)
    {
      this.dbDname = valDname;
    }

    public String getdbLoc()
    {
      return this.dbLoc;
    }

    public void setdbLoc(String valLoc)
    {
      this.dbLoc = valLoc;
    }
  }
```

Next, the methods for the Bean functionality can be defined. These correspond to obtaining a database connection and performing DML operations on the `DEPT` table. The code for these methods follows the standard JDBC syntax and uses the classes defined in `java.sql.*` package.

The code for obtaining a database connection is defined in the no-arg constructor of the Bean. For this purpose, in addition to the properties defined above, the `DeptBean` will have a private variable that corresponds to the database requirements for the DML operations. This is a variable that is an instance of `Connection` object as per JDBC specifications.

```
private Connection Conn;
```

The code for the constructor is as follows:

```
public DeptBean()
{
 try {
        DriverManager.registerDriver(new oracle.jdbc.driver.OracleDriver());
        Conn = DriverManager.getConnection
              ("jdbc:oracle:thin:@training:1521:Oracle",
                "oratest", "oratest");
        Conn.setAutoCommit(false);
    }
    catch (SQLException e) {Conn = null; }
}
```

The above piece of code is a sample that demonstrates how to connect to the database with the Oracle alias on the training host using the oratest user ID with a password of oratest.

This Bean will also have a `finalize()` method to close the connection once the DML operation is over. This looks as follows:

```
protected void finalize()
{
  try {
          Conn.close();
  } catch (SQLException e) { }
}
```

Next, we define the methods that implement the DML operations of INSERT, UPDATE, and DELETE.

```
public int InsertDept()
    throws SQLException {
  int ret_val = 0;
  int numRows = 0;
  try {
     if (Conn == null)
       {ret_val = -1;}
     else
     {
```

```
            String sql = "INSERT INTO dept VALUES (?,?,?)";
            PreparedStatement pstmt = Conn.prepareStatement(sql);
            pstmt.setInt(1, this.dbDeptNo);
            pstmt.setString(2, this.dbDname);
            pstmt.setString(3, this.dbLoc);
            numRows = pstmt.executeUpdate();
            Conn.commit();
          }
      } catch(SQLException e){ ret_val = -1; Conn.rollback()}
      return (ret_val);
   }

   public int UpdateDept()
        throws SQLException {
      int ret_val = 0;
      int numRows = 0;
      try {
            if (Conn == null)
              {ret_val = -1;}
            else
            {
               String sql = "UPDATE dept SET dname =?, loc = ? WHERE deptno = ?";
               PreparedStatement pstmt = Conn.prepareStatement(sql);
               pstmt.setString(1, this.dbDname);
               pstmt.setString(2, this.dbLoc);
               pstmt.setInt(3, this.dbDeptNo);
               numRows = pstmt.executeUpdate();
               Conn.commit();
            }
        } catch(SQLException e){ ret_val = -1; Conn.rollback()}
     return (ret_val);
   }

   public int DeleteDept()
        throws SQLException {
      int ret_val = 0;
      int numRows = 0;
      try {
            if (Conn == null)
              {ret_val = -1;}
            else
            {
```

```
            String sql = "DELETE dept WHERE deptno = ?";
            PreparedStatement pstmt = Conn.prepareStatement(sql);
            pstmt.setInt(1, this.dbDeptNo);
            numRows = pstmt.executeUpdate();
            Conn.commit();
         }
      } catch(SQLException e){ ret_val = -1; Conn.rollback()}
  return (ret_val);
}
```

With these methods in place, the code for the DeptBean is as follows:

```
import java.io.*;
import java.sql.*;
public class DeptBean implements Serializable {
  private int dbDeptNo;
  private String dbDname;
  private String dbLoc;

  private Connection Conn = null;

  // default constructor
  public DeptBean()
  {
   try {
         DriverManager.registerDriver(new oracle.jdbc.driver.OracleDriver());
         Conn = DriverManager.getConnection
              ("jdbc:oracle:thin:@training:1521:Oracle",
                "oratest", "oratest");
         Conn.setAutoCommit(false);
     }
     catch (SQLException e) {Conn = null; }
  }

  protected void finalize()
  {
    try {
           Conn.close();
    } catch (SQLException e) { }
  }

  public int getdbDeptNo()
  {
```

```
    return this.dbDeptNo;
  }
  public void setdbDeptNo(int valDeptNo)
  {
    this.dbDeptNo = valDeptNo;
  }
  public String getdbDname()
  {
    return this.dbDname;
  }
  public void setdbDname(String valDname)
  {
    this.dbDname = valDname;
  }
  public String getdbLoc()
  {
    return this.dbLoc;
  }
  public void setdbLoc(String valLoc)
  {
    this.dbLoc = valLoc;
  }
  public int InsertDept()
    throws SQLException  {
    int ret_val = 0;
    int numRows = 0;
    try {
       if (Conn == null)
         {ret_val = -1;}
       else
       {
         String sql = "INSERT INTO dept VALUES (?,?,?)";
         PreparedStatement pstmt = Conn.prepareStatement(sql);
         pstmt.setInt(1, this.dbDeptNo);
         pstmt.setString(2, this.dbDname);
         pstmt.setString(3, this.dbLoc);
         numRows = pstmt.executeUpdate();
         Conn.commit();
       }
   return (ret_val);
   } catch(SQLException e){ ret_val = -1; Conn.rollback();return (ret_val);}
}
```

```
public int UpdateDept()
    throws SQLException {
  int ret_val = 0;
  int numRows = 0;
  try {
        if (Conn == null)
          {ret_val = -1;}
        else
        {
           String sql = "UPDATE dept SET dname =?,loc = ? WHERE deptno = ?";
           PreparedStatement pstmt = Conn.prepareStatement(sql);
           pstmt.setString(1, this.dbDname);
           pstmt.setString(2, this.dbLoc);
           pstmt.setInt(3, this.dbDeptNo);
           numRows = pstmt.executeUpdate();
           Conn.commit();
        }
       return (ret_val);
   } catch(SQLException e){ ret_val = -1; Conn.rollback();return (ret_val);}
 }

 public int DeleteDept()
     throws SQLException {
   int ret_val = 0;
   int numRows = 0;
   try {
         if (Conn == null)
           {ret_val = -1;}
         else
         {
           String sql = "DELETE dept WHERE deptno = ?";
           PreparedStatement pstmt = Conn.prepareStatement(sql);
           pstmt.setInt(1, this.dbDeptNo);
           numRows = pstmt.executeUpdate();
           Conn.commit();
         }
        return (ret_val);
    } catch(SQLException e){ ret_val = -1; Conn.rollback();return (ret_val);}
  }

}
```

The next step is to execute the above Bean from a container program. One of the ideal examples of a container program is a servlet that

- Displays an HTML page—This page accepts input from user-enterable text fields and calls for the user to click on one of three buttons labeled ADD, MODIFY, and DELETE.
- Invokes methods pertaining to INSERT, UPDATE and DELETE operations. Each of these methods instantiates the `DeptBean`, passes the input parameters to the Bean, and calls the corresponding Bean method to execute the INSERT, UPDATE, or DELETE operation on the `DEPT` table.

For an understanding of servlets, refer to Chapter 12, "Java Servlet Programming." The example servlet is termed `Department`. It displays an HTML form that has three user-enterable input fields, namely, `deptNo`, `deptName`, and `deptLoc`. There are also three buttons ADD, MODIFY, and DELETE each corresponding to the user-clicked actions for INSERT, UPDATE, and DELETE respectively. Clicking one of these buttons invokes one of three servlet procedures named `addDepartment()` corresponding to ADD, `modifyDepartment()` corresponding to MODIFY, and `deleteDepartment()` corresponding to DELETE. The function of these procedures is briefly described below:

`addDepartment()` performs the following:

1. Instantiates the `DeptBean()`.
2. Sets the Bean properties `dbDeptNo`, `dbDname`, and `dbLoc`.
3. Calls the `InsertDept()` Bean method that returns a status of 0 on success and –1 on failure.

`modifyDepartment()` performs the following:

1. Instantiates the `DeptBean()`.
2. Sets the Bean properties `dbDeptNo`, `dbDname`, and `dbLoc`.
3. Calls the `UpdateDept()` Bean method that returns a status of 0 on success and –1 on failure.

`deleteDepartment()` performs the following:

1. Instantiates the `DeptBean()`.
2. Sets the Bean property `dbDeptNo`. The other two properties are not needed for the DELETE operation.
3. Calls the `DeleteDept()` Bean method that returns a status of 0 on success and –1 on failure.

In addition to these three procedures, the Department servlet has four methods named printHeader(), printForm(), printMessage(), and printFooter() that correspond to the HTML interface of the servlet.

To execute the servlet, a Web server supporting servlets must be installed and started. Examples of such Web servers are Tomcat, Netscape Web Server, and so on. To compile the Department servlet, the following environment variables need to be set up:

1. Set the PATH variable to include %JAVA_HOME%\bin directory. (Here a Windows environment is assumed. For an UNIX environment, use the appropriate syntax such as $JAVA_HOME, and so on.)
2. Set the CLASSPATH variable to include the current working directory.
3. Set the CLASSPATH variable to include the servlet.jar file located in the lib subdirectory of the Web server home directory.
4. Set the CLASSPATH variable to include the [Oracle Home]\jdbc\lib\classes12.zip or [Oracle Home]\jdbc\lib\classes111.zip. (Refer to Chapter 3, "Basic JDBC programming").

To run the Department servlet, the steps are as follows:

1. Copy the compiled class files DeptBean.class and Department.class to the appropriate Web server directory for accessing servlets. This directory can be obtained from the setup instructions while installing the Web server. The CLASSPATH variable must be set to include this directory.
2. Start the Web server.
3. Invoke the servlet from a browser using the URL http://localhost:8080/servlet/Department.

The complete code for the servlet example is listed below:

```
import java.io.*;
import javax.servlet.*;
import javax.servlet.http.*;
import java.util.* ;

public class Department extends HttpServlet
{

public void service (HttpServletRequest request, HttpServletResponse response)
 throws ServletException, IOException {
response.setContentType("text/html");
```

```
PrintWriter out = response.getWriter() ;

String action = request.getParameter("action") ;
if ( (action == null)|| (action.equals("")) )
{
printInitialForm(request, out) ;
return ;
}

if (action.equals("ADD") ) addDepartment(request, out) ;
if (action.equals("MODIFY") ) modifyDepartment(request, out) ;
if (action.equals("DELETE") ) deleteDepartment(request, out) ;
}

private void printInitialForm(HttpServletRequest request, PrintWriter out)
 throws ServletException, IOException
{
printHeader(out) ;
printForm(request, out) ;
printFooter(out) ;
}

private void addDepartment(HttpServletRequest request, PrintWriter out)
 throws ServletException, IOException
{
printHeader(out) ;
printForm(request, out) ;
String mesg = new String("") ;
String deptNo = request.getParameter("deptNo") ;
String deptName = request.getParameter("deptName") ;
String deptLoc = request.getParameter("deptLoc") ;
if( (deptNo == null) || deptNo.equals("")||(deptName == null) ||
deptName.equals("")||(deptLoc == null)||deptLoc.equals("") )
{
mesg = "One or more of the input fields are blanks" ;
}
else
{
int status = -1 ;

//Here is where you instantiate the bean and use it.

try {
```

```
    DeptBean myBean = new DeptBean() ;
    myBean.setdbDeptNo(Integer.parseInt(deptNo)) ;
    myBean.setdbDname(deptName) ;
    myBean.setdbLoc(deptLoc) ;
    status = myBean.InsertDept() ;
   } catch (Exception e) { }

   if(status == 0) mesg = "Department Successfully Added" ;
   else mesg = "Failure to add Department" ;
   }

   //printHeader(out) ;
   //printForm(request, out) ;
   printMessage(out, mesg) ;
   printFooter(out) ;
   }

   private void modifyDepartment(HttpServletRequest request, PrintWriter out)
    throws ServletException, IOException
   {
   String mesg = new String("") ;
   String deptNo = request.getParameter("deptNo") ;
   String deptName = request.getParameter("deptName") ;
   String deptLoc = request.getParameter("deptLoc") ;
   if( (deptNo == null) || deptNo.equals("")||(deptName == null) ||
   deptName.equals("")||(deptLoc == null)||deptLoc.equals("") )
   {
   mesg = "One or more of the input fields are blanks" ;
   }
   else
   {
   int status = -1 ;

   //Here is where you instantiate the bean and use it.
   try {

    DeptBean myBean = new DeptBean() ;
    myBean.setdbDeptNo(Integer.parseInt(deptNo)) ;
    myBean.setdbDname(deptName) ;
    myBean.setdbLoc(deptLoc) ;
    status = myBean.UpdateDept() ;
   } catch (Exception e) { }
```

```
if(status == 0) mesg = "Department Successfully Modified" ;
else mesg = "Failure to modify Department" ;
}

printHeader(out) ;
printForm(request, out) ;
printMessage(out, mesg) ;
printFooter(out) ;

}

private void deleteDepartment(HttpServletRequest request, PrintWriter out)
 throws ServletException, IOException
{
String mesg = new String("") ;
String deptNo = request.getParameter("deptNo") ;
String deptName = request.getParameter("deptName") ;
String deptLoc = request.getParameter("deptLoc") ;
if( (deptNo == null) || deptNo.equals(""))
{
mesg = "One or more of the input fields are blanks" ;
}
else
{
int status = -1 ;

//Here is where you instantiate the bean and use it.
try {

 DeptBean myBean = new DeptBean() ;
 myBean.setdbDeptNo(Integer.parseInt(deptNo)) ;
 myBean.setdbDname(deptName) ;
 myBean.setdbLoc(deptLoc) ;
 status = myBean.DeleteDept() ;
} catch (Exception e) { }

if(status == 0) mesg = "Department Successfully Deleted" ;
else mesg = "Failure to delete Department" ;

}

printHeader(out) ;
printForm(request, out) ;
```

```
printMessage(out, mesg) ;
printFooter(out) ;

}
private void printHeader(PrintWriter out)
{
out.println("<HTML>") ;
out.println("<HEAD>") ;
out.println("<TITLE> Department Maintenance Page </TITLE>") ;
out.println("</HEAD>") ;
out.println("<BODY>") ;
out.println("<H1> Department Maintenance Page </H1>") ;
out.println("<B>") ;
out.println(
"(Please enter department details and click on INSERT, UPDATE or DELETE. )") ;
out.println("</B>") ;
out.println("<BR>") ;
out.println("<BR>") ;
}

void printFooter(PrintWriter out)
{
out.println("</BODY>") ;
out.println("</HTML>") ;
}

void printForm( HttpServletRequest request, PrintWriter out)
{
String deptNo = request.getParameter("deptNo") ;
if(deptNo == null) deptNo = "" ;

String deptName = request.getParameter("deptName") ;
if(deptName == null) deptName = "" ;

String deptLoc = request.getParameter("deptLoc") ;
if(deptLoc == null) deptLoc = "" ;

//out.println("<FORM METHOD=GET ACTION='/deptServlet'>") ;

out.println("<FORM METHOD=GET ACTION=Department>") ;

out.println("<TABLE>") ;
out.println("<TR>") ;
```

```
out.println("<TD> Department No: </TD>") ;
out.println("<TD> <INPUT TYPE=text NAME=deptNo VALUE='" + deptNo +"'>") ;
out.println("</TR>") ;
out.println("<TR>") ;
out.println("<TD> Department Name:</TD>") ;
out.println("<TD> <INPUT TYPE=text NAME=deptName VALUE='" + deptName + "'>") ;
out.println("</TR>") ;
out.println("<TR>") ;
out.println("<TD> Department Loc: </TD>") ;
out.println("<TD> <INPUT TYPE=text NAME=deptLoc VALUE='" + deptLoc + "'>") ;
out.println("</TR>") ;
out.println("</TABLE>") ;
out.println("<BR><BR>") ;
out.println("<INPUT TYPE=SUBMIT VALUE='ADD' NAME=action>") ;
out.println("<INPUT TYPE=SUBMIT VALUE='MODIFY' NAME=action>") ;
out.println("<INPUT TYPE=SUBMIT VALUE='DELETE' NAME=action>") ;
out.println("</FORM>") ;
}

void printMessage(PrintWriter out, String mesg)
{
out.println("<BR>") ;
out.println("<B>") ;
out.println(mesg) ;
out.println("</B>") ;
}

} //END of Servlet CLASS
```

Register Events

Events can be registered by specifying the Event source, Event object, and Event Listeners. One example of an event for the `DeptBean` Bean is to have an extra Bean method called `QueryDept()` and specify a `noRows` event when no rows are returned by the query on the `Dept` table.

The `BeanInfo` Class

Usually, the information about a Bean is exposed by means of design patterns. This way of default or implicit introspection was possible by means of a standard convention for properties and events when a Bean was coded. For example, the `DeptBean` had `get()` and `set()` methods defined for its properties and these methods were defined using a standard pattern such as `getPropertyName()` and `setPropertyName()`. Following these design patterns, the Java reflection mechanism determined that there is a property named PropertyName. In situations where this implicit way of exposing a Bean is not enough, the `BeanInfo` class comes into effect. Using the `BeanInfo` class is a way of providing information about a Bean explicitly. This class implements the `java.bean.BeanInfo` interface that specifies a set of methods that can be used to determine information about a Bean such as the Bean name, properties, methods, and events. This information is necessary whenever it is required to develop a utility or program to get meta-information of a Bean and designate exactly the information needed to interface with and use a Bean. Also certain development licenses require information about a Bean to be specified. Separating the Bean from its meta-information is a good way of designing as it allows for making the Bean a run-time only object. The methods of the `BeanInfo` interface are listed below in Table 7.1.

Table 7.1 Methods of the `BeanInfo` ***Interface***

Method	Description
`getAdditionalBeanInfo()`	Returns any additional `BeanInfo` objects pertaining to the associated Bean
`getBeanDescriptor()`	Returns the Bean descriptor object
`getDefaultEventIndex()`	Returns the default event index
`getDefaultPropertyIndex()`	Returns the default property index
`getEventSetDescriptors()`	Returns the event set descriptors corresponding to the events of the Bean
`getIcon()`	Returns the specified graphic icon for the Bean that can be used in visual development tool
`getMethodDescriptors()`	Returns the method descriptors for each of the methods defined in the Bean
`getPropertyDescriptors()`	Returns the method descriptors for each of the properties in the Bean

Of these, the primary methods that are of importance are the `getAdditionalBeanInfo()` and `getBeanDescriptor()` methods and the following three methods corresponding to the properties, events, and methods of the Bean respectively:

```
PropertyDescriptor[] getPropertyDescriptors()
EventSetDescriptor[] getEventSetDescriptors()
MethodDescriptor[] getMethodDescriptors()
```

These three methods return arrays of corresponding objects regarding the properties, events and methods of a Bean. Here `PropertyDescriptor`, `EventSetDescriptor`, and `MethodDescriptor` are classes in the `BeanInfo` interface. The most general form of constructors of these three classes are as follows:

```
public PropertyDescriptor(String property, Class beanClass)
   throws IntrospectionException

public MethodDescriptor(Method method)
```

```
public EventSetDescriptor(Class sourceClass,
                          String eventSetName,
                          Class listenerType,
                          String listenerMethodName)
    throws IntrospectionException
```

Generating the `BeanInfo` Class

The class `java.beans.SimpleBeanInfo` provides the default implementation of the `BeanInfo` interface. Generating the `BeanInfo` class for a Bean consists in extending this `SimpleBeanInfo` class and overriding those methods that return the information to be provided explicitly. The following example shows how to generate a `DeptBeanInfo` class for the `DeptBean` as a subclass of `SimpleBeanInfo`. It overrides the `getPropertyDescriptors()` to specify which properties are presented to a Bean user. This method creates `PropertyDescriptor` object for the `dbDeptNo` property. The name of the class is formed by adding the string `BeanInfo` to the Bean class.

```
import java.beans.*;
public class DeptBeanInfo extends SimpleBeanInfo {
  public PropertyDescriptor[] getPropertyDescriptors() {
    try {
      PropertyDescriptor dbDeptNo =
        new PropertyDescriptor("dbDeptNo", DeptBean.class);
      PropertyDescriptor pd[] = {dbDeptNo};
      return pd;
    } catch (IntrospectionException e) { return null; }
  }
}
```

The Introspector

Of particular importance is the `java.beans.Introspector` class that is used to get a `BeanInfo` object for a specified class. It provides a `getBeanInfo()` method that takes as an argument a Bean class. It first checks if there is a `BeanInfo` class available for the Bean class. If not, it constructs a `BeanInfo` object for the specified Bean class.

A Generalized Example of the `BeanInfo` Interface

A more generalized example of the `BeanInfo` interface is to use it to get the properties, methods, and events for a specific Bean class. The following example illustrates this with respect to the `DeptBean` created earlier.

```
import java.beans.*;
public class GeneralizedBeanInfo {
  public static void main(String[] args) {
```

```
    try {
      BeanInfo bi = Introspector.getBeanInfo(DeptBean.class);
      BeanDescriptor bd = bi.getBeanDescriptor();
      String beanName = bd.getName();
      System.out.println("The Bean Name is " + beanName);
      System.out.println("The properties of the bean are: ");
      PropertyDescriptor pd[] = bi.getPropertyDescriptors();
      int plen = pd.length;
      for (int i = 0;i < plen;i++)
      {
        String pname = pd[i].getName();
        System.out.println("\t" + pname);
      }
      System.out.println("The Methods of the bean are: ");
      MethodDescriptor md[] = bi.getMethodDescriptors();
      int mlen = md.length;
      for (int i = 0;i < mlen;i++)
      {
        String mname = md[i].getName();
        System.out.println("\t" + mname);
      }
      System.out.println("The events of the bean are: ");
      EventSetDescriptor ed[] = bi.getEventSetDescriptors();
      int elen = ed.length;
      for (int i = 0;i < elen;i++)
      {
        String ename = ed[i].getName();
        System.out.println("\t" + ename);
      }
    } catch (Exception e) { System.out.println("Error: " + e); }
  }
}
```

The output of the above program is as follows:

```
The Bean Name is DeptBean
The properties of the bean are:
        dbDeptNo
        class
        dbLoc
        dbDname
```

```
The Methods of the bean are:
        getdbDname
        getdbLoc
        notify
        UpdateDept
        DeleteDept
        wait
        equals
        setdbDeptNo
        getdbDeptNo
        notifyAll
        wait
        getClass
        hashCode
        InsertDept
        toString
        setdbDname
        setdbLoc
        wait
The events of the bean are:
```

Summary

This chapter outlined the use of JavaBeans for component-based development in Java. Essentially, the method of developing a JavaBean in terms of writing the JavaBean class, setting the JavaBean properties, defining methods and events and finally, using it in a container program is described in detail. Also a method of obtaining meta-data about a JavaBean using the `BeanInfo` class is described.

USING ENTERPRISE JAVABEANS

ESSENTIALS

- Use Enterprise JavaBeans (EJB) to build server-side reusable components.
- An EJB has a Remote Interface, a Home Interface, an actual Bean class, a deployment descriptor, and a client program to access the EJB.
- Understand the EJB architecture, the types of EJBS the deployment environments for EJBS, and the role of the client program.
- Choose between using Session Beans and Entity Beans.

This chapter presents the use of Enterprise JavaBeans (EJBs) as reusable Java components. Specifically, it explains the architecture and concepts of Enterprise JavaBeans.

Overview of EJBs

As mentioned in Chapter 7, "Using JavaBeans," one of the major goals of object-oriented software is the ability to reuse software components of one application in developing another. Once a component is developed, it can be distributed and used in other applications. Sun's EJB specification defines EJBs as follows:

The Enterprise JavaBeans architecture is a component architecture for the development and deployment of object-oriented distributed enterprise-level applications. Applications written using the Enterprise JavaBeans architecture are scalable, transactional and multi-user secure. These applications may be written once, and deployed on any server platform that supports the Enterprise JavaBeans specification.

In simple terms, Enterprise JavaBeans is a server-side component model for enterprise level Java. It is based on distributed object technology and is designed to manage distributed objects in a three-tier architecture. From the EJB perspective, a component can be a `Department` business object that can be deployed in any EJB server. Once deployed, this object can be used to develop any application. Server-side components are based on a specification. For EJBs, there is the EJB specification by Sun. The `Department` object is created using a set of classes and interfaces that conform to this EJB specification. This makes it easier to define and implement an object model that can accommodate distributed components.

In the EJB architecture, the Bean is deployed in an EJB container (which comes with every application server that supports EJBs). The EJB container acts as the interface between the client (who uses the EJB) and the Bean.

For writing an EJB and deploying it, we need the following components:

1. The Bean itself
2. The Home Interface, which is used by the client code to get an instance of the EJB
3. The Remote Interface, which is used by the client code to invoke methods on the Bean
4. The deployment descriptor, which gives the name of the Home Interface, Remote Interface, and other properties that specify the way persistence, transaction management, and so on is handled by the EJB container

The container interprets requests from the client and passes it to the Bean. It also takes the response from then Bean and passes it back to the client. In addition, the Container also provides services like transaction management, security, persistence, and resource-pooling. Once deployed, the Bean can make use of these features of the container. Thus the Bean programmer is relieved of taking care of these features and can focus more on the application logic.

Types of EJBs

Enterprise JavaBeans are primarily of two types, Entity Beans and Session Beans. Entity Beans in turn are classified as Container-managed Entity Beans and Bean-managed Entity Beans. Session Beans are further classified as Statefull and Stateless Session Beans. This section discusses the primary purpose of each of these types of Beans.

Entity Beans

Entity Beans are Beans that represent business objects. They represent persistent data that is stored in a permanent data store such as a database. Persistent data is data that is permanent until explicitly deleted. Examples are Employee, Book, and so on. The following are the characteristics of Entity Beans:

- Can implement business objects.
- Can represent data in a database.
- Can represent behavior—By means of methods that change the data.
- Are identified by a primary key—The primary key identifies each instance of an Entity Bean.
- Are created either by inserting data directly into the database or by creating an object using a `Create()` method.
- Are persistent—Permanent until deleted explicitly.
- Are transactional and fine-grained components.
- Are recoverable after a system crash.
- Are shared by multiple clients—This provides fast and reliable access to data while preserving data integrity. All clients see changes to data as it changes.
- Can manage their own persistence or can transfer persistence services to their container. With the former method they are called Bean-managed Entity Beans, with the latter method they are called Container-managed Entity Beans.

Session Beans

Session Beans are Beans that represent business processes. They represent transient objects and exist only for the duration of a single client/server session. Unlike Entity Beans, they don't represent data that is stored in a permanent data store such as a database. Examples are Employee Salary Raise, Book Issuance and Returns, and so on. There will be no Salary Raise record in the database even though the Salary Raise procedure updates the Employee data. Session Beans are created by a client. The following are the characteristics of Session Beans:

- Can implement business processes
- Can represent actions such as those pertaining to queries in a database or performing calculations. This may have side effects on the database, however.
- Are created as an extension of the client application—changes to the Session Bean do not affect the client code.
- Are transient—cease to exist after action is completed
- Can be transactional and are coarse-grained components—most of the details of the process are hidden from the client.
- Are not recoverable after a system crash.
- Are usually accessible to a single client. However, when properly defined can be shared by many clients.
- Can reduce network traffic and connections required by the client—they limit the number of method invocations by the client. This improves the performance of the EJB server.
- Must manage their own persistence.
- Can be statefull or stateless. Stateful Session Beans maintain conversational state across methods and transactions. The state of the Session Bean can change as each method of the Bean is invoked and this can in turn affect subsequent method invocations. Stateless Session Beans do not maintain any conversational state. It deals with independent method calls. Stateless Session Beans drastically improve the performance in terms of throughput.

EJB Architecture and Concepts

The Enterprise JavaBeans component model forms the basis of EJBs and is a logical extension of JavaBeans component model to support server components. Server components are reusable Java components that are designated to run in an application server. They can interact with other components and are assembled to form customized applications. EJB components can be deployed by tools provided by an EJB-compliant application server. Oracle 8i JServer and Oracle Application Server 9i are both EJB-compliant and provide two good deployment environments for EJBs.

EJB Architecture

The EJB architecture is comprised of the following:

- An EJB Server
- An EJB Container
- An EJB Component
- A Client application

These are described below:

Figure 8.1 shows a typical EJB architecture scenario.

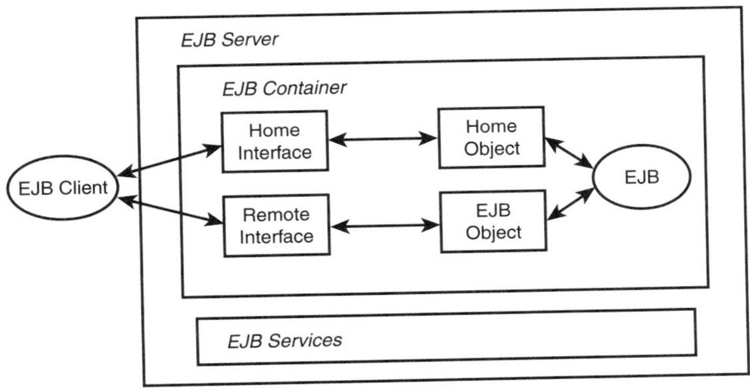

FIGURE 8.1
A typical EJB architecture.

- EJB Server

  An EJB Server is a program that provides an environment for the execution of EJB applications. Since EJB components are transactional, the EJB Server also provides for distributed transaction services. In addition, it also provides a set of system services such as naming, resource pooling, concurrency, and security. The EJB Server also provides for an EJB Container for the EJBs. Examples of EJB Servers are Oracle 8i JServer, which is a part of Oracle 8i Server and Oracle 9i Application Server. EJBs run in an EJB container which in turn runs in an EJB Server. The EJB Server also provides for low-level services to the container such as network connectivity. EJB servers conform to EJB specifications, namely, EJB 1.0 and EJB 1.1 specifications. As per EJB 1.1 specification, an EJB Server must also provide for services to look up an EJB object using JNDI as also distributed transaction services.

- EJB Container

  An EJB Container is an environment that provides a home for the EJBs. It acts as an intermediate layer between the Bean class and the EJB Server. It provides services to the Enterprise Bean. For each Enterprise JavaBean object, it registers the object, provides a remote interface for the object, and creates and removes object instances. It also provides

  - Automatic lifecycle management
  - Implicit transaction control—Starting, Enrollment, Committing, and Rollback of transactions
  - Persistence—managing persistent data, which includes selection and storage of persistent object data from a database
  - Security—Authentication of users and checking authorization levels
  - State Management—Saving and restoration of object state

  A single vendor would provide for both the EJB Server and an associated EJB Container. Also, the EJB container vendor provides tools that are used for deploying the EJBs and other functions. Oracle provides the `deployejb` and `ejbdescriptor` tools for deploying EJBS into Oracle 8i Server or Application Server.

  The container must adhere to the Bean-Container contract that is a set of services that the container must provide. Specifically, it must provide for publishing the names of the EJBs it includes and providing for client lookups. The publishing of names is done by using the JNDI naming service and client lookup is done by the `lookup()` method of the `javax.naming.Context` interface.

  An EJB interacts with its container using the `javax.ejb.EJBContext` interface that is implemented by the container and is a part of the Bean-Container contract. Entity Beans use a subclass of `javax.ejb.EJBContext` called `javax.ejb.EntityContext` and Session Beans use the subclass called `javax.ejb.SessionContext`. These contexts provide the Bean class with information about its container, the client using the Bean, and the Bean itself.

- EJB Component

  To implement an Enterprise Bean, four components must be defined. These components are interrelated and are as follows:

  - The Bean Remote Interface
  - The Bean Home Interface
  - The Bean Class

- The Primary Key Class (only for Entity Beans)
- The Bean Deployment descriptor

These are described in detail below.

The Bean Remote Interface

The Remote Interface for an EJB defines the Bean's business methods. These are methods that the clients can call. This constitutes the public interface of the Bean that the client can call. EJB specification requires that the Remote Interface follow standard RMI (Remote Method Invocation) interface conventions. However, the underlying protocol used by Oracle 8i is IIOP. The Bean Remote interface must comply with the following conditions for its definition:

- It must extend `javax.ejb.EJBObject`, which in turn extends `java.rmi.Remote`.
- All the methods must declare that they throw `java.rmi.RemoteException` exception. This is a requirement of the Java RMI interface.
- The Bean class must declare a corresponding method for each method declared in the Remote Interface. These corresponding methods must have the same name and signature as those defined in the Remote interface.

`EJBOBject`

The object that actually implements the Remote Interface is called the EJB Object. An EJB Object class is generated for each Bean class. The definition of the `javax.ejb.EJBObject` is as follows:

```
public interface javax.ejb.EJBObject
    extends java.rmi.Remote {
public EJBHome getEJBHome() throws RemoteException;
public Object getHandle() throws RemoteException;
public void remove() throws RemoteException;
}
```

On the server side, the EJBObject is a distributed object that implements the remote interface of the Bean. Based on the Bean class and the information in the deployment descriptor, the EJB Object is generated at deployment time by the `deployejb` tool provided by Oracle 8i. Also client stubs are generated. The client using the generated client stub classes remotely invokes the EJBObject.

The EJBObject works in unison with the EJB container to render the services required by the container.

The Bean Home Interface

The Bean Home Interface defines the Bean's lifecycle methods. These are methods for creating new Beans, finding Beans, and removing Beans. These methods are used by the client program to create, find, and remove an EJB from its container. The Bean Home interface must comply with the following conditions for its definition:

- It must extend `javax.ejb.EJBHome`, which in turn extends `java.rmi.Remote`.
- All the methods must declare that they throw `java.rmi.RemoteExecption` exception. This is a requirement of the Java RMI interface.
- The interface must define one or more `create()` methods. The `create()` method is used to instantiate an instance of the Bean. For each `create()` method in the home interface, there must be a corresponding `ejbCreate()` method in the Bean class with the same signature. The return type of the `create()` method should be the Bean's remote interface type. The `create()` method must also throw the `javax.ejb.CreateException` exception.
- Entity Beans must additionally define a `findByPrimaryKey()` method corresponding to a Primary Key class defined separately. This find method should provide as argument an object of the Primary Key class. In addition, this method must also throw the `javax.ejb.FinderException` exception.

EJBHome

The object that implements the home interface is called the `EJBHome`. The `EJBHome` is generated on the server-side, by the `deployejb` tool when an EJB is deployed in Oracle 8i. The definition of the `javax.ejb.EJBHome` is as follows:

```
public interface javax.ejb.EJBHome
    extends java.rmi.Remote {
public abstract EJBMetaData getEJBMetaData() throws RemoteException;
public HomeHandle getHomeHandle() throws RemoteException;
public abstract void remove(Handle handle)
     throws RemoteException, RemoteException;
public abstract void remove(Object primaryKey)
     throws RemoteException, RemoteException;
}
```

Out of these methods, the last `remove()` method is used only by Entity Beans.

The `EJBHome` identifies the Enterprise Bean class and is used to create, find and remove Enterprise Bean instances. The EJB container creates an `EJBHome` that implements the home interface. The client does a look-up of the home object and the container makes the home interface available to the client using JNDI. The `EJBHome` locates, creates, and removes Enterprise Beans from the container. For example, when a `create()` method is invoked on the home interface, the `EJBHome` creates an instance of the EJB object providing it with a Bean instance. Then the corresponding `ejbCreate()` method is called. In case of an Entity Bean, a new record is inserted into the database. In case of Session Beans, the Bean instance is initialized. After the `ejbCreate()` is executed, the `EJBHome` provides a remote reference called stub to the client. The client then uses the stub to invoke business methods.

The Bean Class

This is a Java class implementing business logic. It also provides implementations of the methods defined in the Bean Remote and Home interfaces. The Bean can use JDBC or SQLJ to access Oracle 8i. The actual Bean class resides in an EJB container. The definition of the Bean class must comply with the following conditions:

- It must be declared as public.
- It must implement either the `javax.ejb.EntityBean` or `javax.ejb.SessionBean` interface. The former is for Entity Beans and the latter for Session Beans.
- It must implement the `ejbCreate()` method corresponding to the `create()` method in the Home interface. In addition, it can implement `ejbPostCreate()` method in case of Entity Beans.
- In case of Bean-managed Entity Beans, implement the `findByPrimaryKey()` method defined in the home interface. This is implemented as `ejbFindByPrimaryKey()` method. Note that in case of container-managed Entity Beans, this method need not be implemented in the Bean class.
- It must implement the business methods as defined in the Remote interface. The business methods are the only methods that can be accessed by the client application. All other methods are visible only to the EJB container.

There are methods specific to the `javax.ejb.EntityBean` interface and the `javax.ejb.SessionBean` interface. The following listings provide the definition of these two interfaces:

```
public interface javax.ejb.SessionBean
   extends javax.ejb.EnterpriseBean {
   public abstract void ejbActivate();
   public abstract void ejbPassivate();
   public abstract void ejbRemove();

   public abstract void setSessionContext(SessionContext ctx);
}

public interface javax.ejb.EntityBean
   extends javax.ejb.EnterpriseBean {
```

```
    public abstract void ejbActivate();
    public abstract void ejbLoad();
    public abstract void ejbPassivate();
    public abstract void ejbRemove();
    public abstract void ejbStore();

    public abstract void setEntityContext(SessionContext ctx);
    public abstract void unsetEntityContext();
}
```

A brief description of the methods is as follows:

- `ejbCreate()` and `ejbPostCreate()` methods initialize instance of the Bean class whenever a record is added to the database, in case of Entity Beans. In case of Session Beans, the `ejbCreate()` method initializes the Bean's state. There is no `ejbPostCreate()` method for Session Beans. The code for these methods can be as follows:

  In case of container-managed Entity Beans, the `ejbCreate()` method can initialize the Bean public variables and should return `void`. In case of Bean-managed Entity Beans, the `ejbCreate()` should include code for inserting a record into the database and should return the Primary key class. The `ejbPostCreate()` method can perform additional initialization.

  In case of a session Bean, the `ejbCreate()` method need not do anything and so it can be an empty implementation or can be code to initialize the Bean public variables or can just display a message. There is no need to implement the `ejbPostCreate()` method for session Beans. An empty implementation means coding the method as a null method as shown below:

  ```
  public void ejbCreate() {
  }
  ```

- The methods defined in the `javax.ejb.EntityBean` interface or the `javax.ejb.SessionBean` interface are called *state management callback methods*. For example, in case of an Entity Bean, the `ejbRemove()` method notifies the Bean that its data is about to be deleted from the database. In case of a Session Bean, it notifies the Bean that the client no longer needs it. In case of Entity Beans, this method can be coded as follows:

  For container-managed persistence, an empty implementation of this method is enough. However, for Bean-managed persistence, this method must provide code to delete a record from the database.

  In case of a Session Bean, this method can be an empty implementation or just give a remove message.

- The `ejbLoad()` and `ejbStore()` methods notify an Entity Bean that its state is about to be synchronized with the database. A Session Bean does not need these two methods as they have no persistent state. These methods are not required for Session beans. In case of Entity Beans, for container-managed persistence, these methods can just be empty implementations. This is because the synchronization between the Bean instance the database is automatically taken care of. For Bean-managed persistence, the `ejbLoad()` method must read from database directly and hence must provide code for the `SELECT` operation. The `ejbStore()` method must provide code for the `UPDATE` operation.
- The `ejbActivate()` and `ejbPassivate()` methods notify the Bean that it is about to be activated or deactivated. These can be empty implementations or can just display a message such as "Bean Activated."
- The `setEntityContext()` or `setSessionContext()` methods provide an entity or Session Bean respectively with an interface to the EJB server that in turn provides the Bean with information about itself and its surroundings. It helps the Bean instance to set a reference to its context. The code for `setEntityContext()` or `setSessionContext()` methods should initialize the Bean context defined as a variable in the Bean class.
- In case of Entity Beans, the `unsetEntityContext()` method notifies the Bean that it is about to be included for garbage collection. The code for this method should set the Bean context to `null`.

The Primary Key Class

This class is needed in case of Entity Beans and provides a pointer to the database to find the Beans. It must implement `java.io.Serializable` interface. The persistent fields of a Bean instance are located by means of a primary key. An object of the primary key class is used as an argument for the `findByPrimaryKey()` method of the home interface. In Oracle 8i, the primary key attributes map to a primary key column in a table. With Container-managed Entity Beans, the find methods need not be implemented in the Bean class. However, with Bean-managed persistence, there should be an `ejbFindByPrimaryKey()` method in the Bean class corresponding to the `findByPrimaryKey()` method in the Home interface. If additional `find()` methods are defined in the Home interface, corresponding `ejbFind()` methods should be declared in the Bean class.

The Deployment Descriptor

A deployment descriptor is a property file for the EJB that specifies the rules associated in regard to lifecycle, transactions, and other runtime behavior of the EJB. These are specified declaratively. At runtime, the EJB container automatically executes the services by looking up the values in the deployment descriptor. In Oracle 8i Release 3, the deployment descriptor is defined in the form of an XML file. This is as per EJB 1.1 specifications. Earlier versions of Oracle 8i defined this as a serialized file.

Table 8.1 summarizes the interfaces and classes for Entity and Session Beans.

Table 8.1 A comparison of Entity and Session Bean Characteristics

	Entity Bean	Session Bean
Remote Interface	Extends javax.ejb.EJBObject	Extends javax.ejb.EJBObject
Home Interface	Extends javax.ejb.EJBHome	Extends javax.ejb.EJBHome
Bean Class	Extends javax.ejb.EntityBean	Extends javax.ejb.SessionBean
Primary key	Defined as a separate class	Not defined
Deployment Descriptor	Defined	Defined
Client Code	Defined as a class	Defined as a class

The Client Application

The client application should perform the following steps to run the EJB:

1. Look up the Bean's home interface using the Java naming and directory interface.
2. Authenticate itself to the server.
3. Create the Bean's remote interface instance using the `create()` method of the Bean's home interface object.
4. Invoke the methods defined in the Bean's remote interface.
5. Destroy the Bean using the `remove()` method after it is no longer needed.

These steps are discussed in detail below.

Looking up the Bean's Home Interface

To do this, two things must be known, namely, the name of the object and the location of the name server. In case of EJB's, the name of the object is the EJB Home interface and this is located using JNDI. In case of Oracle 8i, JNDI serves as an interface to the `CosNaming` service. Initially, a JNDI `Context` object is retrieved using the JNDI methods and then a reference to the home interface is obtained. As regards to the JNDI `Context` object, the first `Context` object received is bound to the root naming context of the Oracle8i publishing context. The root naming context is obtained by creating a JNDI `InitialContext` as follows:

First create an environment Hash table using a Hash table constructor.

```
Hashtable env = new Hashtable();
```

Set the properties in the environment object:

```
env.put(javax.naming.Context.URL_PKG_PREFIXES, "oracle.aurora.jndi");
// This specifies the username to sess_iiop
```

```
env.put(Context.SECURITY_PRINCIPAL, "ORATEST");
// This specifies the password to sess_iiop
env.put(Context.SECURITY_CREDENTIALS, "ORATEST");
// This specifies the sess_iiop to use non-SSL login authentication
env.put(Context.SECURITY_AUTHENTICATION, ServiceCtx.NON_SSL_LOGIN);
```

Create an `InitialContext` object using the `InitialContext` constructor:

```
Context ictx = new InitialContext(env);
```

Once the context is obtained, the reference to the home object can be obtained by calling the `lookup()` method of the `Context`. To do this, the following must be known:

- The published full path name of the object
- The host system where the object is located
- The IIOP port for the listener on the system
- The database SID

The code for this looks as follows:

```
String serviceURL = "sess_iiop://training:2481:Oracle";
String objectName = "/test/MyBean";
MyBeanHome home = (MyBeanHome) ictx.lookup(serviceURL + objectName);
```

Here `objectName` is constructed as a concatenation of the default Oracle namespace name which is `/test`, with the Bean's class name.

Authenticate Itself to the Server

The client program cannot access an Oracle 8i database without first authenticating itself to the database server. Since the EJBs execute within Oracle 8i, the client must authenticate itself to the database server in order to invoke methods of the EJB. This authentication is done in two ways, namely, using a username and password over a non-SSL TCP/IP connection or over a SSL (Secure Socket Layer) connection. By default, when the typical installation of Oracle 8i is done, Oracle 8i provides a database configuration using non-SSL connection. The database initialization parameter mts_dispatchers (in the init.ora file) is set as follows:

```
mts_dispatchers="(protocol=tcp)(PRE=oracle.aurora.server.SGiopServer)"
```

A SSL is an authentication protocol used to send encrypted data over a connection, generally the Internet. It is implemented as a layer between the TCP/IP protocol and the client application.

Since a client logs onto the database, it must use either the non-SSL or SSL connection to authenticate itself to the server. In case of non-SSL, this is done by setting the `Context.SECURITY_AUTHENTICATION` property of the env environment variable to the value `ServiceCtx.NON_SSL_LOGIN`. By doing this, the client uses a non-SSL login to authenticate itself to the server. To specify an SSL connection, the above-mentioned parameter in init.ora should be set as follows:

mts_dispatchers="(protocol=tcps)(PRE=oracle.aurora.server.SGiopServer)"Also, the `Context.SECURITY_AUTHENTICATION` property of the env environment variable should be set to the value `ServiceCtx.SSL_LOGIN`. The other options for specifying an SSL connection are `ServiceCtx.SSL_CREDENTIAL` and `ServiceCtx.SSL_CLIENT_AUTH`. When using these options, all the data passing over is encrypted and the client authenticates using the standard SSL protocol.

Create the Bean's Remote Interface Instance Using the `create()` *Method of the Bean's Home Interface Object*

This done by invoking the `create()` method on the Bean's home interface object looked up in the previous step:

```
MyBean mybean = null;
mybean = home.create();
```

Activate the Methods Defined in the Bean's Remote Interface

Now that the remote interface instance has been obtained, the Bean methods defined in the remote interface and implemented in the Bean class can be activated on this instance. Here we assume `method1()` is one such method in the Bean class. The invocation is as follows:

```
mybean.method1();
```

Deploying an EJB

Once the interfaces, classes, and deployment descriptor for the EJB have been completed, the next step is to compile the code and package the class files into a `.jar` file. Compilation can be done using the `javac` command. Note that the two interfaces and the Bean class file have to be compiled.

After compilation, the EJB has to be packaged into a `.jar` file for deployment into the Oracle 8i server. This jar file should include all the classes including dependent classes for the EJB. The advantages of packaging individual class files into a jar file are twofold:

- The jar file serves as a container for all the components of the EJB, namely, the home interface, the remote interface, the Bean implementation, and the deployment descriptor. It is much easier to deploy a jar file rather than deploy several components independently.
- A jar file can be downloaded faster as the elements in a jar file are compressed.

Packaging can be done using the jar command as follows:

```
jar cf <jar-file-name>.jar *.class
```

Once these steps are done, the EJB has to be deployed into the Oracle 8i server. This is done by using the `deployejb` tool provided by Oracle 8i that loads and publishes the JARed Bean. The `deployejb` tool is a command-line utility and is provided as a batch file `deployejb.bat`. This is located in the `[Oracle Home]\bin` directory. To execute this batch file, the `PATH` environment variable must be set up to include the `[Oracle Home]\bin` directory.

SETUP TIPS

The `%JAVA_HOME%\bin` directory must be included in the PATH.

The packaged jar file must be included in the CLASSPATH for client execution.

The standard Java library archive must be included in the CLASSPATH.The Oracle 8i supplied jar files `aurora_client.jar` and `mts.jar` must be included in the CLASSPATH. `These are located in [Oracle Home]\lib directory.`

The class files `vbjapp.jar` and `vbjorb.jar` must be included in the CLASSPATH. `These are located in [Oracle Home]\lib directory.`

If using JDBC, the files `classes111.zip` or `classes12.zip` (as the case may be for JDBC 1.1 and 2.0 respectively), must be included in the CLASSPATH. `These are located in [Oracle Home]\jdbc\lib directory.`

Here `%JAVA_HOME%` refers to the Java Home directory on Windows. For UNIX, the variable `$JAVA_HOME` should be used instead of `%JAVA_HOME%`.

Executing the Client Program

The final step is to execute the client as follows:

```
java -classpath %CLASSPATH% client sess_iiop://training:2481:ORCL /test/MyBean
ORATEST ORATEST
```

The above command is Windows-based and works well when run from the command prompt. In a UNIX environment, the $CLASSPATH environment variable should be used instead of %CLASSPATH%.

Differences Between EJBs and JavaBeans

EJBs are a server-side component models. EJB Components can be created and deployed on a database server or an application server based on classes and interfaces provided in the `javax.ejb.*` packages. JavaBeans are also component model but are not server related. They just use the java.Beans package in the core Java API to build components that can be used generally by a visual environment or for a visual purpose. However JavaBeans can be designed for non-GUI purposes. Whatever the purpose, JavaBeans components are not deployed in any server. Both EJBs and JavaBeans provide APIs to build components that are tailored towards a specific functionality. Except for this difference, there is no other relation between the two technologies.

Table 8.2 summarizes the basic differences between JavaBeans and Enterprise JavaBeans.

Table 8.2 Differences Between JavaBeans and Enterprise JavaBeans

Enterprise JavaBeans	JavaBeans
A server-side component model	Not a server-side component model—generally used for developing client applications for GUI purposes.
Deployed in a database server or an application server	Not deployed
Use the `javax.ejb.*` packages	Use the `java.Beans.*` packages
Suited for inter-process components	Suited for intra-process components
Can model and manage distribute objects	Not suited for distributed applications
Governed by an EJB specification, namely, the EJB 1.1 and 1.0 specifications	JavaBeans specification exists—governed by special characteristics
Examples are Department, Person business objects	Examples are push-button GUI object

Advantages of EJBs

The advantages of EJBs are manifold. EJBs can be developed and deployed in multi-tier architectures and are quite easy to program. Oracle 8i offers EJBs as fast, scalable, secure, and easy-to-use components that can be deployed in the Oracle 8i JServer or Oracle 9i Application Server. The following is a list of advantages offered by EJBS:

- EJBs are easy to develop and use. Developers don't need to worry about low-level issues while developing the EJBs. The EJB Server automatically handles these. The issues of transaction management and security correspond to RDBMS transaction management and security. Also, the deployment tools such as `deployejb` make it easy to package and deploy EJBs in Oracle 8i.
- EJBS provide a declarative method of specifying transaction rules and security policies by means of the deployment descriptor. This can be done at deployment time rather than programmatically at development time. The EJB server automatically handles the start, commit, and rollback of transactions depending on the transaction attribute specified in the deployment descriptor.

- EJBs offer portability by making clients independent of server interfaces and classes. By means of client classes and client stubs, clients are independent of the EJB server implementation.
- EJBS offer customizability by means of the declarative way of defining attributes. These attributes can be changed as desired without modifying source code.
- EJBs are fast to execute in the Oracle 8i server. As standard Java applications they can benefit from the features of the Java VM to provide fast execution. Also, EJBs access persistent data in Oracle 8i via the embedded JDBC driver, SQL data access is very efficient from EJBs.
- EJBs can scale to 1000 concurrent users.
- EJBs deployed in Oracle 8i can take advantage of all the security features of the database as they are tightly integrated into the database. Oracle 8i implements the RunAs mechanism of the EJB 1.0 specification to provide a good access control method to invoke EJB methods by specific users.

Summary

This chapter outlined the use of Enterprise JavaBeans for component-based development in Java. Essentially, the concepts and architecture of EJBs were described in detail. An outline of deploying EJBs and an account of the client application for running EJBs was described. Finally, the difference between JavaBeans and EJBs and the advantages of EJBs was presented.

DEVELOPING AND DEPLOYING ENTERPRISE JAVABEANS

ESSENTIALS

- Implement a session EJB by creating the remote interface, the home interface, the Bean class, and the deployment descriptor.
- Use the packages javax.ejb.* and java.rmi.* to define the remote and home interfaces and the actual Bean class. Use XML to define the deployment descriptor. Use the `jar` utility to package all of these into a .jar file.
- Oracle8i provides an in-built EJB container in its JServer for deployment of EJBS.
- Deploy a session EJB into Oracle8i database by first writing an Oracle deployment descriptor file. The use the *deployejb* utility to deploy the EJB into the database.
- Write a client program as a JNDI application to access the deployed EJB from the database. Use the classes in the packages javax.naming.*, java.util.*, and oracle.aurora.jndi.*.
- Use JDBC in an EJB component to implement an entity EJB with Bean-managed persistence by creating the remote interface, home interface, the primary key, and the actual Bean class. Write the extra method for locating by means of the Primary Key.

This chapter explains the use of Enterprise JavaBeans (EJB) for creating and deploying reusable Java components. The chapter also discusses Enterprise JavaBeans as a development model particular to Oracle8i JServer, including details about implementing Session and Entity Beans.

Overview

The architecture of EJBs was presented in Chapter 8, "Using Enterprise JavaBeans—Architecture and Concepts," along with details of the EJB Component. This chapter presents the implementation details of EJBs and describes how the EJB can be developed and deployed in Oracle8i. The EJB Server and EJB Container are provided in the Oracle8i JServer and the functions to be performed by these are automatically taken care of by the JServer. The role of the developer is to provide the EJB Component and perform the deployment steps.

Developing EJBs

Developing an EJB consists in developing the EJB Component. Specifically, the EJB Component consists of

- The remote interface
- The home interface
- The Bean class
- The deployment descriptor

Implementing an EJB

We will implement a `Person` Session Bean. The following are the steps involved:

1. Define a remote interface for the Bean. This interface is named `Person`.
2. Define a home interface for the Bean. This interface is named `PersonHome`.
3. Define the actual Bean class. This class implements `javax.ejb.SessionBean` class. This is a class named `PersonBean` and defined in a file named `Personbean.java`.

   There is no specific reason for the above naming. It is just a convention that is followed. The EJB specification does not put any restrictions on the names of the Home Interface, Remote Interface or the Bean class.
4. Define the deployment descriptor.

TIP:

Set the environment variables as follows:

JAVA_HOME to include the location where the JDK is installed

CLASSPATH to include

- `tools.jar` and `dt.jar` for JDK 1.2 and `%JAVA_HOME%\lib\classes.zip` for JDK 1.1
- the Oracle8i supplied JAR files, `aurora_client.jar` and `mts.jar`. `These are located in` [Oracle Home]\lib `directory`.
- the class files `vbjapp.jar` and `vbjorb.jar`. `These are located in` [Oracle Home]\lib `directory`.
- If using JDBC, the `classes111.zip` for JDBC 1.0 support and `classes12.zip` for JDBC 2.0 support. These are located in `[Oracle Home]\jdbc\lib` directory.
- If using SSL, then

  `javax-ssl-1_1.jar` and `jssl-1_1.jar` for SSL 1.1 support or

  `javax-ssl-1_2.jar` and `jssl-1_2.jar` for SSL 1.2 support. These files are located in `[Oracle Home]\jlib` directory.
- PATH to include `%JAVA_HOME%\bin`

The Remote Interface

As mentioned in Chapter 8, the remote interface defines methods that are callable by a client. This interface is named `Person` and defined in a file named `Person.java`. This interface extends `javax.ejb.EJBObject`. The code for the `Person` remote interface is as follows:

```
package personp;
import javax.ejb.* ;
import java.rmi.Remote ;
import java.rmi.RemoteException ;
public interface Person extends Remote, EJBObject {
    public String getName()  throws RemoteException ;
    public int  getAge()  throws RemoteException ;
}
```

It provides for the definition of two methods, namely, `getname()` and `getAge()` for a person.

The Home Interface

The home interface specifies how an EJB can be created, located, and destroyed. This interface is named `PersonHome` and defined in a file named `PersonHome.java`. This interface extends `javax.ejb.EJBHome`. A `create()` method that returns a `Person` type is defined here.

A corresponding `ejbCreate()` method is defined in the actual Bean class, as we will see later. The code for the `PersonHome` home interface is as follows:

```
package personp;

import javax.ejb.* ;
import java.rmi.RemoteException ;
import java.util.Hashtable ;
public interface PersonHome extends EJBHome {

    public Person create() throws RemoteException, CreateException ;
  }
```

Here `create()` is a Bean life-cycle method that creates `Person` Beans. There is no need to define the `remove()` method. It is inherited from the `javax.ejb.EJBHome` interface.

The home interface and remote interface define the client-side API for creating and using the `Person` Bean.

The Actual Bean Class

The actual Bean class is an implementation of the `Person` Bean on the server side. It provides an implementation of

- The `ejbCreate()` method corresponding to the `create()` method defined in the home interface `PersonHome`.
- The callback methods, `ejbActivate()`, `ejbPassivate()`, and `ejbRemove()`.
- The remote interface methods. For the `Person` Bean, these are `getName()` and `getAge()` methods.

When a client calls the `create()` method on the home interface, this triggers the container to call the `ejbCreate()` method with the same signature on the Bean instance class.

The actual Bean class is named as `PersonBean` class and defined in a file named `PersonBean.java`. The complete code for the actual Bean class is shown below:

```
package personp;

import javax.ejb.* ;
import java.rmi.RemoteException ;

public class PersonBean implements  SessionBean {
```

```
    private SessionContext mContext = null ;

    public void setSessionContext(SessionContext context)
    {
        mContext = context ;
        System.out.println("PersonBean context set") ;
    }

    public void ejbCreate()
    {
        System.out.println("PersonBean Created") ;
    }

    public void ejbActivate()
    {
        System.out.println("PersonBean Activated") ;
    }

    public void ejbPassivate()
    {
        System.out.println("PersonBean Passivated") ;
    }

    public void ejbRemove()
    {
        System.out.println("PersonBean Removed") ;
    }

    public String getName() throws RemoteException
    {
       String str = new String("aName") ;
       return str ;
    }

    public int getAge() throws RemoteException
    {
      return 99 ;
    }
}
```

The `ejbCreate()` method and the callback methods return `void`. The remote interface implementation methods return `String` and `int` respectively following their signatures defined in the remote interface. It is not mandatory for the methods `getName()` and `getAge()` to throw `RemoteException`. The `setSessionContext()` sets the session context of the Session Bean instance.

The Deployment Descriptor

The deployment descriptor provides the property file for the EJB and is used by the EJB container to handle transaction and other run-time behavior. The EJB 1.1 specification defines an XML format for writing the deployment descriptor. The complete XML descriptor for the `Person` EJB is defined as shown below (in a file named `person.xml`).

```
<?xml version="1.0"?>
<!DOCTYPE ejb-jar PUBLIC "-//Sun Microsystems Inc.//DTD Enterprise JavaBeans 1.1
//EN" "ejb-jar.dtd">
<ejb-jar>
  <enterprise-Beans>
    <session>
      <description>Session Bean Person Example</description>
      <ejb-name>PersonEjb</ejb-name>
      <home>personp.PersonHome</home>
      <remote>personp.Person</remote>
      <ejb-class>personp.PersonBean</ejb-class>
      <session-type>Stateless</session-type>
      <transaction-type>Container</transaction-type>
    </session>
  </enterprise-Beans>
  <assembly-descriptor>
    <security-role>
      <description>Public</description>
      <role-name>PUBLIC</role-name>
    </security-role>
    <method-permission>
      <description>public methods</description>
      <role-name>PUBLIC</role-name>
      <method>
        <ejb-name>PersonEjb</ejb-name>
        <method-name>*</method-name>
      </method>
    </method-permission>
    <container-transaction>
      <description>no description</description>
      <method>
        <ejb-name>PersonEjb</ejb-name>
```

```
        <method-name>*</method-name>
      </method>
      <trans-attribute>Supports</trans-attribute>
    </container-transaction>
  </assembly-descriptor>
</ejb-jar>
```

This XML descriptor contains the following parts:

XML Version Number

```
<?xml version="1.0"?>
```

DTD Filename

```
<!DOCTYPE ejb-jar PUBLIC "-//Sun Microsystems Inc.//DTD Enterprise JavaBeans 1.1
//EN" "ejb-jar.dtd">
```

`ejb-jar` Element

This is the first element that is to be defined in the XML descriptor. This element has two sections: the `<enterprise-beans>` section and `<assembly-descriptor>` section. The former section contains definitions about the EJB, either Session or entity. The latter pertains to application description and is used to specify transaction and security attributes.

```
<ejb-jar> //Start of ejb-jar elemnent
  <enterprise-beans> //Start of the enterprise beans element
    ... //Home Interface, Remote Interface and bean class  definition
  </enterprise-beans>
  <assembly-descriptor> //Application Descriptor section
    ... //Transaction and security attributes
  </assembly-descriptor>
</ejb-jar>
```

Enterprise JavaBeans Element

Here the home and remote interfaces and the Bean class are specified. This element also specifies the type of Bean (Entity or Session) and the subtype of the Bean type—namely, Stateful or Stateless in case of a Session Bean, and Container or Bean managed in case of Entity Bean. For the `Person` Session Bean, this is shown below.

```
  <enterprise-beans>
    <session>
      <description>Session Bean Person Example</description>
      <ejb-name>PersonEjb</ejb-name>
```

```
      <home>personp.PersonHome</home>
      <remote>personp.Person</remote>
      <ejb-class>personp.PersonBean</ejb-class>
      <session-type>Stateless</session-type>
      <transaction-type>Container</transaction-type>
    </session>
  </enterprise-beans>
```

<session> describes that the Bean is a Session Bean. PersonEjb within the <ejb-name> element specifies the logical name of the Bean. This can be a true JNDI name or a logical name (as shown above) for the EJB. In the case of a logical name, it should be mapped to a true JNDI name using an Oracle descriptor map file. <home>, <remote>, and <ejb-class> refer to the home interface, remote interface, and actual Bean class for the Person Bean. <session-type> specifies that the Session Bean is a Stateless Session Bean. <transaction-type> states that the transaction is managed by the container and not by the Bean.

Assembly Descriptor Element

This describes the security and transaction attributes for the EJB. Security is defined by the <security-role> element. This defines roles used in the application. These roles are assigned to specific methods within the Bean and specified within the <method-permission> element. This is shown below:

```
<assembly-descriptor>
  <security-role>
    <description>Public</description>
    <role-name>PUBLIC</role-name>
  </security-role>
  <method-permission>
    <description>public methods</description>
    <role-name>PUBLIC</role-name>
    <method>
      <ejb-name>PersonEjb</ejb-name>
      <method-name>*</method-name>
    </method>
  </method-permission>
```

Here it specifies that all methods of the Person Bean are to be accessed within the PUBLIC role.

The transaction settings are defined by the <container-transaction> element. The type of transaction support for each method is declared within this element. For the Person Bean this is shown here:

```
  <container-transaction>
    <description>no description</description>
```

```
    <method>
      <ejb-name>PedrsonEjb</ejb-name>
      <method-name>*</method-name>
    </method>
    <trans-attribute>Supports</trans-attribute>
  </container-transaction>
</assembly-descriptor>
```

Deploying the EJB Class to the EJB Server

Once the remote interface, home interface, and Bean class have been defined for an EJB, the EJB is ready to be deployed in Oracle8i JServer. The following steps are required for deployment:

1. Compile the code for the Bean and package the classes into a JAR file. This JAR file includes the remote interface, home interface, and Bean classes along with any dependent classes. To compile the code for the `Person` EJB, use the following command:

   ```
   javac Person.java PersonHome.java PersonBean.java
   ```

   To package the obtained classes into the JAR file, use the following command(from within the `personp` subdirectory):

   ```
   jar cvf pers.jar *.class
   ```

2. Define the XML deployment descriptor for the EJB. This is typically the `Person.XML` file described above for a Session Bean.

3. Define the Oracle Mapping deployment descriptor file. This is required only if you used a logical name in the deployment descriptor file in step 2. For example, substitute the `/test/MyBean` with a logical name, say `PersonEjb`. Then the Oracle deployment mapping file looks something like the following:

   ```
   <?xml version="1.0"?>
   <!DOCTYPE oracle-descriptor PUBLIC "-//Oracle Corporation.//DTD Oracle
   1.1//EN" "oracle-ejb-jar.dtd">
   <oracle-descriptor>
     <mappings>
       <ejb-mapping>
         <ejb-name>PersonEjb</ejb-name>
         <jndi-name>/test/MyBean</jndi-name>
       </ejb-mapping>
     </mappings>
     <run-as>
       <description>no description</description>
   ```

```
        <mode>CLIENT_IDENTITY</mode>
        <method>
          <ejb-name>MyBean</ejb-name>
          <method-name>*</method-name>
        </method>
      </run-as>
    </oracle-descriptor>
```

4. Invoke the `deployejb` tool provided by Oracle8i. This tool has the following functions:
   - Reads and verifies the deployment descriptor.
   - Performs a mapping of the logical EJB names to the true JNDI names.
   - Reads the jar file and loads the Interfaces and classes defined in the EJB jar file (`pers.jar` in our example) into the Oracle8i database.
   - Generates the EJBHome and EJBObject classes in the database server.
   - Generates the client-side and server-side stub classes and any other classes as required by the EJB server and container. It generates a second jar file to store these stub classes. A filename can be specified for this jar file using the `-generated` option of the `deployejb` command. The default name for this is the packaged jar file name (created in step 1 of the deployment process) suffixed by `_generated`.
   - Publishes the home interface.

We will deploy the `Person` ejb into Oracle8i as follows (this command is issued from the `personp` subdirectory):

```
deployejb -user ORATEST -password ORATEST -service
sess_iiop://training:2481:Oracle -descriptor person.xml -oracledescriptor ora-
cle_person.xml -temp c:\tmp -generated persClient.jar pers.jar
```

The output from the `deployejb` command is as follows:

```
Reading Deployment Descriptor...done
Verifying Deployment Descriptor...done
Gathering users...done
Generating Comm Stubs.......................................done
Compiling Stubs...done
Generating Jar File...done
Loading EJB Jar file and Comm Stubs Jar file...done
Generating EJBHome and EJBObject on the server...done
Publishing EJBHome...done
```

This generates a file named `persClient.jar`. The next step is to write a client program that uses the `Person` EJB. This is described in the next section.

SETUP TIP

Both the *pers.jar* and *persClient.jar* files (generated by `deployejb`) must be included in the classpath. This is for the client program to execute.

The Client Application—A Java Applet or a JNDI Application

Now that the `Person` EJB is deployed in the database, a client program has to be defined to use the `Person` EJB. This client program can be a Java applet, a Servlet, a stand-alone Java program (i.e., an application), or a Java Server Page (JSP). For the purposes of this chapter we define a stand-alone Java program that uses the `Person` EJB. This client program is defined in the class `PersonClient`, which in turn is defined in the file named `PersonClient.java`. The `PersonClient` class must perform the following steps (as defined in Chapter 8):

1. Locate a reference to the `PersonHome` home interface.
2. Authenticate itself to the EJB server.
3. Instantiate a remote interface object of the `Person` EJB using the home reference obtained above.
4. Invoke the EJB remote interface methods on the above remote interface object.

The `PersonClient` class is shown below:

```
package personp;

import javax.ejb.* ;
import javax.naming.* ;
import java.rmi.* ;
import java.util.Hashtable;
import oracle.aurora.jndi.sess_iiop.ServiceCtx;

public class PersonClient {

  public static void main(String[] args) {
      try {
        Hashtable env = new Hashtable();
        env.put(javax.naming.Context.URL_PKG_PREFIXES, "oracle.aurora.jndi");
        env.put(Context.SECURITY_PRINCIPAL, "oratest");
        env.put(Context.SECURITY_CREDENTIALS, "oratest");
        env.put(Context.SECURITY_AUTHENTICATION, ServiceCtx.NON_SSL_LOGIN);
```

```
        Context ictx = new InitialContext(env);
        String serviceURL = "sess_iiop://training:2481:Oracle";
        String objectName = "/test/MyBean";
        PersonHome pHome = (PersonHome) ictx.lookup(serviceURL + objectName);

    Person person = pHome.create() ;

    String name = person.getName() ;
    int     age  = person.getAge() ;

    System.out.println("Name from Bean: " + name) ;
    System.out.println("\nAge from Bean: " + age) ;

      }
      catch(Exception e)
      {
     System.out.println("Error while creating/using person.") ;
      }
    }
  }
```

This example performs the following functions:

1. Import the required classes. The following classes are imported:

   - `java.naming.*` class—To make available the `Context` and `InitialContext` classes. The `InitialContext` is needed to look up the Bean's home interface.

     ```
     import javax.naming.* ;
     ```

   - `ServiceCtx` class—To set up the Security Authentication needed for the database connection. This is an Oracle class that extends the JNDI `Context` class.

     ```
     import oracle.aurora.jndi.sess_iiop.ServiceCtx;
     ```

   For this class to work, set the CLASSPATH environment variable to include the JAR files aurora_client.jar and mts.jar.

   - `java.util.Hashtable`—to create a `Hashtable` instance that stores the security environment properties of the Bean.

     ```
     import java.util.Hashtable;
     ```

2. Declares a class called `PersonClient`.

   ```
   public class PersonClient {
   ```

3. Creates a `Hashtable` instance and stores the environment properties that pertain to the security of the Bean.

   ```
   Hashtable env = new Hashtable();
   env.put(javax.naming.Context.URL_PKG_PREFIXES, "oracle.aurora.jndi");
   env.put(Context.SECURITY_PRINCIPAL, "oratest");
   env.put(Context.SECURITY_CREDENTIALS, "oratest");
   env.put(Context.SECURITY_AUTHENTICATION, ServiceCtx.NON_SSL_LOGIN);
   ```

4. Creates a `Context` object as an instance of the `InitialContext` class.

   ```
   Context ictx = new InitialContext(env);
   ```

5. Obtains a reference to the `PersonHome` home interface of the Bean via the `lookup()` method.

   ```
   String serviceURL = "sess_iiop://training:2481:Oracle";
   String objectName = "/test/MyBean";
   PersonHome pHome = (PersonHome) ictx.lookup(serviceURL + objectName);
   ```

6. Obtains an instance of the remote interface using the `create()` method of the `PersonHome` home interface.

   ```
   Person person = pHome.create() ;
   ```

7. Invokes the `getName()` and `getAge()` Bean methods on the above created remote interface instance.

   ```
   String name = person.getName() ;
   int    age  = person.get'Age() ;
   ```

TIP

The actual Bean class, namely, `PersonBean` is not used by the client program. The client communicates with the EJB using the Remote and home interfaces only.

Compiling and Executing the Client

Once the client program is complete, the next step to compile the client program. This can be done using the standard java compiler command `javac` as shown below:

```
javac -classpath  %CLASSPATH% PersonClient.java
```

The above command is for Windows environments that use the %CLASPATH% environment variable, when used from the command line. When run in an UNIX environment, use the $CLASSPATH environment variable instead of %CLASSPATH%.

The final step in the EJB development and deployment process is to run the client. This is done as shown below (this command is issued from the parent directory of the `personp` subdirectory).

```
java -classpath %CLASSPATH% personp/PersonClient
sess_iiop://training:2481:Oracle /test/MyBean ORATEST ORATEST
```

Here `personp/PersonClient` is the name of the client class, sess_iiop://training:2481:ORCL is the session service URL with the server specified as training, the port as 2481 and Oracle representing the tnsnames alias; and /test/MyBean is the published EJB name. The schema username and password are both ORATEST. The output of the above command is as follows:

```
Name from Bean: aName
Age from Bean: 99
```

Parameter Passing

Parameter passing comes into picture when programming the client class that invokes EJB methods. The following points are relevant to parameter passing:

- A parameter passed to a Bean method or the return value of a Bean method must be a serializable Java type.
- In case of complex non-remote objects, any object that implements the `java.io.Serializable` interface can be passed. The corresponding class is to be declared as `public`.
- Parameter passing uses call by value in case of non-remote objects. This means that if the parameter value is changed inside a Bean method, the change is not reflected to the client program.
- In case of remote objects, the stub for the remote object is passed.

Using JDBC and SQLJ in an EJB Component

Using JDBC and SQLJ in an EJB component uses the database server-side JDBC internal driver. The JDBC connection is obtained from the default connection of the database session in which the JVM was invoked. For the purposes of this chapter we will demonstrate the implementation of a Bean-managed Entity Bean that uses JDBC for performing DML on the `DEPT` table. Using SQLJ is similar to using JDBC except that SQLJ statements in the actual Bean class replace JDBC statements. The home interface and remote interface remain the same. However, the SQLJ implementation calls for defining SQLJ iterators.

TIP

When using JDBC or SQLJ in an EJB component, an explicit commit or rollback should not be specified. The EJB Container commits or rolls backs the transaction according to the transaction attribute value specified in the deployment descriptor.

When using JDBC or SQLJ in an EJB component, the default Oracle connection should not be closed even if all the JDBC calls or SQLJ statements have been executed.

The steps for implementing our `Department` EJB are as follows:

1. Create a directory named `DeptBeanManaged` to include the home interface, remote interface, Bean class, and client program as part of a package named `DeptBeanManaged`. Then, set the classpath to include this directory.
2. Define the remote interface named `Department` (defined in the file `Department.java`). The code for this is shown below.

```
package DeptBeanManaged;

import java.rmi.RemoteException;
import javax.ejb.EJBObject;

public interface Department extends EJBObject {

  /**
     sets the name of the department
   */
  public void setDeptName(String deptName)
    throws RemoteException;

  /**
   sets the location of the department
   */
  public void setDeptLocation(String deptLocation)
    throws RemoteException;

  /**
    return the name of the department
   */
  public String getDeptName()
```

```
        throws RemoteException;

  /**
        return the location of the department
      */
    public String getDeptLoc()
        throws RemoteException;
  }
```

3. Define the home interface named `DepartmentHome` (defined in the file `DepartmentHome.java`). The code for this is shown below.

```
package DeptBeanManaged;

import javax.ejb.CreateException;
import javax.ejb.EJBHome;
import javax.ejb.FinderException;
import java.rmi.RemoteException;

public interface DepartmentHome extends EJBHome {

public Department create(Integer deptNo, String deptName, String deptLoc)
    throws CreateException, RemoteException;

  public Department findByPrimaryKey(Integer deptNo)
    throws FinderException, RemoteException;

 }
```

4. Define the actual Bean class named `DepartmentBean` (defined in the file `DepartmentBean.java`). This Bean class has the following methods implemented in it:
   - An empty constructor `DepartmentBean()` for the container to create the Bean instance.
   - An `ejbCreate()` method matching the signature of the `create()` method in the home interface. This implements the `INSERT` operation.
   - An `ejbPostCreate()` method.
   - `ejbActivate()` and `ejbPassivate()` methods.
   - An `ejbLoad()` method to implement the `SELECT` operation and an `ejbStore()` method to implement the `UPDATE` operation.
   - An `ejbRemove()` method to implement the `DELETE` operation.

- An ejbFindByPrimaryKey() method corresponding to the findByPrimaryKey() defined in the home interface. This method locates the department name and its location based on the primary key deptNo.
- setEntityContext() and unsetEntityContext() methods to set and unset the Entity Context.

TIP

In case of Bean-managed Entity Beans, the ejbCreate() must implement the INSERT operation into the database. Also, this method must return the datatype of the primary key of the Bean. In case of container-managed Entity Beans, the ejbCreate() just initializes a few fields and returns void.

In case of Bean-managed Entity Beans, the Bean class must implement the ejbLoad() and ejbStore() methods to perform SELECTs to ensure that the Bean always represents most current data and UPDATEs directly into the database. In case of container-managed Entity Beans, the container takes care of this synchronization.

In case of Bean-managed Entity Beans, the Bean class must manage the deletion of an entity from the database using the ejbRemove() method. In case of container-managed Beans this is taken care of by the container and only an empty definition of the ejbRemove() method is included in the Bean class.

In case of Bean-managed Entity Beans, the implementation of the find methods in the home interface must be done in the actual Bean class. For this an ejbFindByPrimaryKey() has to be defined in the Bean class that locates the matching record in the database. In case of container-managed persistence, this method is left empty in the Bean class.

With all these methods in place, the DepartmentBean class looks as shown here:

```
package DeptBeanManaged;

import java.io.Serializable;
import java.sql.*;
import oracle.sql.*;
import oracle.jdbc.driver.*;

import javax.ejb.*;
import javax.naming.*;
import java.rmi.*;

public class DepartmentBean implements EntityBean {

  private EntityContext ctx;
  private int deptNo; // This is the primary Key
  private String deptName ;
  private String deptLoc ;
```

```
// Empty constructor for the container to create the Bean instance

public void DepartmentBean() { }

public void setEntityContext(EntityContext ctx) {
    System.out.println("setEntityContext called");
    this.ctx = ctx;
  }

public void unsetEntityContext() {
    System.out.println("unsetEntityContext called");
    this.ctx = null;
  }

public void ejbActivate() {
    System.out.println("ejbActivate called");
  }

public void ejbPassivate() {
    System.out.println("ejbPassivate called");
  }

  public void ejbLoad() throws RemoteException {

    Connection conn = null;
    PreparedStatement pstmt = null;
    ResultSet rset = null;
    deptNo =(int) Integer.parseInt((String) ctx.getPrimaryKey());
    try {
      conn = getConnection();
      pstmt  = conn.prepareStatement("select dname, loc from dept where
deptNo = ?");
      pstmt.setInt(1, deptNo);
      rset = pstmt.executeQuery();
      if (rset.next()) {
        deptName = rset.getString(1);
        deptLoc = rset.getString(2) ;
      } else {
        String error = "ejbLoad: Department (" + deptNo + ") not found";
        System.out.println(error);
        throw new NoSuchEntityException (error);
       }
```

```
    } catch (SQLException e) {
      try {
      System.out.println("SQLException: " + e);
      throw new EJBException;
      } catch (EJBException ee) {System.out.println(ee);}

    } catch (NoSuchEntityException e) {System.out.println; }
      finally {
        try {
        if (rset != null) rset.close();
        if (pstmt != null) pstmt.close();
        } catch (SQLException e) {}
    }
  }

  public void ejbStore() throws RemoteException {

    Connection conn = null;
    PreparedStatement pstmt = null;

    try {
      conn = getConnection();
      pstmt = conn.prepareStatement("update dept set dname = ?, loc = ?
where deptNo = ?");
      pstmt.setString(1, deptName);
      pstmt.setString(2, deptLoc);
      pstmt.setInt(3, deptNo) ;
      if (!(pstmt.executeUpdate() > 0)) {
        String error = "ejbStore: Deptartment (" + deptNo + ") not
updated";
        System.out.println(error);
        throw new NoSuchEntityException (error);
      }
    } catch(SQLException e) {
      try {
      System.out.println("SQLException: " + e);
      throw new EJBException ;
      } catch (EJBException ee) {System.out.println(ee);}
    } catch (NoSuchEntityException e) {System.out.println ;}
      finally {
        try {
        if (pstmt != null) pstmt.close();
```

```
            } catch (SQLException e) {System.out.println ;}
    }
   }


public Integer ejbCreate(Integer deptNo, String deptName, String deptLoc)
      throws CreateException, RemoteException
{
    this.deptNo = deptNo.intValue();
    this.deptName = deptName;
    this.deptLoc = deptLoc ;

    Connection conn = null;
    PreparedStatement pstmt = null;
    try {
      conn = getConnection();
      pstmt = conn.prepareStatement("insert into dept (deptNo, dname, loc)
values (?, ?, ?)");
      pstmt.setInt(1, deptNo.intValue());
      pstmt.setString(2, deptName);
      pstmt.setString(3, deptLoc) ;
      int retval = pstmt.executeUpdate();
      if (retval != 1) {
        String error = "No Department row created";
        System.out.println(error);
        throw new CreateException (error);
      }
      else
      {
        System.out.println("Department created:");
      }
    } catch (SQLException e) {
            System.out.println("SQLException: " + e);
      try {
      System.out.println("SQLException: " + e);
      throw new EJBException ;
      } catch (EJBException ee) {System.out.println(ee);}
    } finally {
         try {
        if (pstmt != null) pstmt.close();
         } catch (SQLException e) {System.out.println; }
```

```
    }
    return (deptNo);
  }

public void ejbPostCreate(Integer deptNo, String deptName, String deptLoc)
{
    System.out.println("ejbPostCreate called");
  }

  public void ejbRemove() throws RemoteException {

    Connection conn = null;
    PreparedStatement pstmt = null;

    try {
      conn = getConnection();
      deptNo = (int) Integer.parseInt((String) ctx.getPrimaryKey());
      pstmt = conn.prepareStatement("delete from dept where deptNo = ?");
      pstmt.setInt(1, deptNo);
      if (!(pstmt.executeUpdate() > 0)) {
        String error = "DepartmentBean (" + deptNo + " not found";
        System.out.println(error);
        throw new NoSuchEntityException (error);
      }
    } catch (SQLException e) {
      try {
      System.out.println("SQLException:  " + e);
      throw new EJBException ;
      } catch (EJBException ee) {System.out.println(ee);}
    } catch (NoSuchEntityException e) {System.out.println;}
      finally {
         try {
         if (pstmt != null) pstmt.close();
           } catch (SQLException e) {System.out.println;}
    }
  }

  public Integer ejbFindByPrimaryKey(Integer pk)
       throws FinderException, RemoteException
  {
     System.out.println("ejbFindByPrimaryKey (" + pk + ")");
```

```
      Connection conn = null;
      PreparedStatement pstmt = null;
      ResultSet rset = null;

      try {
        conn = getConnection();
        pstmt  = conn.prepareStatement("select dname, loc from dept where
 deptNo = ?");
        pstmt.setInt(1, pk.intValue());
        rset = pstmt.executeQuery();
        if (rset.next()) {
          deptName = rset.getString(1);
          deptLoc = rset.getString(2) ;
          System.out.println("ejbFindByPrimaryKey (" + pk + ") found");
        } else {
          String error = "ejbFindByPrimaryKey: Department (" + pk + ") not
found";
          System.out.println(error);
          throw new FinderException(error);
         }
     } catch (SQLException e) {
         try {
        System.out.println("SQLException:  " + e);
        throw new EJBException ;
          } catch (EJBException ee) {System.out.println(ee);}
     } catch (FinderException f) {System.out.println("Non-existent Dept:" +
f);}
       finally {
         try {
         if (rset != null) rset.close();
         if (pstmt != null) pstmt.close();
        } catch (SQLException e) {System.out.println("SQLException:  " +
e);}
     }

     return (pk);
   }

public void setDeptName(String deptName)
    throws RemoteException
{
    this.deptName = deptName ;
```

```
}

public void setDeptLocation(String deptLoc)
    throws RemoteException
 {
     this.deptLoc = deptLoc ;
 }
  /**
    Return the name of the department
   */
  public String getDeptName()
    throws RemoteException
    {
        return deptName ;
    }
  /**
    Return the location of the department
   */
  public String getDeptLoc()
    throws RemoteException
    {
        return deptLoc ;
    }


 private Connection getConnection()
     throws SQLException
   {
     try {
             Connection conn = new OracleDriver().defaultConnection();
             return conn;

      } catch (SQLException e) { System.out.println("Error getting
 Connection: " + e); return null;}
   }

 }
```

5. Define the deployment descriptor:

```
<?xml version="1.0"?>
<!DOCTYPE ejb-jar PUBLIC "-//Sun Microsystems Inc.//DTD Enterprise
JavaBeans 1.1
```

```
//EN" "ejb-jar.dtd">
<ejb-jar>
  <enterprise-Beans>
    <entity>
      <description>no description</description>
      <ejb-name>DeptEjb</ejb-name>
      <home>DeptBeanManaged.DepartmentHome</home>
      <remote>DeptBeanManaged.Department</remote>
      <ejb-class>DeptBeanManaged.DepartmentBean</ejb-class>
      <persistence-type>Bean</persistence-type>
      <prim-key-class>java.lang.Integer</prim-key-class>
      <reentrant>False</reentrant>
    </entity>
  </enterprise-Beans>
  <assembly-descriptor>
    <security-role>
      <description>no description</description>
      <role-name>PUBLIC</role-name>
    </security-role>
    <method-permission>
      <description>no description</description>
      <role-name>PUBLIC</role-name>
      <method>
        <ejb-name>DeptEjb</ejb-name>
        <method-name>*</method-name>
      </method>
    </method-permission>
    <container-transaction>
      <description>no description</description>
      <method>
        <ejb-name>DeptEjb</ejb-name>
        <method-name>*</method-name>
      </method>
      <trans-attribute>Required</trans-attribute>
    </container-transaction>
  </assembly-descriptor>
</ejb-jar>
```

6. Define the Oracle deployment descriptor:

```
<?xml version="1.0"?>
<!DOCTYPE oracle-descriptor PUBLIC "-//Oracle Corporation.//DTD Oracle
1.1//EN"
```

```
"oracle-ejb-jar.dtd">
<oracle-descriptor>
<mappings>
<ejb-mapping>
<ejb-name>DeptEjb</ejb-name>
<jndi-name>/test/DeptBean</jndi-name>
</ejb-mapping>
</mappings>
<run-as>
<description>no description</description>
<mode>CLIENT_IDENTITY</mode>
<method>
<ejb-name>DeptEjb</ejb-name>
<method-name>*</method-name>
</method>
</run-as>
</oracle-descriptor>
```

Once the interface classes, the Bean class, and the deployment descriptor are defined, the next step is to create the jar file containing these classes. This can be done as follows:

```
jar cvf dept.jar *.class
```

Once this is done, the `Department` EJB is ready to be deployed.

Handling Transactions

A transaction is a logical unit of work and is a collection of subtasks. A transaction is executed as a single operation and the success of the entire transaction comprises in the success of all the individual subtasks. The failure of any one subtask means that all the changes done by all subtasks are undone and the transaction is said to be *rolled back*. From an EJB perspective, subtasks are implemented as Bean methods and the transaction as a whole is the combination of every Bean method invoked. Each and every Bean involved in a transaction defines the scope of the transaction. A transaction is characterized by four properties called ACID properties, namely, Atomic, Consistent, Isolated, and Durable. These are defined briefly as follows:

- **Atomic**—This means that a transaction is either a total success or a failure. What this means is that every subtask comprising a transaction is a success and the transaction gets committed. If any subtask fails, the transaction is a failure and is rolled back.
- **Consistent**—The transaction must adhere to the integrity of the underlying database and changes made during the transaction do not affect this integrity resulting in inconsistent data.

- **Isolated**—The transaction executes independent of other transactions and the data changes during this transaction are not visible outside the scope of the transaction.
- **Durable**—The data changes taking place during a transaction must be committed and stored in a permanent manner before the transaction is completely executed or all the changes are rolled back.

Transactions in Oracle8i comply with the ACID properties. Oracle8i uses the Java Transaction API (JTA) for managing transactions in EJBS. Transactions can be handled either by the Bean or by the container. In case of the former, the transaction is explicitly demarcated—that is, started and stopped and the latter type is implicitly demarcated by specifying in the deployment descriptor. In other words, Oracle8i offers two ways of transaction management: first, implicit transaction demarcation by means of container-management and, second, explicit demarcation either managed by the Bean or client-demarcated. When specifying explicit management, the demarcation can be on the client-side or the server-side. For implicit demarcation, the demarcation is on the server-side.

EJBs support declarative transactional management by means of setting attributes in a deployment descriptor. These attributes can be set either at the Bean level or at the individual method level. When specified at the method level, these attributes override those specified at the Bean level. These attributes are as follows:

```
TX_NOT_SUPPORTED
TX_SUPPORTS
TX_REQUIRED
TX_REQUIRES_NEW
TX_MANDATORY
TX_BEAN_MANAGED
```

Managing transactions implicitly by specifying transactional attributes is more efficient and easier than explicitly managing them.

Table 9.1 describes these attributes in detail.

Table 9.1 EJB Transaction Attributes

Attribute	Description
TX_NOT_SUPPORTED	This postpones the client transaction execution until the Bean method has completed execution.
TX_SUPPORTS	This includes the Bean or its methods as part of the client's transaction.
TX_REQUIRED	This includes the Bean method within the client's transaction if one exists. If not, it starts a new transaction and commits the transaction once the Bean method has completed execution.

Table 9.1 Continued

Attribute	Description
TX_REQUIRES_NEW	This starts a new transaction before invoking a Bean's method irrespective of whether there exists a client's transaction or not. The transaction is committed on the completion of the Bean method. If a client transaction already exists, it is suspended until the Bean's method is executed, and then it resumes execution.
TX_MANDATORY	This mandates that the Bean be included as part of a client's transaction. If no such client transaction exists, the Bean method execution fails, throwing a `javax.transaction.TransactionRequired` exception.
TX_BEAN_MANAGED	This provides for explicit transaction demarcation using the JTA.

TX_BEAN_MANAGED

All the attributes other than TX_BEAN_MANAGED when specified provide for implicit transaction management—that is, container-managed.

In case of implicit transactional attributes, different methods of the same Bean can declare different attributes.

In case of TX_BEAN_MANAGED, all methods of the same Bean must specify TX_BEAN_MANAGED only.

We will first discuss Container Managed method of managing Transactions. The steps involved are as follows:

1. Specify the <transaction-type> element as Container in the deployment descriptor.
2. Specify the <trans-attribute> element as one of the transactional attributes other than TX_BEAN_MANAGED. This should be specified within the <container-transaction> element in the deployment descriptor.

ENTITY BEANS

Entity Beans can specify only container-managed transactions. Session Beans can specify either Bean-managed or container-managed transactions.

For the `Person` Session Bean discussed earlier, the deployment descriptor specified the above two elements in the XML file, for implementing container-managed transaction management. This is shown below as highlighted:

```
<?xml version="1.0"?>
<!DOCTYPE ejb-jar PUBLIC "-//Sun Microsystems Inc.//DTD Enterprise JavaBeans 1.1
//EN" "ejb-jar.dtd">
<ejb-jar>
  <enterprise-Beans>
    <session>
      <description>Session Bean Person Example</description>
```

```
        <ejb-name>PersonEjb</ejb-name>
        <home>personp.PersonHome</home>
        <remote>personp.Person</remote>
        <ejb-class>personp.PersonBean</ejb-class>
        <session-type>Stateless</session-type>
        <transaction-type>Container</transaction-type>
      </session>
    </enterprise-Beans>
    <assembly-descriptor>
      <security-role>
        <description>Public</description>
        <role-name>PUBLIC</role-name>
      </security-role>
      <method-permission>
        <description>public methods</description>
        <role-name>PUBLIC</role-name>
        <method>
          <ejb-name>PersonEjb</ejb-name>
          <method-name>*</method-name>
        </method>
      </method-permission>
      <container-transaction>
        <description>no description</description>
        <method>
          <ejb-name>PersonEjb</ejb-name>
          <method-name>*</method-name>
        </method>
        <trans-attribute>Supports</trans-attribute>
      </container-transaction>
    </assembly-descriptor>
  </ejb-jar>
```

Next, the explicit method of transaction management is described. Explicit demarcation can be of two types:

- Bean-managed demarcation on the server-side
- Client-side demarcation

These are described below.

Bean-Managed Demarcation on the Server Side

Only Session Beans can opt for this type of demarcation. The steps involved are as follows:

1. Specify the following in the EJB deployment descriptor file:

   ```
   <transaction-type>Bean</transaction-type>
   ```

2. Start a transaction by invoking the `begin()` method on a `UserTransaction` object.
3. Commit or rollback the transaction using the `commit()` or `rollback()` methods on the `UserTransaction` object.

The `UserTransaction` object is obtained by using the `UserTransaction` interface of the JTA in either of the following two ways, depending on whether the implementation follows EJB 1.0 or EJB 1.1 specifications:

- **EJB 1.0 specification**—Use the `getUserTransaction()` method of the `SessionContext` object. This object should be defined in the `setSessionContext()` method of the EJB Bean Class. The steps are as follows:
  1. Define a `SessionContext` variable as follows:

     ```
     SessionContext ctx;
     ```

  2. Invoke the `getUserTransaction()` method on this object. The code for the transaction management looks as follows:

     ```
     SessionContext ctx;
     UserTransaction ut;
     .....
     ut = ctx.getUserTransaction();
     ut.begin();
     .....
     ut.commit();
     ```

- **EJB 1.1 specification**—Use the session look-up with a prespecified JNDI name: `java:comp//UserTransaction`. Then follow these steps:
  1. Get an `InitialContext` object.
  2. Get the `UserTransaction` object by calling the `lookup()` method on the obtained `InitialContext` object with `java:comp//UserTransaction` as a parameter to it. This is shown below:

     ```
     import javax.transaction.*;
     i_ctx = new InitialContext ( );
     ```

```
UserTransaction ut = (UserTransaction)i_ctx.lookup
("java:comp/UserTransaction");
ut.begin ();
.....
ut.commit();
```

Client-side Demarcation

For a client to control transactions explicitly, the steps are as follows:

1. Use a `UserTransaction` object and bind it in the JNDI namespace. This is done by using the sess_sh and bindut commands as follows:

   ```
   sess_sh -u scott/tiger -s jdbc:oracle:thin:@training:1521:Oracle -command
   "@bind.txt /test/UserTransaction/DeptUT sess_iiop://training:2481:Oracle"
   ```

   The bind.txt file contains the bindut command as shown below.

   ```
   bindut &1 -rebind -url &2
   ```

   The sess_sh utility is available as a command-line utility provided as a batch file `sess_sh.bat` while installing Oracle8i. This batch file is located in the `[Oracle Home]\bin` directory. To execute this batch file, the `PATH` environment variable must be set to include the `[Oracle Home]\bin` directory.

2. Register the JDBC driver. This is for obtaining JDBC connection to retrieve `UserTransaction` object from namespace.

   ```
   DriverManager.registerDriver(new oracle.jdbc.driver.OracleDriver());
   ```

3. Retrieve the `UserTransaction` object from the JNDI namespace.

   This is done by first obtaining an initial context object and authenticating the client. This is the same as we showed in the `PersonClient.java` program discussed earlier.

   ```
   import javax.transaction.*;
   .....
   Context ctx = new InitialContext(env);
   UserTransaction ut = (UserTransaction)ctx.lookup("jdbc_access://test/
   ➥UserTransaction/DeptUT");
   ```

The prefix `jdbc_access://` must be prefixed to the bound `UserTransaction` object.

4. Invoke on it the `begin()` and `commit()` methods to explicitly start and commit. Any Bean methods can be included inn the transaction by invoking these methods after starting and before committing the transaction.

```
ut.begin();
......
ut.commit();
```

EJB Tools

Oracle8i provides the following tools for EJBs:

- deployejb
- ejbdescriptor

These tools are available for the Oracle8i Enterprise Edition typical installation option. These are provided as batch files `deployejb.bat` and `ejbdescriptor.bat` and are located in the `[Oracle Home]\bin` directory. To execute these batch files, the `PATH` environment variable must be set up to include the `[Oracle Home]\bin` directory. Both these tools are provided as command-line utilities.

The deployejb tool deploys the Enterprise JavaBean in the Oracle8i server or Oracle Application Server so that client programs can invoke the EJB methods.

The ejbdescriptor tool converts a text form of deployment descriptor to serialized object form and vice-versa.

These tools are described below.

deployejb

deployejb performs the following functions in the process of deployment of an EJB into Oracle8i:

- Reads and verifies the deployment descriptor.
- Performs a mapping of the logical EJB names to the true JNDI names.
- Reads the jar file and loads the Interfaces and classes defined in the EJB jar file into the Oracle8i database.
- Generates the EJBHome and EJBObject classes in the database server.

- Generates the client-side and server-side stub classes and any other classes as required by the EJB server and container. It generates a second jar file to store these stub classes. A file name can be specified for this jar file using the -generated option of the deployejb command. The default name for this is the packaged jar file name (created in step 1 of the deployment process) suffixed by _generated.
- Publishes the home interface in the session namespace for clients programs to look-up with JNDI.

The syntax for invoking deployejb is as follows:

```
deployejb {-user | -u} <username> {-password | -p} <password>
{-service | -s} <serviceURL> -descriptor <file> -temp <temp_dir> <Beanjar>
[-addclasspath <dirlist>]
[-Beanonly]
[-credsFile <credentials>]
[-describe | -d]
[-generated <clientjar>]
[-help | -h]
[-iiop]
[-keep]
[-oracledescriptor <file>]
[-republish]
[-resolver "resolver_spec"]
[-role <role>]
[-ssl]
[-useServiceName]
[-verbose]
[-version | -v]
```

The arguments are described below:

- *-user*—The schema username into which the EJB classes will be loaded.
- *-password*—The password for above username.
- *-service*—The URL identifying database in whose session namespace the EJB is to be published. This has the form:

  ```
  sess_iiop://< host>:<listener_port>:<sid>
  ```

  where `<host>` is the computer that hosts the target database; `<listener_port>` is the listener port configured to listen for session IIOP; `<sid>` is the database instance identifier. An example is `sess_iiop://training:2481:Oracle`

- *-addclasspath*—The directories containing remote and home interfaces or implementation dependency classes not contained in <Beanjar>. The format of <dirlist> is the same as javac's CLASSPATH argument. This argument is required if -Beanonly is specified.
- *-Beanonly*—Skips generation of interface files. This option enables you to reload the Bean implementation if none of the interfaces have changed.
- *-credsFile*—A text file with credentials instead of a username and password for the connect. Exporting a wallet into a text version creates this file.
- *-descriptor*—The XML text file containing the EJB deployment descriptor.
- *-temp*—A temporary directory for intermediate files deployejb creates. deployejb removes the files and the directory when it completes unless -keep option is specified in which case it retains the temp directory.
- <Beanjar>— The name of the JAR containing the Bean interfaces, the actual class, and any dependent class files.
- *-describe*—Prints a summary of the deployejb operation.
- *-generated*—Specifies the name of the output (generated) client JAR file. By default the output JAR file has the name of the input JAR file with _generated appended.
- *-help*—Prints the deployejb syntax.
- *-iiop*—Connects to the target database with IIOP instead of the default session IIOP. Use this option when deploying to a database server that has been configured without session IIOP.
- *-keep*—Do not remove the temporary files generated by the tool.
- *-oracledescriptor*—The text file containing the Oracle-specific deployment descriptor. This is need to map the logical Bean name to the true JNDI name when a logical name is used in the deployment descriptor.
- *-republish*—Replaces the published BeanHomeName attributes if the BeanHomeName has already been published, otherwise publishes it.
- *-resolver*—An explicit resolver spec, which is bound to the newly loaded classes. The default resolver spec includes current user's schema and PUBLIC.
- *-role*—The role to assume when connecting to the database; there is no default for this.
- *-ssl*—Connects to the database with SSL authentication and encryption.
- *-useServiceName*—Specifies a service name instead of an SID in the URL.
- *-verbose*—Prints detailed status information while executing.
- *-version*—Lists the deployejb version.

A typical example of deployejb is the one we used while deploying the Person Session Bean earlier. This is as follows:

```
deployejb -user ORATEST -password -service sess_iiop://training:2481:Oracle -
descriptor person.xml -oracledescriptor oracle_person.xml -temp c:\tmp -gener-
ated persClient.jar pers.jar
```

ejbdescriptor

The ejbdescriptor tool converts

- A text deployment descriptor file to a serialized deployment descriptor
- A XML deployment descriptor file to a text deployment descriptor file
- A serialized deployment descriptor file to a text deployment descriptor
- A text deployment descriptor file to a XML deployment descriptor file

Here the XML deployment descriptor file refers to Oracle 8.1.7 and the text and serialized descriptor files refer to Oracle 8.1.6. The syntax for the ejbdescriptor is as follows:

```
ejbdescriptor [-options] <infile> <outfile>
[-parse]
[-parsexml]
[-dump]
[-dumpxml]
[-encoding]
```

- *-parse*—This takes as input a .ejb text deployment descriptor file <infile> and translates it to a serialized deployment descriptor <outfile>.ser.
- *-parsexml*—This takes as input a XML deployment descriptor file <infile> and translates it to a .ejb text deployment descriptor <outfile>.
- *-dump*—This takes as input a serialized deployment descriptor <infile>.ser and translates it to a .ejb deployment descriptor text file <outfile>.
- *-dumpxml*—This takes as input a text deployment descriptor <infile> and translates it to a XML deployment descriptor file <outfile>.
- *-encoding*—Specifies the source file encoding for the compiler, overriding the matching value, if any, in the JAVA$OPTIONS table. Values are the same as for the javac -encoding option.

PACKAGE EJBS!

Now that you know the steps for writing EJBs, either session or entity beans, you can start to write your first EJBs. "Hey, at first it seems trivial to do this, but be careful," I said to one of the programmers. He had the Remote Interface, Home Interface, and the Bean class for the Library EJB written. All these compiled correctly. The deployment descriptor and the oracle deployment descriptor files also seemed okay to me. He started to deploy the EJB using the deployejb command. The initial steps such as Reading deployment descriptor, verifying the deployment descriptor, and Generating CommStubs, Compiling Stubs, Generating Jar file, Loading EJB Jar file, and Comm Stubs Jar file went on well. When it came to Generating EJBHome and EJB Object on the server, it bounced back saying, "An exception occurred during code generation: Class not found:.LibraryHome.class."

He was confused as to what happened. It was surprising as the LibraryHome.class file was there and also compiled correctly. He checked the deployment descriptor once again to see whether he had specified it correctly and that too was right. What was causing the above error was a hard nut to crack. I quickly examined the three files once again and suggested that he include them in a Java package, recompile them, and then deploy them again. To my astonishment, it worked well this time and the deployment process completed with the last step, Publishing EJBHome, being successful.

The moral of the lesson is, "With Oracle 8.1.7, EJBs cannot be deployed when classes are not in a package and a class not found exception occurs if all classes are in the same level without a package."

BE CAREFUL WHEN USING PRIMARY KEY DATA TYPES

One of the things to keep in mind when working with Entity EJBs is defining the data type of the primary key, especially when defining bean managed persistence. If the primary key is defined as type *String*, there seems to be no hassle. However, when using integer data types, specifying Java primitive types such as int for the Primary Key class in the deployment descriptor, the corresponding Home interface, and the actual Bean implementation is not acceptable. It generates errors such as "Can't convert java.lang.Integer to int." during the deployment process.

The moral of this lesson is, "When you create the bmp entity bean, the ejbFindByPrimaryKey method takes a parameter of type *Integer* instead of *int*. This is the default while creation of the bmp entity bean." The solution is to use the Java wrapper class for int—that is, *java.lang.Integer*—while specifying the primary key class in the deployment descriptor and also in the Home interface and performing the necessary conversions in the actual Bean class.

Summary

This chapter outlined the detailed procedure for implementing Enterprise JavaBeans for component-based development in Oracle8i. Specifically the method of developing and deploying Session and Entity EJBs in Oracle8i was discussed. The use of JDBC in developing EJBs was highlighted. Finally, the EJB tools provided by Oracle8i were discussed.

10 USING BUSINESS COMPONENTS FOR JAVA (BC4J)—INTRODUCTION AND DEVELOPMENT

ESSENTIALS

- Use Oracle's Business Components for Java (BC4J) for building the business-logic tier of an application.
- Create a BC4J application by creating the database schema and defining the BC4J components. Oracle provides the JDeveloper tool with numerous Wizards to build a BC4J application.
- Defining the BC4J components consists of creating a new work area, creating a new project, establishing a connection, adding the BC4J components, and testing the application.
- Define Data manipulation components such as Entity objects, Associations, and Domains. Define Data manipulation components such as View Objects and View Links. Define storage components such as Workspaces, Projects, Application Modules, and Packages.
- Define Validation rules using Java and XML by using the Wizards as well as adding custom code to the .java and .xml files generated during the process.
- Run the created application using the Business Components Browser.

This chapter explains the advantages of using Business Components for Java and the method of building BC4J components using Oracle JDeveloper.

Overview of BC4J

This section gives a brief outline of BC4J along with its advantages. It compares BC4J framework with the EJB component model. It also gives a brief account of creating a BC4J application along with the BC4J components involved in a BC4J application.

About BC4J

Oracle Business Components for Java (BC4J) is Oracle JDeveloper's programming framework for building scalable, multi-tier database applications. The Enterprise JavaBeans (EJB) model provides services like transaction, security, persistence, and resource management. But it does not make development of business logic any easier, nor does it provide services for reusing business logic across multiple applications. The BC4J framework facilitates the development of the business logic tier of the application. The principle behind this is that the business logic of any application is closely tied to the underlying database design.

Business logic developed using BC4J can be deployed as an EJB server object in the Oracle 8i JServer. Thus, BC4J rides on the popularity of the EJB model rather than competing with it.

Advantages of BC4J

The advantages of BC4J are as follows:

- Is a component-based architecture.
- Facilitates development of Business logic.
- Allows reuse of business logic across applications.
- Provides database transaction management.
- Provides an easy interface between the front end (HTML/Java code) and the data views.
- Allows layered customization of business logic after deployment.
- Generates most of the code needed for the application.
- Implemented using XML and Java
- Provides "write once, deploy everywhere" capability.

Differences Between BC4J and EJB

EJBs have a widely accepted role as model that allows transaction management, concurrency, and so on. However, the model is quite complex and has less flexibility. BC4J as model for writing the business logic tier of an application has the following advantages over EJBs:

- It is simple and easy to develop in conjunction with JDeveloper.
- It is more flexible enabling customization at all stages.
- An application developed with BC4J can be deployed without any code changes in multiple configurations such as an EJB session bean or CORBA server object in Oracle 8i or in the application server or locally with a Java client or on a Web server for access by a JSP or Servlet.

Creating a BC4J Application—An Overview

An application incorporating the BC4J framework can be developed using Oracle JDeveloper. JDeveloper provides a wizard-based development and deployment environment that enables you to create the BC4J components and generates most of the code needed for encapsulating the business logic needed for the application. The basic steps needed for creating a BC4J application are as follows:

1. Create the database schema. This involves creating the database tables and various integrity constraints involved therein.
2. Create the Business Components. These components correspond to the business objects pertaining to the application, as do their attributes, relationships, and business rules that make up the application logic. Oracle JDeveloper generates the necessary Java and XML code for integrating and using all of these components that can be customized with minimal effort. Typically, components that make up a BC4J application are as follows:
    - Application tasks
    - Business Entities
    - Views of data
    - Validation rules
    - Domains
    - Business rules

3. Deploy the application. Once a BC4J application is written, it is easy to deploy it in different ways, with different interfaces without any changes to the business components. The various deployment options available are as follows:
    - As a local application, with a Java client
    - As an EJB session bean in an Oracle 8I database or on an EJB server
    - As a CORBA object, in an Oracle 8I database or on a middle tier
    - On a Web server, for access by a JSP or a Servlet.

4. Create a client. Once a BC4J application is developed and deployed, a client program needs to be built. The client for the application can be HTML, Java GUI, or a non-GUI client.

Oracle JDeveloper provides wizards that facilitate deployment and creation of a client.

BC4J Components

As outlined, a BC4J application consists of components that correspond to the business objects involved in the particular application. These components fall into three major categories, namely,

- Data definition and validation components. These components pertain to the data definition and validation of the business objects and are as follows:
    - Entity objects
    - Attributes
    - Associations
    - Domains
    - Properties

- Data manipulation components. These components pertain to the presentation and manipulation of the data contained in the Entity and Association objects. These components are as follows:
    - View Objects
    - View Links

- Storage components. These components are for packaging all the components in a BC4J application and are as follows:
    - Application Modules
    - Packages

Figure 10.1 shows a typical BC4J framework.

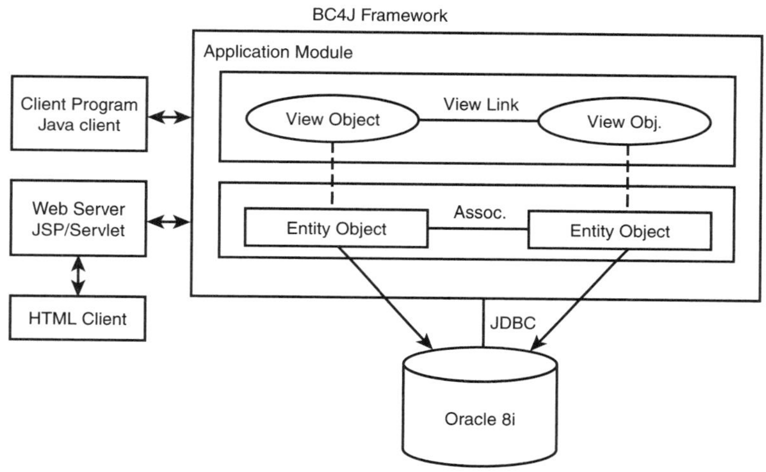

FIGURE 10.1
A typical BC4J framework.

A brief description of these components is given below.

Entity Objects

Entity Objects are the first components created in a BC4J application. These objects represent business objects or business entities based on database tables or views and contain database storage specifications. The characteristics of an entity object are as follows:

- Each entity object maps to a specific database table or view.
- An entity object contains attributes corresponding to the column definitions of a database table or view.
- An entity object handles database interaction and caches data before committing any changes to the database.

An entity object implements validation rules. An example of an Entity object is a Dept entity object. It has the following attributes:

- It contains information about the DEPT table.
- It defines the attributes of a department including data type and database column mapping.
- It implements validation rules. Validation rules are attached to specific entity object attributes. These are implemented as JavaBeans that encapsulate validation logic; they are easily created using a wizard. Complex validation rules are enforced by means of Domains. A Domain is created as a separate business component and code is added to this domain object to enforce validation logic. Once defined, multiple entity objects can reuse a domain. As an example, a domain can specify the list of valid values for an entity object attribute.
- It implements business rules in the form of business methods.

Association

An association is a BC4J component that defines a master-detail relationship between two entity objects. Typically, this corresponds to a foreign key relationship existing between the underlying database tables of an entity-objects pair. However, an association can be defined between any pair of Entity Attributes. Multiple attributes can also be specified on each side of the association as long as the same number of attributes is on each side. An association is bidirectional.

View Objects

A view object contains a subset of the data contained in the entity object. A view object uses the operations of join, filtering and sorting to give data that is required by a business process of the application. The characteristics of a view object are as follows:

- Each view object contains a SQL query that retrieves data from one or more entity objects.
- A view object can contain attributes that are of two types, namely, attributes based on an attribute of an entity object and calculated attributes based on a SQL calculated field.
- A view object specifies columns, filters records, specifies row order, and is updateable.
- A view object has get() and set() accessor methods that enable the data operations of SELECT, INSERT, UPDATE, and DELETE by client applications.

View Link

A view link is a BC4J component that defines a master-detail link between two view objects. Unlike an association, a view link is unidirectional. In a master-detail relationship, a view link coordinates master-detail view objects, by getting the filtered rows for the detail table for the current row selected in the master table.

VIEW AND ENTITY OBJECTS

View Objects and Entity Objects coordinate to enforce business logic. When the data in a view object is updated, the underlying entity objects validate the changed data and apply business rules before committing the data to the database.

View Objects are SQL-based and are executed against the database.

Application Modules

An application module defines the data definition, business logic, and methods that correspond to a specific application function. More specifically, it packages all the entity objects, Associations, View objects, View Links, and Domains related to a specific application function. For example, `DeptEmpApp` can be an application module that performs the function of managing departments and their related employees in an organization.

Also, an application module defines the database session. Custom methods can be added to an application module to perform any processing required by the specific application function. A BC4J application can consist of multiple application modules. In addition, application modules can be nested.

BC4J and XML

This section briefly describes what is XML and how it is used in the BC4J framework.

About XML and Advantages of Using XML

XML stands for Extensible Markup Language. It is a markup language that annotates text. In fact, XML is a markup metalanguage that enables the definition of one's own language and extend that language. This is a key feature not found in HTML. XML specifies information that contains information about information or, in other words, metadata. It lays down rules on how to mark up a document. HTML enables you to display data, whereas XML enables you to find out what the data is all about.

The advantages of XML are as follows:

- A metalanguage that allows one to describe one's own language.
- Data defined using XML is portable as it is stored as an ordinary text file.

- Allows semistructured data to be organized in a consistent manner.
- Allows easy parsing.
- Stores metadata and as such stores information also, not just data.
- Compatible with standard browsers.
- Is convertible to HTML.

How XML Fits into BC4J?

Oracle JDeveloper uses XML to organize project contents. In addition, with regard to BC4J, for the business components such as Application Module, Entity Objects, and View Objects, JDeveloper generates an .xml file that stores the metadata pertaining to the corresponding business component. The metadata represents the declarative settings and features of the BC4J object. For example, an entity object's XML file contains information about the entity as well as information about links to other objects. Also, validation rules specified for entity attributes are stored in XML rather than Java source code. In addition, easy customization of BC4J components is possible by changing XML rather than Java source code.

XML Syntax and Document Type Definition

XML syntax consists of defining tags that are pieces of text that describe specific units of data. Tags are identified as markup rather than data as they are surrounded by angle brackets (<>). Tags can also describe data. XML is hierarchical by design. A tag can contain nested tags. A simple file looks as follows:

```
<?xml version="1.0"?>
<resultset>
 <row num="1">
  <employeeid>7369</employeeid>
  <name>SMITH</name>
  <salary>800</salary>
 </row>
</resultset>
```

XML documents are free formatted.

The syntactic rules are as follows:

- XML documents should start with an XML declaration. This is like a prolog and must contain the following at the minimum:

  ```
  <?xml version="1.0"?>
  ```

- Can contain empty and nonempty tags. Empty tags end with `/>`. Nonempty tags must match. For example, if there is a `<employeeid>` tag, it must end with the tag `</employeeid>`.
- Tags in an XML document must nest properly. In the above example, the `<employeeid>`, `<name>`, and `<salary>` tags are nested properly within the `<row>...</row>` tag.

XML allows you to create custom tags. Tags can be stylistic tags, structural tags, or semantic tags. A stylistic tag is a tag to indicate the formatting of data. A structural tag is a tag that defines a structure such as a `<begin>` tag and an `<end>` tag. A semantic tag is a tag that identifies metadata content, such as `<employeeid>`.

- In addition, XML documents must include an opening and closing tag that contains the whole document. This is called a ROOT tag.
- When a tag is an empty tag, it need not be terminated by a `</tag>` notation. It can be specified as `<tag/>`.
- Comments are specified by the `< !---` tag.
- An XML document can have tags that have attributes. Attribute values must be enclosed in quotation marks (single or double).

Domain-specific constraints are specified by a scheme called Document Type Definition (DTD). Here *domain-specific* refers to the particular component such as project, package, or entity for which the DTD is specified. These are constraints that allow you to determine aspects such as what tags are allowed to be empty, what tags are valid for a particular application and the like. DTD is optional for XML. It specifies the kinds of tags that can be included in an XML document and the valid arrangements of those tags. In this way, it prevents you from creating an invalid XML structure. A DTD has its own syntax. A DTD tag starts with `<!`. A DTD can be specified inline or it can be specified elsewhere and referred to in the XML document. In addition, an XML can have processing instructions that instruct commands to an application that is processing XML data. These instructions are included within `<?target instructions?>` where target is the name of the application processing the XML data and instructions is a string of characters that defines the command for the application to process. As an example of specifying a DTD, consider the following XML:

```
<?xml version="1.0" encoding='WINDOWS-1252'?>
<!DOCTYPE JboProject SYSTEM "jbo_03_01.dtd">

<JboProject
   Name="DeptEmpPRJ"
   SeparateXMLFiles="true"
   PackageName="" >
```

```
    <DesignTime>
       <Attr Name="_NamedConnection" Value="Connection1" />
    </DesignTime>
    <Containee
       Name="deptemppkg"
       FullName="deptemppkg.deptemppkg"
       ObjectType="JboPackage" >
    </Containee>
</JboProject>
```

This specifies that when a document consists of an element `JboProject` ROOT level element, it is to be validated against the DTD. This is indicated by the DOCTYPE identifier. The SYSTEM identifier syntax specifies the location of the DTD file named jbo_03_01.dtd. This means that this XML document must conform to the DTD specified in this file. This file is located in the same directory as the XML file. Inside the DTD jbo_03_01.dtd, we specify which element the document must contain and how each of these elements must be structured.

XSL and DOM

As mentioned earlier, an XML document specifies how to identify data, not how to display it. To be able to display an XML document, an XML document must have associated with it an external style that provides the "how-to-display" information. Cascading Style Sheets (CSS) and Extensible Style Language (XSL) are ways that achieve this functionality. The XSL is an alternative to CSS that specifies a translation mechanism that converts an XML tag into something that can be displayed—for example, in HTML. XSL can be used to display the same data in different ways. The XSL specification consists of two languages, namely, XSLT that is a Transformation language and XSL Formatting Object that is used to describe XML documents for display. XSLT is well-formed and also outputs HTML. XSLT works on structures called templates. Templates are defined by the XSLT `<xsl:template>` tag. It consists of a `match` attribute and the contents of the template. For example,

```
<xsl:template match="initials">Initials of Person available</xsl:template>
```

outputs the text `Initials of Person available` on finding the pattern <initials> in the source XML.

DOM stands for Document Object Model. This provides specifications that convert an XML document into a collection of objects. This is necessary when a program needs to extract the information contained in an XML document into a Java program. In this process, it may alter the content and structure of the XML document and output a second XML file.

There is an alternative architecture for reading XML documents called SAX (Simple API for XML). It is used also to analyze XML documents and extract information out of them. SAX and DOM are complementary technologies. However, SAX has an advantage over DOM in that it provides efficient analysis of large XML documents. DOM when used to analyze an XML document first constructs an in-memory copy of it. This consumes space and time and is inefficient for extracting a specific part of information. SAX follows an event-driven approach enabling the SAX parser to trigger events whenever it finds a specific part of information; and then catches these events. Then the specific information is extracted. For example, the events can be "document start" or "located an <empid> element". The whole document need not be on memory at once.

Parsing XML

An Oracle XML parser included as a Java package parses XML. For example, the package `oracle.xml.parser.v2` is one such XML parser package. Including the parser in a Java program enables you to write applications that search and extract XML documents. The parser uses DOM to process the XML document as standard XML objects. The parser also performs validation checking to ensure that the XML document is well formed and is valid. The XML parser also has an integrated XSL processor for displaying XML documents. An example of parsing XML can be to write an application program that parses an XML string and produces and XML document. This is accomplished by stringing the classes in the Oracle XML parser package along with the Simple API for XML (SAX) package. The steps involved are as follows:

1. Read in the input string.
2. Parse the string.
3. Format the XML string and create an XML document as output.

An example program of parsing XML is given below.

```
import oracle.xml.parser.v2.*;
import org.w3c.dom.*;
import org.xml.sax.*;
public class ParseXMLAndDisplayDocument {
  public static void main (String[] args) {
    String parse_string = "?xml version='1.0' ?> <!DOCTYPE JboProject
    SYSTEM 'jbo_03_01.dtd'>" + ...;
    XMLDocument currDoc = parseCore(parse_string);
    currDoc.print(System.out);
  }

  public static XML Document parseCore (String string_to_parse) {
    XMLDocument doc = null;
    DOMParser parser = new DOMParser();
    ByteArrayInputStream myStream = new ByteArrayInputStream(string_to_
```

```
    parse.getBytes() );
    parser.setValidationMode(true);
    try {
      parser.parse(myStream);
      doc = parser.getDocument();
    }
    return doc;
  }
}
```

Developing a BC4J Application

As outlined earlier, there are four steps for developing a BC4J application, namely,

- Creating the database schema
- Creating the BC4J components
- Deploying the application
- Creating a client program

This section discusses the first two steps involved. The last two steps are dealt with in Chapter 11, "Using Business Components for Java (BC4J)—Deployment and Customization."

Creating the Database Schema

Creating the database schema involves creating the database tables and the related integrity constraints as well as creating data. Our sample application will use the DEPT and EMP_WITH_TYPE tables in the `oratest/oratest@oracle` schema, where oratest is the schema, the second oratest is the password, and oracle is the tnsnames alias in tnsnames.ora, which we used throughout from Chapter 2, "Java Stored Procedures," onwards.

Creating the BC4J Components

This is done using the Business Components Project Wizard in Oracle JDeveloper. This involves the following steps:

1. Create a new work area.
2. Create a new project.
3. Establish a connection.

4. Add the BC4J components.
5. Test the application.

These steps are described below in detail.

Create a New Work Area

First, a new work area needs to be created and the appropriate workspace and project files added to it. By default, JDeveloper puts the workspace files in the default source root directory. The recommended practice is to use a new workspace in a new folder. To do this, follow the steps below:

1. The Navigation Pane of JDeveloper automatically displays a new default workspace named "Untitled.jws."
2. Select File, Save Workspace.
3. Select the Create New Folder icon in the File Dialog box and name the folder "deptemppkg."
4. Double-click the deptemppkg folder to navigate to that folder.
5. Name the workspace file as "DeptEmpWS" and click Save. The name changes to DeptEmpWS.jws.

Figure 10.2 shows this.

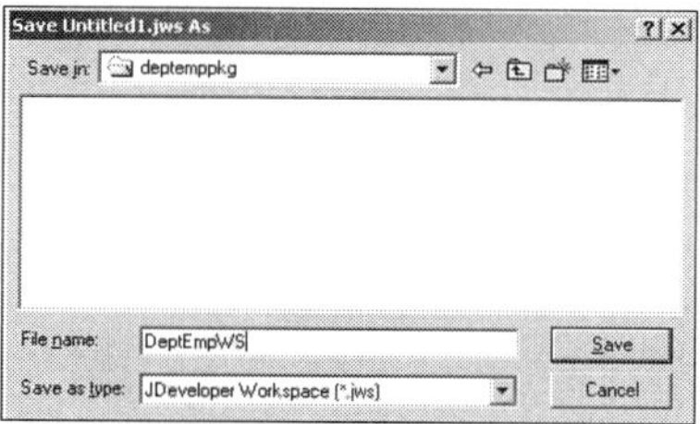

FIGURE 10.2
Creating a new work area.

Create a New Project

A new project needs to be created that will contain the Business Components. Launching the Business Components Project Wizard does this. The steps for this are as follows:

1. Select File, New Project. Click Next.
2. This displays the Project Type page and *A project containing Business Components* is selected as the default type. This is shown in Figure 10.3.

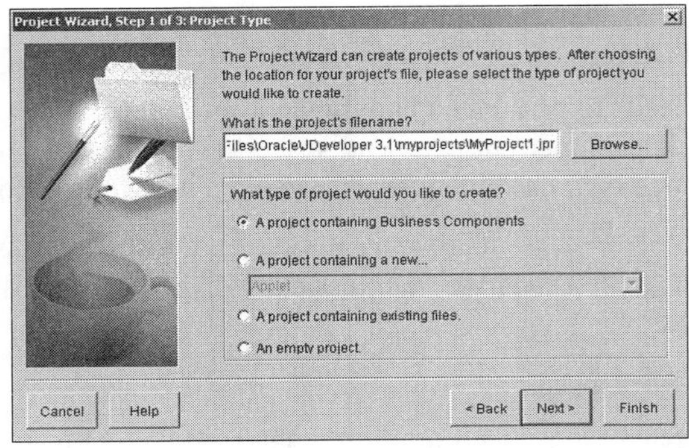

FIGURE 10.3
Project Type page of Project Wizard.

3. On the Project Type page, click Browse to display the Select Project dialog. Double-click deptemppkg to select the package to store the project files.
4. Name the project file as "DeptEmpPRJ." Click Open.
5. Click Next. On the Project Options Page, open the Package Browser by clicking Browse next to "What is the name of the project's default package?" Select "deptemppkg" and click OK. This is shown in Figure 10.4. Click Next to complete the Project Options page.

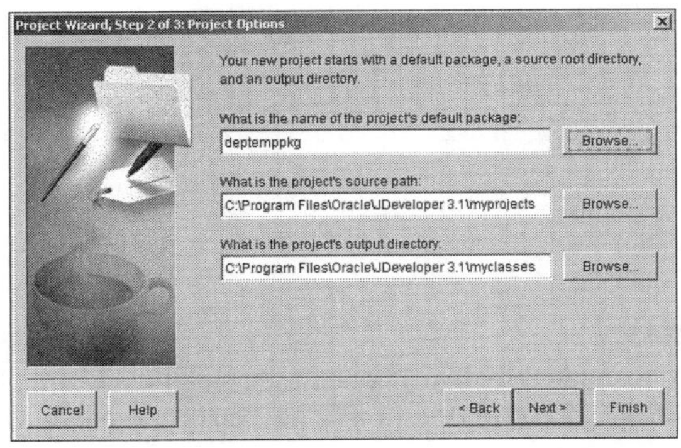

FIGURE 10.4
Project Options page of Project Wizard.

6. On the Project Information Page, enter the designated information describing the project and click Next to continue.

7. A summary page is displayed showing the options selected. This is shown in Figure 10.5.

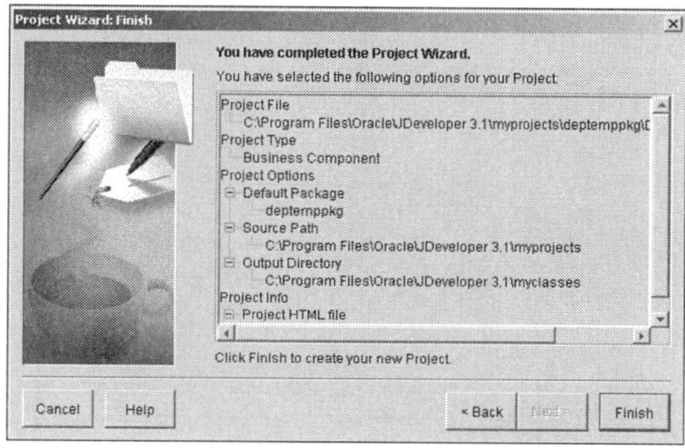

FIGURE 10.5
Summary page of Project Wizard.

Click Finish to create the project. This starts the Business Component Project Wizard and displays the Welcome page. Proceed to the next section, "Establish a Connection."

Establish a Connection

Once a new workspace and a new project have been created, the next step is to establish a connection for the BC4J components. The steps for this are as follows:

1. Open the Connections page by clicking Next on the Welcome page displayed in the above step.

2. Click New to open the Connection Dialog Box and create a new database connection as follows:

   a. Enter the Name of the connection.

   b. Select the Connection Type as JDBC to connect to a database.

   c. IIOP is specified to connect to an EJB or ORB and HTTP is specified to connect to an HTTP server. For a first application, select JDBC.

   d. Enter the username and password as oratest and oratest for the database connection.

   e. The Role field is specified for IIOP connections only.

f. Select Oracle JDBC Thin for the JDBC driver.

g. Specify Connection Method as Named Host. The other choices are Existing TNS Names or Net Name-Value Pair.

h. Specify localhost, Oracle, 1521 as the Host ID, SID and port. This is shown in Figure 10.6.

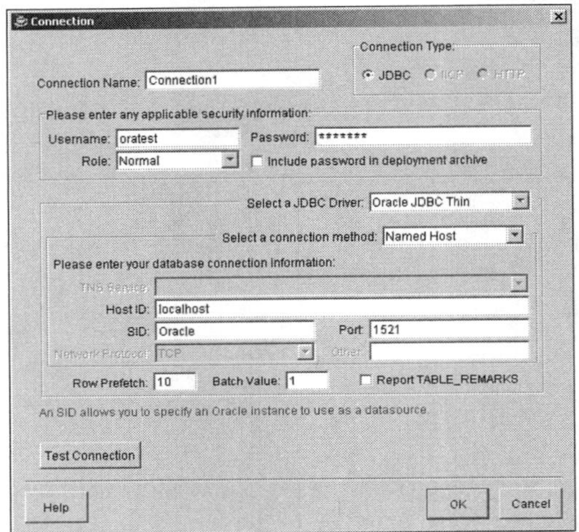

FIGURE 10.6
Connection dialog box.

Click OK.

3. Click Next to establish the connection and display the Package Name page.
4. Accept the default package name "deptemppkg" and click Next. This displays the Business Components Page as shown in Figure 10.7.
5. The database schema shows "ORATEST".
6. Click Next and Finish to end and exit the Business Components Project Wizard.
7. Save all these changes by selecting File, Save All.

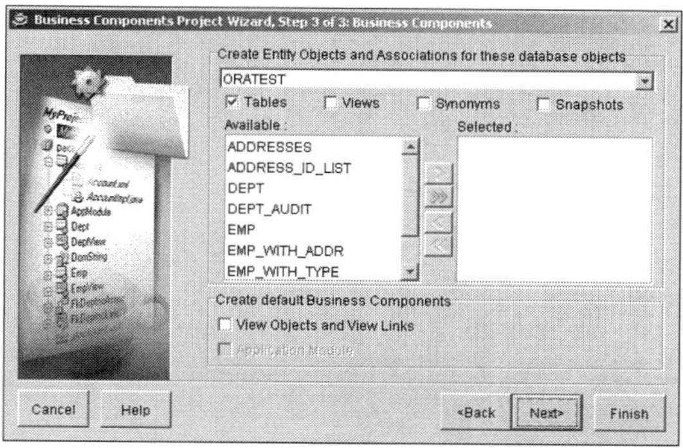

FIGURE 10.7
Business Components page of Project Wizard.

Add the BC4J Components

The next step is to build and modify BC4J objects at the component level. Basically, it adds

- An entity object for each database table
- An association object for each foreign key constraint
- A view object corresponding to each entity
- A link object corresponding to each association
- An application module containing all views and view links

For our sample application, the following components are added:

- An entity object for DEPT
- An entity object for EMP_WITH_TYPE
- Association objects
- A view object for DEPT
- A view object for EMP_WITH_TYPE
- View links
- An application module

The step-by-step procedure for each of these is described below.

Add an Entity Object for DEPT

The steps for doing this are as follows:

1. Select File, New and choose the Business Components tab. Select the Entity Object icon. Click OK. This starts the Entity Object Wizard.
2. Click Next and in the Database Objects area select DEPT for the Select object field. This is shown in Figure 10.8.

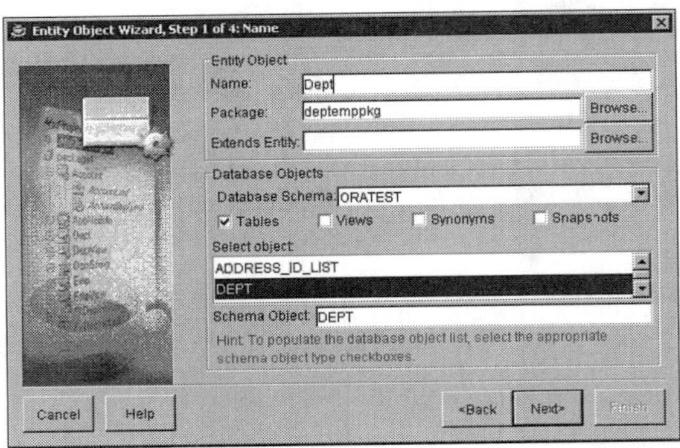

FIGURE 10.8
Name page of Entity Objects Wizard.

3. Click Next to navigate to the Attributes page. The columns of the DEPT table are listed as attributes for the Dept entity. This is show in Figure 10.9.

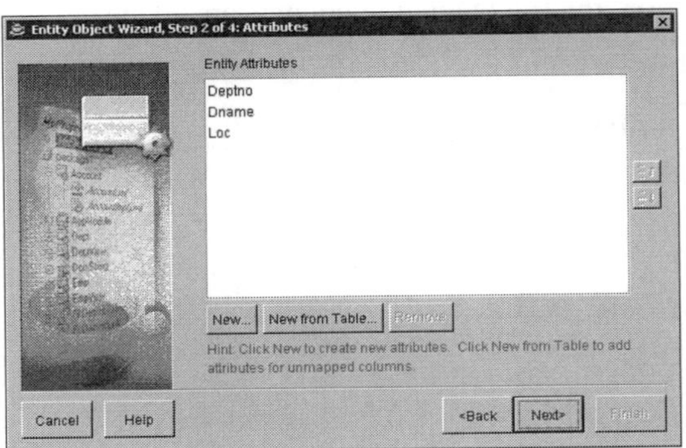

FIGURE 10.9
Attributes page of Entity Objects Wizard.

4. Accept all the defaults in succeeding pages and then click Finish to save the Entity Object and end the wizard.
5. Save the work by selecting File, Save All.

This generates a .java file named `DeptImpl.java` and an .xml file named `Dept.xml` for the entity object corresponding to DEPT. These files are located in the Navigator pane below the DEPT entity node. The contents of these files can be viewed by double clicking each of them. The sample `DeptImpl.java` file looks as follows:

```
package deptemppkg;

// ---------------------------------------------------------------
// ---    File generated by Oracle Business Components for Java.
// ---------------------------------------------------------------


import oracle.jbo.server.*;
import oracle.jbo.RowIterator;
import oracle.jbo.domain.Number;
import oracle.jbo.Key;

public class DeptImpl extends oracle.jbo.server.EntityImpl {
  protected static final int DEPTNO = 0;
  protected static final int DNAME = 1;
  protected static final int LOC = 2;

  private static EntityDefImpl mDefinitionObject;
  /**
    * This is the default constructor (do not remove)
    */
  public DeptImpl() {
  }


  /**
    * Retrieves the definition object for this instance class.
    */
  public static synchronized EntityDefImpl getDefinitionObject() {
    if (mDefinitionObject == null) {
      mDefinitionObject = (EntityDefImpl)EntityDefImpl.findDefObject
      ("deptemppkg.Dept");
    }
```

```
    return mDefinitionObject;
  }


  /**
   * Gets the attribute value for Deptno, using the alias name Deptno
   */
  public Number getDeptno() {
    return (Number)getAttributeInternal(DEPTNO);
  }


  /**
   * Sets <code>value</code> as the attribute value for Deptno
   */
  public void setDeptno(Number value) {
    setAttributeInternal(DEPTNO, value);
  }


  /**
   * Gets the attribute value for Dname, using the alias name Dname
   */
  public String getDname() {
    return (String)getAttributeInternal(DNAME);
  }


  /**
   * Sets <code>value</code> as the attribute value for Dname
   */
  public void setDname(String value) {
    setAttributeInternal(DNAME, value);
  }


  /**
   * Gets the attribute value for Loc, using the alias name Loc
   */
  public String getLoc() {
    return (String)getAttributeInternal(LOC);
  }
```

```
  /**
    * Sets <code>value</code> as the attribute value for Loc
    */
  public void setLoc(String value) {
    setAttributeInternal(LOC, value);
  }

  /**
    * Creates a Key object based on given key constituents
    */
  public static Key createPrimaryKey(Number deptno) {
    return new Key(new Object[]{deptno});
  }
}
```

The sample `Dept.xml` file looks as follows:

```
<?xml version="1.0" encoding='WINDOWS-1252'?>
<!DOCTYPE Entity SYSTEM "jbo_03_01.dtd">

<Entity
   Name="Dept"
   DBObjectType="table"
   DBObjectName="DEPT"
   AliasName="Dept"
   BindingStyle="Oracle"
   CodeGenFlag="4"
   RowClass="deptemppkg.DeptImpl" >
   <DesignTime>
      <Attr Name="_isCodegen" Value="true" />
      <AttrArray Name="_publishEvents">
      </AttrArray>
   </DesignTime>
   <Attribute
      Name="Deptno"
      Type="oracle.jbo.domain.Number"
      ColumnName="DEPTNO"
      ColumnType="NUMBER"
      SQLType="NUMERIC"
      IsNotNull="true"
      Precision="4"
      Scale="0"
```

```
      TableName="DEPT"
      PrimaryKey="true" >
      <DesignTime>
         <Attr Name="_DisplaySize" Value="0" />
      </DesignTime>
   </Attribute>
   <Attribute
      Name="Dname"
      Type="java.lang.String"
      ColumnName="DNAME"
      ColumnType="VARCHAR2"
      SQLType="VARCHAR"
      IsNotNull="true"
      Precision="20"
      TableName="DEPT" >
      <DesignTime>
         <Attr Name="_DisplaySize" Value="20" />
      </DesignTime>
   </Attribute>
   <Attribute
      Name="Loc"
      Type="java.lang.String"
      ColumnName="LOC"
      ColumnType="VARCHAR2"
      SQLType="VARCHAR"
      IsNotNull="true"
      Precision="15"
      TableName="DEPT" >
      <DesignTime>
         <Attr Name="_DisplaySize" Value="15" />
      </DesignTime>
   </Attribute>
   <Key
      Name="SysC001268" >
      <DesignTime>
         <Attr Name="_DBObjectName" Value="SYS_C001268" />
         <Attr Name="_isPrimary" Value="true" />
         <AttrArray Name="_attributes">
            <Item Value="deptemppkg.Dept.Deptno" />
         </AttrArray>
      </DesignTime>
   </Key>
```

```
  <Key
     Name="SysC001266" >
     <DesignTime>
        <Attr Name="_DBObjectName" Value="SYS_C001266" />
        <Attr Name="_checkCondition" Value="&#34;DNAME&#34; IS NOT NULL" />
        <Attr Name="_isCheck" Value="true" />
        <AttrArray Name="_attributes">
           <Item Value="deptemppkg.Dept.Dname" />
        </AttrArray>
     </DesignTime>
  </Key>
  <Key
     Name="SysC001267" >
     <DesignTime>
        <Attr Name="_DBObjectName" Value="SYS_C001267" />
        <Attr Name="_checkCondition" Value="&#34;LOC&#34; IS NOT NULL" />
        <Attr Name="_isCheck" Value="true" />
        <AttrArray Name="_attributes">
           <Item Value="deptemppkg.Dept.Loc" />
        </AttrArray>
     </DesignTime>
  </Key>
</Entity>
```

An Entity Object for EMP_WITH_TYPE

Repeat steps 1 to 5 for adding an entity object for EMP_WITH_TYPE by selecting the EMP_WITH_TYPE table instead of DEPT in the Database objects area for the Select object field.

Add Association Objects

Corresponding to the foreign key between DEPT and EMP_WITH_TYPE, add an association object as a BC4J component. This maintains a master-detail relation between the entity objects for DEPT and EMP_WITH_TYPE. Master-detail data verification is done in the BC4J layer as per the referential integrity constraint in this layer. The steps involved are as follows:

1. Select File, New and choose the Business Components tab. Select the Association Object icon. Click OK. This starts the Association Object Wizard.
2. Click Next and rename the Name field to "FKDeptNoAssoc."
3. Click Next to navigate to the Association Entities page. Specify Dept for Select Source Entity Object and EmpWithType for the Select Destination Entity Object. The Source corresponds to the Entity object with the primary key and the Destination corresponds to the Entity object with the foreign key.

4. Click Next to navigate to the Source Role Attributes page. Select Deptno and add this attribute to the Selected Attributes field.
5. Click Next to navigate to the Destination Role Attributes page. Select Deptno again and add this attribute to the Selected Attributes field.
6. Click Next to go to the Associations Properties page. Set the cardinality for Dept to "0..1" and for EmpWithType to "*."
7. Check the Composite Association check box. Doing this enables master-detail data validation.
8. Click Next and Finish to exit the wizard.

This generates a .xml file named `FKDeptNoAssoc.xml` for the association just built. This file is as follows:

```
<?xml version="1.0" encoding='WINDOWS-1252'?>
<!DOCTYPE Association SYSTEM "jbo_03_01.dtd">

<Association
   Name="FKDeptNoAssoc" >
   <DesignTime>
      <Attr Name="_isCodegen" Value="true" />
   </DesignTime>
   <AssociationEnd
      Name="Dept"
      Cardinality="0"
      Source="true"
      Owner="deptemppkg.Dept" >
      <AttrArray Name="Attributes">
         <Item Value="deptemppkg.Dept.Deptno" />
      </AttrArray>
      <DesignTime>
         <Attr Name="_aggregation" Value="0" />
         <Attr Name="_isUpdateable" Value="true" />
         <Attr Name="_finderName" Value="Dept" />
         <Attr Name="_foreignKey" Value="deptemppkg.Dept.SysC001268" />
      </DesignTime>
   </AssociationEnd>
   <AssociationEnd
      Name="EmpWithType"
      Cardinality="-1"
      Owner="deptemppkg.EmpWithType"
      HasOwner="true" >
```

```
      <AttrArray Name="Attributes">
         <Item Value="deptemppkg.EmpWithType.Deptno" />
      </AttrArray>
      <DesignTime>
         <Attr Name="_aggregation" Value="0" />
         <Attr Name="_isUpdateable" Value="true" />
         <Attr Name="_finderName" Value="EmpWithType" />
         <Attr Name="_foreignKey" Value="deptemppkg.EmpWithType.SysC001283" />
      </DesignTime>
   </AssociationEnd>
</Association>
```

Add a View Object for DEPT

The steps for doing this are as follows:

1. Select File, New and choose the Business Components tab. Select the View Object icon. Click OK. This starts the View Object Wizard.
2. Click Next and select View1 and change its name to DeptView. Note that the default package is specified as deptemppkg and the Extends View field is left blank. This is shown in Figure 10.10.

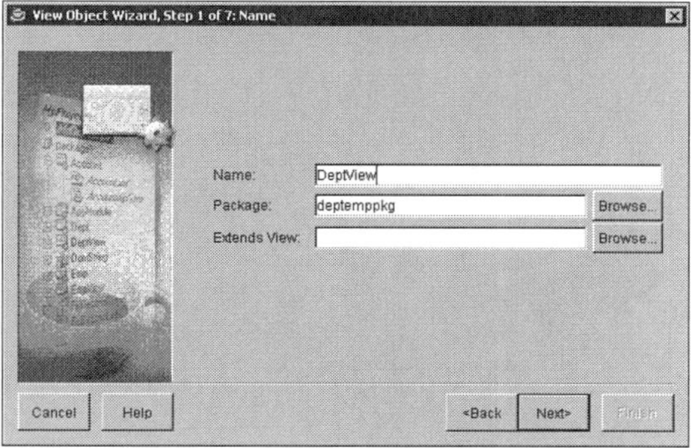

FIGURE 10.10
Name page of View Objects Wizard.

3. Click Next to navigate to the Entity Objects page.
4. Select Dept as the Entity Object for this view and add an instance of this entity to the Selected field by clicking >. This is shown in Figure 10.11.

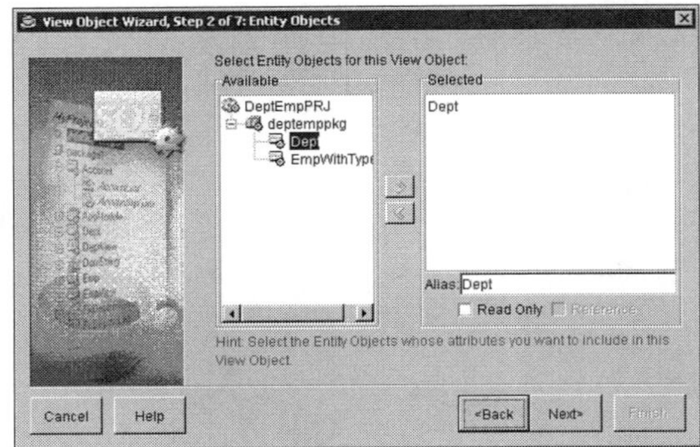

FIGURE 10.11
Entity Objects page of View Objects Wizard.

5. Click Next to navigate to the Attributes page. Here the columns for the view are selected. Select the columns to be included in the view and click > or click >> to include all the columns. In addition, user-defined attributes can be added to the view object by clicking New here. This is shown in Figure 10.12.

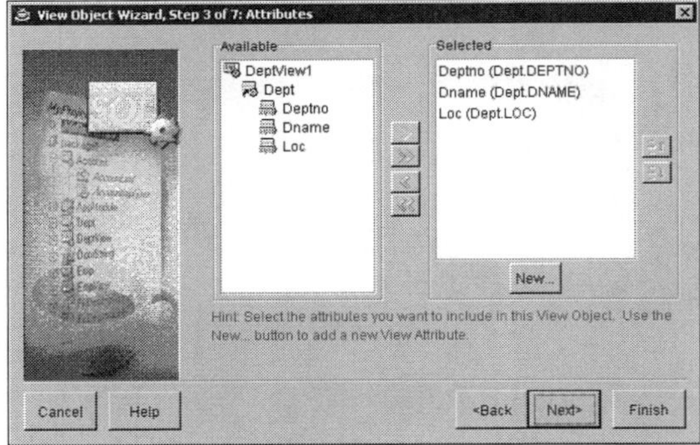

FIGURE 10.12
Attributes page of View Objects Wizard.

6. Click Next to navigate to the Attribute Settings page.

7. Click Next to access the Query page. This page is for modifying the query. Check the Expert Mode check box to enter any valid SQL query. Click Test to test that the query is valid. This is shown in Figure 10.13.

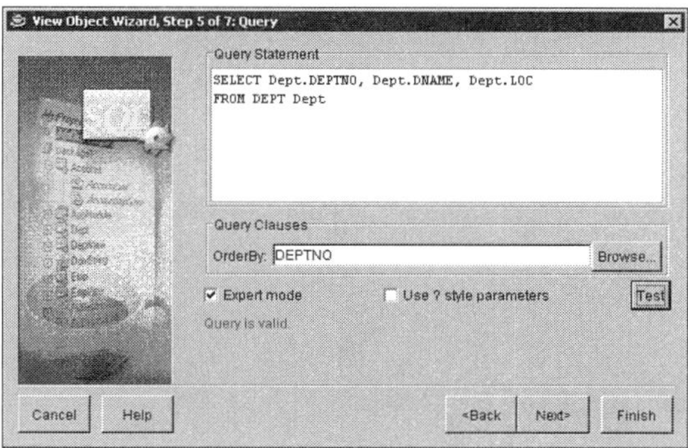

FIGURE 10.13
Query page of View Objects Wizard.

Click Next to go to the Attribute Mappings Screen.

8. Click Next to go to the final screen. Here specify any additional classes to be generated by the wizard such as those for setting default values. Click Finish to exit the wizard and generate the source files. This is shown in Figure 10.14.

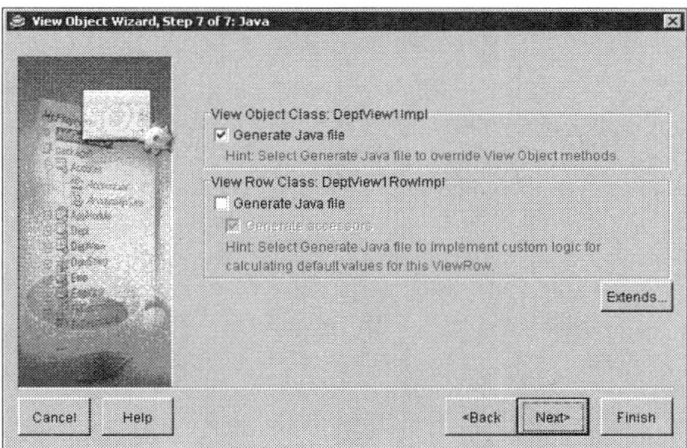

FIGURE 10.14
Java page of View Objects Wizard.

9. Save the work by selecting File, Save All.

This generates a .java file named DeptViewImpl.java and an .xml file named DeptView.xml for the view object corresponding to DEPT entity object. Also a second .java file named DeptViewRowImpl.java is generated based on the specifications in the final screen of the View Objects Wizard. A listing of these files is given below.

DeptViewImpl.java

```
package deptemppkg;

// ---------------------------------------------------------------
// ---    File generated by Oracle Business Components for Java.
// ---------------------------------------------------------------


import oracle.jbo.server.*;
import oracle.jbo.RowIterator;

public class DeptViewImpl extends oracle.jbo.server.ViewObjectImpl {

  /**
    * This is the default constructor (do not remove)
    */
  public DeptViewImpl() {
  }

}
```

DeptView.xml

```
<?xml version="1.0" encoding='WINDOWS-1252'?>
<!DOCTYPE ViewObject SYSTEM "jbo_03_01.dtd">

<ViewObject
   Name="DeptView"
   OrderBy="DEPTNO"
   BindingStyle="Oracle"
   CustomQuery="true"
   RowClass="deptemppkg.DeptViewRowImpl"
   ComponentClass="deptemppkg.DeptViewImpl" >
   <SQLQuery><![CDATA[
SELECT Dept.DEPTNO, Dept.DNAME, Dept.LOC
FROM DEPT Dept
   ]]></SQLQuery>
   <DesignTime>
      <Attr Name="_isCodegen" Value="true" />
      <Attr Name="_codeGenFlag" Value="20" />
   </DesignTime>
   <EntityUsage
```

```
      Name="Dept"
      Entity="deptemppkg.Dept" >
      <DesignTime>
         <Attr Name="_ReadOnly" Value="false" />
         <Attr Name="_EntireObjectTable" Value="false" />
         <Attr Name="_queryClause" Value="false" />
      </DesignTime>
   </EntityUsage>
   <ViewAttribute
      Name="Deptno"
      EntityAttrName="Deptno"
      EntityUsage="Dept"
      AliasName="DEPTNO" >
      <DesignTime>
         <Attr Name="_DisplaySize" Value="0" />
      </DesignTime>
   </ViewAttribute>
   <ViewAttribute
      Name="Dname"
      EntityAttrName="Dname"
      EntityUsage="Dept"
      AliasName="DNAME" >
      <DesignTime>
         <Attr Name="_DisplaySize" Value="0" />
      </DesignTime>
   </ViewAttribute>
   <ViewAttribute
      Name="Loc"
      EntityAttrName="Loc"
      EntityUsage="Dept"
      AliasName="LOC" >
      <DesignTime>
         <Attr Name="_DisplaySize" Value="0" />
      </DesignTime>
   </ViewAttribute>
   <ViewLinkAccessor
      Name="EmpWithTypeView"
      ViewLink="deptemppkg.FKDeptNoLink"
      Type="oracle.jbo.RowIterator"
      IsUpdateable="false" >
   </ViewLinkAccessor>
</ViewObject>
```

DeptViewRowImpl.java

```
package deptemppkg;

// ---------------------------------------------------------------
// ---    File generated by Oracle Business Components for Java.
// ---------------------------------------------------------------

import oracle.jbo.server.*;
import oracle.jbo.RowIterator;
import oracle.jbo.domain.Number;

public class DeptViewRowImpl extends oracle.jbo.server.ViewRowImpl {
  /**
   * This is the default constructor (do not remove)
   */
  public DeptViewRowImpl() {
  }

  /**
   * Gets Dept entity object.
   */

  public DeptImpl getDept() {
    return (DeptImpl)getEntity(0);
  }

  /**
   * Gets the attribute value for DEPTNO using the alias name Deptno
   */
  public Number getDeptno() {
    return (Number)getAttributeInternal("Deptno");
  }

  /**
   * Sets <code>value</code> as attribute value for DEPTNO using the
     alias name Deptno
   */
  public void setDeptno(Number value) {
    setAttributeInternal("Deptno", value);
  }
```

```
  /**
    * Gets the attribute value for DNAME using the alias name Dname
    */
  public String getDname() {
    return (String)getAttributeInternal("Dname");
  }

  /**
    * Sets <code>value</code> as attribute value for DNAME using the
      alias name Dname
    */
  public void setDname(String value) {
    setAttributeInternal("Dname", value);
  }

  /**
    * Gets the attribute value for LOC using the alias name Loc
    */
  public String getLoc() {
    return (String)getAttributeInternal("Loc");
  }

    /**
    * Sets <code>value</code> as attribute value for LOC using
      the alias name Loc
    */
  public void setLoc(String value) {
    setAttributeInternal("Loc", value);
  }

  /**
    * Gets the associated <code>RowIterator</code> using master-detail
      link EmpWithTypeView
    */
  public oracle.jbo.RowIterator getEmpWithTypeView() {
    return (oracle.jbo.RowIterator)getAttributeInternal("EmpWithTypeView");
  }

}
```

Add a View Object for EMP_WITH_TYPE

Repeat steps 1 to 9 for adding a view object for EMP_WITH_TYPE by selecting EMP-WITHTYPE instead of DEPT as the entity object for this view. In step 2, name the view as EmpWithTypeView.

Add View Links

We add a view link from the view object for DEPT to the view object for EMP_WITH_TYPE. The steps for doing this are as follows:

1. Select File, New and choose the Business Components tab. Select the View Link icon. Click OK. This starts the View Link Wizard. Click Next.
2. A default name appears in the Name field. Change the name to "FKDeptNoLink." Note that the default package is specified as deptemppkg and the Extends View field is left blank.
3. Click Next to navigate to the Association Views page. Set the source view for the link as DeptView by selecting DeptView for the Select Source View Object field. Set the destination view for the link as EmpWithTypeView by selecting EmpWithTypeView for the Select Destination View Object field.
4. Click Next to go to the Source Role Attribute page. This is for adding the source attribute that view link will be based on. Either one of the available attributes can be selected or an association can be specified for this. We will use the FKDeptNoAssoc based on DEPTNO, previously created. Select FKDeptNoAssoc in the Available Associations dialog and then click > to add the attribute to the Selected Attributes field.
5. Click Next to go to the Destination Role Attribute page. This is for adding the destination attribute that the view link will be based on. We will use the association FKDeptNoAssoc based on DEPTNO for this. Select FKDeptNoAssoc in the Available Associations dialog and then click > to add the attribute to the Selected Attributes field.
6. Click Next to navigate to the Association SQL page. This displays the results of the query that the View Objects are based on. Click Test to test the query generated for the view link. A dialog with a "Valid" message shows that the query is correct.
7. Click Next and Finish to exit the wizard. This generates the source code. A .xml file is generated for the view link created.
8. Save the work by selecting File, Save All.

Create an Application Module

The steps for doing this are as follows:

1. Click the DeptEmpPRJ BC4J Project in the Navigation Pane and under it right-click the deptemppkg Business Component.
2. Click the Create Application Module to invoke the Application Module Wizard. Click Next.
3. Change the Name to deptemppkgM. Click Next to navigate to the Data Model page.
4. Here we select Views and View Links to include them in the application module. In the Available Views dialog, select DeptView by clicking it. Objects in the Data Model must have unique names. The names can be changed manually or else the wizard assigns unique names for duplicate objects. Change the name to "DeptView1" and click > to move it to the Data Model field.
5. Expand the DeptView node, then select "EmpWithTypeView Via FKDeptNoLink" in the Available Views field by clicking it. Then click DeptView1 to select the parent for the view link in the Data Model field. Then click > to add the view link to the model. This ensures that the view link is automatically updated to display only rows with employees belonging to the current DEPTNO that is selected in the DeptView.
6. Click Next and Finish to create the application Module.
7. Save the work by selecting File, Save All.

Jdeveloper creates two files namely, deptemppkgMImpl.java and deptpkgempM.xml for the application module just created. The listing for the .java file is given below.

```
package deptemppkg;

//  ---------------------------------------------------------------
//  ---    File generated by Oracle Business Components for Java.
//  ---------------------------------------------------------------


import oracle.jbo.server.*;
import oracle.jbo.ViewObject;

public class deptemppkgMImpl extends oracle.jbo.server.ApplicationModuleImpl {

  protected DeptViewImpl DeptView1;
  protected EmpWithTypeViewImpl EmpWithTypeView;
  protected ViewLinkImpl FKDeptNoLink;
  /**
```

```
   * This is the default constructor (do not remove)
   */
  public deptemppkgMImpl() {
  }


  /**
   * Container's getter for DeptView1
   */
  public DeptViewImpl getDeptView1() {
    if (DeptView1 == null) {
      DeptView1 = (DeptViewImpl)findViewObject("DeptView1");
    }
    return DeptView1;
  }


  /**
   * Container's getter for EmpWithTypeView
   */
  public EmpWithTypeViewImpl getEmpWithTypeView() {
    if (EmpWithTypeView == null) {
      EmpWithTypeView = (EmpWithTypeViewImpl)findViewObject(
      "EmpWithTypeView");
    }
    return EmpWithTypeView;
  }


  /**
   * Container's getter for FKDeptNoLink
   */
  public ViewLinkImpl getFKDeptNoLink() {
    if (FKDeptNoLink == null) {
      FKDeptNoLink = (ViewLinkImpl)findViewLink("FKDeptNoLink");
    }
    return FKDeptNoLink;
  }

}
```

The listing for the .xml file is as follows:

```
<?xml version="1.0" encoding='WINDOWS-1252'?>
<!DOCTYPE AppModule SYSTEM "jbo_03_01.dtd">

<AppModule
   Name="deptemppkgM"
   ComponentClass="deptemppkg.deptemppkgMImpl" >
   <DesignTime>
      <Attr Name="_isCodegen" Value="true" />
      <Attr Name="_deployType" Value="0" />
      <Attr Name="_exportName" Value="deptemppkgM" />
   </DesignTime>
   <ViewUsage
      Name="DeptView1"
      ViewObjectName="deptemppkg.DeptView" >
   </ViewUsage>
   <ViewUsage
      Name="EmpWithTypeView"
      ViewObjectName="deptemppkg.EmpWithTypeView" >
   </ViewUsage>
   <ViewLinkUsage
      Name="FKDeptNoLink"
      ViewLinkObjectName="deptemppkg.FKDeptNoLink"
      SrcViewUsageName="deptemppkg.deptemppkgM.DeptView1"
      DstViewUsageName="deptemppkg.deptemppkgM.EmpWithTypeView" >
      <DesignTime>
         <Attr Name="_isCodegen" Value="true" />
      </DesignTime>
   </ViewLinkUsage>
</AppModule>
```

Running the Application Using Business Component Browser

Once the BC4J components have been created and packaged in an application module, the new created application can be run and tested by using the built-in Business Component Browser. This eliminates the need of a client application. The Business Component Browser automatically constructs a default set of panels and generates a simple single-table User Interface to test the view and entity objects or a master-detail UI to test the view links. Data can be input to test the underlying data-validation code. The steps for running the above-created application are as follows:

1. In the navigation pane, select the deptemppkgM application module node and right-click it. Then click Test. This displays a connection screen.
2. Accept the default connection parameters. Click Connect to start the Tester. This constructs the UI. It takes a few moments to do this.
3. Select DeptView and right-click it. Then click Show. This generates a test application.
4. The DML operations of SELECT, INSERT, UPDATE, and DELETE can be tested now using the UI generated.

Creating Entity Objects

In the earlier sections, we saw what are entity objects and how to create entity objects using JDeveloper. This section expands more on the use of entity objects and explains how to add validation rules and business rules to an entity object.

Defining Entity Objects

An entity object is the first BC4J component to be defined in a BC4J application. It represents a business object in an application and is based on a data source such as a table or a view. As such, it handles database interaction.

In our case study, the Dept Entity object that was added is based on the DEPT table. An entity object's attributes map to the columns of the database table or view. The Dept entity object has attributes called DeptNo, Dname, and Loc (for location) and these map to the respective columns of the DEPT table.

Similarly, the EmpWithType entity object is based on the EMP_WITH_TYPE table and has attributes that map to the columns in this table.

Creating a New Entity Object

An Entity Object is created using the Entity Object Wizard. There are two ways to create a new entity object, namely,

- Select the Entity Object icon in the Business Components Tab.
- Right-click the package name in the navigator and in the resulting context menu, select Create Entity Object.

This brings up the Entity Object Wizard. The following steps are as follows:

1. Enter a name for the Entity Object. This is optional.
2. Click Next and in the Database Objects area select a database object (a table or a view) (such as DEPT) for the Select object field.
3. Click Next to navigate to the Attributes page.
4. Accept all the defaults in succeeding pages and then click Finish to save the Entity Object and end the wizard.
5. Save the work by selecting File, Save All.

Using Entity Object Wizard to Modify an Existing Entity Object

An entity object already created can be edited for modifications using the Entity Object Wizard. The steps are as follows:

1. Right-click the entity name in the navigator.
2. Select Edit <entity-name> from the context menu to display the Entity Object Wizard.
3. Use the tabs in the Entity Object wizard to make modifications. Modifications such as adding or removing attributes, changing attribute settings, defining the Java classes for the entity object, adding validation rules, and adding custom properties to the entity.
4. In the Java tab page, the check boxes under Generate methods, namely, Accessor, Create Method, Data Manipulation methods, Remove Method can be checked to generate code for each of these operations.

JDeveloper generates Java and XML files for the changes done and applied using the Entity Object wizard. These files are as follows:

<entity-name>.xml—This contains metadata for the entity object and is always generated.

<entity-name>Impl.java—This is the entity object class containing getter and setter methods for each attribute defined in the entity. This class extends the EntityImpl class. A listing of these two files for the DEPT entity object created above is given in the previous section "Developing a BC4J Application."

In addition, one more class file can be generated from Entity Object Wizard as follows:

<entity-name>DefImpl.java—This is the entity definition class and extends the EntityDefImpl class.

Adding Business Rules to an Entity Object

An entity object can incorporate business rules and can contain custom business methods. For example, the set() methods of the <entity-name>Impl.java class can be modified by adding code to implement business rules.

As a simple example, let us assign a database sequence to an attribute. This initializes the value of attribute DeptNo to the next value in the sequence DEPTNO_SEQ. Here we assume that DEPTNO_SEQ is an Oracle sequence created using the CREATE SEQUENCE command. The steps are as follows:

1. Add the code to the `create()` method in DeptImpl.java. Entity objects have a `create()` method that is invoked automatically when the entity is instantiated.
2. Use the `SequenceImpl` class. The code for this is given below:

```
public void create(AttributeList attributeList) {
   super.create(attributeList);
   SequenceImpl s = new SequenceImpl("deptno_seq", getDBTransaction());
   Integer next = (Integer)s.getData();
setDeptNo(new Number(next.intValue()));
}
```

The above code has the following:

`SequenceImpl` is the `oracle.jbo.server.SequenceImpl` class that represents a sequence. The constructor for this class is called in order to create a sequence object based on deptno_seq sequence in the database.

`getDBTransaction()` is the method that retrieves the `DBTransaction` object for this entity object. The `DBTransaction` object represents a database transaction.

`setDeptNo()` is one of the setter methods generated in the `DeptImpl` class. It sets the value of the `DeptNo` attribute of the entity.

Associations and Compositions

As mentioned earlier, an association is a link between two entity objects that maintains a master-detail relationship between them. The two entities are called the source and the destination. The entity containing the primary key is usually the source and the entity containing the foreign key is the destination. Once an association is created, its components can be viewed by selecting the association in the navigator pane. This displays the

- Source entity and its attributes
- Destination entity and its attributes

JDeveloper generates one file named <association-name>.xml that consists of the metadata.

The Association Wizard enables you to create or modify an association. The following can be specified:

- Source and destination entities
- Source Role attributes and destination role attributes
- Cardinality and accessor methods for the association
- Mark the association as a composition

An example of an association is the FKDeptNoAssoc created earlier. This indicates that the Dept entity references the EmpWithType entity. The cardinality for this association is 0..1 on the Dept side and * on the EmpWithType side. This means that an employee should belong to at least one Dept and a dept may or may not have zero, one, or multiple employees. The example .xml file generated when the association is created is given in the previous section, "Developing a BC4J Application."

Compositions

A composition is an association in which one entity contains another. It is the strongest type of association. An example of a composition is the association between the entities Order and Item.

A composition has the following characteristics:

- When a change is made to the destination entity, a validate message is sent to the source entity. At this point, the source entity's `validate()` method is called when the transaction is committed.
- The master entity cannot be deleted until all the corresponding details have been deleted.

To create a Composition,

1. Create an association.
2. Check the Composition checkbox in the Association Wizard.

For the FKDeptNo Assoc association created earlier, this is shown in Figure 10.15.

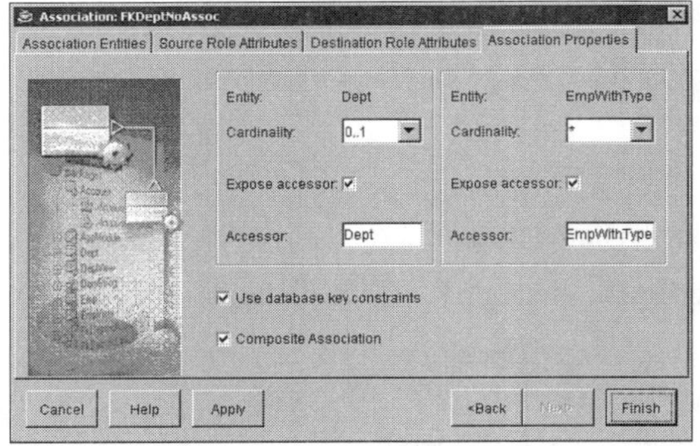

FIGURE 10.15
Association Properties page of Association Wizard showing a Composition.

Validation of Business Data

An entity object has the ability to encapsulate attribute-level, entity-level, and domain-level validation logic. Entity-level validation is validation at the row-level. Attribute-level and entity-level validation can be defined using XML and Java. Domain-level validation is for adding complex validation and is specified using domain objects.

Using Validation Rules

Validation rules are specified to validate an entity attribute. The Validation Tab of the Entity Object Wizard can be used to add and edit validation rules. There are two ways to specify a validation rule for an attribute, namely

- Use XML to validate the attribute.
- Use Java to validate the attribute.

Use XML to Validate the Attribute

XML can be used to perform simple checks to determine whether an attribute's new value against a list of valid values or a comparison or range of values. It is based on adding tags to the XML file to define basic validation rules. These tags are generated when the Entity Object Wizard is used to specify simple checks. As an example, we demonstrate how to validate the emp_type attribute of the EmpWithType Entity Object against a list of valid values, JUNIOR and SENIOR. The steps for doing this are as follows:

1. In the Navigation pane, right-click the EmpWithType BC4J component and then click Edit to invoke the Entity Object Wizard.

2. Select the Validation Tab and select the EType attribute from the Attribute list. This is shown in Figure 10.16.

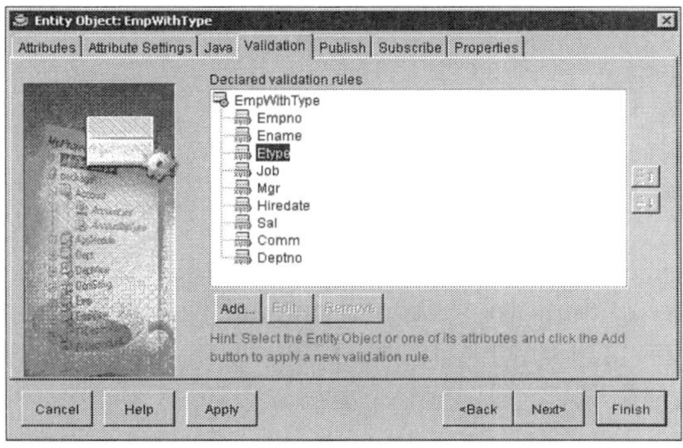

FIGURE 10.16
Validation Tab of Entity Object Wizard showing Entity Attributes.

3. Click Add to navigate to the "Add Validation Rule for EType" dialog box.
4. From the drop-down list box to the right of the Operator field, choose Equals.
5. The Compare With field is set to "Literal Value." In the Enter Literal Value area, type in JUNIOR and SENIOR, one below the other. This is shown in Figure 10.17.

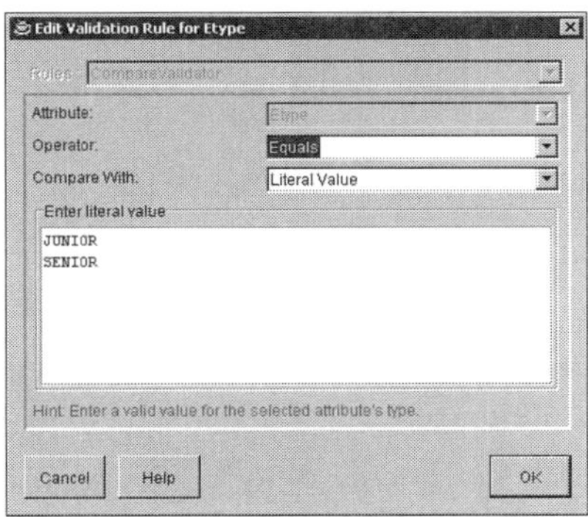

FIGURE 10.17
Edit Validation Rule Screen.

6. Click OK to return to the Entity Object Wizard and then Finish to end the Wizard.

This generates a XML file with the following code in it:

```
...
<CompareValidationBean
   OnAttribute="Etype"
   OperandType="LITERAL"
   CompareType="EQUALTO"
   CompareValue="JUNIOR SENIOR" >
</CompareValidationBean>
```

This validation rule specifies that the valid values for the EmpType attribute are JUNIOR or SENIOR and only either of these values can be entered for it. The list of values can also be retrieved from a SQL query or a view object attribute. The SQL query is a simple SELECT from a look-up table.

Use Java to Validate the Attribute

Using XML for validation enables only simple field-level checks and complex validations cannot be performed using this method. For complex validations, validation rules have to be specified in the <entity-name>Impl.java file. To do this, add the code to the `set()` method of the particular attribute in the above .java file.

As an example, we will show how to validate the Sal attribute of the EmpWithType entity object against a zero or a negative value. The steps for doing this are as follows:

1. Open the EmpWithTypeImpl.java file in the source editor.
2. Add the following import statement to the end of the existing import statements:

   ```
   import oracle.jbo.JboException;
   ```

   This adds the error handling class.
3. In the `setSal()` method, add the following code:

   ```
   if (value.floatValue() <= 0) {
      throw new JboException("Salary cannot be zero or negative");
   }
   ```

   The `setSal()` now looks as follows:

   ```
   public void setSal(Number value) {
     if (value.floatValue() <= 0) {
      throw new JboException("Salary cannot be zero or negative");
     }
     setAttributeInternal(SAL, value);
   }
   ```

4. Save the work by selecting File, Save All. When the user navigates out of a field or commits the changes, the validation is triggered.

Using Domain Objects

A domain is a user-defined datatype that is used to specify validation that is more complex. The domain constructor does validation. A domain is not bound to a particular entity or attribute. Once a domain is defined, it can be used by any of the attributes of any entity relevant to the domain specification.

Once a domain containing validation is attached to an attribute field, when the control navigates out of the field, the field value is validated against the validation logic. If the validation fails, an error message is displayed.

There are two ways to create a domain, as follows:

1. Right-click the Business Components package in the Navigation pane, and from the resulting context menu choose Create Domain.
2. Select File, New and select the Business Components tab. Double-click the Domain object.
3. JDeveloper creates a .java file for the domain object created. This .java file contains a `validate()` method. Add code for custom validation logic to this method.

When multiple validation levels have been defined in an application using domains—at the attribute level using XML, Java code, or row-level validations—the order in which the validation code will be executed is as follows:

First, all domain level validations fire.

Attribute-level validation using Java code in the `set()` methods.

Row-level validation using entity validation method.

Attribute-level validation using XML rules.

Master-detail constraint validation based on a composition.

Creating View Objects

In the earlier sections, we saw what are view objects and how to create view objects using JDeveloper. This section elaborates more on the use of view objects and explains how to create view objects, modify an existing view object, define relationships between view objects, and calculate attributes to a view object.

Defining View Objects

A view object presents a subset of business data in an application and is based on one or more entity objects. As such, it represents a database query and is used for joining, projecting, filtering, and sorting data contained in entity objects. A view object can be constructed from a SQL SELECT statement.

In our case study, the DeptView View object that was added is based on the Dept entity object. This means the DeptView is bound to the Dept entity object. A view object's attributes map to the attributes of the underlying entity object. The DeptView entity object has attributes called DeptNo, Dname, and Loc (for location) and these map to the respective attributes of the Dept entity object.

Similarly, the EmpWithTypeView view object is based on the EmpWithType entity and has attributes that map to the attributes of this entity.

Creating a New View Object

A View Object is created using the View Object Wizard. There are two ways to create a new view object, namely

- Select the View Object icon in the Business Components Tab.
- Right-click the package name in the navigator and, in the resulting context menu, select Create View Object.

This brings up the View Object Wizard. The steps are as follows:

1. Enter a name for the View Object. This is optional. For the DeptView View Object created earlier, this is shown in Figure 10.10.
2. Click Next to navigate to the Entity Objects page.
3. Select one or more entities on which the view will be based and click the > button to move the selections to the Selected list. For the DeptView View Object created earlier, this is shown in Figure 10.11.
4. Click Next to navigate to the Attributes page. Select one or more entity attributes to include in the view and click > or click >> to include all the columns. In addition, user-defined attributes can be added to the view object by clicking New here. For the DeptView View Object created earlier, this is shown in Figure 10.12.
5. Click Next to navigate to the Attribute Settings page.

6. Click Next to access the Query page. This page is for modifying the query. Check the Expert Mode check box to enter any valid SQL query. Click Test to test the query is valid. For the DeptView View Object created earlier, this is shown in Figure 10.13.

   Click Next to go to the Attribute Mappings page.

7. Click Next to go to the final screen. Here specify any additional classes to be generated by the wizard such as those for setting default values. Click Finish to exit the wizard and generate the source files. For the DeptView View Object created earlier, this is shown in Figure 10.14.

8. Save the work by selecting File, Save All.

Using View Object Wizard to Modify an Existing View Object

A view object already created can be edited for modifications using the View Object Wizard. The steps are as follows:

1. Right-click the view name in the navigator.
2. Select Edit <view-name> from the context menu to display the View Object Wizard.
3. Use the tabs in the View Object wizard to make modifications. Modifications such as adding or removing attributes, changing attribute settings, and changing the query Where clause and Order By clause.

JDeveloper generates Java and XML files for the changes done and applied using the View Object wizard. These files are as follows:

<view-name>.xml—This contains metadata for the view object and is always generated. The View Object Wizard gets all its information from this file.

<view-name>Impl.java—This is the view class for the defined View object. This class extends the ViewObjectImpl class.

In addition, one more class file can be generated from View Object Wizard as follows:

<view-name>RowImpl.java—This is the view row definition class and extends the ViewRowImpl class. This contains methods to get and set view object attribute values.

The example listings of these three files for the DeptView and EmpWithTypeView view objects are given in the previous section, "Developing a BC4J application."

We can use two classes in the `oracle.jbo.server` package to write code for customizing view objects. These are as follows:

- ViewObjectImpl class. This is the view object class. This class contains methods that are applicable to the whole view object, and is updateable. Some of the methods are:

  `setWhereClause()`—This is to set the WHERE clause of the SQL query.

  `findByKey()`—This is for retrieving all rows that match a given key.

  `first()`, `last()`, `next()`—These are for scrolling through the rows in the view object's resultset.

- ViewRowImpl class. This is the view row class. This class contains methods to get and set view attribute values.

Calculated Attributes

Calculated attributes are attributes based on calculated fields and function calls rather than on underlying entity attributes. Calculated attributes can be added to a View Object as follows:

1. Open the View Object Wizard for the View Object and navigate to the Attributes Tab.
2. Click new in the Attributes Tab. This is shown in Figure 10.18.

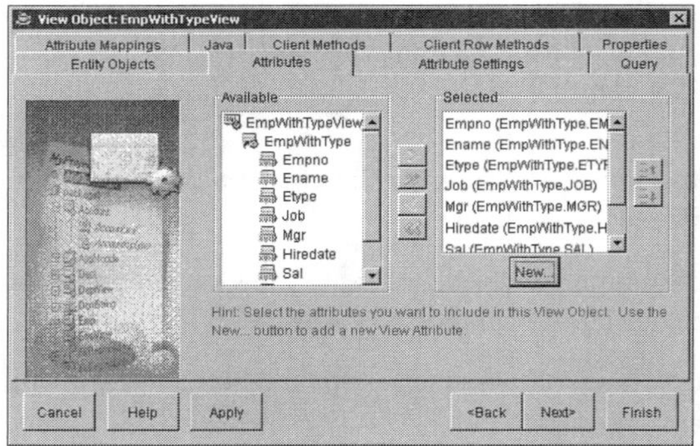

FIGURE 10.18
Attributes Page of View Object Wizard.

3. Specify the Name, Type (i.e., the datatype), Alias, and check the Selected in Query checkbox. Enter the Expression for the calculated attributed. Here Expression denotes a calculation on which the new attribute will derive its value. For example, we can add a calculated attribute called BONUS based on the Sal attribute of the EmpWithType View object. For the Expression field enter 0.5*sal. This is shown in Figure 10.19.

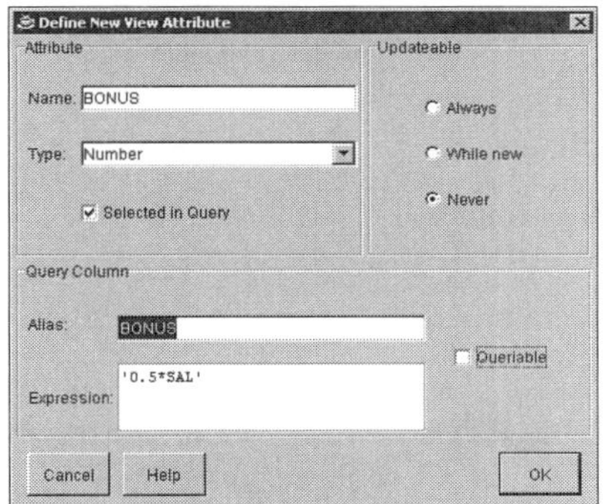

FIGURE 10.19
Screen showing adding Calculated Attributes to View Object.

RECALCULATE ATTRIBUTES

To recalculate the new attribute whenever the view row changes, add code to the appropriate setter methods in the <view-name>RowImpl.java file. In addition, this attribute should be marked as updateable in the View Object Wizard.

View Links

A view link represents a master-detail relationship between two view objects. Generally, the relationship between the view objects is a single master with multiple details. In this case, the first two view objects should be created and then both joined with a link.

Creating View Links

The two views involved are called the source and the destination. Specifying the source and destination views and the source and destination attributes can create a View Link. A View Link is created using the View Link Wizard. There are two ways to do this:

1. Right-click the package name in the Navigator pane. Select Create View Link from the resulting Context Menu.
2. Select File, New and then from the Business Components Tab choose the View Link object.

Either of the above steps can display the View Link Wizard that is used to specify the source and destination View objects.

Once a view link is created, its components can be viewed by selecting the view link in the navigator pane. This displays the

- Source view and its attributes
- Destination view and its attributes

JDeveloper generates one file named <association-name>.xml that consists of the metadata used by the View Link Wizard.

An example of a View Link is the FKDeptNoLink created earlier.

When View Links represent master-detail relationships between view objects, three types of relationships can be specified as follows:

Master to single detail

Master to multiple detail

Cascading master-detail to any depth

Traversing View Links

A View Link is traversed from source to destination. This is in contrast to associations that are bidirectional. Traversing a view link is similar to traversing an association from source to destination. The file <view-name>RowImpl.java contains an accessor method to get the associated row iterator (RowIterator). This accessor method in defined in the source view object. The row iterator contains all the associated rows in the destination view object.

Creating Application Modules

As mentioned earlier, an application module acts a container for the views and entities in a BC4J application. In addition, it is responsible for transaction management. An example of an application module is the deptemppkgM module created earlier.

Defining Application Modules

Defining an application module consists of defining the data model and business processes for specific functional tasks in an application. It contains views and view links. A top-level application module maintains one connection to the database. It can contain other application modules and service methods. It keeps track of all changes that modify data in the database. It is the interface for the BC4J application that client programs interact with. It does this by means of remotely accessible methods. It is a discrete unit that is reusable by multiple applications and can be deployed in multiple configurations such as an EJB session bean in the database tier or as a CORBA object in the middle tier or locally without having to modify its code.

To create an application module,

1. Click the BC4J Project in the Navigation Pane and under it right-click the package icon.
2. From the context menu, click the Create Application Module to invoke the Application Module Wizard.

For each application module created, JDeveloper generates two files, as follows:

1. <App-module-name>Impl.java—This is the application module class and is a subclass of oracle.jbo.server.ApplicationModuleImpl class. It is responsible for controlling the behavior of the application module.
2. <App-module-name>.xml—This is the file that contains the metadata for the application module. The Application Module Wizard gets all its information from this file.

   The example listings of these two files for the deptemppkgM application module are given in the previous section, "Developing a BC4J Application."

Defining a Data Model for an Application Module

Defining a Data Model for an application module consists in defining the set of views and view links in the application. The data model consists only of views and view links. The underlying entities and associations are included by implication. Views and Views links are added to the data model of an application module. A view added to the data model can be marked as restricted or unrestricted. Restricted views display data pertaining to the current record under consideration whereas unrestricted views display all rows associated with the view object.

To define a data model for an application module:

1. Select the Data Model tab of the Application Module Wizard.
2. Add Views and View Links to it. From the Data Model tab, select a view from the Available Views Pane. Then select an insertion point in the Data Model pane. Finally, click the > button to add the view to the Data Model.

   Note that the Available Views pane displays views based on the View Links to which they belong.
3. The > is the add button and is disabled for invalid selections. This ensures that the Data model is a valid one.
4. Click Next and Finish to create the application Module.
5. Save the work by selecting File, Save All.

For the deptemppkgM application module created earlier, the data model is shown in Figure 10.20.

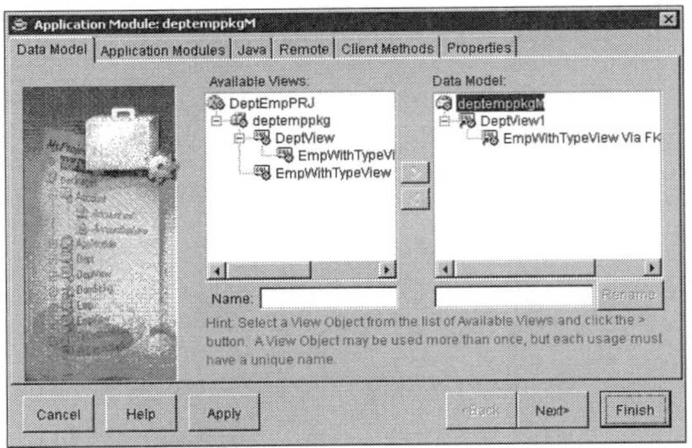

FIGURE 10.20
Screen showing Data Model of an Application Module.

Nesting Application Modules

Nesting of application modules consists of including one application module in another. A nested application module can be made to behave differently depending on the context it is used. For example, it can be made to display one data set when used as a nested module and a different data set when used on its own as a top-level module. Adding custom code to the nested application module's .java file or adding custom properties to the nested application module does this.

The steps to nest an Application Module are as follows:

1. In the Application Module Wizard, select the Application Modules tab.
2. Select the application module in the Available list. Click > to move it to the Selected list.
3. Click Finish.

Adding Custom Code to an Application Module

Custom code can be added to the application module by adding the code to the <App-module-name>Impl.java class file. Adding application-specific code implements the behavior of the application module. The point is when to add custom code to an application module. There are two cases to be considered:

1. When a view object contains code that is used only in a single application module, move the custom code to the application module, so that it is used by only those applications that need it. This way it is more efficient than adding the code to the view object. The rule of thumb is: Add code to an application module only if that module needs the code to be executed.
2. When a view object is being reused in multiple application modules and behaves differently in different application modules, do not add the custom code to the application module. Instead, add it to the view object. As an example of this, add custom code to change the WHERE or ORDER BY clause of a view object.

Adding Custom Properties to an Application Module

Custom properties can also be added to an application module. Specifying name-value pairs of metadata does this. The client accesses these properties at runtime.

The steps are as follows:

1. Invoke the Application Module Wizard and select the Properties tab.
2. Specify the name and value of the custom property and click Add.
3. Click Finish to add the property to the application module.

The value of the added custom property can be accessed and set at runtime using the `getProperty()` and `setProperty()` methods in the `oracle.jbo.server.ApplicationModuleImpl` class.

For example to access a `String` property named `Prop1`, use the following code:

```
String prop1 = (String) getProperty("Prop1");
```

Service Methods are added to the file <App-module-name>Impl.java file.

Summary

This chapter outlined the detailed procedure for implementing Business Components for Java in Oracle 8i. Specifically the method of developing BC4J components in Oracle 8i in terms of creating the database schema and then creating the BC4J components was discussed. The technique for adding validation rules was highlighted. Finally creating an Application Module that incorporates the created BC4J components and running it using the Business Components Browser was presented.

USING BUSINESS COMPONENTS FOR JAVA (BC4J)—DEPLOYMENT AND CUSTOMIZATION

ESSENTIALS

- Use JDeveloper to deploy a created Business Components for Java (BC4J) application in various configurations.
- A BC4J application can be deployed as a local application or as a session Bean or CORBA object in the Oracle8i database or an application server.
- Deploying an application module consists of selecting methods to export, making the application module remotable, deploying in the particular configuration chosen using a deployment profile, and testing the deployed application. JDeveloper provides wizards for performing all of these steps.
- Develop a JSP client and a Java GUI client using data-aware controls for the BC4J application using JDeveloper.
- Generate database objects from BC4J components using forward engineering in JDeveloper. More specifically create a database table from an entity object and a database constraint from an entity constraint.

This chapter outlines the different ways of deploying a Business Component application and the ways of customizing BC4J. Specifically, the various deployment configurations for BC4J applications along with developing a client program for accessing BC4J components are discussed. It also explains event and error handling in BC4J.

Deploying BC4J

Chapter 10, "Using Business Components for Java (BC4J)—Introduction and Development," outlines the steps for developing a BC4J application as follows:

1. Create the database.
2. Create the BC4J components.
3. Deploy the BC4J application.
4. Create a client.

The initial two steps were discussed in Chapter 10. This section discusses the third step of deploying the BC4J application. The fourth step is discussed in the next section.

Deployment Options

Once a BC4J application is written, it has to be deployed in one of several different ways for use in a production environment. The deployment involves using different interfaces without any changes to the business components. The various deployment options available are as follows:

- As a local application, with a Java client
- As an EJB session bean in an Oracle8i database or on an EJB server such as Oracle Application Server
- As a CORBA object, in an Oracle8i database or on a middle tier
- On a Web server, for access by a JSP or a servlet

JDeveloper generates the necessary code for the deployment option used. The deployment is done by using the Application Module Wizard and the Deployment Dialog Box (wherein the deployment option is specified) in JDeveloper.

Local Deployment

In local deployment, the Java client runs in the same JVM as the business components application. However, the BC4J application can run on a servlet-compatible Web server for access by a JSP or servlet. The JSP or servlet accesses an instance of the application module and the

BC4J application is accessed through an HTML client. The BC4J objects interact with the database using JDBC. An alternative configuration is when the BC4J components reside on the client machine and are accessed through a Java GUI client.

Deployment in the Oracle8i Server

There are two options for deploying a BC4J application in Oracle8i database, namely,

- As an EJB session bean
- As a CORBA object

In this case, the BC4J application runs inside the database server and accesses SQL through Oracle's server-side JDBC driver. The client accesses the application module by means of RMI over IIOP if deployed as an EJB session bean or by means of IIOP if deployed as a CORBA server object. RMI stands for Remote Method Invocation and is an easy-to-use Java-based distributed computing facility. It is a set of APIs that enables you to build distributed applications by treating Java remote objects and their methods as normal Java objects. It also takes care of passing objects themselves from machine to machine over a network. IIOP stands for Internet Inter-ORB Protocol and is a transport protocol that defines a set of message formats that allow data to be passed across a network from one computer to another. RMI, when used with IIOP protocol, enables you to convert normal method invocations into remote method invocations. RMI over IIOP combines the usability of Java Remote Method Invocation with the interoperability of IIOP.

Deployment as an EJB Session Bean on an Application Server

In this case, the BC4J application runs as a session bean on an application server and accesses the database using JDBC. The client accesses the application module by means of RMI over IIOP.

The option you should choose depends on the logical and physical environments present. The following points highlight when to consider one option over another:

- The local deployment is useful for two-tier client/server applications or servlets.
- When the environment consists of a logical three-tier and physical two-tier setup with the application tier running inside the database server, the deployment in the Oracle8i server can be used.

Steps in Deploying an Application Module

Certain classes and interfaces need to be generated that allow a client program to access the deployed BC4J application module and any of its service methods. The following are the steps involved in deploying a BC4J application module:

1. Select methods to export.
2. Make the application module remotable.
3. Deploy in the particular configuration chosen.
4. Test the deployed application.

These steps are described in detail in what follows.

Select Methods to Export

The first step is to select methods in the application module that a remote client needs to access and export them. Exporting a method makes it remotely accessible. JDeveloper adds exported methods to the application module interface. The steps for exporting methods are as follows:

1. Select the Application Module, right-click and choose Edit. This brings up the Application Module Wizard.
2. Select the Exported Methods tab.
3. Select the methods to export and move them to the Selected list.
4. JDeveloper adds the methods selected for export to the application module interface while deploying.

Make the Application Module Remotable

An application module is called remotable if it can be accessed from an object running in a different JVM using normal method calls. Before deploying, an application module must be made remotable. JDeveloper generates classes and interfaces that allow the client program to access the application module and any of its service methods. The steps for making an application module remotable are as follows:

1. Select the Application Module, right-click and choose Edit. This brings up the Application Module Wizard.
2. Select the Remote tab.
3. Select "Remote Application Module" and then select the deployment option.
4. Click Finish to make the application module remotable.

This is depicted in Figure 11.1

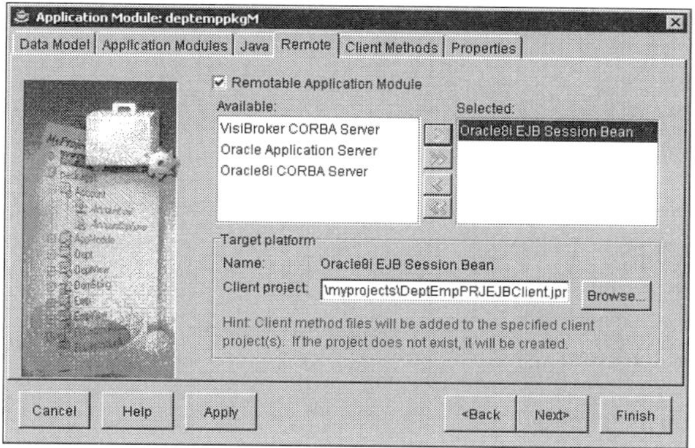

FIGURE 11.1
Figure showing the Remote tab of Application Module Wizard.

Architecture of a Remotable Application Module

In case of a remote application module, the client and server modules implement the same interface. This enables an instance of one class to be cast to an instance of the other. JDeveloper generates the following code when making an application module remotable:

1. An application module interface named <app-module> with method stubs that correspond to the exported methods in the application module.
2. A new declaration in the .java file corresponding to the application module (<app-module>Impl.java) making the corresponding class <app-module>Impl a class that implements the above module interface.
3. A client application module class Client<app-module>Module for each deployment platform that also implements the interface generated in step 1.
4. Stub and skeleton classes for each deployment platform. The stub is a class that translates remote method class into network communication setup and parameter passing. The skeleton takes as input the network connections from the stub and translates them into method calls on the remote application module.

Figure 11.2 shows a typical architecture of a remotable application module.

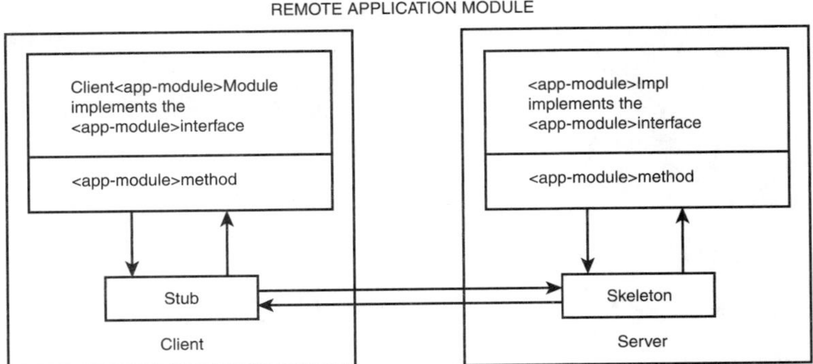

FIGURE 11.2
A typical Remote Application Module.

It works as follows:

1. The remote application module has a method called <app-module>method().
2. The client instantiates the application module class generated by JDeveloper. This class also contains the same method with the same signature as the in the remote application module class.
3. When the client calls the Client<app-module>Module.<app-module>method(), the corresponding remote method is executed.

Deploying an Application Module Using a Deployment Profile

The next step is to deploy the BC4J application to the chosen deployment configuration. This consists of the following steps:

1. Load the BC4J framework archives.
2. Create deployment profiles.
3. Deploy the BC4J application from the profiles.

JDeveloper generates all the necessary files and deploys the application module.

The above steps are described below.

Load the BC4J Framework Archives

This is necessary only when deploying to Oracle8i. The BC4J framework archives should be loaded into the database schema. While loading the archives, sometimes an "out of memory" error may occur. After deploying the archives, the resolver script should be run to fix any resolver errors such as these in the database. Information about the resolver script is listed in the release notes for Oracle JDeveloper.

TIP

Loading of archives needs to be done only once. All application modules deployed to the same schema use the same BC4J framework archives.

It is best to load the archives from the command line as this enables you to check that the archives have loaded correctly before loading the application module.

Create Deployment Profiles

A deployment profile needs to be created for deploying the BC4J application. After the deployment profile is created, the application can be deployed to the target platform. The procedure for creating a deployment profile is as follows:

1. Select the project name in the navigator and right-click in it. Then select Create Deployment Profiles. This brings up the Deployment dialog box.
2. Select the deployment platform(s) such as Oracle8i EJB session bean.
3. Specify connections. When deploying to an Oracle8i database, two connections need to be specified, namely, a JDBC connection for deploying the Java classes and an IIOP connection for creating EJB session bean or CORBA object.
4. Check the Deploy check box to deploy the application module immediately after creating the deployment profile. Then click OK. Doing this creates the deployment profiles and then deploys the application module. Alternatively, click OK without checking the Deploy checkbox to only create the deployment profile and deploy the application module later using the profile created.

This is shown in Figure 11.3.

Three deployment profiles are added to the navigator pane in a folder called Deployment. These are as follows:

- Two profiles that create .jar files on the client.
- One profile that deploys to the server.

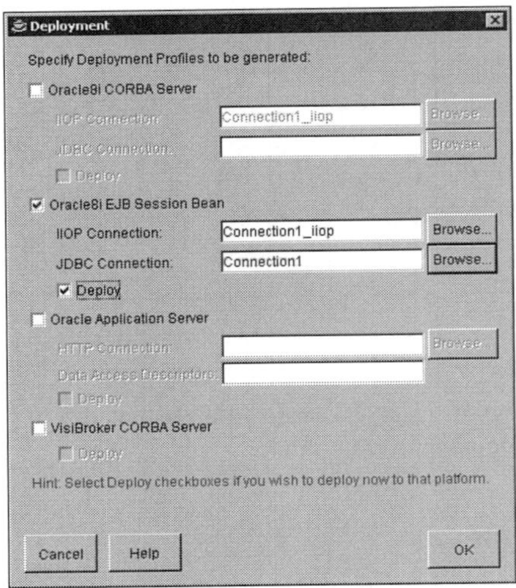

FIGURE 11.3
Creating a deployment profile.

The example output is shown in Figure 11.4.

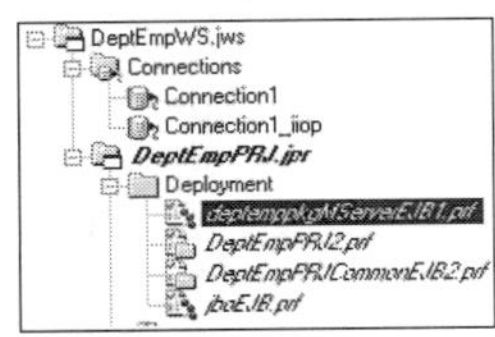

FIGURE 11.4
The created deployment profiles.

Deploy the BC4J Application from the Profiles

There are two ways to deploy an application module from the deployment profiles. These are:

- Deploy while creating the deployment profile. This is by checking the Deploy checkbox in the Deployment dialog box at the time of creating the deployment profile. This method was highlighted above.
- Deploy from an existing profile. To do this, select the first deployment profile from the navigator pane and right-click it. Select Deploy. Repeat these steps for the second and third profiles.

JDeveloper displays deployment messages as it deploys the BC4J components to the database. JDeveloper generates the following files during deployment:

- <App-module>EJBClient.jar
- <App-module>ServerEJB.jar
- Deploy.jar
- DeployCommonEJB.jar

These files have to be copied to the jdev/myclasses folder.

Once deployed, the application can be verified as published to the database. The steps for this are as follows:

1. In the navigator pane, open the Connection folder and double-click the IIOP connection. This brings up a Connection window.
2. Navigate to the folder `Published Jserver Objects/test/<username>/ejb`. Here, the application is deployed as an EJB session bean.
3. In the navigator pane, double-click the JDBC connection.
4. In the Connection window, navigate to the folder Database Schemas/<username>/Deployed Java Classes. In this folder, there will be a list of deployed packages such as com, oracle, oraclex, org, and <workspace> (the deployed BC4J components). Here workspace refers to the BC4J workspace created in the very beginning containing all the BC4J components.

The deployed Java classes for the JDBC connection appear as shown in Figure 11.5.

Deleting a Deployed Application Module

A deployed application module such as a deployed EJB can be deleted from the command line. The steps involved are as follows:

1. Delete the Java classes. This is done using the `dropjava` command as follows:

   ```
   dropjava -u <username>/<password> <package-name>
   ```

2. Remove the bean home interface from the published object name space. This is done using the session shell invoked as follows:

   ```
   sess_sh -user <username> -password <password> -service
   session_iiop://<host-name>:2481:<SID>
   $ rm -r /test/<username>/ejb
   $exit
   ```

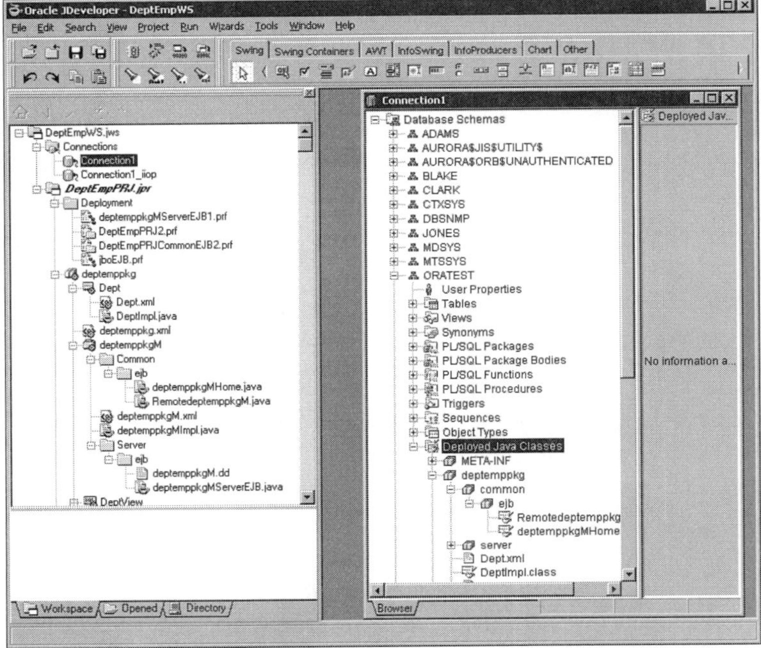

FIGURE 11.5
The deployed Java classes of the published application.

Here /test/<username>/ejb refers to the default JNDI path.

For the connection1_iiop connection this can be specified as follows:

```
sess_sh -user oratest -password oratest -service
session_iiop://training:2481:ORCL
$ rm -r /test/oratest/ejb
$exit
```

Testing a Deployed Application

This is for testing the deployed application module before creating a client application. The steps involved are as follows:

1. Invoke the Business Components Browser.
2. Select a value for the middle-tier server type. For example, for an EJB deployed to Oracle8i, select EJB as the middle-tier server type. For a CORBA object deployed to Oracle8i, select Oracle8i.

3. Enter the Client jar path and the JNDI path. The Client jar path is the name of the .jar file generated by the deployment wizard. The JNDI path is the location of the EJB or CORBA object in the database. This can be obtained as follows:
   a. In the navigator pane, open the Connections folder and double-click the name of the IIOP connection. This brings up a Connection window.
   b. Navigate to the folder `Published Jserver Objects/<username>/ejb`. This can be obtained by navigating through the tree until the deployed component is obtained.
4. Select Application Module for Application Type and enter the name of the deployed Application Module.

   With these settings in place, the Business Components Browser appears as shown in Figure 11.6.

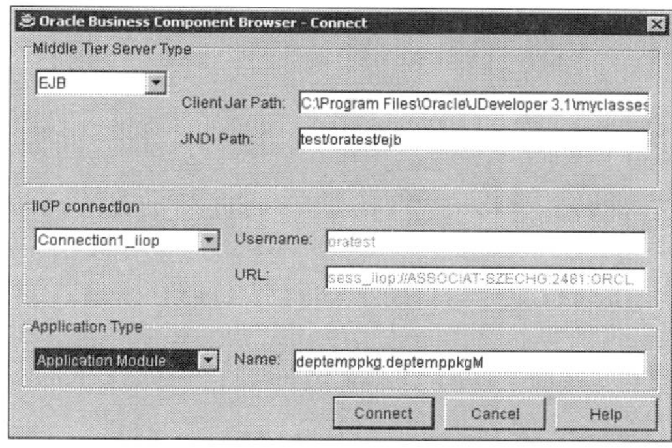

FIGURE 11.6
The Business Components Browser for testing the deployed Application Module.

5. Click Connect. This starts the tester.
6. Click in the Views and View Links in the deployed application.

Developing a Client for BC4J Application

This is the last step in creating a BC4J application. Once deployed, a BC4J application can run with any type of client without changes to the application module. The client can be an HTML, Java GUI, or non-GUI client. This section discusses three ways of defining a client as follows:

- An HTML client using Java Server Pages (JSP)
- A Java GUI client using JDeveloper's data-aware controls
- Hand-coding a Java client

Developing an HTML Client Using JSP

A Java Server Page (JSP) dynamically generates HTML content displayed as a JSP page. This is done using JSP-specific tags and Java-based JSP scriplets. These encapsulate the logic that dynamically generates the content for the JSP page. The formatting of the Web page is done using HTML.

Creating a JSP client in JDeveloper involves using Web beans and data Web beans in the JSP. A JSP client interacts with BC4J components using data Web beans. A Web bean is a JavaBean that generates a user-interface component such as navigation toolbar. A data Web bean is a Web bean that maps to a view object and generates a visual component.

The steps for creating a JSP client are as follows:

1. Create a BC4J application.
2. Create a new Project for the JSP client. This is done by selecting File, New Project to start the Project Wizard. Then select "A Project Containing a New…" and the select Business Components JSP Application from the list. Enter the project name and package name. This is shown in Figures 11.7 and 11.8.

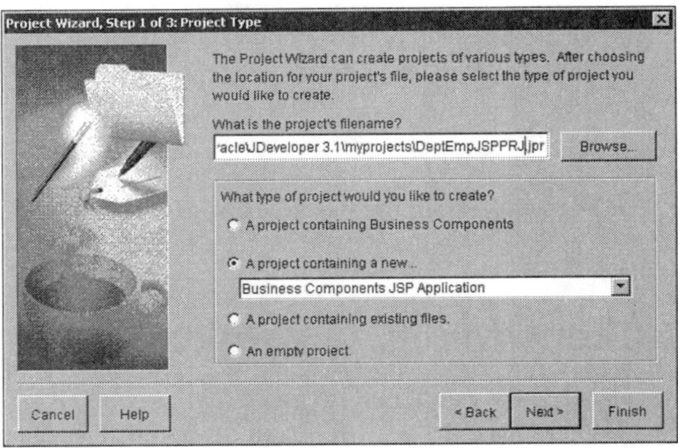

FIGURE 11.7
The Project Type page of Project Wizard for creating a JSP client.

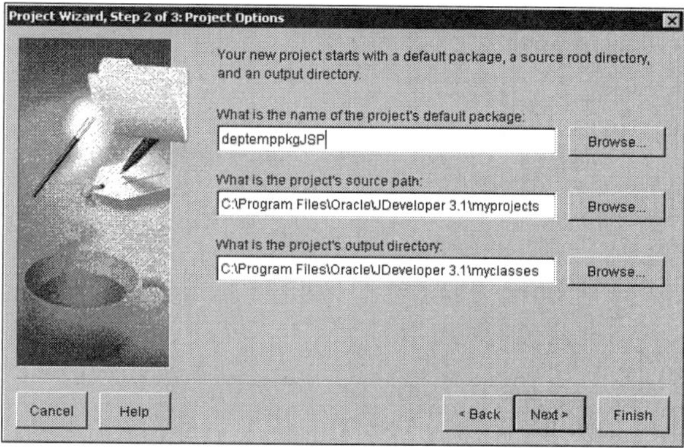

FIGURE 11.8
The Project Options page of Project Wizard for creating a JSP client.

3. Select File, New and then Select the Web Objects tab. Double-click the Business Components JSP Application icon. This starts the JSP Application Wizard. This is shown in Figure 11.9.

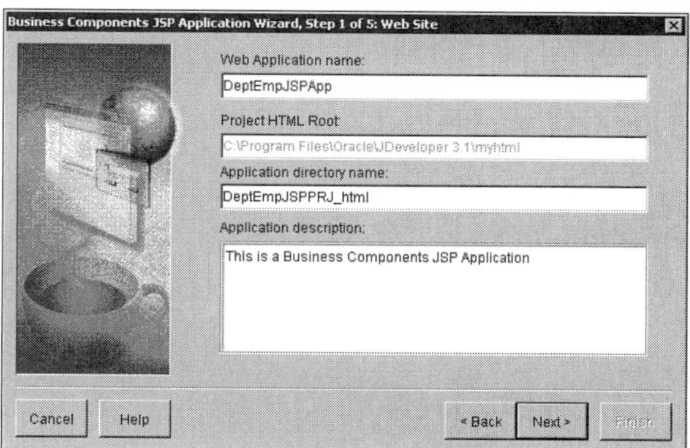

FIGURE 11.9
The Web Site page of Business Components JSP Application Wizard.

4. Select the BC4J application already created. This is shown in Figure 11.10.

   Click Next.

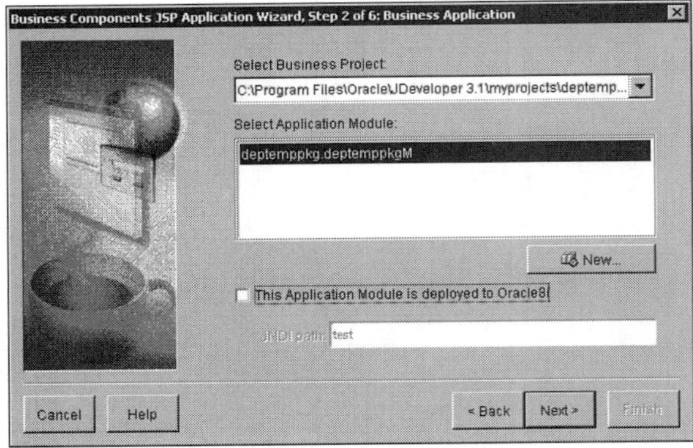

FIGURE 11.10
The Business Application page of Business Components JSP Application Wizard.

5. Make sure that the JDBC connection is selected. This is shown in Figure 11.11.

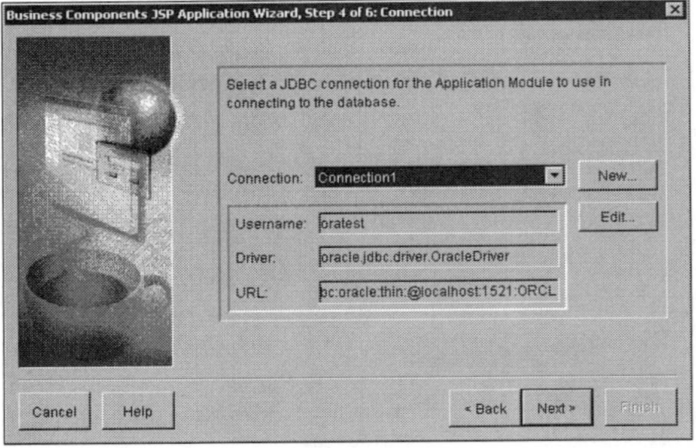

FIGURE 11.11
The Connection page of Business Components JSP Application Wizard.

Click Next.

6. Select the Forms to generate for each view object such as Query Form, Browse Form, Edit Form, and New Record Form. Click Next.
7. Click Next and then Finish.
8. Save the work using File, Save All.

9. This generates a JSP application along with some files that include a property file for the JSP that contains information about the application module, the database connection, and a .jsp file named `main.jsp` for the client. It also generates a UI containing a toolbar and a record viewer for viewing the selected records. Run the JSP client application by right-clicking the main.jsp file in the navigator and selecting Run from the resulting context menu. This is shown in Figure 11.12.

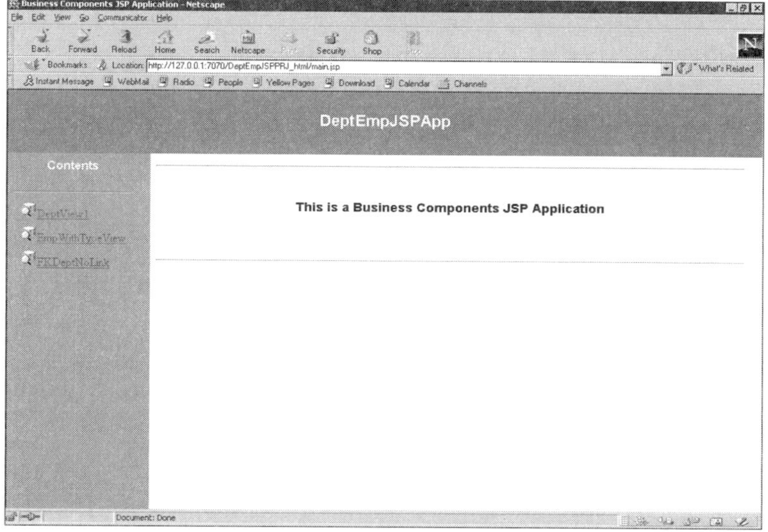

FIGURE 11.12
The JSP Client Application.

The .jsp code works as follows:

1. Each data Web bean is bound to a view object.
2. The JSP registers the application module that it runs against using the name of the properties file generated by the JSP Application Wizard. The properties file is named as <package-name>_<App-module-name>.properties. The code for registering looks similar to the following:

```
<%
oracle.jbo.html.jsp.JSPApplicationRegistry.
registerApplicationFromPropertyFile( session, "<property-file-name>");
%>
```

3. A toolbar is added to the form. The code for this looks as follows:

```
<jsp:useBean
   class="oracle.jbo.html.databeans.NavigatorBar" id="tb" scope="page" />
```

4. The toolbar generated is bound to a particular view object, that is, mapped to a data source. For the `DeptView`, the code looks as follows:

```
<%
  tb.initialize(application, session, request, response, out,
"deptemppkg_deptemppkgM.DeptView");
%>
```

Here `deptemppkg` is the package and `deptemppkgM` is the name of the application module created. (This was done in Chapter 10).

Developing a Java GUI Client Using Data-Aware Controls

Using data-aware controls (DAC) is an alternative way for developing a Java GUI client. It consists of generating a DAC for that which is based on a BC4J application module. The BC4J components can be local to or remote from the DAC components. The steps involved are as follows:

1. Create the DAC form and the InfoProducer components. The DAC form is an InfoSwing Form and the InfoProducer components are data-aware components. The steps for this are as follows:

    a. Create a new Project for the DAC Client. Select the project name from the navigator pane and select File, New. Double-click the InfoBus Data Form. This starts the Business Components Data Form Wizard.

    b. Follow the instructions on each step of the wizard.

    c. Finally, select Invoke the UI designer after creating the form and then click Finish. JDeveloper creates a frame1.java file and invokes the UI designer. This is shown in Figure 11.13.

    A DAC form running against a remote BC4J application runs as a thin client. In this case, the DAC form and the InfoProducer components run on the client. The BC4J components run on the middle tier.

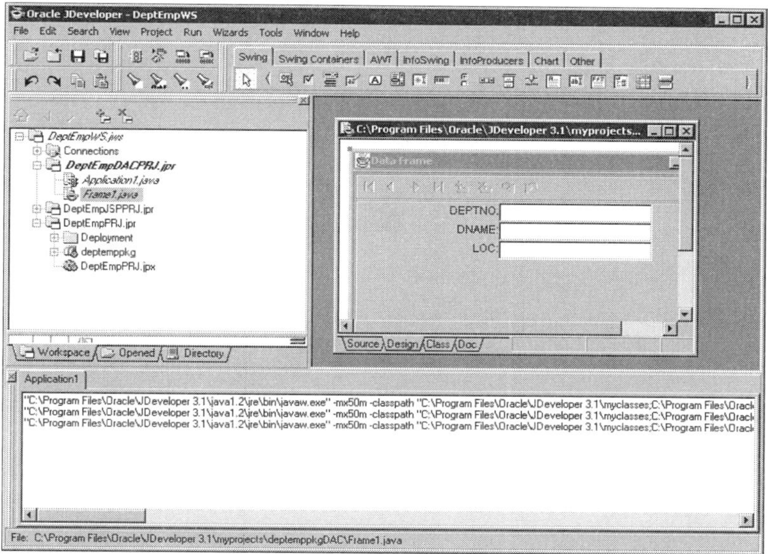

FIGURE 11.13
The UI Designer for a DAC form.

2. Configure the DAC form for middle-tier deployment. The steps for this are as follows:

   a. Set the properties in SessionInfo control. This can be done by selecting sessionInfo mode in the structure pane under InfoBus Data Items. For running against an EJB deployed to Oracle8i, the properties are as follows:

```
deploymentPlatform - EJB
        iiopConnectionName - <iiop_conn>
        remoteApplicationPath = test/<username>/ejb
```

   b. Add the client .jar that was generated while deployment, to the classpath and add the appropriate libraries. For deployment as an EJB in Oracle8i, the libraries to add are JBO EJB Client and JBO EJB Runtime.

   c. Deploy the client .jar file along with the DAC application.

   d. Save the changes by choosing File, Save All.

3. Create an application and run it. This is done as follows:

   a. Select File, New and double-click Application.

   b. Select Use an Existing Frame as your default frame and enter the name of the frame created in step 1.

c. Save the changes and rebuild the project.

d. It creates an Application1.java file. Right-click this and select Run. This brings up the run-time data form as shown in Figure 11.14.

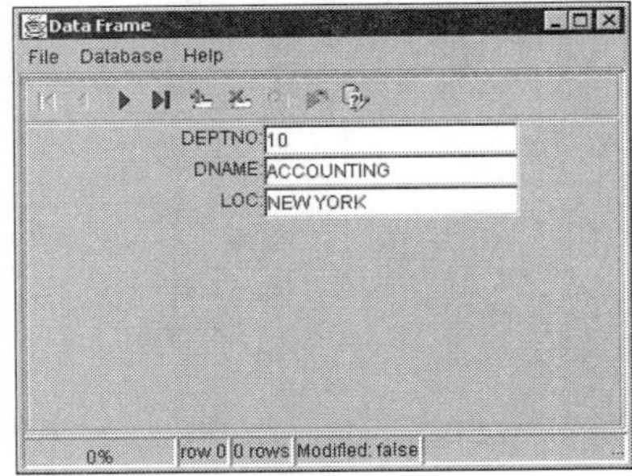

FIGURE 11.14
The runtime DAC form.

Hand-coding a Java Client

This is needed for the following reasons:

- Creating a non-GUI client
- For a client driven by a command-line interface
- For batch processing

When hand-coding the client for a BC4J application, classes from the javax.naming package of the JNDI protocol are used. The hand-coding works as follows:

1. The client application is constructed on a server by a context factory. The factory knows what application module to construct, given the JNDI environment set by the client. For BC4J, the context factory is JBO_CONTEXT_FACTORY.
2. The constructed application is then passed to the client.

The detailed steps involved in hand-coding a client are as follows:

1. Set the environment for a JNDI context. All JNDI methods are invoked relative to a context. For a local connection, this is done as follows:

```
Hashtable env = new Hashtable(10);
env.put(Context.INITIAL_CONTEXT_FACTOR, JboContext.JBO_CONTEXT_FACTORY);
env.put(JboContext.DEPLOY_PLATFORM, JboContext.PLATFORM_LOCAL);
```

For other connection types, there are more variables to be set. Use the code segments provided by JDeveloper by selecting File, New from the main menu and then selecting the Snippets tab.

2. Create a JNDI context based on the environment set. The code for this is as follows:

```
Context ic = new InitialContext(env);
```

3. Instantiate a server Application Module on the client by passing the name of the application module to the context. This calls the context factory to create the instance of the application module. The code for this is as follows:

```
ApplicationModuleHome home = (ApplicationModuleHome)ic.lookup(AppModName);
ApplicationModule AppMod = home.create().
```

   Here `AppModName` is the name of the application module interface generated while making the application module remotable.

4. Connect to the database using the `getTransaction()` method on the application module. The code for this is as follows:

```
AppMod.getTransaction().connect(<URL>, <username>,<password>);
```

5. Cast the application module in step 3 to the application module interface generated during the deployment process while making the application module remotable.

```
<app-module> finalModule = (<app-module>) AppMod;
```

Doing this enables you to call any methods on the BC4J application module to perform actions by the client.

Coding a Client for Tier Independence

For tier independence of the client form the server tier, follow the steps below:

1. Do not instantiate a server application module. Use the application module interface generated while deployment (making the application module remotable). Use always the interface name and not the name of the deployed application module.
2. Cast an application module created by the context interface to the generated application module interface.
3. Import only the packages `oracle.jbo.*` and `oracle.jbo.domain.*` from the `oracle.jbo` hierarchy. The other jbo packages such as oracle.jbo.common.* and oracle.jbo.server.* should not be imported.

Handling of Events and Errors

This section explains the event generation methods and exception handling mechanism in BC4J. Specifically, generating, publishing, and subscribing events are outlined and error handling and exception classes in JDeveloper are discussed.

About Events and Publishing of Events

An event is an action performed during the process of running a BC4J application. For example, changing of an attribute value can be recorded as a change event. An event is triggered by a source object and is published by this source. In addition, an event can have zero or more listeners who subscribe to the event. In the BC4J framework, only entity objects can publish or subscribe to events. To the end user, a change event appears as a simple change of attribute value, but a lot of code and logic must be written to trigger an event and publish it. This is the responsibility of the programmer.

As an example, consider the entity object `EmpWithType` created in Chapter 10. It has `EmpType` as one of its attributes. The type of employee is changed by invoking the `setEmpType()` method, which updates the corresponding row in the underlying database table `EMP_WITH_TYPE`. This establishes a change event.

The steps for publishing an event are as follows:

1. In the navigator pane, select the entity object, right-click it and from the resulting context menu choose Edit. This brings up the Entity Object Wizard.
2. Navigate to the Publish tab. JDeveloper lists a set of published events that can be edited.
3. To create a new event, click New. This brings up the Publish Event dialog box. Specify the name of the event. For example, specify `EmpTypeChange`. Specify the attributes to which the event handler is to have access. For the `EmpTypeChange` event, select `EmpType` attribute. Click OK to close the dialog box and then click Finish to exit the Entity Object Wizard.
4. An event is mapped to a set of Java methods. When the New Event dialog box is closed, JDeveloper generates a number of methods in the .java file for the entity object. These methods are as follows:

    a. A method to create the event data. The signature for this method is

    ```
    public JboEventObject createEmpTypeChangeEventData() {...}
    ```

    b. A method to publish the event. The signature for this method is

    ```
    public void EmpTypeChange(...) {...}
    ```

c. A method to add listeners. The signature for this method is

```
public void addEmpTypeChangeListener(JboEventListener l) {...}
```

JDeveloper provides a list of valid arguments to these methods based on the attributes selected for the event while publishing it. These methods are necessary to connect the publisher with the subscriber.

However, JDeveloper doesn't write code to determine when to fire the event. This is the responsibility of the programmer. The code for this should be written in the `set()` methods of the entity object. For example, the `EmpTypeChange` event should be fired whenever the `EmpType` is changed, so the right place to code the event is in the `setEmpType()` method. The code for this looks as follows:

```
public void setEmpType(String value) {
  setAttributeInternal(EMPTYPE, value);
  EmpTypeChange(...);
}
```

Subscribing to Events

When an event is defined, JDeveloper does determine what the event handler does. It is the responsibility of the programmer to add objects that subscribe to the event. The steps for subscribing to an event are as follows:

1. In the navigator pane, select the entity object, and right-click it. From the resulting context menu, choose Edit. This brings up the Entity Object Wizard.
2. Navigate to the Subscribe tab. JDeveloper lists a set of events that are available to this entity object. Select the event in the Published Events list and click the > to move it to the Subscribed Events list.
3. Select the moved event in the Subscribed Events section and click Add. This brings up the Define Method dialog box.
4. Select the desired method as the event handler method. Then select the desired attribute if any.

Error Handling

JDeveloper and the BC4J framework use the Java exception mechanism to handle exceptions. Java exceptions can be implicit in which case they extend the `java.lang.RuntimeException` exception or can be explicit. When a Java method uses an explicit exception to handle an error, it is required to use a `throws` clause in the method signature that specifies the type of exception the method will throw. For example, the `getDname()` method of the DeptImpl.java file can be modified to throw an explicit exception called `NameNotFoundException` as follows:

```
public String getDname(Dept dept) throws NameNotFoundException {
  String dept_name = dept.Dname;
  if (dept_name == null) {
    throw new NameNotFoundException();
  }
  return dept_name;
}
```

Exception Classes in JDeveloper

JDeveloper extends Java exception handling by providing the JboException class. This is included in the package oracle.jbo and is fully declared as `oracle.jbo.JboException`. This class extends `java.lang.RuntimeException` class. The constructor for the JboException class has two signatures as follows:

```
JboException(String message, String errorCode, Object[] params)

JboException(Class resBundleClass, String errorCode, Object[] params).
```

The second type of constructor is used in NLS translation and message formatting.

BC4J methods can throw the `JboException` exception without the `throws` clause in the signature.

Handling Exceptions

Handling of exceptions in the BC4J framework can be done in two ways as follows:

1. The Java way—Here use the `try-catch-finally` method as done in any standard Java program.
2. The JDeveloper way—Here use the `JboExceptionHandler` class.

The normal Java way works if the application module runs locally. However, as the BC4J framework is a multi-tier scenario, exceptions may have propagated across tiers and the best way to use the `JboExceptionHandler` class as the normal Java way may not detect all the errors. In fact, it handles only the top-level exception. Using the `JboExceptionHandler` class can handle exceptions occurring in the top-level as well as middle tiers. The technique for doing this is as follows:

Invoke the `handleException()` method in the `JboExceptionHandler` class. This will uncover all the piggyback exceptions that are piled up one over the other on all tiers. The `handleException()` method has the following signature:

```
void handleException(Exception ex, boolean lastEntryInPiggyback)
```

where `ex` is the exception unloaded from the piggyback and `lastEntryInPiggyback` is a flag that indicates whether this exception was the last one in the piggyback pile.

Miscellaneous Topics

This section discusses the concept of forward engineering from a BC4J perspective. It also outlines the process of transaction control in BC4J.

Forward engineering is the process of generating database objects from BC4J components. Specifically, the method of creating a database table from an entity object and a database constraint from and entity constraint are highlighted.

Creating a Database Table from an Entity Object

JDeveloper allows creating a database table from the definition of an existing Entity Object. The steps for doing this are as follows:

1. Select a package from the navigator pane and right-click it. From the resulting context menu, select Create Database Objects.
2. Select the entity objects on the left and click the > to move them one by one to the right. Then click OK.

This is shown in Figure 11.15.

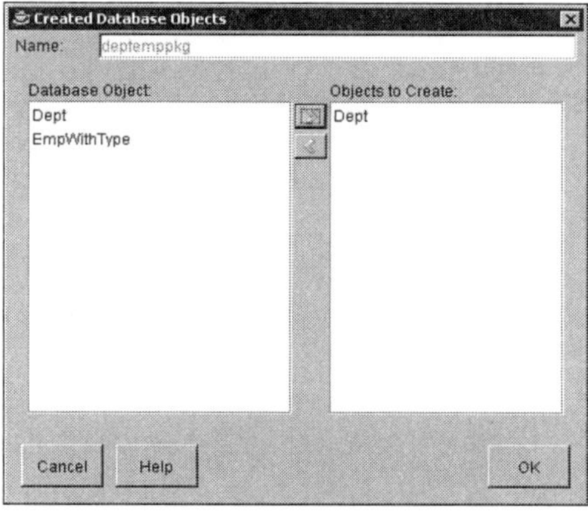

FIGURE 11.15
The Created Database Objects page during Forward Engineering.

JDeveloper creates one table for each entity object selected, even if a table of the same name exists or not. If a table already exists, it is dropped and re-created. This means any existing data is lost.

Creating a Database Constraint from an Entity Constraint

An entity constraint represents a key constraint in the database and is defined in terms of entity objects and attributes. An entity constraint can be a primary key constraint, unique key constraint, foreign key constraint, or a check constraint. It is created using the Entity Constraint Wizard. The steps for creating an entity constraint are as follows:

1. Select the entity name in the navigator pane and right-click it. From the resulting context menu, choose Create Entity Constraint. This starts the Entity Constraint Wizard.
2. Enter the constraint name and the name to be used in the database. Select the attributes of the constraint. Select the constraint type and validation options. For a foreign key constraint, also enter a value for the "references:" field as the name of the primary key that the foreign key references.

This is shown in Figures 11.16, 11.17, and 11.18.

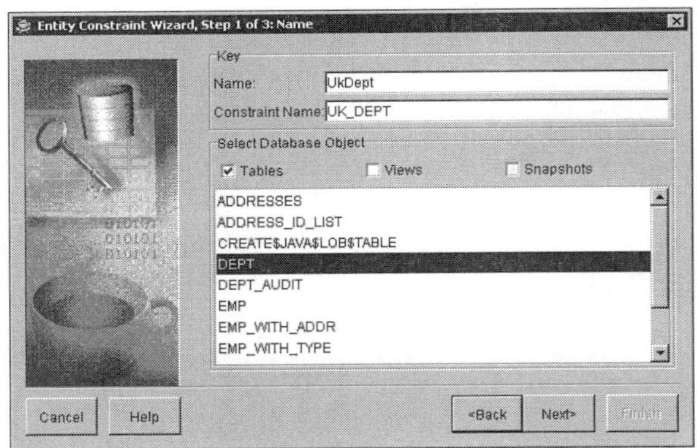

FIGURE 11.16
The Name page of the Entity Constraint Wizard.

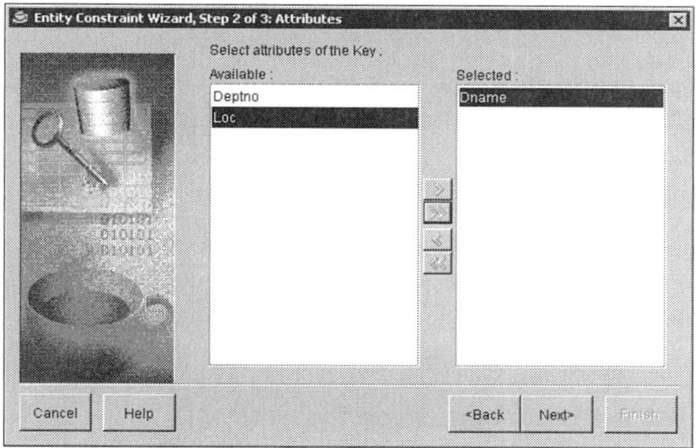

FIGURE 11.17
The Attributes page of the Entity Constraint Wizard.

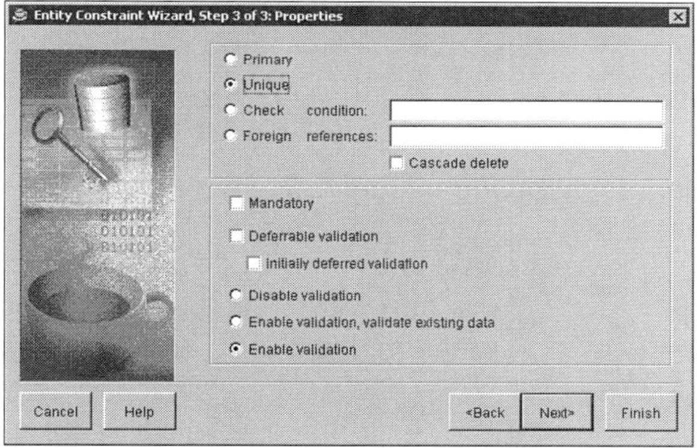

FIGURE 11.18
The Properties page of the Entity Constraint Wizard.

JDeveloper allows creation of a database constraint based on an entity constraint. The steps for doing this are the same as for creating a database object from an entity object. Simply select the entity with entity constraints defined in the Create Database Objects dialog box and click OK.

This creates the database table based on the entity object along with integrity constraints corresponding to the entity constraints defined on the entity object.

Expert Mode View Objects

As outlined in Chapter 10, view objects are based on a SQL query. By default, this query is in normal mode meaning that only its `WHERE` and `ORDER BY` clauses can be altered for the operations of filtering and sorting respectively. The `SELECT` clause of the query cannot be changed. In normal mode, JDeveloper ensures that the `SELECT` columns are in sync with the view object's attributes.

Alternatively, a query can be placed in Expert Mode that enables you to enter any valid SQL `SELECT` statement for the view object's query. For example, SQL built-in functions can be used on the individual columns and defined using an alias. The steps to do this are as follows:

1. Invoke the View Object Wizard and select the Query tab.
2. Check the Expert Mode checkbox and enter any valid SQL SELECT statement.

This is shown in Figure 11.19 for the DeptView View object.

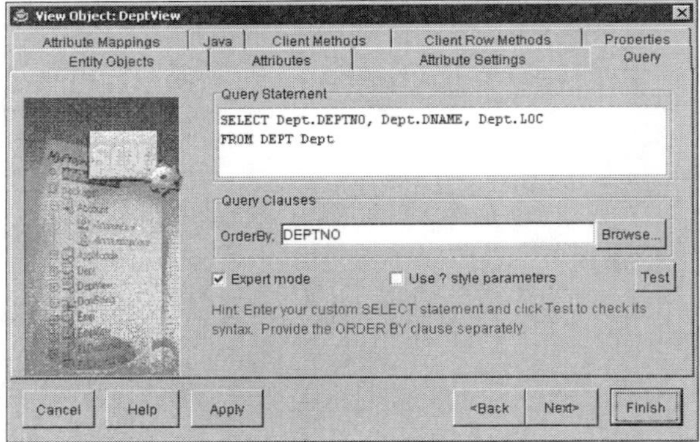

FIGURE 11.19
The Expert Mode View Objects.

TIP

Unchecking a checked Expert Mode check box reverts the query to the default. Any changes made to the query are lost.

When editing a query in expert mode, the default mappings between the entity attributes and database columns are lost. For example, specifying the following query results in the value of the ename attribute not matching with the value in the underlying `EMP_WITH_TYPE` table:

```
SELECT empno, UPPER(ename) ename FROM EMP_WITH_TYPE
```

To preserve the mapping, do the following:

1. Delete the default ename attribute.

2. Create a new calculated attribute called `ename`.
3. Specify ename as the alias to map to the `ename` alias defined in the edited query.
4. Enter * for the expression field.
5. However, the actual expression will be obtained from the edited query.

Transaction Control in BC4J

The BC4J framework provides support for transaction management and concurrency control. It handles all transactions at the application module level. The application module gets a transaction context from a single database connection. For nested application modules, the outermost application module provides the transaction context for all the inner application modules.

BC4J provides two interfaces named `Transaction` and `DBTransaction` for defining database transactions. These interfaces have methods to access transactions. The methods are as follows:

```
getTransaction()
getDBTransaction()
```

These methods can be invoked on an instance of the `ApplicationModuleImpl` class to commit or rollback changes in a transaction. A sample code for committing is shown below.

```
ApplicationModuleImpl testMod;
TestMod.getTransaction().commit();
```

The process of commit is done in the following manner:

1. Changes made to the entity data are cached by the entity objects until commit time.
2. At the time of commit, pending updates are validated by calling each entity's `validate()` method. If the validation is a success, the changes are posted—that is, they're written to the database.
3. When all pending changes have been posted, the transaction is committed.
4. Uncommitted changes are lost.

Summary

This chapter outlined the detailed procedure for deploying Business Components for Java in Oracle8i. Specifically the method of deploying BC4J applications, writing a client program to access BC4J components, customizing BC4J applications, and handling of exceptions and transactions was discussed.

JAVA SERVLET PROGRAMMING

ESSENTIALS

- Deploy Java in a Web environment using Java Servlets. Java Servlets can be deployed in the Oracle8i database and run using the Oracle Servlet Engine.
- Developing a servlet involves importing the servlet-specific packages javax.servlet.* and javax.servlet.http.*, defining the servlet class, defining the service methods, and interacting with the client using the service request and response objects.
- Access a servlet from a Web server such as Apache JServ or Tomcat using a configured URL.
- Deploy servlets on the database tier using database dispatcher servicing HTTP by creating a service, adding an endpoint for a port, registering it to the Web service, granting ownership to the servlet user for the service created, creating a Web domain, creating a servlet context, compiling and loading the servlet class into the database, and publishing the servlet in the Oracle8i Web server. Use the session shell tool `sess_sh` and the `loadjava` utility for the above steps.
- Access the deployed servlet from a Web browser using a URL `http://<hostname>:<port>/<virtual-path>`.

This chapter explains the use of servlets in Java. It highlights the method to incorporate Java servlets that run against an Oracle8i database. The method of accessing the servlet from a HTML page is explained. The method of servlet deployment in Oracle8i server and exception handling are covered. Initially, writing a servlet and running it in a Web server (more specifically using Apache JServ and Apache Web Server) is discussed. Subsequently, the deployment of servlets in the Oracle8i database and running it using the Oracle Servlet Engine is presented.

Overview of Servlets

Java servlets are one of the server-side frameworks for Java application deployment. A servlet can be defined as a logical extension program of the Web server. In this respect, it serves as a Java-based replacement for CGI scripts. Servlets can be invoked from HTML code exactly in the same way CGI programs are invoked. However, unlike CGI programs, servlets are persistent across invocations and hence are much faster than CGI programs. Being written in Java, servlets have access to all the APIs of the Java platform and are portable across operating systems.

The servlet model works in the following way:

1. The user makes a request of the Web server.
2. The Web server invokes a servlet designed to handle the request.
3. The servlet fulfills the request. They servlet may invoke other Java APIs to achieve this.
4. The servlet returns the results to the user (in HTML format).

Since the servlet is persistent across invocations, it is initialized only once. This initialization process can set up I/O-intensive resources like database connections that can then be used across multiple invocations thus saving the overhead of doing the initialization for each request to the servlet. But the programmer can choose not to retain the state information across invocations. For example, in a situation where there are limited number of database connections, the connections can be released at the end of the servlet invocation. The servlet can also retain persistent data at session level. This is favorable from a security perspective because once the user closes the session, all the information pertaining to user's session will be destroyed.

Java provides a servlet API that makes life easy for the servlet developer. Among other things, it takes care of tasks like decoding HTML form parameters and dealing with sessions and cookies. It also provides classes that can be used for communication between the Web server and the servlet.

Servlets Basics

This section presents a discussion of servlet basics in respect of servlet life cycle, MIME types and the advantages of using servlets.

Servlet Life Cycle

Every servlet has the following life cycle:

- Creation and initialization
- Handling of client requests
- Destroying the servlet and garbage collection

The Java servlet API has provided an interface that handles the life cycle of a servlet. This is the `javax.servlet.Servlet` interface. There are life-cycle methods defined in this interface. First we discuss the setup steps required to develop and deploy servlets followed by and explanation of the life cycle steps.

To execute a servlet, a Web Server supporting servlets must be installed and started. Examples of such Web servers are Tomcat, Netscape Web Server, Apache JServer, and so on. To develop and deploy servlets, the following environment variables need to be set up:

1. Set the `PATH` variable to include `%JAVA_HOME%\bin` directory. (Here a Windows environment is assumed. For a UNIX environment, use the appropriate syntax such as $JAVA_HOME etc.).
2. Set the `CLASSPATH` variable to include the current working directory.
3. Set the `CLASSPATH` variable to include the `servlet.jar` file located in the `lib` subdirectory of the Web server home directory.
4. If using JDBC inside the servlet, set the CLASSPATH variable to include the `[Oracle Home]\jdbc\lib\classes12.zip` or `[Oracle Home]\jdbc\lib\classes111.zip`. (Refer to Chapter 3, "Basic JDBC Programming.")

Creation and Initialization

When a servlet is invoked from a Web URL, the Web server loads and instantiates the servlet. Then it calls the servlet's `init()` method. The `init()` method is called only once even when the servlet runs in multi-threaded servers. The invocation of the `init()` method calls for creation and initialization resources necessary for handling requests. The Web server calls the `init()` method each time the servlet is reloaded. A servlet can be reloaded only after it has been destroyed.

The signature of the init() method is as follows:

```
public void init(ServletConfig config) throws ServletException;
```

As is evident from the above signature, the ServletConfig object is passed as a parameter to the init() method. This object can be referenced later and should be saved by calling the super.init() method with the config object as an argument. This is shown below:

```
public void init(ServletConfig config) throws ServletException
{
  super.init(config);
}
```

Also, the init() throws a ServletException exception when the initialization fails.

Handling of Client Requests

Once initialized, the servlet handles client requests. The HTTP client requests are handled by the service() method. Every request from a client results in a call to the servlet's service() method. This method then interprets the method type stored in the client's request and handles it by assigning the request to a method that handles that request. The servlet then responds to the request. A typical implementation of the service() method is defined in the javax.servlet.HttpServlet class. The HttpServlet class is a subclass of javax.servlet.Servlet class. Its signature is as follows:

```
protected void service(HttpServletRequest req, HttpServletResponse res)
  throws ServletException, IOException;
```

The request and response objects are defined as parameters to the service() method as well as to the methods that service() calls to handle requests. The methods that service() assigns HTTP requests are as follows:

- doGet() for handling GET requests
- doPost() for handling POST requests
- doPut() for handling PUT requests
- doDelete() for handling DELETE requests
- doOptions() for handling OPTIONS requests
- doTrace() for handling TRACE requests

The HTTP request methods can be any of the following: GET, HEAD, POST, DELETE, OPTIONS, and TRACE. The HttpServlet provides different methods to handle each type of HTTP request.

When a request is made to a `HttpServlet`, the `service()` method in the servlet is invoked. This method determines the type of HTTP request and invokes the appropriate method in the servlet. For example, if the HTTP request uses the POST method, then the doPost() method of the servlet is called.

Let us consider the following HTML form:

```
<HTML>
<HEAD> <TITLE> Greet Me </TITLE>
<BODY>
<FORM METHOD=GET ACTION=GreetingServlet">
<H1> See a Greeting ! </H1>
Please enter your name here:
<INPUT TYPE=TEXT NAME=username >
<BR><BR>
<INPUT TYPE=SUBMIT VALUE="View Greeting">
</FORM>
</BODY>
</HTML>
```

When the user clicks the "View Greeting" Button, the `GreetingServlet` is invoked. The HTTP method used is GET (because of the "METHOD=GET" line in the above HTML). When the call reaches the servlet, the `doGet()` method is invoked which will return the greetings to the user. The servlet code is shown below:

```
 import java.io.*;
 import javax.servlet.*;
 import javax.servlet.http.*;

 public class GreetingServlet extends HttpServlet
 {
   public void doGet(HttpServletRequest req,
                         HttpServletResponse res)
             throws ServletException, IOException
    {
      res.setContentType("text/html");
      PrintWriter out = res.getWriter();
      out.println("<HTML>");
      out.println("<HEAD><TITLE> Greetings from a Servlet </TITLE></HEAD>");

      out.println("<BODY><H1> Hello, " + req.getParameter("username") +
" Wish you a very happy and prosperous year ahead! </H1>");
       out.println("</BODY></HTML>");
}
}
```

REGARDING HTTP REQUESTS

The most common HTTP requests are GET and POST. The servlet class should override one or more of these methods by providing a definition of them in it.

In addition to handling client requests, a servlet can provide a description of itself. This can be done by overriding the method `getServletInfo()` that returns a description as a `String`.

```
public String getServletInfo() {
  String myString = "My Servlet Information";
  return myString;
}
```

Destroying the Servlet and Garbage Collection

The handling of client requests and servlet responses continues until the server destroys the servlet. When a service destroys a servlet, the servlet's `destroy()` method is invoked. This performs any garbage collection and cleanup. This method is also run once.

Winding up operations are done in the `destroy()` method. For example, if the servlet were using database connections, then the connections will be closed in the destroy method. A banking servlet would write the account balance (and other details) to the database before it is destroyed.

MIME Types

A servlet processes HTTP client requests and responds back to the client by returning any MIME types. These MIME types can be one of the following:

HTML

XML

Images

This is specified using the `setContentType()` method of the `HttpServletResponse` object inside the `service()` method. We will learn more about this in the section "Developing a Servlet."

Advantages of Java Servlets

The advantages of Java servlets are varied as follows:

- Java servlets are portable and platform-independent. This is based on the fact that the Java servlet API is a standard extension.
- The Java servlets API is very easy to use.

- Java servlets run within the context of an HTTP request and an environment context. This greatly reduces maintenance problems that are otherwise present in CGI and server-side extension programs. A single process can serve multiple servlet responses as opposed to CGI where a new process is to be created to serve each request. Therefore, Java servlets are scalable, stable, and persistent.
- Java servlets enable resource sharing, such as database connections and so on.
- Java servlets are secure as they run within the context of a security manager. The Java servlets run within the context of the Web server's security manager. The user authentication is done by the web server's security manager. The servlet can access the user information from the HttpServletRequest Object that it receives from the web server.
- Java servlets provide built-in session management. This relieves the burden of providing an explicit session management mechanism.

Developing a Servlet

A Java servlet is implemented as a Java class that extends `javax.servlet.Servlet` class or one of its subclasses such as `javax.servlet.HttpServlet`. A servlet does not have a `main()` method; that is why it is required to extend the `javax.servlet.Servlet` class. Servlets are of two types: generic servlets and HTTP-specific servlets. A generic servlet extends the `javax.servlet.Servlet` class and an HTTP-specific servlet extends the `javax.servlet.HttpServlet` class which is a subclass of the `javax.servlet.Servlet` class.

TIP

Any type of servlet can extend the `javax.servlet.HttpServlet` class.

The Java servlet API primarily defines two packages that can be used to implement servlets. These are `javax.servlet` and `javax.servlet.http` packages. The former package consists of interfaces and classes that are used by all servlets. The latter package consists of classes that are specific to HTTP-specific servlets. These packages must be imported by any program that implements servlets. Three classes in the `javax.servlet` package are of primary importance while developing servlets:

`javax.servlet.Servlet` class—This is the class all servlets classes must inherit. This provides an abstract `service()` method that must be overridden to define application-specific functionality. It also provides methods that facilitate communication of a servlet with its server environment and with clients.

`javax.servlet.ServletRequest`—This provides a `ServletRequest` object available with each client request. This object stores data from the client and might include information about the request such as the protocol type, the host originating the request, and any request parameters.

`javax.servlet.ServletResponse`—This provides a `ServletResponse` object available with each servlet response to a client request.

TIP

If the servlet extends `HttpServlet` instead of `Servlet`, then `ServletRequest` and `ServletResponse` objects must be replaced by `HttpServletRequest` and `HttpServletResponse` objects respectively.

For the purposes of this chapter, we assume we are dealing with a generic type of servlets.

Creating a Servlet

We will use the `Department` servlet that was defined in Chapter 7, "Using JavaBeans." To avoid duplication with the `Department` class of Enterprise JavaBeans, we rename this servlet class as `DepartmentS`.

Creating a servlet involves the following steps:

- Import the servlet specific packages.
- Define the servlet class.
- Define the service methods.
- Interact with the client using the service request and response objects.

These steps are described below.

Importing the Servlet Specific Packages

Import the packages `javax.servlet` and `javax.servlet.http` as shown below:

```
import javax.servlet.*;
import javax.servlet.http.*;
```

Defining the Servlet Class

This is done by defining a class that typically extends the `javax.servlet.Servlet` or the `javax.servlet.HttpServlet` class. The `DepartmentS` servlet in our example extends `HttpServlet` as shown below.

```
public class DepartmentS extends HttpServlet {
......
```

Defining the Service Methods

This is done by implementing a `service()` method that overrides the default service method and defines application-specific functionality. This method must be defined in case of a generic servlet. In case of an HTTP-specific servlet, there are the `doGet()`, `doPost()`, `doPut()`, and `doDelete()` methods that need to be defined to handle the corresponding type of HTTP request. The `service()` method or one of the other methods accept two parameters, namely, a `ServletRequest` or `HttpServletRequest` object and a `ServletResponse` or `HttpServletResponse` object. For the `DepartmentS` servlet, this is shown below.

```
public void service(HttpServletRequest req, HttpServletResponse res)
  throws ServletException, IOException {
... ...
}
```

Interacting with the Client Using the Service Request and Response Objects

In the body of the service methods, use the `ServletRequest` or `HttpServletRequest` and `ServletResponse` or `HttpServletResponse` objects, as the case may be, to interact with the server environment and client.

HttpServletRequest Object

An `HttpServletRequest` object enables to obtain the arguments that the client sent as part of the request.

REQUEST PARAMETERS

The `HttpServletRequest` object defines a `getParameter()` method that returns the value of a named parameter. If the parameter is multi-valued, the `getParameterValues()` returns an array of values for the named parameter. The names of the parameters can be explicitly specified or can be obtained from the method `getParameterNames()`.

HttpServletResponse Object

An `HttpServletResponse` object enables to return data to the client. It provides a `getWriter()` method returns a `Writer`. Generally, this is the method that is used to return text data. Otherwise, the `getOutputStream()` method can be used to return a `ServletOutputStream`, i.e., binary data.

TIP

HTTP header data must be set before accessing the `Writer` or `OutputStream`. The `HttpServletResponse` class provides methods to access the header data. For example, the `setContentType()` method sets the content type.

TIP

Close the `Writer` or `ServletOutputStream` after response has been sent.

For the DepartmentS servlet this is shown here:

```
response.setContentType("text/html");

PrintWriter out = response.getWriter() ;

String action = request.getParameter("action") ;

if ( (action == null)|| (action.equals("")) )
{
printInitialForm(request, out) ;
return;
}

if (action.equals("ADD") ) addDepartment(request, out) ;

if (action.equals("MODIFY") ) modifyDepartment(request, out) ;

if (action.equals("DELETE") ) deleteDepartment(request, out) ;

}
```

Here response is an instantiation of HttpServletResponse class and can be declared as shown below:

```
HttpServletResponse response;

// Omit the semicolon at the end if declaring as a parameter
```

The entire servlet program is shown here. The example demonstrates how to extract the parameters from the request object and how to set the HTML response back in the response object. Comments are given explaining each of these. This program also uses the DeptBean JavaBean defined in Chapter 7.

```
//Import the Java IO package and the
//Servlet packages
import java.io.*;
import javax.servlet.*;
import javax.servlet.http.*;
import java.util.* ;

public class DepartmentS extends HttpServlet
{
//The HttpServlet's "service" method is overwritten.
```

```
//Alternatively (since the HTTP GET method is used), the doGet() method
//could have been over-written
public void service ( HttpServletRequest request, HttpServletResponse response)
throws ServletException, IOException {

response.setContentType("text/html");
PrintWriter out = response.getWriter() ;

//Finds out which of the buttons was pressed by the
//user (ADD, MODIFY, DELETE).
//The value will be blanks the first time the servlet is
//invoked
String action = request.getParameter("action") ;

//First time the servlet is invoked
if ( (action == null)|| (action.equals("")) )
{

printInitialForm(request, out) ;
return;

}

//Call the method corresponding to each of the
//action buttons
if (action.equals("ADD") ) addDepartment(request, out) ;
if (action.equals("MODIFY") ) modifyDepartment(request, out) ;
if (action.equals("DELETE") ) deleteDepartment(request, out) ;

}

// Prints the HTTP header, the form and the footer first time
private void printInitialForm(HttpServletRequest request, PrintWriter out)
 throws ServletException, IOException
{

printHeader(out) ;
printForm(request, out) ;
printFooter(out) ;

}
```

```
//Adds the department (whose details are contained in the
//'request' object) to the database.
private void addDepartment(HttpServletRequest request, PrintWriter out)
 throws ServletException, IOException
{

printHeader(out) ;
printForm(request, out) ;
String mesg = new String("") ;

//Extract the user supplied parameters from the 'request' object
String deptNo = request.getParameter("deptNo") ;
String deptName = request.getParameter("deptName") ;
String deptLoc = request.getParameter("deptLoc") ;

//Field validation for null values
if( (deptNo == null) || deptNo.equals("")||(deptName == null) ||
deptName.equals("")||(deptLoc == null)||deptLoc.equals("") )
{

mesg = "One or more of the input fields are blanks" ;

}
else //if all fields are valid
{

int status = -1 ;

try {

//use the Department Bean to add the new department
//to the database.
 DeptBean myBean = new DeptBean() ;
 myBean.setdbDeptNo(Integer.parseInt(deptNo)) ;
 myBean.setdbDname(deptName) ;
 myBean.setdbLoc(deptLoc) ;
 status = myBean.InsertDept() ;
} catch (Exception e) { }

//Check the status returned by the bean and accordingly
//report success or failure
```

```
if(status == 0) mesg = "Department Successfully Added" ;
else mesg = "Failure to add Department" ;

}

printMessage(out, mesg) ;
printFooter(out) ;

}

//Modifies the attributes of an already existing department
//(whose details are contained in the 'request' object)
private void modifyDepartment(HttpServletRequest request, PrintWriter out)
 throws ServletException, IOException
{

String mesg = new String("") ;

//Extract the user supplied parameters from the 'request' object
String deptNo = request.getParameter("deptNo") ;
String deptName = request.getParameter("deptName") ;
String deptLoc = request.getParameter("deptLoc") ;

//Field Validation for null values
if( (deptNo == null) || deptNo.equals("")||(deptName == null) ||
deptName.equals("")||(deptLoc == null)||deptLoc.equals("") )
{

mesg = "One or more of the input fields are blanks" ;

}
else //if all fields are valid
{

int status = -1 ;
try {

//use the Department Bean to modify the
//attributes of the department
 DeptBean myBean = new DeptBean() ;
 myBean.setdbDeptNo(Integer.parseInt(deptNo)) ;
 myBean.setdbDname(deptName) ;
```

```
 myBean.setdbLoc(deptLoc) ;
 status = myBean.UpdateDept() ;
} catch (Exception e) { }

//Check the status returned by the bean and accordingly
//report success or failure
if(status == 0) mesg = "Department Successfully Modified" ;
else mesg = "Failure to modify Department" ;

}

printHeader(out) ;
printForm(request, out) ;
printMessage(out, mesg) ;
printFooter(out) ;

}

//Delete and already existing department
//(whose details are contained in the //'request' object)
private void deleteDepartment(HttpServletRequest request, PrintWriter out)
 throws ServletException, IOException
{

String mesg = new String("") ;

//Extract the user supplied parameters from the 'request' object
String deptNo = request.getParameter("deptNo") ;
String deptName = request.getParameter("deptName") ;
String deptLoc = request.getParameter("deptLoc") ;

//Field Validation for null values
if( (deptNo == null) || deptNo.equals(""))
{

mesg = "One or more of the input fields are blanks" ;

}
else //if all fields are valid
{
```

```
int status = -1 ;

try {

//use the Department Bean to do the deletion
 DeptBean myBean = new DeptBean() ;
 myBean.setdbDeptNo(Integer.parseInt(deptNo)) ;
 myBean.setdbDname(deptName) ;
 myBean.setdbLoc(deptLoc) ;
 status = myBean.DeleteDept() ;
} catch (Exception e) { }

//Check the status returned by the bean and accordingly
//report success or failure
if(status == 0) mesg = "Department Successfully Deleted" ;
else mesg = "Failure to delete Department" ;

}

printHeader(out) ;
printForm(request, out) ;
printMessage(out, mesg) ;
printFooter(out) ;

}

//Prints the first few lines of the output HTML
private void printHeader(PrintWriter out)
{

out.println("<HTML>") ;
out.println("<HEAD>") ;
out.println("<TITLE> Department Maintenance Page </TITLE>") ;
out.println("</HEAD>") ;
out.println("<BODY>") ;
out.println("<H1> Department Maintenance Page </H1>") ;
out.println("<B>") ;
out.println("(Please enter department details and click on INSERT, UPDATE or
DELETE. )") ;
out.println("</B>") ;
out.println("<BR>") ;
out.println("<BR>") ;
```

```
}

//Print the HTML footer
void printFooter(PrintWriter out)
{

out.println("</BODY>") ;
out.println("</HTML>") ;

}

//Print the resulting output HTML form
void printForm( HttpServletRequest request, PrintWriter out)
{

String deptNo = request.getParameter("deptNo") ;

if(deptNo == null) deptNo = "" ;

String deptName = request.getParameter("deptName") ;

if(deptName == null) deptName = "" ;

String deptLoc = request.getParameter("deptLoc") ;

if(deptLoc == null) deptLoc = "" ;

out.println("<FORM METHOD=GET ACTION=Department>") ;
out.println("<TABLE>") ;
out.println("<TR>") ;
out.println("<TD> Department No: </TD>") ;
out.println("<TD> <INPUT TYPE=text NAME=deptNo VALUE='" + deptNo +"'>") ;
out.println("</TR>") ;
out.println("<TR>") ;
out.println("<TD> Department Name:</TD>") ;
out.println("<TD> <INPUT TYPE=text NAME=deptName VALUE='" + deptName + "'>") ;
out.println("</TR>") ;
out.println("<TR>") ;
out.println("<TD> Department Loc: </TD>") ;
out.println("<TD> <INPUT TYPE=text NAME=deptLoc VALUE='" + deptLoc + "'>") ;
out.println("</TR>") ;
out.println("</TABLE>") ;
```

```
out.println("<BR><BR>") ;
out.println("<INPUT TYPE=SUBMIT VALUE='ADD' NAME=action>") ;
out.println("<INPUT TYPE=SUBMIT VALUE='MODIFY' NAME=action>") ;
out.println("<INPUT TYPE=SUBMIT VALUE='DELETE' NAME=action>") ;
out.println("</FORM>") ;

}

//Displays a messge at the bottom of the output HTML page
//Used to display status messages
void printMessage(PrintWriter out, String mesg)
{

out.println("<BR>") ;
out.println("<B>") ;
out.println(mesg) ;
out.println("</B>") ;

}

} //END of CLASS
```

Accessing a Servlet

Accessing the servlets consists of invoking the servlet from a `http://` based URL. To do this, the servlet has to be first installed on a Web server. To do this there are two steps, as follows:

- Once a servlet class has been defined, compile the .java file. This requires the servlet API to be included in the CLASSPATH.
- Install the servlet on the Web server by moving the generated `.class` file to the Web server's servlet directory. The steps for configuring the servlet directory for Apache JServ are listed below. The setup assumes a Windows environment.

1. There are three configuration files where changes have to be made:
   - jserv.conf located in the conf directory of the Apache JServ home directory
   - `jserv.properties` located in the `conf` directory of the Apache Jserv home directory
   - `zone.properties` located in `servlets` directory of the Apache Jserv home directory
2. Add the following line to the `jserv.conf` file.

   ```
   ApJServMount /servlets /root
   ```

3. Modify the `jserv.properties` file to include the following:

   ```
   #jserv.properties
   zones=root
   root.properties=%APACHE_JSERV_HOME%\servlets\zone.properties
   wrapper.classpath=%ORACLE_HOME%\jdbc\lib\classes12.zip
   ```

   Here `%APACHE_JSERV_HOME%` refers to the home directory where Apache JServ is installed. On Windows it may be `C:\Program Files\Apache JServ 1.1.2`.

4. Modify the zone.properties file to include the following:

   ```
   #zone.properties
   repositories=%APACHE_JSERV_HOME%\servlets
   servlets.startup=DepartmentS
   servlets.DepartmentS.code=DepartmentS
   ```

   Here DepartmentS in the third line the name with which the servlet will be accessed. This can be different from the actual servlet class name (that is given in the last line to the right of the = sign).

5. Copy the DepartmentS.class and DeptBean.class files to the servlets directory under Apache Jserv home directory.

6. Start Apache. If already running, shutdown and restart it.

Once the servlet has been installed on the Web Server, it can be accessed in two ways:

- By referencing its name in a URL. For the `DepartmentS` servlet, this is shown here:

  ```
  http://localhost/servlets/DepartmentS
  ```

- From an HTML page.

Specify the servlet URL in the appropriate HTML tag.

Exception Handling

Servlets provide a clean way for handling exception conditions. The `HttpServletResponse` object provides a `sendError()` method that takes a HTTP error code and the error message as parameters. The `Response` object defines constants for all major HTTP error codes. For example, a servlet can contain the code:

```
response.sendError(HttpServletResponse.SC_NOT_FOUND, "Could not find file");
```

The Web server checks the `Response` code and returns the appropriate error message to the browser.

The Servlet API also defines two Exception classes, namely, `ServletException` and `UnavailableException`. `UnavailableException` is derived from `ServletException`. For typical errors, the servlet throws the `ServletException`. However, it throws the `UnavailableException` when there is a fatal error—for example, unable to connect to a database. This will notify the Web server that the servlet is unavailable to take user requests.

Any servlet class method is required to throw the `ServletException` exception. In addition it might throw the `IOException` exception as is the case with the `service()` method. When using JDBC within a servlet, the SQLException must also be thrown by the servlet methods.

The following shows the code for the GreetingServlet with exceptions included:

```
import java.io.*;
import javax.servlet.*;
import javax.servlet.http.*;

public class GreetingServlet extends HttpServlet
{
  public void doGet(HttpServletRequest req,
                     HttpServletResponse res)
          throws ServletException, IOException
   {
     res.setContentType("text/html");
     PrintWriter out = res.getWriter();

     String name = req.getParameter("username") ;

     if (name == null || name.equals("") )
   {
       throw(new ServletException("Your name is missing!") );
   }
    else
     {
     out.println("<HTML>");
     out.println("<HEAD><TITLE> Greetings from a Servlet </TITLE></HEAD>");

     out.println("<BODY><H1> Hello, " + req.getParameter("username") +
" Wish you a very happy and prosperous year ahead! </H1>");
      out.println("</BODY></HTML>");
     }
}
}
```

Managing Sessions in Servlets

From an Oracle Servlet Engine(OSE) perspective, there are two types of sessions involved with servlets:

- Database sessions
- HTTP servlet sessions

Managing sessions consists of tracking the database session and HTTP sessions resulting out of a client's HTTP requests. When the first HTTP request is received from a client (that is, a browser), an HTTP session is created for the client. Any subsequent requests from the client are delegated to this session. OSE manages these sessions using two methods:

- Cookies
- URL rewriting

These methods are described in the section "Managing Sessions" later on.

REGISTER THE END POINT WHILE ADDING IT TO ACCESS A PUBLISHED SERVLET

Don't forget to register the end point while adding it to access a servlet published in Oracle 8i from a Web browser. Otherwise, you get the error such as "Unable to locate server localhost:8080" while accessing the servlet from the Web browser.

One of the ways to configure a servlet running in the Oracle Servlet Engine (OSE) is via the database dispatcher servicing HTTP.

The database DISPATCHER technique requires creating an endpoint and *registering* it on the OSE service that is created. This endpoint is for the HTTP protocol. This can be done using the *-register* option with the *addendpoint* command of the session shell.

Another trick of the trade is to log in to the session shell as SYS instead of an ordinary user account so that it has the necessary privileges to store the port in the dynamic tables associated with the ports.

Database Sessions

Whenever an HTTP client connects to an instance of Oracle8i, (that is, to the JServer within Oracle8i), a database session is created. This session runs its virtual JVM. Each database session combines several HTTP sessions within it. The database session remains active as long as all HTTP sessions have responded to the client requests or when the timeout period has occurred. The database timeout period is set by the service parameter `service.globalTimeout`. This can be set when the Web service is created (using the `createservice` command) or can be configured at a later time.

TIP

Only one database session exists per client.

TIP

When a database session terminates because of a timeout, it causes all HTTP sessions within it to terminate. This also causes any uncommitted SQL changes to be rolled back.

TIP

When all the HTTP session requests have been processed, it causes the database session to be terminated automatically.

HTTP Servlet Sessions

An HTTP session is created when the servlet executes within the database to process the client request. An HTTP session is set up for each servlet that the client activates in a stateful servlet context. This causes the `getSession(true)` method be invoked.

The HTTP session terminates when its timeout value has occurred. This can cause the corresponding database session to be terminated when there are no more session objects left inside the database session. The architecture of sessions regarding servlets can be depicted as in Figure 12.1.

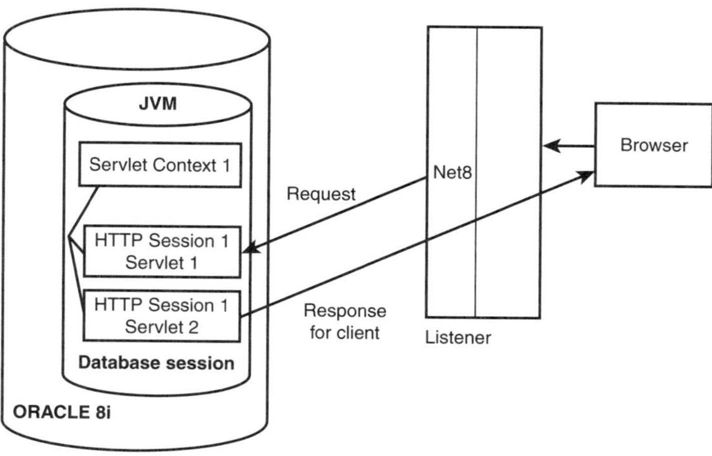

FIGURE 12.1
A typical architecture showing Servlet sessions within Oracle8i.

Managing Sessions

OSE manages servlet sessions by means of cookies or URL rewrites.

A *cookie* is a unit of data that is created by the servlet engine and stored by the client browser. Each browser has a list of unique cookies stored in it. A stateful session sends a cookie to the client to enable the client information to be readily available to the server. The servlet sends a response with a cookie in it. This helps in session tracking by opening a dialogue between the client and the servlet. The Java servlet API has built-in support for cookies by means of a Cookie class and the following two methods:

```
HttpServletResponse.addCookie()
HttpServletRequest.getCOokies()
```

Sometimes a browser might support cookies, but the user can turn them off for security purposes. In such cases or if the client browser does not support cookies, OSE uses URL rewriting for session tracking. This method works as follows:

- The servlet processes a request.
- Encode a URL with the session ID appended to it.
- Redirect the client to the new URL.
- The servlet processing the redirection request determines the current user based on the appended session ID and performs a database lookup on the user based on the session ID.

Servlets Deployment

Oracle8i provides an Oracle Servlet Engine (OSE) for deployment of servlets. The OSE functions by means of services. Each service consists of one or more Web domains. Each Web domain, in turn, consists of one or more servlet contexts. Finally, the servlet context contains servlets. A Web domain is configured to map a virtual path to a servlet context. A servlet context is configured to map a virtual path to a servlet.

Deploying a Servlet to a JAR File

The servlet class as well as any other dependent classes can be deployed to a JAR file using the JAR command. Once deployed to a JAR file, it can be loaded into the Oracle8i database and then published into the servlet context.

Packaging JAR Files

The servlet class as well as other dependent classes can be packaged into a JAR file using the `jar` command. This is shown below.

```
jar cvf deptS.jar *.class
```

Deploying Java Servlets on the Database-tier in Oracle8i (Oracle 8.1.7)

Servlets that are database-bound rather than application-bound can be deployed inside the Oracle8i database for efficient execution.

There are two methods to configure a servlet running in the Oracle Servlet Engine (OSE):

- Via the database dispatcher servicing HTTP
- Via the Oracle supplied module for Apache (MOD_OSE)

The database DISPATCHER technique requires creating an endpoint and registering it on the OSE service that is created. This endpoint would be for the HTTP protocol. The other technique is to configure an endpoint for listening for requests from MOD_OSE which are communicated via Net 8 protocol.

We will demonstrate the deployment of servlets in Oracle8i Release 3 using a configuration via the database dispatcher servicing HTTP.

Deployment of servlets on the database-tier in Oracle8i requires the following steps:

1. Create a service.
2. Add an endpoint for a port and register it to the Web service.
3. Grant ownership to the servlet user for the service created.
4. Create a Web domain.
5. Create a servlet context.
6. Compile and load the servlet class into the database.
7. Publish the servlet in the Oracle8i Web server.

These steps are detailed below.

TIP

Creating a service, a Web domain, and a servlet context and publishing the servlet require the use of the session shell command `sess_sh` invoked as follows:

sess_sh –u SYS/<password> –s sess_iiop://training:2481:Oracle

Here

`sess_iiop` is like a keyword and should be specified for a SESS_IIOP URL.

`training` refers to the hostname of the computer that has Oracle8i.

`2481` is the listener port configured to listen to session IIO.

`Oracle` is the tnsnames alias corresponding to the SID of the database.

Only the DBA or the DBA priviled users can logon as SYS.

TIP

There should be an entry for `mts_dispatchers` in the init.ora file to set up MTS dispatchers.

mts_dispatchers = "(PROTOCOL=TCP)"

Create a Service

A Web service is created using the `createwebservice` command at the $ prompt of the session shell.

This creates basic information for a Web-based service that is used during service installation, using the HTTP protocol for connecting. This information includes the basic level of a service, the service name, property groups, and the root location.

The syntax is as follows:

```
createwebservice [options] <service_name>
-root <location>
[-properties <prop_groups>]
[-ip]
[-virtual]
```

`<service_name>` is the user-defined name of the new service.

`-root <location>` is the JNDI location for the Web service configuration.

`-properties <prop_groups>` is the property group to be used as the default for this service.

`-ip` is the Web service allowing IP-based multi-homed domains.

`-virtual` is the Web service allowing VirtualHost multi-homed domains.

If neither -ip nor -virtual is specified, the Web service is a single domain Web service. The name given will be the service root name.

The following example creates a Web service, deptService, that is defined in the /deptDomain directory. The /deptDomain directory should have been created by the createwebdomain command.

```
createwebservice -root /deptDomain deptService
```

Add an Endpoint for a Port and Register It to the Web Service

An end point should be created to specify a port for the servlet engine to listen and this endpoint should be registered with the Web service created above. This is done with the addendpoint command at the $ prompt of the session shell. This is shown below.

```
addendpoint - port 9494 -register deptService endpt9494
```

Here endpt9494 is the name of the endpoint.

Grant Ownership to the Servlet User for the Service Created

The user using the servlet must be granted ownership for the service created. This is done using the chmod command at the session shell $ prompt. For the deptService Web service created above, this is shown below.

```
chmod -R +rwx ORATEST deptDomain
```

Here -R denotes the option to change the execute rights recursively, +rwx denotes the read (r), write(w) and execute(x) privileges to be added(+) to the user ORATEST for the domain deptDomain of the service deptService.

Create a Web Domain

A Web domain is created within a service root using the createwebdomain command at the $ prompt of the session shell. Each Web domain is initialized with a default servlet context named /default. The syntax for the createwebdomain command is as follows:

```
createwebdomain [options] <domain_name>
```

The options are:

```
[-docroot <location>]
[-properties <prop_groups>
```

Here `<domain_name>` is the full path of where the domain should be located and its name.

`-docroot <location>` is the location of the servlet pages for this Web domain's default context. Other context's docroot location is specified in the `createcontext` command.

`-properties <prop_groups>` specifies the property groups to use as the defaults for this service. The properties are specified as the name-value pairs.

The following creates a Web domain named `webdomain`:

```
createwebdomain -docroot c:\dept /deptDomain
```

Create a Servlet Context

A servlet context is created using the `createcontext` command at the $ prompt of the session shell. A servlet context is located in `contexts` directory within the Web domain root. A servlet context can support either stateless or stateful servlets.

The syntax for the `createcontext` command is as follows:

```
createcontext [options] <domain_name> <context_name>
-virtualpath <path>
[-recreate]
[-properties <prop_groups>]
[-docroot <location>]
[-stateless]
```

Here `<domain_name>` specifies the directory and name for the domain where the servlet context is to be created. This domain must already exist and should have been created using the `cre-atewebdomain` command.

`<context_name>` is the user-defined name for the servlet context to be used within the domain. The default context is `default`.

`-virtualpath <path>` is the virtual path to which the servlet is bond. This is used while invocation of the servlet from a Web browser.

`-recreate`—If a context with this name already exists, delete it before adding an empty context with this name. This destroys any servlets currently associated with this context.

`-properties <prop_groups>` specifies the property groups to use as the defaults for this service. This is specified as name-value pairs.

`-docroot <location>`—All of the servlet static pages are located in this directory in the server machine's filesystem.

`-stateless` specifies that all servlets in this context are stateless.

```
createcontext -virtualpath /testing -docroot c:\dept /deptDomain deptContext
```

Compile and Load the Servlet Class into the Database

Compile the servlet class to obtain a `.class` file which will be loaded into the database. Compilation of a servlet class requires the following jars in your CLASSPATH:

- The jar containing the http classes:

```
$(ORACLE_HOME)/jis/lib/servlet.jar
```

- If the servlet accesses the database, the JDBC classes file `classes12.zip` must be in the class path:

```
%(ORACLE_HOME)/jdbc/lib/classes12.zip
```

For the DepartmentS servlet this is shown below.

```
javac DepartmentS.java DeptBean.java
```

The reason for compiling DeptBean.java along with DepartmentS.java is that the DepartmentS servlet uses the DeptBean for instantiation and invokes the Bean methods InsertDept(), UpdateDept(), and DeleteDept() on this object instance. Once compiled, the `.class` files can be packaged into a `.jar` file as follows:

```
jar cvf deptS.jar *.class
```

The resulting jar file is to be loaded into the database using the `loadjava` utility. This is shown below.

Alternatively the individual class files can be loaded.

```
loadjava -thin -user oratest/oratest@training:1521:oracle -r DepartmentS.class
DeptBean.class
```

Publish the Servlet in the Oracle8i Web Server

Once the servlet has been loaded into the database, it has to be published in the Oracle8i Web server. This requires a servlet context created earlier or the servlet can be published in the `default` context. The servlet is published into the servlet context subdirectory `named_servlets` by name. This is done using the `publishservlet` command at the $ prompt of the session shell. The syntax of this command is as follows:

```
publishservlet [-virtualpath <path>] [-stateless] [-reuse] [-properties props]
contextName <servletName> [className]
```

Here `-virtualpath option` and *`path:`* `virtual path` are specified to associate with this servlet for invocation.

`-stateless flag`—Specifies the OSE that the servlet is stateless. When this is set, the servlet has no access to the HTTPSession.

`contextName`—The name assigned to this context servlet directory.

`servletName`—The name assigned to this servlet in the named_servlets directory.

`className`—The name of the class implementing the HttpServlet interface.

This command publishes a servlet by name in the context and associates a virtual path with the named servlet.

The following must be specified as arguments to the `publishservlet` command:

- A virtual path that the servlet is mapped to.
- The servlet context name.
- The servlet name. This specifies identifying the servlet by a name and the servlet is said to be published by name using this name.
- The Oracle schema name suffixed by a colon and followed by the actual servlet class name.

For the `DepartmentS` servlet this is shown here:

```
publishservlet -virtualpath /tdept /deptDomain/contexts/deptContext tdept ORAT-
EST:DepartmentS
```

Here we are publishing the servlet in the `deptContext` context we created above.

After publishing, to verify that the servlet is published use the following:

```
ls /deptDomain/contexts/deptContext/named_servlets
```

We obtain the following:

```
tdept
```

Access the Servlet from a Web Browser

Once the servlet has been published in the database, it can be accessed from any Web browser using the virtual path specified while publishing the servlet. The servlet is accessed using the URL `http://<hostname>:<port>/<virtual-path>`.

For the DepartmentS servlet, this is shown here:

```
http://localhost:9494/testing/tdept
```

Summary

This chapter outlined the detailed procedure for implementing Java servlets in Oracle8i using the Oracle Servlet Engine inside the database. Specifically the method of developing and deploying servlets in Oracle8i was discussed.

USING JAVA SERVER PAGES

ESSENTIALS

- Deploy Java in a Web environment using Java Server Pages (JSP).
- Create a JSP by writing the HTML involved in displaying a Web page. Then embed JSP-specific tags in the HTML to provide for dynamic content and save the resulting file with .jsp extension.
- JavaBeans components can be referenced in a JSP using a special `<jsp:useBean>` tag. Implement a JSP using a JavaBean.
- A JSP can be deployed on various Oracle environments such as Oracle8i database server, Release 8.1.7, Oracle Internet Application Server or Oracle HTTP Server powered by Apache.
- Deploying a JSPs on the database-tier in Oracle8i using the OSE involves compiling any dependent classes, translating the JSP on the server side or pre-translating the JSP pages on the client side, loading the translated JSP pages into the Oracle8i database, and publishing the JSP pages to make them accessible from the database for execution.
- Use the command-line tools *loadjava* and *session_sh* to translate, load, and publish the pages. Then access the JSP using a URL.

This chapter explains the use of Java Server Pages for building Java-enabled Web sites. A comparison is made between Java servlets and Java Server Pages and a detailed account of creating a JSP and running it is provided. The method of deploying a JSP in Oracle8i is explained.

Overview of JSP

Java Server Pages (JSP) are Sun's solution for developing dynamic Web sites. JSP allows us to mix regular static HTML with dynamically generated HTML. The dynamic part of the code is enclosed in special tags. The JSP page looks more like an HTML page and is normally stored using the .jsp extension. But behind the scenes, the JSP page is converted into a servlet with the static HTML simply printed to the servlet's `HttpResponse` object. JSP allows nothing that cannot be implemented using a servlet.

The JSP page is translated to a servlet the first time it is accessed. Subsequent requests to the JSP page use the servlet. Since translation is not done for every request, JSPs are significantly faster than CGI programs.

JSP offers the advantage of separating the front-end components from the business components. A JSP/HTML programmer can write the JSP code. The code can make use of JavaBeans that can be designed and developed independently by a Java programmer.

We will give the basic setup procedure for running JSPs followed by a typical directory structure for placing the JSP files using the Tomcat Web Server that supports JSPs. The setup of the development environment for running JSPs depends on what classes we are using in the JSP code. A typical setup might include the following steps:

1. Set the `PATH` variable to include `%JAVA_HOME%\bin` directory. (Here a Windows environment is assumed. For an UNIX environment, use the appropriate syntax such as $JAVA_HOME.)
2. Set the `CLASSPATH` variable to include the current working directory. Also set the CLASSPATH variable to include the directory of the Web server (such as Tomcat) where utility classes such as dependent JavaBean classes are located.
3. If using servlet-specific classes, set the `CLASSPATH` variable to include the `servlet.jar` file located in the `lib` subdirectory of the Web server home directory.
4. If using JDBC inside the JSP, set the CLASSPATH variable to include the `[Oracle Home]\jdbc\lib\classes12.zip` or `[Oracle Home]\jdbc\lib\classes111.zip`. (Refer to Chapter 3, "Basic JDBC Programming").

Regarding the Tomcat Web Server, the following is the directory structure:

1. The root directory where the Tomcat server is installed—On Windows it may look like `C:\jakarta\jakarta-tomcat-3.2.1>`. We refer to this directory as <SERVER_ROOT>.
2. The subdirectory under <SERVER_ROOT> directory that corresponds to the root directory of the Web application where the JSPs will be located—On Windows this may look like `C:\jakarta\jakarta-tomcat-3.2.1\webapps`.
3. The subdirectory `WEB-INF` under the Web application root directory that contains all resources associated with the application that are not in the document root of the application—Every Web application root directory must have this subdirectory. On Windows this may look like `C:\jakarta\jakarta-tomcat-3.2.1\webapps\WEB-INF`.
4. The subdirectory `classes` under WEB-INF where utility classes such as JavaBean classes are loaded—On Windows this may look like `C:\jakarta\jakarta-tomcat-3.2.1\webapps\WEB-INF\classes`.

JSP Basics

A JSP adheres to the JSP 1.1 specification defined by Sun. It has various elements that are defined as per the specifications outlined in this specification set. This section discusses the various syntax elements that make up a JSP page. Specifically, it discusses how to include directives, declarations, expressions, objects (both implicit and explicit), scriptlets, and actions.

JSP Tags

A JSP page can include within it the above-mentioned elements using special characters called tags. For example, to include a directive the tag `<%@ ... %>` is used. This subsection discusses how to specify directives in a JSP page. The next two subsections describe how to include other types of JSP elements in a JSP page.

Directives are specified using the `<%@ ... %>` tag. A directive instructs the JSP container with information regarding the entire JSP page. This is used in translating or executing the JSP page.

The syntax is as follows:

```
<%@ directive attribute1="value1" attribute2=" value2"... %>
```

Here directive refers to one of the following:

- page—This directive is used to specify any page-dependent attributes such as the scripting language to use, a class to extend, a package to import, an error page to use, or the JSP page output buffer size. For example,

  ```
  <%@ page language="java" %>
  ```

  sets the scripting language to "java". In OracleJSP, the default scripting language is java.

- include—This directive is used to specify a file that contains text or code to be inserted into the JSP page when it is translated. The path of the file is specified relative to the URL specification of the JSP page. For example,

  ```
  <%@ include file="abcd.jsp" %>
  ```

  specifies that the JSP should use the text or code in the file abcd.jsp at the time of translation. This is not similar to a Java include that makes classes available, but is code that is actually executed.

- taglib—This directive is used to specify a library of customized JSP tags that will be used in the JSP page. When using this directive, specify the location of a *tag library description* file and a prefix to distinguish use of tags from that library.

Declarations, Scripting, and Expressions

This subsection discusses how to specify declarations, expressions, scriptlets, and comments in a JSP page.

Declarations

Declarations create new objects in a JSP page. A declaration is specified by the `<%! ... %>` tag and it specifies the name, the data type, and an initial value for the object being created.

For example,

```
<%! int cnt = 0; %>
```

declares a variable cnt of type int with an initial value of 0. This uses standard Java syntax within the tag.

TIP

Using this tag, only member variables can be declared. Method variables are declared within scriptlets. Member variables have instance scope and are associated within an instance of the servlet built by the JSP container.

The semicolon is necessary to mark the end of a Java statement.

Multiple variables can be declared by separating them by a comma.

Once a variable has been declared, it can be used in expressions.

Expressions

An expression is a small segment of Java code that is evaluated, converted into string values, and displayed when encountered in the JSP. An expression is specified by the `<%= ... %>` tag.

For example,

```
<HTML>
<BODY>
<%! int i=4; %>
<P> The initial value of i is <%= i %>.</P>
<P> The computed value of i is <%= i+2 %>.</P>
</BODY>
<HTML>
```

Scriptlets

Scriptlets are segments of Java code mixed with HTML that are executed every time the JSP is accessed. They provide the basis for dynamic behavior and are written using a special tag called the scriptlet tag as shown below.

```
<% ... %>
```

For example,

```
<% DeptBean myBean = new DeptBean(); %>
The name is <%= myBean.getName() %>
```

Here the line `<% DeptBean myBean = new DeptBean(); %>` is executed every time the page is requested, creating myBean as a new instance each time. Then the expression displays the current value each time.

TIP

The declaration is made only once, whereas the scriptlet and an expression are executed each time the page is accessed.

Variables can be declared in scriptlet tags and these have local scope as opposed to variables declared in declaration tags that have instance scope. These local scope variables are also called method variables.

Comments

Comments are programmatic text comments included within the JSP page. Comments are specified by the tag `<%-- ... --%>`. Unlike HTML comments, these comments are not visible when a user views the page source.

For example:

```
<%-- This is a Department JSP returning the name of a particular dept. --%>
```

Objects and Actions

A JSP object is a Java class instance declared within a JSP page. JSP objects are of two types, explicit and implicit. Explicit objects are declared within the JSP page and are accessible to that page or to other pages based on their scope. An example of an explicit object is an instance variable declared within the JSP.

Implicit objects are those created by the JSP Container. An example of an implicit object is the *request* object that is of type `javax.servlet.HttpServletRequest`. This object can be used as follows:

```
<%= request.getParameter("<param-name>") %>
```

Other commonly used implicit objects are as follows:

application—This is associated with the `javax.servlet.ServletContext` object and has Application scope.

session—This is associated with the `javax.servlet.HttpSession` object and has Session scope.

response—This is associated with the servlet `javax.servlet.HttpServletResponse` object and has Page scope.

out—This refers to the `javax.servlet.jsp.PrintWriter` object that is sent back to the client (that is, the browser) and has Page scope.

exception—This is associated with the `java.lang.Throwable` object and has Page scope.

page—This is associated with the `java.lang.Object` object and has Page scope.

The OracleJSP mechanism defines four standard JSP scopes for event-handling for any Java objects used in a JSP application:

- Page—The object can be referenced from only within the JSP page within which it was created. Changes made to an object with page scope are retained as long as the page exists and are lost when the page exits. Whenever the JSP page is accessed, an entirely new page is generated at request time and sent to the user. This indicates page scope.
- Request—The object can be referenced from any JSP page servicing the same HTTP request that is serviced by the JSP page that created the object. Although the request object exists for the duration of a page, request scope can be separated from page scope.
- Session—The object can be referenced from any JSP page executing within the same session as the JSP page that created the object. Session scope implies that the data is associated with a user of a page.
- Application—The object can be referenced from any JSP page that is being executed within the same Web application as the page that created the object. This scope spans over all users and all pages and can be used to access data appearing on multiple pages and accessible across multiple sessions. An example of an object in application scope is a database connection object that is shared by multiple pages of an application.

Scope setting can be done manually using scriptlets or automatically using Beans. The latter method is discussed in the section "Referencing a JavaBeans Component from a JSP" later in the chapter.

Actions

An action in a JSP page refers to any activity occurring within the execution process such as instantiating a Java object, referencing a JavaBean, and so on. The actions are described by means of action tags specified in the JSP specification. The main action tags are the following:

`jsp:useBean`

The `jsp:useBean` action defines an instance of a specified JavaBean class, gives the instance a specified name, and defines the scope within which it is accessible. For example,

```
<jsp:useBean id="myBean" scope="request" class="NameBean" />
```

This is described in the section "Referencing JavaBean Components."

`jsp:setProperty`

The `jsp:setProperty` action sets one or more bean properties. (The bean must have been previously specified in a `useBean` action.) The value of the property can be directly specified or get it from an associated HTTP request parameter.

```
<jsp:setProperty name="nameBean" property="Name" value="Bulusu" />
```

`jsp:getProperty`

The `jsp:getProperty` action retrieves a bean property value, converts it to a Java string, and stores the string value into the implicit out object so that it can be displayed as output. (The bean must have been previously specified in a `jsp:useBean` action.) For example,

```
<jsp:getProperty name="NameBean" property="Name" />
```

`jsp:include`

The `jsp:include` action includes static or dynamic resources into the page at request time as the page is displayed. The resource is specified with a relative URL. As of the Sun Microsystems *JavaServer Pages Specification, Version 1.1*, you must set flush to true, which results in the buffer being flushed to the browser when a `jsp:include` action is executed. (The flush attribute is required and a setting of false is currently invalid.)For example,

```
<jsp:include page="test.jsp" flush="true" />
```

`jsp:forward`

The `jsp:forward` action terminates execution of the current page, discards its output, and sends a new page—either an HTML page, a JSP page, or a servlet. For example,

```
<jsp:forward page="test.jsp" />
```

Putting all the above basics of JSP together, we can write a sample JSP page. The following code saved in a file named `SimpleJSP.jsp` demonstrates a JSP that connects to an Oracle database and runs a simple query. Here we use directives, declarations, scriplets, and expressions mixed with HTML to construct the JSP and display the results.

```
<%@ page import="java.sql.*" %>
<%@ page import="oracle.sql.*" %>
<%@ page import="oracle.jdbc.driver.*" %>

<%! Connection conn; %>
<%! Statement stmt; %>
<%! ResultSet rset; %>
<%  DriverManager.registerDriver(new oracle.jdbc.driver.OracleDriver()); %>
<%  conn = DriverManager.getConnection
            ("jdbc:oracle:thin:@training:1521:Oracle",
             "oratest", "oratest"); %>
<% stmt = conn.createStatement(); %>
<HTML>
<HEAD>
  <TITLE>List of Departments</TITLE>
```

```
</HEAD>
<BODY>
<H1>List of Departments</H1>
<TABLE BORDER="1">
  <TR><TH>Id</TH><TH>Name</TH><TH>Location</TH></TR>
  <% rset = stmt.executeQuery("SELECT deptno, dname, loc FROM dept"); %>
  <% while (rset.next()) { %>
     <TR>
        <TD><%= rset.getInt(1) %></TD>
        <TD><%= rset.getString(2) %></TD>
        <TD><%= rset.getString(3) %></TD>
     </TR>
  <% } %>
</TABLE>
</BODY>
</HTML>
<% if (rset != null) rset.close(); %>
<% if (stmt != null) stmt.close(); %>
<% if (conn != null) conn.close(); %>
```

To access the JSP from a browser, copy the `SimpleJSP.jsp` file to the root directory of the Web server where JSP files are to be located. Start the Web Server and then access the JSP from a browser using the URL `http://localhost:8080/<root-directory-for-jsp>/SimpleJSP.jsp`. The output of this JSP is displayed as shown in Figure 13.1.

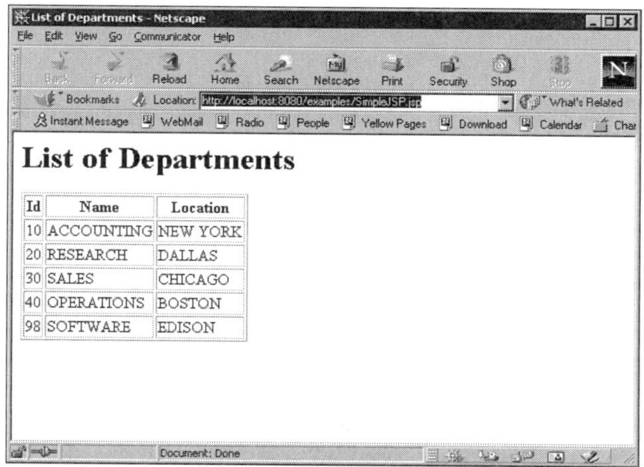

FIGURE 13.1
The output screen of SimpleJSP page.

Advantages of JSPs

JSPs offer several advantages over other server-side technologies. These are as follows:

- JSPs are independent of a specific platform. All that is needed to implement JSPs is a Java Virtual Machine and a JSP Engine. This makes it free from any particular platform or architecture.
- JSPs enable faster development and deployment. JSPs are automatically compiled when first accessed and subsequently run as compiled code. This enables faster deployment. All that is needed then is to place the JSP file in the appropriate Web server directory.
- JSPs allow the definition of presentation logic using special JSP tags and Java scriptlets without worrying about application logic. In addition, JSPs allow the implementation of application logic in JavaBean components that the JSP accesses using a special tag. This provides for a clear demarcation of presentation logic in the JSP file and application logic in the JavaBean.
- JSPs are an extension of Java servlets and as such leverage the benefits of the Java programming language such as cross-platform development and deployment, extensibility, component reusability, and ease of use.
- JSPs are based on an open-standard specification and can be deployed on any platform that supports the JSP specification. These platforms also include Oracle8i database.

Differences Between JSPs and Java Servlets

Although JSPs are an extension of Java servlets, there exist subtle differences between them. These differences are:

- JSPs are a method of embedding Java code in an HTML or XML file whereas servlets incorporate HTML or XML strings in a Java class.
- JSPs are translated into a Java servlet the first time it is accessed.
- JSPs eliminate the need to write Java code to produce static HTML such as HTML formatting and layout markup unlike servlets.

JSP Architecture

Basically, a JSP is a standard HTML or XML page containing JSP-specific tags. The JSP container or the JSP engine is the one that compiles, translates, and executes a JSP and finally processes the requests to the client. The JSP Container is included within the Oracle8i Server Release 3. The following is a typical architecture of a JSP:

1. Request Phase—The client requests the JSP page by means of a URL containing the .jsp filename.
2. Translation Phase—The .jsp filename of the URL triggers the servlet container of the Web server to invoke the JSP container. The JSP container traces the JSP page and translates it into a pure Java source code file containing a Java servlet. It implements the `javax.servlet.jsp.HttpJspPage` interface. This .java source file is then compiled by the JSP container to produce a servlet .class file. Subsequent JSP requests do not involve translation and the existing Java class is used.
3. Execution and Request processing Phase—Once translated, the JSP Container instantiates and executes the resulting servlet. This servlet (that is a JSP instance) will then process the HTTP request, generate an HTTP response, and return the response to the client.

This is shown in Figure 13.2.

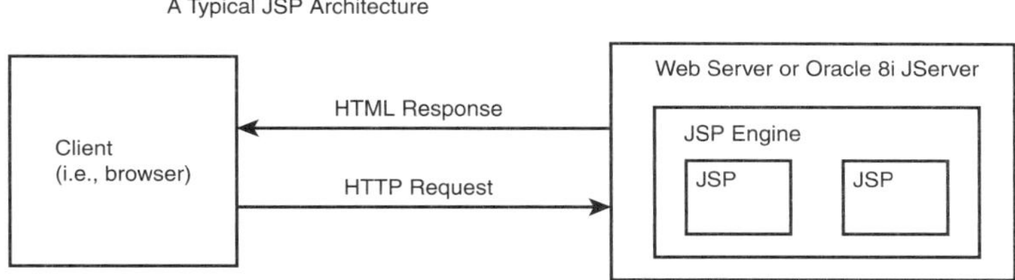

FIGURE 13.2
Figure showing a typical architecture of a JSP.

Creating and Designing a JSP

This section discusses the basic steps for creating a JSP. It also highlights the use of JavaBeans in a JSP.

Create JSPs

Creating a JSP involves the following steps:

1. Write the HTML involved in displaying a page.
2. Embed JSP-specific tags in the HTML to provide for dynamic content.
3. Save the resulting file with a .jsp extension.

We will discuss the creation of name.jsp that prints a name in the client browser. The code for this is as follows:

```
<%@ page import="NameBean"%>
<HTML>
<HEAD> <TITLE> Name JSP </TITLE> </HEAD>
<BODY BGCOLOR="#FFFFFF">
<% NameBean myBean = new NameBean(); %>
The name is <%= myBean.getName() %>
</BODY>
</HTML>
```

Here `NameBean` is a Java class that has the following definition:

```
public class NameBean {
String name;
public String getName()
  {
name = "Bulusu Lakshman";
return name ;
}
}
```

The above JSP is saved in a file named name.jsp and the associated Java class is stored in a file named NameBean.java and then compiled. In the case of Tomcat Web Server, this class file should be copied to the <SERVER_ROOT>/webapps/WEB-INF/classes directory so that it can be assessed when called from the JSP. (Refer to the Tomcat directory structure given in an earlier section).

The JSP presented above performs the following functions:

1. A page directive is used to import the `NameBean` class into the JSP. The following statement does this:

   ```
   <%@ page import="NameBean"%>
   ```

2. The heading title for the page is set using HTML. A chunk of HTML is sent consisting of

   ```
   <HTML>
   <HEAD> <TITLE> Name JSP </TITLE> </HEAD>
   <BODY BGCOLOR="#FFFFFF">
   ```

3. A scriptlet is used to instantiate the `NameBean` class. The following line does this function:

   ```
   <% NameBean myBean = new NameBean(); %>
   ```

4. Another chunk of HTML is sent consisting of

   ```
   The name is
   ```

5. An expression is used to compute the return value of `getName()` function on the instance of the `NameBean` class.

   ```
   <%= myBean.getName() %>
   ```

   The return value is sent to the client.

6. Finally, the last chunk of HTML is sent.

   ```
   </BODY>
   </HTML>
   ```

TIPS

The HTML page can be created first using a GUI HTML editor and then insert the JSP-specific scriplets and other dynamic code into the HTML file. This makes development of the HTML page easier and more correct.

Referencing a JavaBeans Component from a JSP

A JavaBean component can be accessed from within a JSP using the `<jsp:useBean ... />` tag. A typical signature of this tag is as follows:

```
<jsp:useBean id="bean name" class="bean class" />
```

Here `bean name` is any valid Java identifier and must be unique. The ID cannot be the same for two different beans. `bean class` is the name of the JavaBean class.

Once the `useBean` tag is specified, the methods of the bean can be invoked from within the JSP using id.method syntax.

The name.jsp referenced earlier can be written using the `useBean` tag as follows:

```
<%@ page import="NameBean"%>
<HTML>
<HEAD> <TITLE>  Test JSP </TITLE> </HEAD>
<BODY BGCOLOR="#FFFFFF">
```

```
<jsp:useBean id="myBean" scope="request" class="NameBean" />
The name is <%= myBean.getName() %>
</BODY>
</HTML>
```

The scope parameter specifies the scope of Java objects used in the JSP. By default all Beans are in page scope. To specify this explicitly use `scope="page"` in the `useBean` tag. Similarly session and application scope can be specified by replacing `scope="request"` with `scope="session"` and `scope="application"` respectively.

Creating, Initializing, and Using JSP for Calling JavaBeans

In this section, we demonstrate the DepartmentS servlet program presented in Chapter 12, "Java Servlet Programming," using JSP. The JSP so implemented calls the DeptBean JavaBean. The code for the JSP is saved in a file named dept.jsp and is shown below.

```
<%@ page import="DeptBean"%>
<%@ page import="javax.servlet.jsp.JspWriter"%>
<%@ page import="javax.servlet.*" %>
<%@ page import="javax.servlet.http.*"%>

<!-- function declarations -->
<%!
//**************************************************************
private void printInitialForm(HttpServletRequest request, JspWriter out)
throws IOException
{
        printHeader(out) ;
        printForm(request, out) ;
        printFooter(out) ;
}
//****Function to add a new department******************************
private void addDepartment(HttpServletRequest request, JspWriter out)
throws IOException
{
String mesg = new String("") ;
String deptNo = request.getParameter("deptNo") ;
String deptName = request.getParameter("deptName") ;
String deptLoc = request.getParameter("deptLoc") ;
```

```
if( (deptNo == null) || deptNo.equals("") || (deptName == null) ||
                deptName.equals("") ||
                (deptLoc == null) || deptLoc.equals(""))
 {
        mesg = "One or more of the input fields are blanks" ;
 }
else
 {
 int status = -1 ;
 try {
//Instantiate the Bean class and invoke its methods on the instance created
 DeptBean myBean = new DeptBean() ;
 myBean.setdbDeptNo(Integer.parseInt(deptNo)) ;
 myBean.setdbDname(deptName) ;
 myBean.setdbLoc(deptLoc) ;
 status = myBean.InsertDept() ;
 } catch (Exception e) {}
 if(status == 0) mesg = "Department Successfully Added" ;
 else  mesg = "Failure to add Department" ;
 }
        printHeader(out) ;
        printForm(request, out) ;
        printMessage(out, mesg) ;
        printFooter(out) ;
}
//****Function to modify an existing department*****************************
private void modifyDepartment(HttpServletRequest request, JspWriter out)
throws IOException
{

String mesg = new String("") ;
String deptNo = request.getParameter("deptNo") ;
String deptName = request.getParameter("deptName") ;
String deptLoc = request.getParameter("deptLoc") ;

if( (deptNo == null) || deptNo.equals("") || (deptName == null) ||
                deptName.equals("") ||
                (deptLoc == null) || deptLoc.equals(""))
 {
        mesg = "One or more of the input fields are blanks" ;
 }
else
```

```
 {
 int status = -1 ;
 try {
//Instantiate the Bean class and invoke its methods on the instance created
 DeptBean myBean = new DeptBean() ;
 myBean.setdbDeptNo(Integer.parseInt(deptNo)) ;
 myBean.setdbDname(deptName) ;
 myBean.setdbLoc(deptLoc) ;
 status = myBean.UpdateDept() ;
 } catch (Exception e) {}
 if(status == 0) mesg = "Department Successfully Modified" ;
 else  mesg = "Failure to modify Department" ;
 }
        printHeader(out) ;
        printForm(request, out) ;
        printMessage(out, mesg) ;
        printFooter(out) ;
}
//****Function to delete an existing department*****************************
private void deleteDepartment(HttpServletRequest request, JspWriter out)
throws IOException
{

String mesg = new String("") ;
String deptNo = request.getParameter("deptNo") ;
String deptName = request.getParameter("deptName") ;
String deptLoc = request.getParameter("deptLoc") ;

if( (deptNo == null) || deptNo.equals("") || (deptName == null) ||
                deptName.equals("") ||
                (deptLoc == null) || deptLoc.equals(""))
 {
        mesg = "One or more of the input fields are blanks" ;
 }
else
 {
 int status = -1 ;
 try {
//Instantiate the Bean class and invoke its methods on the instance created
 DeptBean myBean = new DeptBean() ;
 myBean.setdbDeptNo(Integer.parseInt(deptNo)) ;
 myBean.setdbDname(deptName) ;
```

```
 myBean.setdbLoc(deptLoc) ;
 status = myBean.DeleteDept() ;
 } catch (Exception e) {}
 if(status == 0) mesg = "Department Successfully Deleted" ;
 else  mesg = "Failure to delete Department" ;
 }
        printHeader(out) ;
        printForm(request, out) ;
        printMessage(out, mesg) ;
        printFooter(out) ;
}
//***********************************************************
private void printHeader(JspWriter out) throws IOException
{

out.println("<HTML>") ;

out.println("<HEAD>") ;
out.println("<TITLE> Department Maintenance Page </TITLE>") ;
out.println("</HEAD>") ;

out.println("<BODY>") ;

out.println("<H1> Department Maintenance Page </H1>") ;

out.println("<B>") ;
out.println("(Please enter department details and click on INSERT, UPDATE or
DELETE.)") ;
out.println("</B>") ;
out.println("<BR>") ;
out.println("<BR>") ;
}

//***********************************************************
void printFooter(JspWriter out) throws IOException
{
out.println("</BODY>") ;
out.println("</HTML>") ;
}
//***********************************************************
void printForm( HttpServletRequest request, JspWriter out) throws
IOException
```

```
{

String deptNo = request.getParameter("deptNo") ;
if(deptNo == null) deptNo = "" ;
String deptName = request.getParameter("deptName") ;
if(deptName == null) deptName = "" ;
String deptLoc = request.getParameter("deptLoc") ;
if(deptLoc == null) deptLoc = "" ;

out.println("<FORM METHOD=GET ACTION='dept.jsp'>") ;
out.println("<TABLE>") ;
out.println("<TR>") ;
out.println("<TD> Department No: </TD>") ;
out.println("<TD> <INPUT TYPE=text NAME=deptNo VALUE='" + deptNo +"'>") ;
out.println("</TR>") ;

out.println("<TR>") ;
out.println("<TD> Department Name:</TD>") ;
out.println("<TD> <INPUT TYPE=text NAME=deptName VALUE='" + deptName + "'>")
;
out.println("</TR>") ;

out.println("<TR>") ;
out.println("<TD> Department Loc: </TD>") ;
out.println("<TD> <INPUT TYPE=text NAME=deptLoc VALUE='" + deptLoc + "'>") ;
out.println("</TR>") ;
out.println("</TABLE>") ;

out.println("<BR><BR>") ;

out.println("<INPUT TYPE=SUBMIT VALUE='ADD' NAME=action>") ;
out.println("<INPUT TYPE=SUBMIT VALUE='MODIFY' NAME=action>") ;
out.println("<INPUT TYPE=SUBMIT VALUE='DELETE' NAME=action>") ;


out.println("</FORM>") ;

}
//**************************************************************
void printMessage(JspWriter out, String mesg) throws IOException
{
 out.println("<BR>") ;
```

```
    out.println("<B>") ;
    out.println(mesg) ;
    out.println("</B>") ;
}
%>
<!-- End of functions -->

<%

                String action = request.getParameter("action") ;

                if ( (action == null)||  (action.equals(""))  )
                        {
                                printInitialForm(request, out) ;
                                return ;
                        }

                if (action.equals("ADD") ) addDepartment(request, out) ;
                if (action.equals("MODIFY") ) modifyDepartment(request, out);
                if (action.equals("DELETE") ) deleteDepartment(request, out);

%>
```

The output of executing this JSP is depicted in Figure 13.3.

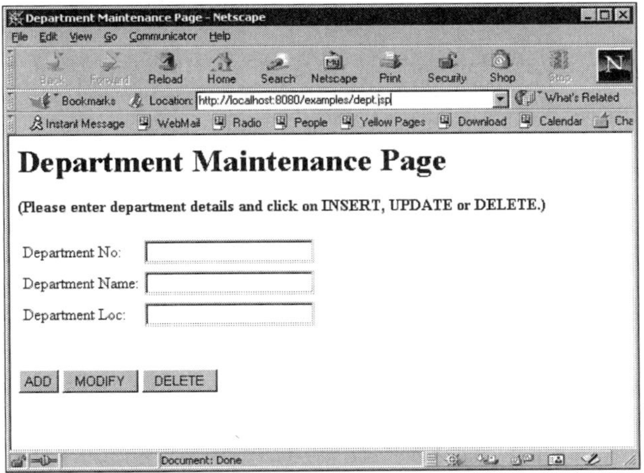

FIGURE 13.3
The output screen of a JSP page.

Deploying a JSP

Once completely written, a JSP can be deployed on various Oracle environments such as:

- Oracle8i database server, Release 8.1.7
- Oracle Internet Application Server
- Oracle HTTP Server powered by Apache

Also, Oracle9i Application Server uses Apache and a JSP can also be deployed in this environment. In fact, the method of building a JSP page as highlighted above works on any JSP 1.1 compliant server such as Allaire or Tomcat and as such the JSP architecture is extensible.

This opens the way for three options for JSPs for execution and access of Oracle8i:

1. Run in the Oracle Servlet Engine and use it as the Web server directly.
2. Run in the ApacheJServ servlet container through the Oracle HTTP Server (using mod_jserv).
3. Run in the Oracle Servlet Engine through the Oracle HTTP Server (using mod_ose).

With these Oracle environments in place, OracleJSP supports two different types of execution of the JSP, namely,

1. Pre-translation method—This is for the Oracle Servlet Engine environment. To execute JSP pages in the Oracle8i database, the OSE translates the pages in advance and loads them into the Oracle8i database as working servlets. Oracle has provided command-line tools to translate the pages, load them, and "publish" them to make them available for execution. Also, the translation can occur in the server or on the client. When the client—that is, a browser—requests the JSP page, it is executed directly, with no translation necessary.
2. On-demand translation method—For the other Oracle environments, the OracleJSP container supports the typical on-demand translation method, typically translating the pages at runtime.

This section discusses the method of deploying a JSP in Oracle8i database server Release 8.1.7 using the Oracle Servlet Engine (OSE).

The Oracle Servlet Engine (OSE), which is included with the Oracle8i JServer, consists of an OracleJSP container. It supports a JSP pre-translation model translating JSPs into servlets prior to or during deployment into the database and subsequently run in the database address space. The resulting servlets run inside a servlet container that is a part of OSE.

Along with the OSE, a JSP can be executed directly inside the database in this way and access to the database is by means of the Oracle JDBC server-side internal driver. Oracle Servlet Engine release 8.1.7 supports the servlet 2.2 and JSP 1.1 specifications, incorporating OracleJSP release 8.1.7 (1.1.0.0.0).

Deployment of JSPs on the database-tier in Oracle8i using the OSE requires the following steps:

1. Compile any dependent classes. These are any classes that the JSP uses.
2. Translate the JSP on the server side or pre-translate the JSP pages on the client side (typically including compilation).
3. Load the translated JSP pages into the Oracle8i database.
4. Optionally "hotload" the generated page implementation classes.
5. "Publish" the JSP pages to make them accessible from the database for execution.
6. Access the JSP using a URL.

Command-line tools are available to translate, load, and publish the pages. The translator creates the page implementation class in a .java file and compiles it into a servlet .class file.

Hotloading can be enabled and accomplished through additional steps. This feature allows more efficient use of literal strings such as the generated HTML tags in a page implementation class.

Deployment to Oracle8i can be performed with the translation being done either in the server or on the client. For the purposes of this chapter, we will describe server-side translation.

Compile Any Dependent Classes

Compile any classes such as JavaBean classes or other dependent classes that the JSP uses. The `name.jsp` uses the `NameBean` class. It is compiled as follows:

```
javac NameBean.java
```

Translate the JSP on the Server Side or Pre-translate the JSP Pages on the Client Side

There are two ways to perform translation of a JSP, either on the server side or on the client side.

For server side translation,

1. Use the `loadjava` command to load the .jsp source file into the database. This is loaded as a Java resource file.
2. Run the `publishjsp` command from the session shell. This automatically translates the .jsp source into a .java source and then compiles it into a .class file. Then it optionally hotloads the page implementation class if the `-hotload` option is specified for `publishjsp`. It then publishes the resulting class for execution.

We will load the `name.jsp` file along with the `NameBean.class` file into the database. This is done as shown below.

```
loadjava -thin -user ORATEST/ORATEST@training:1521:Oracle name.jsp
NameBean.class
```

USE OJSPC

For client-side translation, use the oracle JSP pre-translation tool `ojspc`. This translates the .jsp into a .java source file and then compiles this into a .clas file. Then use the `loadjava` command to load the .class file generated above as a class schema object.

Load the Translated JSP Pages into the Oracle8i Database

This is done by the `loadjava` command. This has already been shown above. There is no need to use the –r option with the `loadjava` command.

Optionally "Hotload" the Generated Page Implementation Classes

This is done by specifying the `-hotload` option with the `publishjsp` command. Hotloading is an Oracle8i feature for efficient use of static final variables.

"Publish" the JSP Pages

Once loaded, the JSP has to be published to make it accessible from the database for execution. Actually, the page implementation class obtained after loading what is published. This is done with the `publishjsp` command from the $ prompt of the session shell. The syntax for the command is as follows:

```
publishjsp [ options] path/name.jsp
```

The options can be any of the following:

```
[-schema schemaname] [-virtualpath path] [-servletName name] [-packageName name]
[-context context] [-hotload] [-stateless] [-verbose] [-resolver resolver]
[-extend class] [-implement interface]
```

The file name.jsp (or name.sqljsp for a SQLJ JSP page) specifies the JSP page resource schema object that is loaded with loadjava and is a mandatory parameter.

By default, if no -virtualpath option is specified, path/name.jsp becomes the servlet path.

By default, if no -context option is specified, the OSE default servlet context is used and "/" is the context path.

Both, the context path and servlet path (along with the host name and port) define the URL to invoke the page.

-schema specifies the schema where the JSP page resource schema object is located, if it is not in the same schema as logged onto sess_sh. No password needs to be specified.

-virtualpath specifies a servlet path for the JSP page. By default, the servlet path is simply the specified .jsp filename itself along with any specified schema path.

-servletName specifies the servlet name (in OSE named_servlets) for the JSP page. The default servlet name is the base name of the .jsp file along with any path you specified.

-packageName specifies a package name for the generated page implementation class. It defaults to the path specification for the .jsp file.

-context specifies a servlet context in the OSE. This should have been created using the session shell createcontext command. The virtual path of this servlet context becomes part of the URL used to invoke the page. By default, the JSP is run in the OSE default context, `/webdomains/contexts/default`, whose context path is simply `/`.

-hotload specifies to perform hotloading.

-stateless specifies that the JSP page is to be stateless. In other words, the JSP page should not have access to the HttpSession object during execution.

-verbose specifies to print the translation steps as it executes.

-resolver specifies a Java class resolver. The default resolver is `((* user) (* PUBLIC))`. The value is specified in double quotes.

-extend specifies a Java class that the generated page implementation class will extend.

-implement specifies a Java interface that the generated page implementation class will implement.

We will publish the `name.jsp` in the `deptContext` servlet context created in Chapter 12. The full name of this context is `/deptDomain/contexts/deptContext`.

First log in to the session shell using the following command:

```
sess_sh -u sys -p <password> -s sess_iiop://training:2481:Oracle
```

At the $ prompt, execute the `publishjsp` command as follows:

```
$ publishjsp -schema ORATEST -context /deptDomain/contexts/deptContext name.jsp
```

Here the context virtual path is `/testing` for the `deptContext` and the servlet path is `name.jsp`.

PUBLISH A JSP IN A SERVLET CONTEXT CREATED EARLIER THAT USES SYS PRIVILEGES

To publish a JSP in the Oracle database, the publishjsp command seems to do the job. However, some routine steps need to be performed before doing this. These steps are creating a Web service, adding an end point and registering it to the Web service, granting ownership to the JSP user for the service created, creating a Web domain, and creating a Servlet Context.

Another important step to follow is to log in to the session shell as SYS instead of an ordinary user account so that it has the necessary privileges to store the port in the dynamic tables associated with the ports. However, while using the publishjsp command, you can specify the schema name where in the JSP is to be published.

Access the JSP Using a URL

Like a servlet, a JSP is invoked by means of an URL. The URL to invoke a JSP running in the Oracle Servlet Engine is formed by a combination of four components:

- The hostname
- The port
- The *context path* of the servlet context in OSE, as determined when the servlet context was created. This is the virtual path specified when creating the context using the create-context command. The context path for the OSE default context, `/webdomains/contexts/default`, is simply `/`.
- The *servlet path* of the JSP page in OSE (often referred to as the "virtual path"), as determined when the JSP page was published. The servlet path is the JSP page "virtual path" and is determined by the way the JSP was published. The virtualpath option, if specified, gives the servlet path. Otherwise, the servlet path is the name of the .jsp itself.

Specifying the four components as above the jsp can be invoked as follows:

```
http://<hostname>:<port>/<virtual-path>/<servlet-path>
```

For the name.jsp, this is shown below.

```
http://localhost:9494/testing/name.jsp
```

Summary

This chapter outlined the detailed procedure for implementing Java Server Pages in Oracle8i. First it discussed an overview of JSP followed by a description of basic JSP elements such as JSP tags, declarations, scripting, and expressions. The architecture of a JSP page was presented. Then the method of creating a JSP page was highlighted with an example. A more specific discussion of developing a JSP with JavaBeans was detailed with a complicated example. Finally the method of deploying JSPs in Oracle8i was discussed.

INDEX

T

U-V

W-Z